beyond Suffering

Discovering the message of Job

32.7-8

LAYTON TALBERT

41.11 Layton Talbert 42.5

Psalm 119.71

BOB JONES
UNIVERSITY PRESS
Greenville, South Carolina

Library of Congress Cataloging-in Publication Data

Talbert, Layton, 1960-
Beyond suffering : discovering the message of Job / Layton Talbert.
p. cm.
ISBN 978-1-59166-620-2 (perfect bound pbk. : alk. paper)
1. Bible. O.T. Job—Commentaries. I. Title.

BS1415.53.T35 2007
223'.107—dc22

2006102510

Cover Photo Credits: Unusual Films

All Scripture is quoted from the Authorized King James Version unless otherwise noted.

The fact that materials produced by other publishers may be referred to in this volume does not constitute an endorsement of the content or theological position of materials produced by such publishers.

Beyond Suffering: Discovering the Message of Job
Layton Talbert, PhD

Design by Nathan Hutcheon
Composition by Michael Boone

Greenville, South Carolina 29614

Printed in the United States of America

ISBN 978-1-59166-620-2

15 14 13 12 11 10 9 8 7 6 5 4 3 2 1

To
Tony & Faye Abbott
and
Charlie & Wendy Naselli,
dear friends and spiritual kin of Job
In memory
of
Cheryl Abbott
(February 15, 1985)
and
Michael Naselli
(June 30, 1995—March 30, 2002)

Contents

Part IV—Human Monologue: Job and Elihu

Part V—Divine Monologue: Job and God

Part VI—Epilogue

Foreword

The overarching message of the inspired wisdom books is the same—satisfaction in life is not found in any component of the creation but in the Creator Himself. Ecclesiastes proves the theme by satiation. Job proves it by deprivation. The central subject of the Bible is God—and thus it is with the book of Job.

The book of Job is about suffering in the same way that the book of Ecclesiastes is about affluence. They are only the anvils of experience upon which the truth of the centrality of God is hammered out in a person's life.

Layton Talbert has captured the essence of Job's experience with clarity, precision, and beauty. To the believer who has found God to be more than enough, there is nothing more he would rather talk about, and it is obvious that Dr. Talbert has seen the Creator in the Scriptures and in his own experience. His writing style is refreshing and energetic, but that is not merely because he is a scholar; it is because he has a refreshing and life-giving topic to write about—the God of heaven.

Beyond Suffering is more than a commentary on a book of the Bible—thought it is truly that. But as you might surmise from the title, it is about much more than suffering. Like the book of Job itself, the work you hold in your hands is about the living God. Read this book slowly. Read it reflectively. Read it reverently. You will see your own story in its pages—and the stories of your friends. But most importantly, you will see God's story in its pages. Not just the story

He tells of one of His servants, but the story He tells of Himself and of His wonderful providence and redemption for the creation He loves—you and me. Breathe in His message deeply and thereby find rest and joy for your soul.

Jim Berg

Preface

Few have suffered, in kind or degree, the devastation that Job endured. I am keenly aware that many others are far more experientially qualified than I am to teach most of the lessons of this book. Others could speak, with more insight and eloquence than I can, out of painful personal encounter with suffering. I have tried to include as many of their voices as possible. We value the voice of experience. Personal encounter lends credibility to counsel, but it does not necessarily bestow authority. Authority rests in the testimony of Scripture, and the lessons of Job are there for all of us. If we will hear it, the timeless message of Job answers our questions about past calamity, consoles and instructs us in present suffering, and prepares us for future affliction.

I am also keenly aware that many within Fundamentalism are admirably equipped to write a more technical commentary on the book of Job. I wish they would. But several factors have compelled me to write a more generally accessible book on the message of Job. One is my deep and longtime love for the book of Job. Another is the urgency of personal discovery; like the lepers in 2 Kings 7, I am constrained to share with others the treasures I have found in this book. Finally, I share Elihu's conviction that there is a spirit in every man to which the breath of the Almighty may grant understanding (Job 32:6-8). To each generation is given a stewardship of the insights granted to it, and it is the duty of each generation to make fresh applications of the timeless truths of God's Word to man.

This is not a verse-by-verse commentary, though it is devoted to unfolding the meaning and application of each passage throughout the book of Job. It is an exposition of the message of Job. The text of this book assumes a deliberately explanatory purpose with a practical posture, while the notes offer the interested reader more detailed and technical commentary on points of particular interest. To readers who dislike endnotes I offer my sincere apology. So do I. However, as in *Not by Chance: Learning to Trust a Sovereign God*, I have tried to write the book on two levels—a lay-friendly text for the general reader, supplemented by technical, elaborative, or corroborative endnotes for the more advanced student of the Scripture. The notes contain additional research and information, corroboration and argumentation, that I hope many will find profitable. My ambition is to make what I write accurate (exegetically rooted), biblical (expositionally based), and relevant (practically oriented). My goal is to make the often intimidating, misunderstood, and misapplied book of Job accessible and interesting to both teacher and student, preacher and layman.

Bible books that are long or difficult are often victimized by oversimplification, selective attention, or outright disregard. Because Job is both long *and* difficult, its own voice is often muted by such treatment. The rarity of contextual teaching and preaching from the book of Job is disappointing, and a serious loss for the people of God. Does anyone preach an expository series through the book of Job? Is any book of the Bible—*all* of which is not only profitable but *essential* to equip Christians (2 Tim. 3:16-17)—unfit for such expositional treatment from the pulpit of God's people? Joseph Caryl spent over forty years preaching through Job; his expositions are collected in volumes. Excessive? Some might think so. But Caryl was preaching to believers during an era of extended suffering. I am not suggesting that preachers and teachers engage in a pedantic, word-by-word sermonic scrutiny of the book. But neither do I mean playing hermeneutical hopscotch from text to popular text in a way that fails to deal substantively with the overall message of the book in its context. I mean a careful expository treatment of the thought and flow of the book's full message. My prayer is that this work will become a helpful tool to that end. If this book ministers not only to individuals but also to congregations through Sunday school lessons, Bible study discussions, and preaching series, I will be more than recompensed for the writing of it.

The book of Job rivets our attention on what it means to work through the principles of God's providence and sovereignty on an intensely intimate and personal level. That case study allows us to take a spiritually surgical look into the mind and soul of someone confronted with perplexing and devastating providences, forced to wrestle with the workings of a sovereignty that seems inexplicably unfair. My hope is that this study will engender a clearer understanding of the nuances of this book of your Bible and a fresh appreciation for the timelessness and relevance of its message about the nature of life, the nature of man, and the nature of God. If you come to love this book and revel in its truths as I have, I could ask for no greater compensation.

The book of Job is one of the practical and theological Himalayas of the Bible. Scaling mountains requires some effort, but as one writer assures us regarding Job, "The task of understanding it is as rewarding as it is strenuous." The best preparation for profiting from this book is a fresh familiarity with the story of Job—the *whole* story. My suggestion is to read through the book of Job first. Ideally this should be done in one sitting. You can read through the entire book at a *comfortable* pace (even aloud) in just a couple of hours. The end of chapter 1 includes several suggestions for maximizing your reading. At the least, reading through the book of Job section by section as you work through the chapters of this book will keep the text before you. That is important since everything in this book is tied to the text of Job. This book is not a topically organized collection of random thoughts; it is a Bible study following the progression of the text. It is the entrance of God's words, not man's, that sheds light (Ps. 119:130); it is the words of God that are, like the spirit to the body, life-giving (John 6:63).

Here is the core of comfort in the message of Job: beyond suffering, past our pain and loss, is a God Who is not only all-knowing and omnipotent, sovereign and free to do as He chooses but also always good and just, loving and wise, purposeful and perfect in all that He chooses to do or to allow—and intimately aware of all its effects on us. In a word, God is always sovereign, God is always benevolent, and ultimately God always rewards (both evil and good). But *He* is the center of all life, not we. When we ignore or doubt or deny these realities in the face of suffering, we not only harm ourselves but also rob others of an opportunity to see God as He truly is.

Abbreviations

The commentary in the notes engages considerable interaction with a wide variety of sources. In order to make the discussion more reader-friendly, frequently cited sources will utilize the following abbreviated forms. Other works by the same author that are infrequently cited will be fully documented in the conventional manner.

Andersen Francis I. Andersen, *Job: An Introduction and Commentary.* Volume 13 of *Tyndale Old Testament Commentaries.* Downers Grove, Ill.: Inter-Varsity Press, 1974.

Archer Gleason L. Archer Jr., *The Book of Job: God's Answer to the Problem of Undeserved Suffering.* Grand Rapids: Baker Book House, 1982.

Carson D. A. Carson, *How Long, O Lord? Reflections on Suffering and Evil.* Grand Rapids: Baker Book House, 1990.

Carter Charles W. Carter, *The Greatest Book Ever Written: The Book of Job (A Commentary).* Grand Rapids: Eerdmans, 1968.

Delitzsch Franz Delitzsch, *Commentary on Job.* Translated by Francis Bolton. Volume 4 of *Commentary on the Old Testament in Ten Volumes* by C. F. Keil and F. Delitzsch. Grand Rapids: Eerdmans, rpr. 1982.

Dhorme E. Dhorme, *A Commentary on the Book of Job.* Translated by Harold Knight. Thomas Nelson and Sons, 1967.

Gordis	Robert Gordis, *The Book of Job: Commentary, New Translation and Special Studies.* New York: The Jewish Theological Seminary of America, 1978.
Green	William Henry Green, *The Argument of the Book of Job Unfolded.* New York: Hurst and Company, 1891.
Holladay	William Holladay, *A Concise Hebrew and Aramaic Lexicon of the Old Testament.* Grand Rapids: Eerdmans, 1971.
Kidner	Derek Kidner, *The Wisdom of Proverbs, Job and Ecclesiastes.* Downers Grove, Ill.: InterVarsity Press, 1985.
LXX	Septuagint
Morris	Henry Morris, *The Remarkable Record of Job.* Grand Rapids: Baker Book House, 1988.
MT	Masoretic Text
NASB	New American Standard Bible
NCV	New Century Version
NEB	New English Bible
NIV	New International Version
NKJV	New King James Version
NSRB	New Scofield Reference Bible
NT	New Testament
OT	Old Testament
Robinson	H. Wheeler Robinson, *The Cross in the Old Testament.* London: SCM Press, 1955.
Rowley	H. H. Rowley, *Job.* Thomas Nelson and Sons, 1970.
Smick	Elmer B. Smick, "Job" in *The Expositor's Bible Commentary.* Volume 4. Grand Rapids: Zondervan Publishing, 1988.
Strahan	James Strahan, *The Book of Job.* Edinburgh: T. and T. Clark, 1914.
Zuck	Roy B. Zuck, *Job.* Everyman's Bible Commentary. Chicago: Moody Press, 1978.

I

Introduction to the Book of Job

1
Introducing the Book of Job

"Behold, God is great, and we know him not—" The grumble of a distant storm stopped the speaker in midsentence. Five men eyed the looming thunderhead, lightning flickering from its black base. The wind gusted. A bolt flashed close and cracked the air with a brassy echo like some unearthly voice. The speaker plunged ahead but a torrent of wind and sound soon swallowed his words. There would be no more speeches today. Not from them. It was time to hear from God.[1]

The book of Job is a tale full of sound and fury—but signifying nothing? Hardly. No stodgy discussions among armchair theologians here! The book bristles with full-bore debate and hot-blooded argument amid intense personal suffering and searching. It affirms faltering faith and challenges right-hearted but wrong-headed religious platitudes. The book represents "a vital, throbbing uprise of the human spirit."[2] Job is the stuff of universal human experience and gnawing questions about the timeless presence of pain. The book of Job "is not simply literature. It is life, distilled life."[3]

The story of Job reads like theater electrified to life by painful personal experience. Animated actors gesture energetically. Their voices rise and fall with entreaty, accusation, even sarcasm. It is a real-life drama brimming with vivid verbal images, passionate prayers, withering insults, soaring soliloquies, arresting frankness of speech to man and God. A no-holds-barred wrestling with questions about disturbing realities, inexplicable inequities, apparent injustice, and, above all, the silence and hiddenness of God. Job challenges traditional assumptions with disarmingly candid observations and the honest questions of an honest faith that pester for equally honest answers.[4] He is unsatisfied with parroted platitudes that fly in the face of obvious realities. The result is not eroded confidence in God or a weakened faith but a matured and settled assurance rooted more firmly in a reliance on God's self-revelation. The result is a spirit willing to submit, even when it may not understand, to a sovereign God Who is unfailingly good, even when it may not look like it.

This first chapter addresses background details that are important for understanding the book of Job as a whole.

The Nature of the Book of Job

No one who is hurting or confused by life hungers for Homer's *Iliad*, or peruses Plato's *Republic*, or thumbs through Shakespeare's sonnets looking for answers. It is the unique ministry of the Bible to speak out of its antiquity in a timeless language that consoles and convicts us even in our modernity.

> The Old Testament book about Job is . . . one of the best gifts of God to men. The task of understanding it is as rewarding as it is strenuous. . . . Job is a prodigious book in the vast range of its ideas, in its broad coverage of human experience, in the intensity of its passions, in the immensity of its concept of God, and not least in its superb literary craftsmanship. . . . It plumbs the depths of human despair, the anger of moral outrage, and the anguish of [apparent] desertion by God.[5]

The driving conviction of this volume is the relevance of the ancient book of Job to the needs of modern experiences. That Job verbalizes universal thoughts and emotions is evident from the fact that ancient literature includes a number of remarkably similar tales.[6] Every reflective soul knows something of its questions and frustrations. The book has never lacked for admirers, and "by any standard of comparison it ranks among the most significant pieces of world literature."[7] Nineteenth-century English essayist and historian Thomas Carlyle expressed his opinion that "there is nothing written, I think, in the Bible or out of it, of equal literary merit."[8] Tennyson reputedly called Job "the greatest poem of ancient or modern times." Its enduring literary influence is apparent in masterpieces such as

Dante's *Divine Comedy*, Milton's *Paradise Lost*, Goethe's *Faust*, and other works artistic and musical that have been inspired by these.[9]

Almost everyone is familiar with the opening two chapters—the so-called "contest," or "wager," scene and Job's resulting calamities. Once we wade into the long-winded and seemingly circular debates between Job and his companions, however, our interest may begin to wane. The persevering reader dutifully plods through thirty-five chapters of speeches by men who sometimes seem more interested in hearing themselves than listening to each other. God's appearance revives the reader's attention (though at times it may be hard to figure out His point), and one manages to tune in again for the final "happily-ever-after."

But is that all God intends for us to get out of it? If so, why not spare us all that belabored dialogue? If not, what does God want us to learn from this book—*all* of it? God did not include thirty-five chapters of dialogue to build the Bible reader's character. If we are accustomed to ignoring the bulk of this book except as an occasional source for useful quotations and proof texts, how do we know we are accurately understanding the portions where we do pay attention?

The book is rich with theological truths and implications. John Walvoord has remarked that

> the knowledge of Job and his friends about God and His ways is proof that prior to written Scripture God had revealed Himself in definite form. The Book of Job furnishes sufficient material in itself for a well-rounded systematic theology . . . and indicates God had not left Himself without adequate testimony.[10]

But Job is not a textbook of static doctrine.[11] The style and form intertwine the theological with the dramatic and the literary. Short stories recount the resolution of a conflict. Job is more like a novel, tracing the growth and transformation of a character in conflict. It is an organic whole, an unfolding drama that uncovers new facets of the central supernatural character (God) and reveals the spiritual metamorphosis of the central human character (Job).

The Structure of the Book of Job

Poetry and prose are the book's building materials. Think of the book of Job as the "logue" cabin of the Bible, constructed of four "logues": a *pro*logue, a *dia*logue, a *mono*logue, and an *epi*logue. These sections are further divided between prose (the prologue and epilogue) and poetry (the dialogue and monologue).[12] Highly structured, it is one of the few books of the Bible where there is little substantive disagreement over its outline. (See pages 12–13 for a structural outline of Job along with a visual diagram that illustrates the relative amount of material dedicated to each section of the book.[13])

The Authorship and Date of the Book of Job

No one knows who wrote Job. The text contains no definitive clue. No consensus of scholarly opinion or rabbinic tradition exists on the question of authorship.[14] Suggestions are as diverse as they are speculative. Guesses include Moses, Solomon, Hezekiah, Isaiah, Jeremiah, Ezra, Elihu (the speaker in Job 32–37), and an unknown intertestamental author.[15] Some see subtle hints that Job himself may have penned the account after his restoration (Job 19:23–24; 31:35). Whoever the author was, "his work has witnessed to the spirits of the faithful through the ages that he was divinely inspired."[16] Nevertheless, the question of authorship does raise the secondary issue of the date of the book.

When discussing the date of Job, it may be necessary to distinguish between the historical *setting* of the events in Job and the time of the *composition* of the story of Job. The story may have been written at or about the time of Job himself, which was almost certainly the pre-Mosaic patriarchal period (ca. 2000 BC). The level of the dialogue in Job along with other textual evidences (see below, "Historical Setting") suggest to many both an author and date of composition close to the actual event. Adding to the attractiveness of this view, a pre-Mosaic date of composition makes it even more likely that the work was "originally composed in some language other than Hebrew, whether in a North Arabian dialect or possibly in Aramaic."[17] That would help explain the unusual difficulty of much of the language in Job. This has historically been the predominant—though not the exclusive—view among conservative scholars.

It is also possible, however, that the written account may have been an inspired product of the later Wisdom movement in the Solomonic era (ca. 950 BC). This, too, is an ancient opinion defended by many with a conservative opinion of the Bible.[18] Several factors seem to support this possibility. The prominence of the wisdom theme in Job suggests a traceable connection between the statements of Solomon (Prov. 1:7; 9:10), David (Ps. 111:10), and Job (Job 28:28). Both Job (28) and Proverbs (8) feature a similar and extended adulation of wisdom. The *Pax Solomonus* afforded an era of "prosperous leisure" for "literary pursuits."[19] The literary output of the Solomonic era displayed a marked concentration on wisdom literature (Proverbs), including a contemplation of the inequities of life (Ecclesiastes). Solomon's unique access to international materials would have placed within his reach any extant records of the northern Arabic Job tradition. The reference to Job as "the greatest of all the men of the East" (Job 1:3) signals a Palestinian composition consistent with the Solomonic era (but not necessarily inconsistent with a patriarchal composition). Though it was a common Palestinian designation for those living east of Palestine (Gen. 29:1; Judg. 6:33; Isa. 11:14),[20] it is not how those living in the East would have described themselves. Finally, the principal designation for God throughout the dialogue segment of the book is the patriarchal title *Shaddai* or the pan-Semitic *'Eloah* or *'Elohim*; but the predominant appearance of the name *Yahweh* in the narrator's prologue (18 times) and epilogue (9 times) also suggests a Palestinian composition consistent with the Solomonic era.[21]

A later date of composition does not threaten the book's inspiration and authority nor compromise its credibility or historicity. After all, Moses recorded the creation and early history of mankind centuries before his time. All the extended dialogue of the Joseph narrative (Gen. 37–50), for instance, occurred some five centuries before Moses penned it. In the end, "there is no convincing evidence for either denying or insisting upon a pre-Mosaic date of composition," but Job is not, on that account, "to be dismissed as mere fiction"; the author, whether early or late, "composed it under the inspiration of the Holy Spirit and accurately represented the sentiments and theological opinions historically expressed by the parties concerned."[22]

The Historical Setting of the Book of Job

The geographical backdrop of the book indicates that "Job was a native of North Arabia, and the whole setting of the story is Arabic rather than Hebrew."[23] Nevertheless, Job and his friends stand among those to whom God graciously revealed Himself prior to and outside the channel of Israel—Pharaoh (Gen. 12), Melchizedek (Gen. 14),[24] Abimelech (Gen. 20), and a later Abimelech (Gen. 26). All the socio-religious and historical details in the book suggest that Job lived about the same time as these individuals as well.

Several elements in the story point to the patriarchal time period (ca. 2000 BC). The text makes no reference to Israelites or Mosaic institutions. The economy is agricultural, with wealth measured principally in livestock (1:3). A family priest structure predominates (1:5). Raids by nomadic Sabeans and Chaldeans fit the second millennium BC (1:15, 17).[25] The Hebrew term for "piece of silver" (Job 42:11) is "a unit of value characteristic of the patriarchal age"[26] and occurs elsewhere only in Genesis 33:19 and Joshua 24:32. Job's longevity fits with the Pentateuchal data regarding patriarchal lifespans (42:16).[27] The preferred name for God in Job, *Shaddai,* is almost exclusively a patriarchal designation.[28]

Scholars have noted striking similarities between the biblical account of Job and other ancient stories, notably one called the "Babylonian Job." This cuneiform composition relates the story of a wealthy, righteous man who lost everything and endured a severe physical illness as well. He appealed to the gods to no avail yet maintained his piety. Finally, the god Marduk stepped in and restored the sufferer to his former condition. The Babylonian version appears to be a pagan adaptation of the original story of Job.[29]

The Literary Setting of the Book of Job

In terms of traditional literary genres, Job is unique and defies relegation to traditional literary categories.[30] Rather, "the book of Job is an astonishing mixture of almost every kind of literature to be found in the Old Testament."[31] Primarily for the sake of description, I have adopted a "theatrical" view of Job. While this is not a technically accurate description of the book's genre,[32] the analogy helps to reflect the atmosphere of the book.

Job fits into the category of ancient wisdom literature. Literature takes a wide variety of forms, and each form must be handled according to its own rules. One does not read and interpret poetry and prose (or even different kinds of prose) in the same way. The Bible itself is filled with a surprising array of literary genres. Biblical wisdom literature includes Job, Proverbs, and Ecclesiastes; but wisdom literature is not unique to the Bible.[33] Though wisdom literature embraces a philosophical approach to life, it is not merely metaphysical or theoretical philosophy. It is practical philosophy because at its roots it is theological philosophy—that is, a philosophical framework for living life that is rooted in revealed theological truth. The wisdom movement has been defined as "the discipline whereby was taught the application of prophetic truth to the individual life in the light of experience."[34]

The book of Job, then, is not simply an interesting but ancient tale of one man's calamity. It is designed by God to instruct, by genre to instruct effectively, by inspiration to instruct accurately, and by preservation to instruct timelessly.

Hints for a Profitable Reading of the Book of Job

Good biography does not just transmit historical facts about a person but makes that person live and move in the reader's mind. The responsibility for attaining that goal falls to both the writer and the reader. The biographer must write engagingly, but the reader must enter sympathetically into the subject's soul and circumstances. That approach is important for a profitable reading of all the biographical and historical narratives in Scripture, especially Job. How can our reading of Job help that happen?

Many do not enjoy reading through the entire book of Job. The main reason for this is the discourses, which seem to go in circles, make the same points, and get nowhere. But the Holy Spirit does not waste space. The dialogue contains indispensable insights into the nature of God, the nature of man, and the relationship between them. Here are some simple suggestions for getting a handle on the book as a whole. The more of them you incorporate, the more Job (or any other book of the Bible) will open up for you.

Read in single sittings. You can listen to a Beethoven symphony fifteen minutes a day, but you will lose the continuity of the music and any clear overall impression of the unity of the piece. The same is true of a lengthy book such as Job. Sometimes, of course, it is helpful to slow down and concentrate thoughtfully on smaller portions. Nevertheless, the single-sitting reading is an irreplaceable method for studying any book of the Bible. It enables you to get your hands around the overall message of the book, to follow its argument and progression, to see recurring themes you would otherwise overlook, to give you a more accurate sense of context into which to fit isolated sayings, and even to avoid misplaced emphases and misconstrued meanings that often arise from a piecemeal approach. You can read through Job at a comfortable reading pace (even aloud) in just over two hours. That suggests a second strategy.

Read aloud. If this strikes you as an odd suggestion for Bible reading, you cannot imagine what you are missing. One of the best ways to enter into the narrator's world and the emotion of the discourses is to read out loud. Adapting this method to a group setting (in a class or Bible study context or as a family), with different individuals reading different roles, elicits profitable discussions about the book's contents and message.[35] The next suggestion is a natural outgrowth of reading aloud.

Read sympathetically. Job is primarily dramatic dialogue. Read it as drama. The atmosphere of Job crackles with intense feeling. Put emotional color into the black-and-white words on the page. Gesture with the actors. Express their pain or their outrage. The result is delightful and invigorating. Characters will spring to life off the pages of this ancient story.

Read in a different version. When it comes to Bible reading, familiarity ought not breed contempt, but it can breed ruts. And even a good rut is still a rut. The problem lies not in the translation but in our acquaintance with it and in our natural intellectual laziness. Familiarity with language that we have read repeatedly can become an impediment to comprehension. Well-known expressions fall off our lips like sacred shibboleths, but shedding little light—not because they fail to communicate but because our overacquaintance reduces our receptivity. A different translation forces us to think freshly about what we are reading, as we reckon with new vocabulary and syntax. It may also alert our attention to things we have previously misunderstood or misconstrued on the basis of a particular wording to which we have become accustomed.

Read synoptically. As you read each discourse, look for one or two or three verses that encapsulate the main point of the speaker. The rest is not insignificant, but it is usually subordinate. Summarize the point in your own words. You can then create a running chart that paraphrases the main point of each speech and traces the progression of the debate—and there *is* progression—in a kind of synopsis of the book. For example, the interaction between Eliphaz and Job in the second cycle of speeches can be boiled down to the following exchange:

> Eliphaz (15): Listen to yourself! Your own words betray your sinfulness (15:1–6)! You think you know everything (15:7–13)? No man can claim to be righteous as you do (15:14–16). Only the wicked suffer like this (15:17–35).
>
> Job's response (16–17): Miserable comforters you are! I've heard all this before (16:1–6)! But God has devastated me (16:7–16) despite my innocence (16:17–22). Come back when you have something intelligent to say (17:10). As for me, I'm just waiting to die (17:11–16).

Or later, the exchange between Zophar and Job in chapters 20–21:

> Zophar (20): Don't you know from experience that the triumph of the wicked is short-lived, and that God always sends them swift judgment like this (20:4ff.)?
>
> Job's response (21): Oh, really? Look around you! Why do the wicked often prosper all their life long even though they reject God (21:7–21)? God sovereignly deals with individual men as he sees fit (21:22–26). Your theology does not match reality (21:34).

Locate the kernel verses of each speech and you can reconstruct the entire discourse in synopsis form, follow its logical progression back and forth from speaker to speaker, and trace the flow of thought throughout.[36]

Structural Outline of the Book of Job

The Narrator's Prologue (1–2)

- Introduction of Job
- Testing of Job
  - Possessional testing; Job's response
  - Personal testing; Job's response

PROSE

The Human Dialogue (3–37)

First Cycle (3–14)

- Job's lament (3)
  - Eliphaz replies (4–5)
- Job responds (6–7)
  - Bildad replies (8)
- Job responds (9–10)
  - Zophar replies (11)
- Job responds (12–14)

Second Cycle (15–21)

  - Eliphaz replies (15)
- Job responds (16–17)
  - Bildad replies (18)
- Job responds (19)
  - Zophar replies (20)
- Job responds (21)

POETRY

Third Cycle (22–31)

  - Eliphaz replies (22)
- Job responds (23–24)
  - Bildad replies (25)
- Job's final response and defense (26–31)

Elihu's Discourse (32–37)

The Divine Monologue (38–42*a*)

- First interrogation (38–39)
  - Job responds (40*a*)
- Second interrogation (40*b*–41)
  - Job responds (42*a*)

The Narrator's Epilogue (42*b*)

- God rebukes Job's three friends
- God rewards Job

PROSE

Visual Diagram of the Book of Job

NOTE: Each unit (◆) represents one chapter. Percentages are based on the number of verses since chapters vary widely in length.

Segment		Chapter Units	Speaker	Chapters
Prologue (3%)		◆◆	*Narrator*	1–2
	First Cycle	◆	*Job*	3
		◆◆	Eliphaz	4–5
		◆◆	*Job*	6–7
		◆	Bildad	8
		◆◆	*Job*	9–10
		◆	Zophar	11
	Second Cycle	◆◆◆	*Job*	12–14
		◆	Eliphaz	15
Dialogue (83%)		◆◆	*Job*	16–17
		◆	Bildad	18
		◆	*Job*	19
		◆	Zophar	20
		◆	*Job*	21
		◆	Eliphaz	22
	Third Cycle	◆◆	*Job*	23–24
		◆	Bildad	25
		◆◆◆◆◆◆	*Job*	26–31
		◆◆◆◆◆◆	Elihu	32–37
Monologue (12%)		◆◆◆◆	**Yahweh**	38–41
Epilogue (2%)		◆	*Narrator*	42

2

Discovering the Theme of Job

What is the first word that comes to mind when you think of Job? For most people, it is probably the word *suffering*. But saying that Job is about suffering is like saying *The Lord of the Rings* is about an adventure or *The Pilgrim's Progress* is about salvation. Besides, not all suffering is the same. The Bible addresses at least four different kinds of suffering.[1] Some suffering is humanly inflicted and some is divinely imposed; some is justified and some is undeserved. None of it is enjoyable, and some form of it is inevitable for everyone. The wealthy, the crafty, even the godly do not escape. The Bible counsels different ways of responding to different kinds of suffering in this life.

Kinds of Suffering

Persecution is undeserved suffering inflicted by people and permitted by God. It may be verbal or physical, inconvenient or torturous. History is full of persecution for many causes, from religious beliefs to ethnic identity to political persuasion.[2] The Bible is, of course, concerned primarily with persecution for one's faith. Acts recounts several examples, but one New Testament book is particularly devoted to dealing with persecution. First Peter addresses this class of suffering and how we should respond to it (1 Pet. 2:18–23; 3:13–17; 4:14, 19).[3]

Punishment is deserved suffering, inflicted by people for a just cause (1 Pet. 2:18; 3:17; 4:15). The fact that Peter addresses both persecution and punishment displays his down-to-earth realism. Because he knew himself, Peter "knew how easily people can rationalize punishments that are deserved and explain them as 'Christian' suffering." Peter wanted believers to "distinguish between genuine Christian suffering and suffering that is a consequence of misbehavior."[4]

Chastisement is deserved suffering inflicted by God, usually through circumstances or people. The most extensive treatment of this kind of suffering is the book of Lamentations, where God's people are experiencing His chastisement for their sin. Chastisement is different from punishment. It is disciplinary, not penal. Chastisement is, by definition, remedial and restorative. It is not a mark of hatred and rejection but of love and relationship (cf. Heb. 12:5–11). The right response to chastisement is trust in God's changeless character and a repentant return to the Lord (Lam. 3:21–38, 40ff.). Job, however, is not about any of these kinds of suffering.

Affliction is suffering that is not only undeserved but not even understood—"what most of us would call irrational evil, incoherent suffering."[5] This kind of suffering comes only through the decision or permission of God (hence it is "permitted" by God). He may or may not originate this kind of suffering; but because He is sovereign, He alone claims ultimate responsibility for it (hence it is "sent" by God). It may come in the form of "natural" circumstances or through the actions (even the sinful actions) of people. It may affect us directly, or indirectly in the form of "collateral damage." How does one interpret and respond to *that* kind of suffering? That is the issue at the eye of the storm swirling around Job.

Suffering as a Test of Faith

Tribulation is pressure. The New Testament word for *tribulation* (*thlipsis*) means pressure. We apply pressure to assess the resilience and reliability of everything from industrial machinery to home repairs. But something about suffering in order to prove one's faith or loyalty sounds a little cruel on the surface. It is the human element that adds the objectionable dimension to suffering. "Besides," pride objects, "why do I have to *prove* my faith? God knows my heart, so why can't people take my word for it?"[6] Because you're a sinner like the rest of us, and you probably don't know yourself any better than Peter did (Mark 14:29–31, 66–72).

None of us is innately honest and trustworthy. All of us are prone to deception, including self-deception. The testing of faith through suffering demonstrates nothing to God; He already knows our hearts (Acts 1:24; 15:8).[7] It demonstrates a great deal to us, to those around us, and to others who are watching. Pressure may reveal that we do not possess the faith or commitment that we thought we had (Luke 8:6, 13). Other pressures expose the anemia and distractibility of our faith (Luke 8:7, 14). But the pressure of suffering tempers and strengthens a faith that is genuine and healthy.

Of all the kinds of suffering listed above—persecution, punishment, chastisement, affliction—it is the last one more than any of the others that represents what James describes as a trial of our faith (James 1:3). Why? Persecution we can understand. It may be cruel and uncomfortable, but it makes sense in a fallen world. Christ was persecuted and warned His followers to expect the same (John 15:18–20). Persecution can galvanize a believer's faith in Christ; there is consolation and confirmation in knowing we are suffering for Christ (Acts 5:40–41; 1 Pet. 4:13–14). Punishment and chastisement work the same way. We can generally see the connection between our actions and our circumstances. Our conscience bears witness against us, and we submit to the rod. It's painful but it makes sense.

But adversity, affliction, calamity, catastrophe—plain old suffering "without cause" (Job 2:3)—rarely seem to make sense. We see no connection between our behavior and our circumstances *because there is none*. That is why this kind of suffering is uniquely a *testing* of our *faith*—its genuineness and sincerity, its motives, its depth, its steadfastness, its object. It is the inexplicability of affliction that generates frustration, questions, and even doubts. That was Job's predicament. But through the process of suffering, Job discovered a great deal about himself and about God. Exploring Job's experience uncovers a great deal about Job's faith and ours, about Job's God and ours.

Searching for the Theme

There is no shortage of competing theories about the theme of Job. Surveying some of the themes proposed by various scholars who have studied the book will broaden our thinking and illustrate how multifaceted the story really is. Weighing the various proposals will enable us to narrow our focus as well.

The problem of suffering. Why do the righteous suffer?[8] In the popular vernacular, why do bad things happen to good people? Some assert that Job sets out to explain the mystery of undeserved suffering and to answer our questions about it.[9] Though God does "answer" Job out of the whirlwind (Job 38:1),[10] He does not explain. No solution to the mystery is forthcoming. "If this was the real aim of the work, it is clearly a conspicuous failure."[11]

Theodicy. Others see the purpose of Job as primarily a justification of God's ways to man. The book seeks to vindicate the justice of all God's ways, to reconcile what we know about God with what we experience—especially when what we experience seems to contradict what we think we know.

The maintenance of faith in the midst of suffering. Job, some insist, is designed to demonstrate that genuine worship exists in the world. It is possible to "keep the faith" even in the face of undeserved, unexplained, and even severe suffering.[12]

Discrediting retribution theology. Retribution theology is the notion that bad things happen only to bad people, that all calamity is traceable to specific evil, that every affliction is caused by some sin. This idea is reflected by the disciples in John 9:1–2. Job sets out to disprove that kind of thinking in his friends.[13]

Doubt as a sign of mature faith. Some think that the book of Job harmonizes skepticism toward orthodox theology with a sincere faith in God. In other words, one can reject orthodox doctrine and still be a true believer. According to one writer, "The principal function of the Book of Job was, and is, to demonstrate dramatically and forcefully that doubt as to the correctness of religious affirmations concerning ultimate reality is a sign of mature faith."[14] This sounds suspiciously self-serving. It smells like a skeptic's excuse to project into this book his own unbelief so that he can turn around and congratulate himself for having a faith that is mature enough to disbelieve.[15] Some even canonize "Job the rebel" as "the patron saint of religious rebellion" for legitimizing "a voice of moral outrage" against God's injustice in the world. This gratuitous reading of self back into the book crashes, however, when "Job the rebel" abandons his "moral outrage" and falls to his knees in submission to God's nonanswer.[16] It is not Job's doubt that creates the tension; it is his faith.[17] "It is precisely because he knows God to be there, and to be loving and just, that he has such a hard time understanding such [apparent] injustice."[18] It is not doubting that relieves this tension; it is faith—the submission of doubt to what God says is so, even (and especially) in the face of the inexplicable.

The incomprehensibility of God's ways to men. Some argue that the whole point of Job is to convince us that there are no ultimate answers to our questions about why God does (or allows) what He does. A more optimistic expression of this view often blends with the following theme.

Beauty versus chaos. We have no answers to the questions that disturb our souls and rankle our sense of justice, but we should not dwell morosely on such matters. We should focus instead on the beauty of life and the wonder of creation around us. By comparison, our sufferings will then seem sufferable, even insignificant. This, it is argued, is the essence of God's response to Job at the end of the book.[19] Folded into this view is an undeniably appealing element of trust and optimism, akin to Paul's perspective on suffering (Rom. 8:18ff.; 2 Cor. 4:17–18). The difference is that Paul focused not on comparisons with the present beauties of this world but on future certainties in the next. Such an analysis of Job 38–41 makes God a Pollyanna, singing songs to a heavy heart (Prov. 25:20).[20] Someone insulated from personal suffering, or agnostic in his view of God as He has revealed Himself in Scripture, may derive comfort from such a diversion. It is difficult to imagine, however, that anyone with Job's view of God (as sovereign, just, and beneficent) who experiences Job's kind of suffering would find such an answer meaningful or satisfying. Moreover, the text of Job 38–41 itself indicates that something altogether different is going on in God's answer.

Putting man in his place. This line of reasoning focuses on the humbling of Job (and us) as the ultimate point of the story. In the final interrogation, God pulls rank and awes Job into submissive silence; so the book is designed to quiet our questions and put us in our place in relation to God.

All of these themes have varying degrees of merit. Even the theory that focuses on Job's doubt as a sign of mature faith suggests a valid insight we will explore later—that God values frankness and honesty over piously repeated platitudes that merely mask the thoughts of our heart. Job was willing to challenge certain tenets of the traditional theology of his day with empirical evidence to the contrary, though it is critical to remember that this took place prior to written revelation. All the themes above recognize legitimate and often major facets of the story, but each one latches onto one segment of the book, often at the expense of other sections.[21]

Questions help us get to the roots of the story. Biblical answers to these questions are essential for settling the story's thematic issues. Proving these answers will be the task of the remainder of the book.

Questions and Answers

Flotsam from a sunken ship testifies that a tragedy occurred, but what caused it? An iceberg? A torpedo? A fire? The surface of the book of Job is scattered with the flotsam of Job's former life. But the debris is only indicative. The suffering is symptomatic. What initiated this calamity? The book's negative answer to that is emphatic: *it was not Job's sin* (1:1, 8; 2:3). The book's positive answer is startling: *it was Job's faith, esteemed by God and impugned by Satan* (1:8–9). Who initiated the chain of events that resulted in this calamity? *God, not Satan, brought up the issue and the name of Job* (1:8). What issue underlies Satan's counteraccusation? *The integrity and basis of the relationship between Job and God* (1:10–11). What specific event precipitated all Job's suffering? *The express permission of God* (1:12; 2:6). Who instigated the incidents that caused Job's sufferings? *Satan, through man and natural elements* (1:12*b*–19; 2:7). Who was in control of all Job's suffering? *God, not Satan, claimed responsibility for everything Job suffered* (2:3). What is Job's chief question throughout the book? *Why God had turned against him* (e.g., 7:20–21). What is the central topic of discussion throughout the debate between Job and his friends? *Not Job and his sufferings, but God—His attributes, His actions, His ways, and His relationship with man.* What does God emphasize in His answer to Job? *His creative sovereignty over, intimate knowledge* *of, and compassionate care for, His creation.* What is Job's response to God's answer? *Confession of God's sovereign freedom to do whatever He pleases* (42:2), *contrition over his rash and ignorant insinuations* (42:3), *and contented submission to his God* (42:4–6). God ignores Job's central question, yet Job finds peace in his relationship to God and in his circumstances.

In the end, the true basis of Job's relationship with God, and God's with Job, has been demonstrated. It is rooted not in possessions ("blessings"), as Satan insinuated, but in a Person. Contentment in that relationship, amid *any* circumstances, is rooted not in understanding everything God does but in trusting what He says He is like. Job maintains his faith in what he knows about God and learns to submit contentedly to what he does not understand.

The Centrality of God

Tracing the names of God in the book of Job is not a pedantic academic exercise. This theological and literary detail quantifies the dominant subject and underlying theme of Job. To identify what the book is about, listen to what Job and the others spend the most time discussing.

Job's suffering may initiate but does not dominate the discussion. Instead, everyone keeps talking about *God.* At least a dozen proper names or titles for God—including Jehovah, Lord, Almighty, Holy One, Redeemer, Judge, Maker, Watcher of men—appear over 180 times in Job.[22] That may not sound very impressive at an average of only four titles per chapter. However, virtually every occurrence of a divine name or title is followed by dozens of pronouns referring back to Him. For example:

- Job's speech in chapters 9–10 contains 70 references to God in 55 verses.
- Zophar's reply in chapter 11 contains 12 references to God in 20 verses.
- Job's rejoinder in chapters 12–13 contains 69 references to God in 75 verses.

Throughout the debate between Job and his friends they talk less about Job's suffering and more about God's character, God's ways, and God's relationship with man.[23] Sometimes the Lord has to take drastic measures to get people to talk about Him seriously and to seek Him in earnest.

This is not to say that "God" is the theme of Job, per se. But recognizing the centrality of God is important—in our understanding of Job and of our own suffering—to move us away from our myopic obsession with our circumstances to something and Someone much bigger, outside ourselves, and over our circumstances. Job's suffering is the occasion for communicating far larger spiritual issues than the problem of personal pain. "The book does not set out to answer the problem of suffering but to proclaim a God so great that no answer is needed, for it would transcend the finite mind if given."[24]

Does this mean the book of Job has nothing to say about how to deal with suffering? Of course not. But the book teaches us very little about *why* we suffer—which is what we, like Job, always want to know. God never explained that to Job. What we learn instead is who is in control when we suffer (and who is not), how to help those who are suffering (and how not to), and how we should respond to suffering (and how we shouldn't).

How we respond to suffering (rather than why we suffer) comes closer to the thematic center of the book.[25] The book ends by showing us Job's response; he is content, patient, and submitted. But why should we respond to adversity that way? There is the book's bull's eye. Our faith relationship to a God Who is sovereign, always just, and unfailingly compassionate despite all contrary appearances—and His right to allow us to suffer without compromising any of those attributes—is the underlying theme. The book of Job unfolds the motive and basis of that relationship (the heart of Satan's challenge in the first place) and our interaction with God in that relationship (the hub around which the discourses revolve) especially in the face of circumstances that challenge that relationship.[26]

What Is Job All About?

A thematic statement of Job needs to be narrow enough to be helpful yet comprehensive enough to encompass every major segment of the book in a meaningful way.

The primary *subject* under discussion throughout the book of Job is God. The concept of suffering is only a secondary subject, the catalyst for the discussion. The *theme* of Job is the nature and basis of the relationship between God and man—founded on faith in God's self-revelation as ultimate reality and God's Person as supremely worthy. The *function* of the book is to display the dynamics of the relationship between God and man—honesty, trust, and submission to a sovereign, wise, and good God. The *thesis* of the book is two-sided: (1) God is unquestionably sovereign, sometimes inscrutable, but always righteous, aware, compassionate, and good in all He does or allows. (2) Man has the privilege and responsibility to know and to trust this one true God in an intimate and infinitely rewarding relationship.

> What is the message of the Book of Job? If the popular idea that the Book of Job is primarily about suffering is correct, then we must conclude that the book is a failure. No real answer is given to the question of why the righteous suffer. The problem of suffering is discussed at length, but this is not the primary theme of the book. Rather, suffering is a channel through which the basic issue is brought to the fore. The real problem discussed by Job and his friends is the question of man's relationship to God. Can a man really know God? The Book of Job raises the question of innocent suffering as a genuinely relevant issue to discuss the whole nature of the relationship between God and man. Why the righteous suffer is discussed to show how a man can truly relate to God.[27]

The message of Job regarding our relationship to God is threefold: (1) reverent worship, with or without reward, because He is worthy; (2) confident faith, with or without evidence, because He has spoken; and (3) trusting submission, with or without understanding, because He is both sovereign and good.

An Analogy: Suffering as a Catalyst

You probably learned about catalysts in high school chemistry. A catalyst initiates or modifies a chemical reaction between elements but is not itself altered by the process. In nonscientific terms, a catalyst precipitates a process or event without being directly involved in or changed by that process or event.

The story of Job begins with God and man in a crucible. For us to observe their relationship and interaction, the catalyst of suffering must be poured in. The debate does not alleviate suffering; it remains until God Himself removes it. He does not remove the suffering until *after* all the issues in this relationship have been resolved. Suffering in the book of Job functions as a catalyst that initiates the relational interaction between God and man.

One writer describes a transformation in his understanding of Job and offers his own analogy:

> If you had asked me when I began my study what the Book of Job was about, I would have been quick to respond. Job? Everybody knows what Job is about. It's the Bible's most complete treatment of the problem of suffering. It's about terrible grief and bewildering pain. Without doubt the bulk of the book does center on the theme of suffering. . . . Job, his three friends, and the enigmatic Elihu . . . are all trying to account for the slings and arrows of outrageous fortune that have fallen upon poor Job, who sits forlorn in the ashes of what used to be his mansion. I now believe I misread the book—or, more accurately, didn't take into account the entire book. . . . I am coming to the conclusion that Job is not really about the problem of pain. Suffering contributes the ingredients of the story, not its central theme. Just as a cake is not about eggs, flour, milk, and shortening, but uses those ingredients in the process of creating a cake, Job is not "about" suffering; it merely uses such ingredients in its larger story, which concerns even more important questions, cosmic questions. Seen as a whole, Job is primarily about faith in its starkest form. . . . The point of the book is not suffering: Where is God when it hurts? The prologue dealt with that issue. The point is faith: Where is Job when it hurts? How is he responding? To understand the Book of Job, I must begin there.[28]

To some this may sound too theological. Whatever we identify as the book's theme or purpose or meaning, the fact remains that it takes place in a context of unparalleled human suffering in every conceivable dimension—physical agony, emotional anguish, mental angst, spiritual desolation. Some may find it hard to believe that the answer to that kind of pain lies in theology.

"For tortured spirits," says one writer, "theology is less satisfying than religion, and religion is encounter, encounter with God. It is in the sphere of religion rather than theology that the meaning of the book is to be found."[29] But without correct (and corrective) theology there *is* no true religion. If our encounter with God is not grounded in theological realities, our religion is fabricated out of our own imagination. Religion that is not rooted in the objective self-revelation of God is no more a solution to our suffering than a narcotic that alters our perception of reality.

It is theology—right thinking about God based on revelation from God—that humbles Job and adjusts his attitude toward his experiences and toward the God of his experiences. But what *comforts* Job is the *Theos* of *theo*logy. What satisfies Job's soul is God Himself.[30] Principles do not minister to people in pain. Only a person can comfort, and only one Person can comfort effectually.

Job's head wanted answers. He asked "Why?" some twenty times. It was a question God never answered. Job's heart wanted God. Christianity can become as hollow and lifeless as any false religion if it becomes removed from Christ, if it is reduced from a Person to mere principles. Speaking from painful personal experience, Joni Eareckson Tada points out that "Why?" is, at its roots, a "me-oriented" question. It is a natural, instinctive, and valid question in the face of suffering, and she explores several biblical answers to that question. In the end, however, even "good answers aren't enough." After all, "answers are for the head." Suffering is the divinely ordained catalyst to draw, or drive, us to Himself. "We must never distance the Bible's answers from God. The problem of suffering is not about some *thing*, but *Someone*. It follows that the answer must not be some thing, but Someone." By our deliberate choice, "God must be at the center of things. He must be in the center of our suffering." And God "doesn't just give advice. He gives himself." In the final analysis, He is "the only answer that ultimately matters," the only One Who can fill and satisfy the suffering soul.[31] This is not a matter of finding where God fits into the picture of our suffering. He *is* the picture. "He is not a missing piece of our life which, once found, can be bolted into place so our spiritual lives run efficiently and smoothly."[32] As Paul says, Christ "is our life" (Col. 3:4).

The story of Job is a paradigm of the relationship between God and man. It is an incarnation—a fleshing out—of man's earthbound relationship to his heavenly Father, a model of how God and man relate and interact in the rough-and-tumble of real life in a fallen world.

II

Prologue: Job, God, and Satan

3

What Kind of People Suffer?

Job 1:1–5

Imagine a pastoral landscape of distant fields dotted with flocks. In the foreground stands a lone figure with a wine-colored robe offset by a cummerbund of gold fabric. His ringed fingers embrace a silver goblet engraved with the serpentine figure of a single leviathan spiraling the cup—from its tail that wreathes the goblet's stem, up to the rim where its mouth gapes at an evening sky of rayed stars. He paces in the pool of a single spotlight, reflecting on all his surrounding wealth. His opening soliloquy is a prayer:

> O Lord, if this were lost instead,
> And all I had was you, I would
> Be rich, and have the greatest Good.
> But I do love my seven sons,
> And all my daughters, Lord, the ones
> Above all land and name and wealth,
> And even, God, above my health.
> For them I praise and bless your name,
> And pray that any sin or blame
> In them would be forgiven by
> The mercy you have shown in sky
> And earth these forty years that they
> Have lived now even to this day.[1]

So opens the drama of Job in my mind's eye. The Holy Spirit begins by introducing us to Job, scattering more data throughout the book about this remarkable, yet remarkably human, person.

A Godly Believer (1:1)

"There was a man in the land of Uz named Job" (Job 1:1).[2] A four-dimensional description of Job is repeated three times in the prologue (1:1, 8; 2:3). Two adjectives describe his character internally ("perfect") and externally ("upright"). Two verbs portray his demeanor vertically (he "feared God") and horizontally (he "eschewed evil"). Each term unshutters a window into his soul.

Perfect does not mean sinless. The Hebrew word (*tam*) denotes "wholeness" or "integrity." In mathematics, "integers" are *whole* numbers; fractions convey incompleteness. On a scale of 1 to 5, Job's character index was not 3½ or even 4¾, but a full 5. He is all he ought to be, everything anyone could expect. We would call such a person "sound"—no character flaws compromise his consistency or dependability.

Upright (*yashar*) depicts what is straight or level, "human behavior that is in line with God's ways."[3] Whereas the previous term highlights *internal* wholeness of character, this word implies *external* straightness in comparison to others.[4] Job is "on the level" in his dealings with others. Both terms combined describe an extraordinary character of the highest caliber.

Job also *feared God,* a classic expression of biblical religion. References to fearing God appear over a hundred times in the Old Testament and several times in the New Testament. In light of the modern innocuous use of "awesome,"[5] the popular paraphrase "reverential awe" dilutes the force of the expression and diminishes the biblical response to a holy and glorious God. The "fear of God" in the Bible is not just an inward awe over His greatness, but an outward obedience because of His God-ness—His authority to command, His ability to discipline, and His awareness of all we are and do. [6] The book of Job contains the first (chronological) references to the fear of God. (See also 6:14; 22:4; 28:28; 37:24.) Fearing God is not an outmoded concept that has no place in Christianity. The New Testament emphasizes it as well.[7] The child of God should fear to disobey His Father. Such fear is an expression of faith that He really does mean what He says about sin and its consequences, and an expression of love that is afraid to mar the relationship by displeasing Him.[8]

Finally, Job *shunned evil.* The KJV translation *eschewed evil* is not an everyday expression, but it captures the outward aspect of the "fear of the Lord." The English word *eschew,* related to the word *shy,* implies being frightened of evil. The Hebrew verb means to recoil and to go out of one's way to avoid. Job feared God and was frightened of evil because he understood the true nature of each. Being frightened of evil is not a sign of immaturity or paranoia. It is the same sane aversion to danger that my nephew has to peanuts; they may appear harmless but he knows they can kill him.

A man of private integrity and public honesty, God-fearing and evil-shunning. This is "an impressive accumulation of epithets to indicate that Job was a model of excellence—a blameless, whole-hearted servant of God who failed in none of his duties to men."[9] The threefold repetition of this four-dimensional description of Job is a deliberate device to establish Job's righteousness firmly in the reader's mind. It is the integrity of Job's character and of his relationship to God that Satan, and later his friends, will attack relentlessly. Armed with this insight, we should not mistake the cause of his troubles as they did. Job is a sinner, to be sure, but the narrator informs us, in a literary version of shouting it at us, that what happens to Job is *not* because of his sin.[10]

Centuries later God brings up Job's name and character again. When the kingdom of Judah slid into idolatry, God decided to judge the nation with national humiliation, devastation, and slavery as He had warned centuries earlier. Her wickedness was terminal, her condition past the power of prayer. God told Ezekiel that even if Noah, Daniel, and Job were living in Judah at that time, they would not be able to persuade Him to deliver anyone but themselves by the skin of their own righteous teeth (Ezek. 14:14, 20).[11] God's repeated emphasis on "their righteousness" expresses His esteem for them as paragons of godly character. Out of all the possibilities—the patriarchs Abraham or Joseph, leaders such as Moses or David, prophets such as Elijah and Elisha, Isaiah and Jeremiah—the three men most noted for their righteousness that came to *God's* mind were Noah, Daniel, and Job.[12] That extraordinary divine assessment must be factored into our understanding of the story of Job.

A Wealthy Man (Job 1:3)

Genuinely godly *and* fabulously wealthy? Here is a combination as intriguing as it is rare (Luke 18:25–27). Centuries before Paul penned his admonition to the wealthy (1 Tim. 6:17–19), Job personified the apostle's exhortation not to be conceited or to trust in wealth (see Job 31:24–25) but to be rich in good works, generous, and ready to share (see Job 31:16–23). Job was not among those who imagine prosperity to be a sign of one's piety and God's approval (1 Tim. 6:5). He understood—not just theoretically when he still had all his stuff, but even in the vise of total loss and devastation—that his wealth was not his just reward for right living. He understood that his wealth was not even *his* (Job 1:21). But it gets even more astonishing.

A Model Father (Job 1:4–5)

Genuinely godly *and* fabulously wealthy *and* a conscientious father? The description of these festive seasons (along with the fact that the cycle is repeating itself again when disaster strikes in 1:19) indicates this was a family tradition. These feasts may have commemorated the yearly birthday celebrations for each of the siblings[13] or the observance of other holidays. Others think that it was the weekly practice of each of the seven sons to take a turn hosting all their siblings for a meal.[14]

Job's sacrifices have become the subject of unfortunate and unnecessary speculation.[15] Job offered atonement not for known or suspected sins but because he knew the potential for sin inherent in human nature ("*it may be* that my sons have sinned, and cursed God *in their hearts*"). To suppose that Job's sacrifices on behalf of his children imply that these festive occasions involved sinful indulgences is unwarranted. The boundaries of the text are always our safest interpretational guide. Here the underlying premise of the entire book comes into play: there was no logical, self-evident, cause-and-effect explanation for what was about to happen (1:1, 8; 2:3). The text casts these feasts in an innocent and positive light. These "delightful family gatherings are part of the atmosphere of well-being that begins the story"—just one more sign of God's blessing on Job.[16] Likewise, the reference to Job's sacrifices is one more way of underscoring his exemplary righteousness.

Job's tireless attentiveness to his children's spiritual welfare ("thus did Job continually") is extraordinary.

> It was the sacred habit of the family to throw the safeguards of religion around every period of mutual entertainment and social enjoyment. Whenever his children gathered, as they regularly did, at each other's houses on festive occasions, cementing and displaying their fond fraternal affection, it was Job's invariable custom to summon all together afterwards, and sanctify them, and offer burnt offerings according to the number of them all.[17]

Job *would send and consecrate them* (NASB). Functioning as the family priest, he regularly and conscientiously dedicated them to God for cleansing and blessing.[18] In addition, he *rose up early in the morning, and offered burnt offerings*—an intercessory offering on behalf of each one to expiate his sins. We even get a glimpse into Job's thinking as the motivation for his actions: *It may be that my sons have sinned, and cursed God in their hearts.* Job's parental example is striking for at least three reasons.

First, Job's concern for his children's spiritual welfare displays his spiritual values. This is not obsessive anxiety.[19] Job was no fretful parent, and his behavior cannot be faulted or connected with his later suffering without undercutting God's admission that there was no just cause for what happened to him (2:3). The whole point of this introduction is to put Job in the show window—to display his model godliness in every area of life—so that when the suffering descends we will not make the same mistaken assumption as his friends. Nevertheless, Job was a godly man who knew human nature and the seriousness of evil. He shunned it himself and rightly feared its effects in his children's lives.

Second, Job's sacrifices for his children reveal his spiritual discernment. It is not enough to produce children who appear outwardly religious and respectable. Job is not merely afraid that his children might commit some public indiscretion that would embarrass the family and mar their reputation in the community. He is focused on the Godwardness of their spirits and their internal purity, lest they have cursed God *in their hearts.* Parents need to make inner purity of heart a priority in praying for their children.

Third, Job's behavior displays his spiritual responsibility. His leadership in this area harmonizes with a refrain repeated throughout Scripture that fathers bear the primary responsibility for the spiritual upbringing and welfare of their children (Eph. 6:4).

An Impeccable Reputation

Though a sinner, Job was an icon of impeccability. Godly, wealthy, and a good father—the narrator's opening testimony to Job's character makes Job's later protests of his innocence that much more believable. He was highly respected in the community (29:7–11), a fair and honorable judge (29:7, 12–17), a wise and influential counselor (29:21–25), an honest and just employer (31:13–15, 38–39), hospitable and generous (31:16–21, 32), scrupulous in moral purity (31:1, 9–12), and memorialized for his patience under severe trial (James 5:11).

Patience? More than one scholar accuses James of ignorance when it comes to crediting this virtue to Job. One writer is particularly audacious: "Everyone who speaks of the patience of Job (Js. 5:11) shows thereby that he has but a vague acquaintance with the poem [of Job], or probably none at all."[20] Another presumes to correct James's misdiagnosis: "Honesty, not patience, is the real virtue of Job."[21] Anyone who dismisses the New Testament writer's inspired assessment of Job exposes an elementary understanding of "patience." This biblical virtue is not a sappy, carefree cheeriness. It is a manly word that means "to remain under" whatever pressure or pain one is presently enduring from the hand of God.[22]

Patience is fortitude under adversity. Job struggled to maintain his integrity and his faith under great duress. The fact that he did not buckle under the pressure to turn against God (2:9–10), nor seek a way out of his circumstances through desertion or death (for which he longed, 6:8–9), nor surrender his integrity in deference to his friends' theology, attests to his patience. At the same time, anyone who supposes that Job's response was always flawless and unfaltering has not read the story with attention. Under provocation, even Job says some shocking things. That does not diminish his patience in the least.

James 5:7–11 is gently persistent in emphasizing our need for patience amid suffering. Six times in five verses James uses two synonyms for "patience" or "endurance." He does not issue a generic command just to "wait" indefinitely. Three times his exhortation to patience is tied to a specific and certain anticipation—the coming of the Lord.

Patience is not suffering in silence (Job certainly didn't), and endurance does not mean being an emotionless stoic (Job certainly wasn't). The first word (*makrothumia,* James 5:7–10) denotes long-suffering, a willingness to put up with someone or something for a long time. The second word (*hupomonē,* twice in James 5:11) describes perseverance, a resolute determination to remain under and work through whatever circumstances a sovereign God ordains.

The prophets, including Job, were fully human. People of "like passions" with us (James 5:17), they were remarkably honest with their God. They suffered at the hands of people and circumstances. Sometimes they cried out to Him. Sometimes they wept before Him. Sometimes they complained to Him. Sometimes they even accused Him. But they *never forsook* Him. They clung to Him and to His Word. They *endured.* And God ultimately proved Himself and His Word entirely worthy of their trust. In the end, their patience was worth the wait and more than repaid.

What Kind of People Suffer Adversity?

Our instinctive question when suffering strikes is "Why?" That question requests an explanation that makes some sense of our suffering. Sometimes we ask it in a slightly different form: "Why *me*?" That question subtly shifts from requesting a reason for the suffering to demanding a justification for aiming the suffering at us. It suggests, "I can understand why this might happen to some other people but I'm a decent person. I haven't done anything to deserve this."

How do we measure up to Job—reputable in society, meticulous in moral behavior, genuine in personal spirituality, conscientious in family life? There was no one else like him then. There have been few like him since. There is a reason the book opens with a portrait of Job's godly character and happy home life, surrounded by all the signs of God's blessing. Job was, quite literally, the last person on earth to deserve what was about to happen to him.

This chapter opened with a question. What kind of people suffer adversity? We expect bad things to happen to bad people. But that's not the kind of suffering Job addresses. The Bible's classic example of suffering inexplicable affliction is Job, one of the best men the world has ever seen. If you don't measure up to Job's level of godliness and yet still find yourself suffering inexplicable adversity, part of the message of Job is this: It happens to the best of us, and it happens to better than us. Someone observed that the story of Job is not about God making a bad man good but making a good man better.

4

What on Earth (and Beyond) Is Going On?

Job 1:6–12

When I was in college, I worked on the floor crew of an auditorium that staged a variety of dramatic productions, everything from musical concerts to Italian operas to Shakespearean plays. We often used a versatile staging device called a scrim, a thin backdrop of finely meshed material painted with scenery. Lit from the front it appears opaque like any other backdrop. When the lighting shifts backstage, however, the scrim's translucence enables the audience to see through it to a separate, simultaneous scene-behind-the-scene.

The introduction to Job (1:1–5) occurs upstage. Job stands amid the pastoral scene (1:1–3), while his sons and daughters make a merry pass across the stage on their way to a family gathering (1:4). Alone again, Job lifts his hands in intercession to God for them (1:5). Cue lights. Between verses 5 and 6, the forestage gradually darkens until a single spotlight illumines Job while the lights come up backstage, behind the scrim, to reveal Satan on a raised platform above and behind Job. The audience becomes privy to a heavenly conversation related in Job 1:6–12—an exchange to which Job is deaf and blind. Facing the audience, Job has no idea what is happening on the set behind him. A masterful stroke of dramatic irony gives the reader a glimpse backstage at a parallel reality beyond.

Dramatic irony is a literary device that lets the audience in on something that a character in the story does not know. The irony may be developed in several ways: "the character acts in a way grossly inappropriate to the actual circumstances, or expects the opposite of what fate holds in store, or says something that anticipates the actual outcome, but not at all in the way he means it."[1] All of these are present to some degree in Job. For example, Job came to believe that God had turned against him and expected to die in disgrace; he never dreamed of recovery and reward. Job repeatedly called for a hearing before God to ask why He had turned against him and sent all this suffering; but he never anticipated it this side of the grave. Job even desired that his words be memorialized in a book!

The prologue divides naturally into four parts, each signaled by a repeated transitional phrase.

"There was a man . . ." (1:1–5) introduces the reader to Job.

"Now there was a day . . ." (1:6–12) informs the reader of the proceedings of the divine council in heaven.

"[Now] there was a day . . ." (1:13–22) recounts the earthly impact of that divine council, namely, Job's possessional losses and his response.

"Again there was a day . . ." (2:1–13) relates the second divine council and its impact on Job's personal suffering and response.

The Scene Backstage (Job 1:6)

"Now there was a day when the sons of God came to present themselves before the Lord, and Satan came also among them." The interchange in Job 1:6–12 is pivotal for understanding the story. This glimpse backstage colors our reading of the rest of the book. This passage epitomizes an old cliché: there is more to Job's circumstances —and ours—"than meets the eye." We are at a distinct advantage over Job and over his friends. After all, we understand exactly what is going on, and why. Or do we?

This is not a "wager" between God and Satan.[2] This is *warfare*. But who fires the first salvo? Who brings up Job's name in the first place (1:8)? God, not Satan, first draws attention to Job. God does not react; He acts. This subtle detail immediately establishes God's sovereignty over all that follows.

The Enemy (Job 1:7)

"Satan" appears fourteen times in Job, all in chapters 1–2.[3] He is consistently identified throughout the Hebrew text as "the adversary" (*ha-satan*). Because Satan is the adversary of God, he is necessarily the adversary of man, for man alone is created in the image of God. Anything that resembles or delights God is the object of Satan's disdain and opposition.

Satan describes himself as "going to and fro through the earth" and "walking up and down in it." The first phrase describes Satan's unrestricted roaming throughout the world, his untethered access to all the earth. No boundaries. The whole world is his realm of observation and operation. The second term is the simple verb for walking (*halak*), but in a form that implies walking around, wandering, exploring (cf. Gen. 13:17), or pacing. The Greek version of the Old Testament here uses a verb *(peripateō)* from which we derive the word *peripatetic*. Peter uses a related verb in the New Testament to describe our "adversary the devil" on the prowl "as a roaring lion *walk[ing] about*, seeking whom he may devour" (1 Pet. 5:8). In Job 1:7, these are not merely descriptions *about* Satan; they are self-descriptions used *by* Satan—the language of "a restless, ubiquitous being, a vagabond among the angels."[4]

These are not encouraging images. Like unarmed natives working by day in jungle-bordered fields and sleeping by night in vulnerable grass huts, we seem to be at the mercy of this cruel predatory beast who roams at will. What is encouraging is how both terms describing Satan's ceaseless activity are also used to describe God's ceaseless activity.

Satan claims to rove the earth at will (Job 1:7; 2:2) but he does not roam unwatched. God's angels also patrol "to and fro through the earth" (Zech. 1:10; 6:7). More reassuring still, "the eyes of the Lord" Himself "run to and fro throughout the whole earth, to show himself strong in the behalf of those whose heart is perfect toward him" (2 Chron. 16:9; cf. Zech. 4:10). He is watching for opportunities to intervene for certain people—not perfect people, but men and women and children who are completely His and whose hearts are loyal to Him alone.[5]

While Satan prowls the world in search of prey, "the Lord thy God *walks* in the midst of your camp, to deliver you and give your enemies over to you" (Deut. 23:14, NKJV). The word *walk* is the same form of the same verb Satan uses to describe himself (Job 1:7; 2:2). God moves constantly about like a general inspecting the condition and morale of his troops, or pacing like a sleepless sentry on constant patrol.[6] A lion roams loose, unbound but not unwatched, ferocious but not unrivaled. He is a trespasser in the territory of another Lion that infinitely outmatches him (Rev. 5:5).

Satan is not God's opposite. Satan is God's archnemesis and opposes all that God does and loves. But if "you mean a power opposite God and, like God, self-existent from all eternity, the answer is certainly No. . . . God has no opposite."[7] Satan may be the opposite of Michael—intelligent and powerful but created and limited—but not of God. God has no remotely comparable evil counterpart. Remembering this reality takes the terror out of his roar: "the terrible *Satan* is only another of the *sons of God*,"[8] angelic creatures summoned to appear before the God of heaven *and earth*.

> There is profound meaning in representing Satan as appearing before God, for he is thereby designated as subordinate and in subjection to divine control. He cannot act on his own discretion or without any boundaries. He must receive permission from the Sovereign Lord.[9]

Rather than puzzling us, the appearance of Satan before the Lord along with all the other angels should comfort us. As powerful and wicked as he may be, he is not independent of God's control. He is under authority and accountable to God. The narrative ahead makes that even clearer.

Ignorance of the enemy leads to underestimation. We should not be ignorant of Satan's character or devices, plots or purposes (2 Cor. 2:11).[10] Boito's opera *Mefistofele* imaginatively captures the character and attitude of Satan, condensing his self-centered arrogance and implacable rebellion into a single monosyllable ("No!"). The relish with which he pronounces it—sometimes roaring, sometimes hissing with icy insolence—is accentuated by his signature shrill whistle of defiance. Satan's true character is revealed by his words and actions in Job, especially as they contrast with God's character.[11]

- God notes our actions and knows our motives (1:8). Satan scrutinizes our actions and suspects our motives (1:9).
- God pities and defends us before Satan (2:3). Satan hates and accuses us before God (1:10–11).
- God grants permission in sovereign confidence (1:12). Satan is a liar and a cheat who tries to change the rules to save face and win (2:4–5).
- God alone grants, withholds, and regulates permission, while Satan's evil designs are circumscribed by the consent of God (1:12; 2:6).
- God is always good in His designs and gracious in His disposition (42:7–17). Satan is cruel whenever unleashed and given the opportunity (1:13–19; 2:7–8).

Robert Bell notes perceptively, "Satan would have us believe that God is not fair, yet we seldom consider the cruelty of the devil. I have never met anyone bitter about what Satan has done to him, but I have met many who were bitter toward God."[12]

The Gauntlet (Job 1:8–11)

In singling out Job, the Lord "brings him into perilous prominence."[13] God initiates the challenge: *Have you considered my servant Job?* Why is this so significant? Because it means that our sufferings do not arise at the whim of Satan's snooping malevolence but out of the considered attention of God Himself.

> It is God who first calls attention to Job, God who permits the trial of his faith . . . and assigns its proper limits. Throughout it is the will of God that is being done. . . . All that comes to Job comes not by blind chance nor by the compulsion of the Adversary. It is the simple development of God's first word: "Hast thou considered my servant Job?"[14]

The "accuser of our brethren" (Rev. 12:10) and the consummate prosecuting attorney has a ready riposte: *Does Job fear God for nothing?* The phrase *for nothing* can carry either the idea of "without compensation" or "without cause [reason]." The details of Satan's indictment in 1:10 imply that the meaning here is "without compensation." Either nuance works since Satan insinuated that the reason Job worshiped God was the remuneration he received from God in the form of prosperity. *Does Job fear God without a payoff? Haven't you meticulously insulated and protected him* ("made an hedge about him") *and his family* ("and about his house") *and his possessions* ("and about all that he hath on every side") *and paid him off* ("blessed the work of his hands") *and compensated him handsomely* ("his substance is increased in the land")*?*

According to Satan, Job is pious only for pay. Job's alleged righteousness (1:8) is not merely a sham but a scam. The sham is that his piety is only pretended. The scam is that despite the payoff, God is not getting what He thinks He is. The popular "health and wealth" gospel of modern "prosperity theology" is the eerie echo of Satan's accusation—the proof that some people are holy for hire.[15] Satan's implication is clear: who wouldn't go through the motions of "fearing" God with that kind of kickback to sweeten the deal? The indictment oozes with insinuation, but not only against Job. After all, if God is omniscient, He cannot be scammed. If He knows Job's heart, then He is aware of the deception. Yet He is paying off Job anyway? That can mean only one thing: God is complicit in Job's hypocrisy. Suddenly neither Job nor God look very righteous. Satan's accusation is against Job on the surface, but it has a devilish undertow. Job and God are both scam artists. Meanwhile, others are watching and listening. Three crucial issues are at stake here—and the stakes are of cosmic proportions.

What Is at Stake?

A close look at Satan's accusation uncovers fault lines that run all the way down to hell. The first and most obvious issue sits on the surface in plain view. A second and larger issue runs deep beneath the surface. A third and wider issue reveals that the fault lines run clear throughout the whole of creation.

The Sincerity of Human Faith. The most obvious target of Satan's accusation is the genuineness and integrity of Job's faith in God, his fear of God, his service to God. The sincerity of man's faith, Satan insinuates, runs only as deep as his pocketbook, his material possessions, his guarantee of God's blessing in return. Take away the dividends, sever the link between piety and payola, and man has no incentive for worshiping God. Satan has a point. Experience and history substantiate that this is true of many people.

Most of the Christians I know are not wealthy. Probably not many of us can be accused of worshiping God because of what we get out of it materially. More common is a superstitious faith that behaves a certain way in order to avoid "bad things." If we are careful to perform our rituals faithfully, we suppose that will shield us from calamity. Some Christians have a rabbit's-foot approach to religion. But the satanic insinuation goes even deeper.

The Integrity of God. The second crucial issue at stake is the integrity of God. This is the more insidious implication underlying Satan's accusation: "Hast not thou made an hedge about him . . . ? *thou* hast blessed the work of his hands." The legal charge is quid pro quo, "this for that"—a trade-off that benefits both parties, mutual favors people do for one another to obtain benefits that are just out of their own reach ("you scratch my back and I'll scratch yours"). It is obvious to Satan what is going on here, for "the treacherous are ever distrustful."[16] If Satan is correct, then the whole pretended relationship between God and Job is a sham on *both* sides.

This is a charge with cosmic consequences. If God's people, including the best of men, honor Him only because He blesses them in return, God is a conniver who buys the flattery of insincere men. If God must *buy* such worship, what does that say of His own worth? Satan's charge not only impugns God's character but also attacks His intrinsic worthiness. Here is the ugly underbelly of Satan's accusation, and the first tip that the book is not ultimately about Job after all. In the final analysis "this book is as much about God being on trial as it is about Job being tested."[17]

"Wait!" someone protests. "Consider the source!" What about the accuser's lack of character and credibility? Why should anyone listen to "that old serpent" (Rev. 12:9; 20:2)?[18] Jesus called him a murderer and a liar (John 8:44). Why is God obligated to prove anything to such a scoundrel as Satan—especially at the expense of an innocent man's suffering? That is where the third issue comes into play.

The Celestial Audience. Job stands center stage as his whole world crumbles around him. But Job is not merely *on* the stage. Job *is* the stage, his soul the arena of a cosmic struggle. On his response to affliction hinges the sincerity of his own faith, the credibility of human faith, and the character of God. From all appearances, God is pinning His own integrity on the response of a mortal.

All this raises a fundamental question: For whose benefit are these events happening? How can God benefit from proving what He already knows to be the case? How can Job benefit if he doesn't even know what is really going on and, apparently, never finds out? How does Satan benefit if he never admits defeat or changes his character? At the root of God's dealings with fallen people is His intention to display dimensions of His character to a spiritual world that we never see and rarely consider.[19]

In Ephesians 3:8–12 Paul piles phrase upon phrase into a single sentence as theologically provocative as it is grammatically complex. He glories in the privilege of preaching Christ's riches to the Gentiles (v. 8) and unfolding the previously unrevealed purpose of God to unite Jews and Gentiles into one body called the church (v. 9; see vv. 1–7). Verses 10–11 unveil God's larger purpose: "to the intent that" someone might somehow come to know something. But who, and how, and what? Work your way thoughtfully through this wardrobe of words and you suddenly find yourself standing on the edge of a snowy wood gazing out onto a whole new world you may have never seen before.[20] Ephesians 3:10 reads literally, "In order that now may be made known *to* the principalities and *to* the powers in the heavenlies, *through* the church, the manifold wisdom of God." God's intent in creating the world (v. 9) and the church (v. 10) is to display more facets of His wisdom to all the angels (cf. Eph. 1:21). God is constantly doing things to and for and in and through us (the church) in order to manifest His perfections to all angelic intelligences for their benefit and for His glory. Before we leave this snowy wood, glance up between the looming evergreens in verse 11 and the star-studded sky snatches away your breath: this grand design is God's "eternal purpose"—literally, *the purpose of the ages which He executed by Christ Jesus our Lord.* This new vista begins to answer our questions back in Job.

First Peter 1:12 informs us that angels peer with eager interest into God's dealings with men.[21] We assume that because angels live in God's presence they know everything that is going on and understand God completely. How could they? They are created like us, not eternal; less limited than us but not infinite; more intelligent than us but not omniscient. "We should presume that angels are ignorant of certain things, and that they long to know more as they see the fulfillment of God's purposes."[22] After all, they are God's servants, just as we are. There are things God does that they do not understand, just like us. And there are things God does to reveal Himself to them, just as He does to reveal Himself to us.[23]

Charles Bridges opens his classic work *The Christian Ministry* with Ephesians 3:10 and 1 Peter 1:12 in mind:

> The Church is the mirror that reflects the whole effulgence of the Divine character. It is the grand scene in which the perfections of Jehovah are displayed to the universe. The revelations made to the Church—the successive grand events in her history and, above all, the manifestation of "the glory of God in the person of Jesus Christ"—furnish even to the heavenly intelligences fresh subjects of adoring contemplation.[24]

If Ephesians 3:10 is a wardrobe portal to another world waiting to be explored, 1 Corinthians 4:9 is a full-color snapshot—straightforward, vivid, and instantly accessible.

First Corinthians 4:9 evokes the same theatrical motif I have used to develop the story of Job. "For I think that God hath set forth us the apostles last, as it were appointed to death: for we are made a spectacle unto the world, and to angels, and to men." *Set forth* is a technical term for "displaying theatrical entertainments."[25] Paul describes the apostles themselves as a *spectacle*—literally a *theatron*.[26] Men are a theater? For whom? Who is the audience? "For the world, for men, *and for angels*!"[27] Shakespeare was right: All the world's a stage!

The link between this New Testament revelation and the book of Job is the celestial audience in Job 1:6 and 2:10. Satan's charges were issued in the presence of the "sons of God" as they appeared before the Lord.[28] Likewise, the "test case" of Job and the silencing of Satan's slander against man and God must take place in as wide an audience as the charges.

Our theological vision has a tendency to become small-minded and man-centered. Anthropocentric by nature, man once assumed that our world was the center of the galaxy and that the sun revolved around the earth. People instinctively see themselves at the center of God's world as well.

We are not at the center of the universe; the Son is (Col. 1:16–19; Phil. 2:9–11). We are not even the center of God's redemptive activity. God is. His saving work is not prompted by our inherent worth (see Rom. 3:9–18), nor is He under any duty or obligation to save us.[29] God justifies every believer "freely" by His grace (Rom. 3:24)—that is, as a gift, without cause or compulsion.[30] That word *freely* is the same term used to describe the fact that Jesus' enemies hated Him "without a cause" (John 15:25). God had no more cause or necessity to save us than Jesus' enemies had to hate Him and hang Him on a cross. But God's saving work is the free choice of His good pleasure (Eph. 1:5, 9, 11) to the praise of His own glory and grace (Eph. 1:6, 12, 14).

This emphasis on the centrality of God does not minimize our genuine value and importance to God. We are valuable because He values us, and He values us uniquely because He created us alone in His own image and for His own glory. Emphasizing the centrality of God sharpens our focus on the real spiritual world around us and the multitude of spiritual beings other than us for whose benefit God does certain things. The angels understand and glorify God more as they learn about Him through His dealings with men. Revelation 5:8–14 describes the ranks of angels that swell the chorus of the redeemed. They lift their voices "to the praise of his glory" because they have seen more of God's power and compassion, sovereignty and mercy, wisdom and tenderness, through all His saving kindnesses to us (cf. Eph. 2:7).

This is what is going on in Job. This is what is at stake. The audience at the original live performance of Job consists of all the spiritual intelligences in the heavenlies.[31] God wants to display for all created beings the mutual genuineness and mutual integrity of the relationship between God and man. If the faith of even the best of men is insincere and rooted in self-interest, God would be a manipulative and deceptive deity who bribes man for worship. The whole created order would collapse into the chaos that follows the overthrow of a tyrant and a fraud. Satan, like Toto, would have pulled back the curtain to reveal a Cosmic Humbug loudly protesting, "Pay no attention to that man behind the curtain!" But that is not how this story ends. This is Uz, not Oz.

Permission Granted (Job 1:12)

God throws Satan's dare ("Put forth now thine hand") back in his face: "Behold, all that he hath is in thy power [lit., thine hand]; only upon himself put not forth thine hand." So whose hand was Job in, God's or Satan's? The technical answer is that Job was in Satan's hand because God says so. The full answer is yes because Job's God put him there and set the parameters. "What the prologue makes clear . . . is that this is indeed permission, not abdication; for in both these chapters it is God who sets the limits of the test. The conditions are all that the challenger could desire, but they are of God's choosing, not his."[32] Satan loses no time capitalizing on his advantage. "So Satan went forth from the presence of the Lord."

What Does This Have to Do with My Suffering?

The prologue is not intended to teach us that every time a believer suffers inexplicably, it is because of another satanic challenge. Job already suffered to prove the integrity of human faith and of God's character. The celestial jury found Satan's lawsuit against man and God to be frivolous and without merit; it has been summarily dismissed. Why give Satan's argument any further hearing just because he files it against some new defendant?

Job suffered to prove, among other things, that there *are* people who serve God "for nothing" other than for Who He is, people who worship God "without cause" (1:9) even when they suffer "without cause" (2:3).[33] What, then, does our suffering accomplish? When we cling to God amid inexplicable affliction, we demonstrate that *we* are some of those people. We are not proving anything further about the character and integrity of God; that was eternally substantiated by the case of Job.[34] But we are proving a great deal about ourselves, about the integrity of our faith and the sincerity of our relationship to God. More than any other kind of suffering, this kind of suffering is a testing of your faith (James 1:2–3).

We also affirm a great deal about our God. We magnify His worthiness and desirability when we are willing to suffer loss or injustice and still maintain our loyalty to the Lord and to His Word. "It demonstrates the enormously high value we attach to Him."[35]

> As you're reading this, tens of thousands of the Lord's pilgrims around the world are threatened with execution, torture, slavery, starvation, homelessness, poverty, imprisonment, and other persecutions designed to destroy their faith in Jesus Christ. And yet . . . they find it "worth [their] while to endure those hardships" because of what they have and hope for in Christ. . . . [O]ur endurance testifies to the worthiness of Christ. Unrelenting faithfulness in the absence of all earthly explanation says to the watching world, "It is worth enduring all this pain and heartache to know Christ and to anticipate the glory of being with Him forever."[36]

Every difficulty we or someone we love faces, every trial we endure, every loss we bear, every experience of inexplicable pain and suffering—and even the misunderstanding and rejection it may bring from friends or family—is a fresh opportunity to stand in the company of Job and to affirm that our faith, our worship, and our devotion to God is rooted in soil far deeper than personal advantage or material blessing or physical well-being. Knowing God is not about me and what I get but about understanding Who and what He is.

Tenacious suffering, though tearful, magnifies God's trustworthiness. It magnifies God in the eyes of others. It even magnifies God in the eyes of angels. And it delights God's heart as nothing else can. God's eventual answer to Job assures us that He takes note, and remembers, and responds. The story of Job is designed, in part, to help us cultivate a greater awareness of the reality of the spiritual warfare in which we are engaged. There is more to our circumstances, and more at stake in our response to them, than meets the eye. T. S. Eliot saw this as well.

> To believe in the supernatural is not simply to believe that after living a successful, material, and fairly virtuous life here one will continue to exist in the best possible substitute for this world, or that after living a starved and stunted life here one will be compensated with all the good things one has gone without: it is to believe that the supernatural is the greatest reality here and now.[37]

Weigh Your Afflictions Biblically

The apostle Paul gloried in the privilege of being God's minister despite wave after wave of suffering because of it. He tells us exactly how he felt sometimes: pressured from every side yet not crushed, perplexed but not hopeless, hounded but not treed, decked but not destroyed (2 Cor. 4:8–9). Then he makes one of the most remarkable statements in the Bible regarding suffering. It would ring hollow were it not for the fact that Paul the persecuted says it. If you are a Christian, your afflictions—however heavy or many—are *light* and *momentary* in comparison to the glory that awaits you beyond the threshold of this fleeting world (2 Cor. 4:17). Your afflictions work for you like an investment. Future glory is exponentially proportional to present pain. How do we achieve that kind of otherworldly perspective? Paul tells us. By consciously redirecting our attention to what we *know* is so but cannot presently see, instead of remaining preoccupied with what is visible. What we can see is temporary but what we cannot see is forever (2 Cor. 4:18). Is Paul talking pious nonsense? How can you look at what you cannot see?

Suppose you want to plan a vacation to a place you've never visited, but first you want to find out what it's like. You read brochures that describe it. You may even talk to others who have been there. But all your information is ultimately based on faith because you still have never seen it for yourself. You are assuming that those who say they have been there are not pulling your leg about how great it is, or whether the place even exists! The Bible is God's brochure of spiritual realities and "heavenly places" (Eph. 1:3, 20; 2:6). When Paul penned 2 Corinthians 4:8–18, he was not speaking prophetically or theoretically. He was speaking from personal experience. He had *been* there and *seen* that (2 Cor. 12:1–6). It is out of the context of that experience that Paul expresses his contentment—even *pleasure*—in the midst of affliction. It is not a sterile knowledge of theological principles but your relationship to a Person that will sustain you in such times (2 Cor. 12:7–10).

5

A Model Response to Devastating Loss

Job 1:13–22

In his epic fantasy, *The Lord of the Rings,* J. R. R. Tolkien describes Sauron—roughly analogous to Satan—as blinded by his own self-absorption. "The only measure he knows is desire, desire for power; and so he judges all hearts."[1] The tendency of fallen beings is to make themselves the standard by which they judge others. Satan does nothing not rooted in self, "and so he judges all hearts." He cannot imagine anyone—especially fragile mortals who crave creature comforts—doing otherwise. He is motivated solely by self-interest, so he supposes everyone else is. Evaluating others by his own self-centeredness, he completely misjudged Job. His warped view of God shows that he does not understand Him any better. For the time being, blindness is bliss. Relishing his nearly unfettered opportunity to humiliate both Job and God, "Satan went forth from the presence of the Lord" (1:12). Satan exits, confident of victory. The adversarial Prosecutor becomes the quintessential Persecutor.

Losing It All (Job 1:13–19)

Job's first test was *possessional.* Satan saw Job's possessions as the key to his soul. God has put a hedge around "all that he has" and blessed "the work of his hands so that "his possessions have increased," but take away "all that he has, and he will surely curse You to Your face" (1:10–11, NKJV). Satan's strategy was to exploit Job's alleged preoccupation with the perks of serving God. Job's first test was also *relational*, for Satan insinuated that Job's devotion was tied to God's protection of his family as well (1:10).

A succession of messengers interrupted one another to report four nearly simultaneous tsunamis aimed directly at Job (1:14, 16, 17, 18).[2] Wave upon wave of sudden devastation swept away everything he had. He lost all tangible resources of wealth (his livestock), all tangible signs of stature (his servants), and all tangible means of personal fulfillment (his children). Satan's malicious strategy saved this cruelest blow for last. Doubled over by three swift punches to the gut, Job receives a final kick to the face that sends him sprawling into the dirt.

Job's loss of reputation and standing within the community added insult to injury (30:1–11). "Obviously the judgment of God," men nodded knowingly to one another. Job now earned no more than a disdainful shaking of the head from passers-by. Unhelpful onlookers are always ready, whether through ignorance or envy, to interpret catastrophe as a sure sign of divine displeasure. It certainly *looked* like divine judgment. One of the messengers implied as much: "The *fire of God* fell from heaven" (1:16, NKJV).[3] Even in Job's mind all this is from the Lord (1:21).

A Model Outward Response (Job 1:20–21)

Surely Satan's jaw dropped in disbelief before it clenched in rage. This was not the outcome he had predicted and promised. Job's reaction grasps the most basic realities of life in a poetic reflection of resolute submission:

> Naked I came from my mother's womb,
> And naked I shall return there.[4]
> Yahweh has given, and Yahweh has taken.
> Blessed be the name of Yahweh.

One writer describes Job's utterance as "the noblest expression to be found anywhere of a man's joyful acceptance of the will of God as his only good."[5] Noble, yes. But joyful? It is possible to read Job's words too victoriously. To a nonsufferer, Job's declaration sounds triumphant and inspiring—the obvious and only biblical reaction one would expect from such a spiritual giant. To someone in the vise of Job-like loss, those words can sound so serene and celebratory that they seem unrealistic, unattainable, untouched by grief. They were nothing of the kind.

To read Job rightly we must view his words in 1:21 through the tears of 1:20—hear his robe rip, watch him shave his head, and see him fall to the ground. These are impassioned actions. Job's response was not a super-spiritual stoicism. Still less was it a superficial shrug of the shoulders and a shallow "Praise the Lord anyhow!" Job is a man in agony, his anguish the overflow of a hemorrhaging heart.

Ripping the garment and shaving the head express abandonment to grief, an external image of how you feel inside, heart-torn and bare. Job's words are neither impassive nor tearless. He displays remarkable resolution in the face of mystifying providences and disturbing events; but it is a resolution voiced through tears. "As the victim of such unparalleled misfortunes, he felt too crushed in heart to put up any false front of cheerful courage."[6] Job was no stranger to weeping (16:16, 20; 30:31). There is no shame in sorrow and tears do not necessarily contradict faith or submission.

There is a glory in a firm declaration of submission to God, come what may. The same resolution, polished by tears, shines even more brightly for the glory of God. Tears testify that though the pain is real God is still worthy of trust, whatever He chooses to do. Tearful resolve attests to our esteem for a "gloriously desirable"[7] God Who deserves our loving loyalty in spite of personal loss or pain. That glorifies God before men and onlooking angels.

Job's philosophy of life is biblical and portable. Everything we possess we received since birth. Everything we have acquired since birth we will leave behind at death. It is all on loan. Solomon echoes Job: "As [man] came forth of his mother's womb, naked shall he return to go as he came, and shall take nothing of his labor, which he may carry away in his hand" (Eccles. 5:15). Paul, too, reminds us that "we brought nothing into this world, and it is certain we can carry nothing out" (1 Tim. 6:7). Man's instinctive response to this certainty is irrational: denial that fuels a frenetic devotion to acquiring, hoarding, and consuming everything possible. The biblical counsel in the face of this reality is quite different. The conclusions of Job and Solomon and Paul dovetail into a single word of wisdom: *learn to be content.*

Contentment is a rational skill learned by grace. To Solomon, the nakedness of death was one of the great enigmas of life (Eccles. 5:15–16), a vexation that prompted him to call the reader to contented enjoyment of the God-given blessings of life (Eccles. 5:18). Paul, having administered the same dose of reality, harmonizes with Solomon's note of contentment: "having therefore food and raiment, let us therewith be content" (1 Tim. 6:7–8). Job models that contentment.

This is not a stoic fatalism that won't complain about the weather because it never does any good anyway. Job will complain about the "weather," though he will complain directly to the One Who controls it. The Bible calls us to a settled conviction that God is the gracious giver and therefore the just taker of all that we have. "All things belong to God, absolutely, to be given as gift, not claim, to be taken back without wrong. There is no talk of 'human rights.' The Lord is the sovereign owner of all."[8]

Job had not done anything to deserve the removal of all God's blessings. God Himself acknowledges this (2:3). *But neither had he done anything to deserve all those blessings in the first place.* Nor have we. Job understands both of these truths (1:21; 2:10). It is not unjust for God to remove any (or all) of the blessings He has bestowed freely and "without cause" upon us in the first place. If we think this is unfair, then we have misunderstood the terms of the arrangement. All life blessings are undeserved loans to be recalled at His will or left behind at death. The spiritual blessings of salvation from sin, life in Christ, and eternity in heaven are also undeserved, but they are not loans; they are unearned possessions that God swears He will never take back.

"I was naked when I was born, and I will be naked when I die" (NCV). Job "began life with nothing but himself; he will go out from life stripped of everything but what he has become. God has given him a rehearsal for death."[9] Hearses don't have trailer hitches. You will take nothing with you but what you have become.

A Model Inward Response (Job 1:22)

Job keeps a close check not merely on his tongue but also on his spirit. "In all this Job did not sin, and did not give folly to God"

(1:22, lit.). The term translated "[charge God] foolishly" is not an adverb but a rare noun (*tiphlah*) denoting what is empty, insipid, unseemly (a different word appears in 2:10). It does not describe what Job said about God but what he did not say about God: he "did not give folly to God."

This may mean that his resolve in 1:21 was not just hot air offering "empty" words to God; his response was not hollow but sincere. Some take it to refer to Job's attitude toward what had happened; he did not "blame" God.[10] It may indicate that Job did not attribute any folly or wrongdoing to God; he refused to say that God did anything inappropriate.[11] Still others suggest that Job acknowledged that God was not acting without reason; He had a purpose in what He was doing.[12] In any case, Job's initial reaction to devastating loss is a model for honoring God. Surely his faith will see him through.

Andersen, however, puts his finger on a bitter irony: "Job's faith does not relieve his agony; it causes it."[13] None of this would have happened to Job had he not been a man of such exemplary character and faith. It is his *faith* that is being tested. It is that very testing that will make it stronger and better founded, less self-reliant and more God-dependent.

> But this faith cannot survive without a terrible struggle. Because Job sees nothing but the Lord's hand in everything, how can he escape the horrible thought that God has done something bad? He knows no cause for such a willful act. . . . Job is hurled into the cauldron of doubt concerning the justice and equity of God's ways with him. He must suffer and grow before he can see why this has happened. So far he has begun superbly.[14]

Did Job "Curse" God?

Satan was so sure he knew what was in man that he swore Job would "curse" (*barak*) God in response to his losses (1:11). This same Hebrew word appears in 1:5, where Job offers sacrifices on behalf of his children in case they might have "cursed God in their hearts." The word occurs again when Job's wife urges him to "curse God, and die" (2:9).

Did Job "curse" God? Yes. Sort of. This very word, *barak,* falls from Job's lips in response to his losses. It is camouflaged by translation: "Blessed (*barak*) be the name of the Lord" (1:21). This is not a mistranslation. It is a dramatic *coup fourré,* a counterthrust as stunning as it is unwitting. Job uttered the very word that Satan said he would, but with the *opposite* meaning than Satan intended.

The Hebrew verb *barak* can mean either to "curse" or to "bless," depending on the context.[15] It works the same way in Southern English.[16] (Maybe Job lived in southern Uz.) Southerners are familiar with *bless* as a euphemism for *curse* or *cuss* or *reprimand.* If cousin Bubba says, "Aunt Lulu really *blessed* me out for trackin' mud all over her clean kitchen floor!" any Southerner worth his grits knows that Aunt Lulu was not happy about Bubba's indiscretion. Job's "coincidental" use of the very word that Satan said he would utter, but in the reverse sense, is an ironic twist of the knife, a subtle, satisfying, extra indignity to Satan's arrogant and erroneous allegation.

Did Satan Make a Tactical Error?

I wonder if Satan overplayed his hand against Job. Was this unintended overkill on Satan's part—a tactical error, a strategic miscalculation? You may notice that Satan doesn't do this very often anymore.

Satan's devices are a product of trial and error, honed to effectiveness over centuries of experimentation. He is not omniscient. He has learned over ages what does and does not work, and on whom. It is not swift and utter devastation that cripples and embitters the spirit so effectively as the constant, nagging, heel-nipping of repeated loss and setback. Satan's strategies today are still just as much under the providential hand of God as they were in the case of Job. But his method with most of us is more incremental—relentless little ambushes that do not demolish us all at once but leave us shell-shocked and weary, eating away at our morale and undermining our confidence in God's presence and control.

Satan's blitzkrieg on Job may have driven Job *to* God rather than away from Him. Job's response to such complete devastation is the only logical one. In the face of desolation so obviously of divine origin, where else *could* he turn? What else could he do? Only the foolish and rebellious child rises from parental discipline and shakes his fist in defiance. Job is no fool and no rebel.

Job deserves credit for his stellar response. It was exemplary. It glorified and pleased God. It humiliated Satan. But as time wore on—with no relief or reply from God, only the relentless accusations of his friends ringing in his ears—Job's conclusions wavered, his patience thinned, his composure crumbled.

What Does All This Have to Do with Me?

The experiences of a man who lived four thousand years ago may be hard to relate to even for the most imaginative and sympathetic reader. Let me try to put a human face on this kind of pain. What do you do

- when your own child—formerly exuberant and healthy and full of all the mischievous life you can pack into a seven-year-old—lies in constant pain on your living room sofa suffering with neuroblastoma?
- when you are preparing to go to Bangladesh as a missionary (how many are willing to do that?) and your three-year-old son is suddenly diagnosed with leukemia? After three excruciating years of treatment he recovers, but in the meantime you have another child whose body and brain are laced with latent tumor cells that trigger seizures?
- when you have to watch your spouse slowly and prematurely dying of cancer?
- when your life and ministry become redefined by the need to care for a parent—once bright, cheerful, and independent—who has, in the puzzling providence of God, now suffers the indignities of Alzheimer's disease?
- when a son or daughter dies suddenly in a car accident or is murdered?
- when your family seems to endure serious illness after illness?
- when you lose everything—including a loved one—in a blaze of outrageous, senseless terrorism?

These are not hypothetical illustrations dreamed up for dramatic effect. I am personally acquainted with individuals (most of them family members, personal friends, or fellow church members) who have faced these very experiences. Most of those reading this book know of comparable situations. Some of you may be presently enduring similar circumstances or their residual effects.

What do you do when your circumstances are chaotic, puzzling, heart-ripping, nonsensical? When there seems to be no cause, and no point? Especially when, in the process, God seems strangely silent, even absent? If you are to sustain not merely your testimony but your faith (remember, such sufferings are uniquely a "trial of your faith") and a sense of security in your own soul, you will need more than a surface knowledge of paper promises in the Word of God. You will need a deepening knowledge of the God of the Word, Who committed those promises to paper.

6

Who Is Responsible for This?

Job 2:1–10

Biblical theology is earthy and practical. Theological questions are the most pertinent kind to ask, like looking for the light switch in a dark room. They have everything to do with seeing and responding to our circumstances. Biblical answers to theological questions put our hand on the light switch. Job 1 raises just such a theological question. Job 2 answers it. Who did all this to Job?

Was Job a casualty of "random violence" at the hands of the Sabeans (1:15) or the target of an orchestrated strike by Chaldean renegades (1:17) or a victim of the merciless blows of irrational nature (1:16, 18–19)? All these events have one thing in common: they are secondary causes. What, or who, was the primary cause? Who was responsible for what happened to Job? Or for what happens to you? Many assume that God is responsible for the "good stuff" and Satan causes the "bad stuff." Is that assumption biblical? The Bible's answer to these questions is not ambiguous.

According to Satan, Job's religion was mercenary. God's blessings were Exhibit A. Satan drew attention to everything God had given Job (1:9–10) and offered a simple test to prove his case: take it all away and see what he does. "Put forth *thine hand*," said Satan (1:11). "Behold, all that he hath is in thine hand," replied the Lord (1:12). The same is true in Satan's second challenge and God's reply (2:4–6). Satan challenges God to stretch out *His hand* ("power") against Job. God relinquishes Job into *Satan's hand* ("power") but, again, with clearly defined parameters ("only upon himself put not forth *thine hand*"). God delegated massive latitude to Satan. As disquieting as the object of that sentence may be ("delegated to *Satan*"), the subject is the major theological point ("*God* delegated").

So who is responsible for what happened to Job, God or Satan? The provisional answer is yes. God proposed the topic of Job (1:8) and Satan countered with an accusation and a proposed test (1:9–11). God authorized Satan to proceed (1:12) and Satan facilitated Job's losses (1:12–19). But Job 2 moves us to an ultimate answer. Who is responsible for what happened to Job? God. He says so.[1]

Systematic theology argues that God is not only good but also omnipotent and therefore must be responsible for what happened to Job. Affliction tempts us to question these two divine attributes. Either God is good but not omnipotent since He wasn't able to prevent the suffering, or God is omnipotent but not so good after all since He permitted something so painful and unfair. Since both options are expressly unbiblical,[2] we are faced with a choice: (1) ignore what the Bible says about God and reevaluate Him on the basis of our limited experience, knowledge, and understanding or (2) accept God's self-description and reevaluate our circumstances in the light of the Bible's depiction of reality.

Interpreting experiences in light of God's revelation rather than interpreting the Bible in light of experiences is a simple adjustment. It is like reminding ourselves that despite contrary appearances, the movement of the sun and moon and stars across the sky really is caused by the earth's rotation. It may not feel as if we are standing on the surface of an orb whirling a thousand miles per hour and rocketing through eighteen miles of space every second. But that is reality. The constellation Pleiades (9:9; 38:31) looks like a cluster of tiny points of light far smaller than the sun; it requires faith in objective reality to believe that they are light-years away from each other and that some of them are larger than our sun. The adjustment of our perception to what God says is so may not be easy, but it is simple. The Bible must refocus our view of reality.

Job was the victim of amoral natural calamity. We usually accept that God is in control of natural calamities like the great wind that killed Job's children or the lightning storm that destroyed his sheep. But he was also the victim of the sinful choices and wicked deeds of others. The Sabeans stole Job's oxen and donkeys and killed his servants. The Chaldeans stole Job's camels and killed his servants.

Everyone in the story understood that God was responsible for what happened to Job; they just misunderstood why He did it and what it meant. When it was all over, Job's acquaintances and relatives came to "comfort him over all the *evil* that the *Lord* had brought upon him" (42:11). Don't let that word *evil* mislead you. The same word is used to describe rotten fruit as "bad" (Jer. 24:2, 8). The Bible often uses *evil* in a nonmoral sense just as we do. We refer to "a *bad* storm" or even "a *wicked* storm" without implying anything about the morality of the weather. The point of 42:11 is that they all understood that it was the *Lord* that had brought all these "bad" things upon Job.

Job understood that God was responsible for what happened to him. He never wavered on this point. It was the Lord Who had "taken away" (1:21). It was from God that he must now "accept adversity" (2:10). If the animals could speak, Job said, even they could tell you "that the hand of the Lord hath wrought this" (12:7–9). No one in the book is arguing over *who* did this. Everyone agrees it was God. If Job never doubted who did all this, why should we?[3] Suppose, however, that everyone in the story is mistaken. Does anyone else settle this question unambiguously? God does.

The Divine Council Reconvenes (Job 2:1–3)

The second half of 2:3 is arresting. God "destroyed" Job after all. He says so Himself. This verse is the key that opens the door into the theology of this book, and a bedrock text for the biblical doctrine of divine providence. "Hast thou considered my servant Job?" asks God. "Still he holdeth fast his integrity, although thou movedst me against him, to destroy him without cause." Such a pivotal verse merits closer scrutiny.[4]

Holdeth fast (*chazaq*) means "to seize, grip firmly, and cling to." In spite of what his losses seemed to imply about God's posture toward him, Job clung tenaciously to his integrity. His lifelong pursuit of righteousness seemed for the moment to have gained him nothing. But then, that is what the test was all about. Job's response proves that he did not follow God for gain. Under such duress, a fair-weather follower would forsake his professed faith for more propitious paths (cf. Luke 8:13). Not Job. He later used this same verb to say he had no intention of abandoning his life of faith out of bitterness or despair: "My righteousness I hold fast, and will not let it go" (27:6).

Integrity (*tamah*)[5] has come to imply ethical morality, especially honesty. The Hebrew word means *wholeness*, *completeness*, *soundness.* Job's integrity signified that he was "whole-hearted in his commitment to the person and requirements of God."[6] No ulterior motive lurked behind his morality, as Satan had accused.

Movedst (*sut*) means to "entice" or "incite." The nuance depends on the context. Sometimes people do this to others in an evil sense of inciting them to do wrong. Jezebel *stirred up* Ahab to do evil (1 Kings 21:25). Ahab *persuaded* Jehoshaphat to join him in battle (2 Chron. 18:2). The Israelites were warned against allowing a friend or relative to *entice* them to worship idols (Deut. 13:6). Sometimes people do this to others in an innocent sense of encouraging or motivating them. Achsah *persuaded* her husband to ask Caleb for an inheritance (Josh. 15:18). Sometimes God does this to people in the sense of inducing them to some action, either directly or through secondary means. God protected Jehoshaphat in battle by *moving* the enemy to leave him alone (2 Chron. 18:31). He also *moved* David against Israel to number them (2 Sam. 24:1; cf. 1 Chron. 21:1).[7]

Job 2:3 is unique. Only here is God the *object* of this verb. Satan *provoked, motivated, prompted, persuaded* God against Job. Whatever translation you choose, the implication is startling: "You caused me to ruin him for no good reason" (NCV). God admits that Satan is the one who got Him to do all this to Job. But if "all this" includes murder and theft by wicked men, how do we reconcile God's admission here with James 1:13? God's purpose in what He permitted was righteous. Satan's purpose in what he pursued was evil. Satan did not move God to do anything morally evil. The secondary means employed to destroy Job, foreknown and permitted by God, were the product of Satan's instigation and man's free choice. To devastate Job without provocation was regrettable but not unjust. It is the prerogative of sovereignty to remove "without cause" what has been freely given "without cause." Job acknowledged this (1:21; 2:10).

To destroy him (*bala'*) is a graphic verbal image, to "swallow up" or "gulp down." The earth "opened her mouth and *swallowed up*" those who rebelled against God's leadership through Moses (Num. 16:32). God "prepared a great fish to *swallow up* Jonah" (Jon. 1:17). What the Lord did to Job at Satan's instigation, He admits, was a similarly overwhelming experience for Job.

Without cause (*chinnam*) can mean either "without compensation" or "without reason." The same term appears in Job 1:9, where the contextual implication is "without compensation." Here it implies the absence of any just cause or reason,[8] as when Saul sought to destroy David *without cause* or *provocation* (1 Sam. 19:5). Psalm 69:4 applies this phrase to Christ and puts even Job's suffering into perspective —"They hated me without a cause." Jesus cited this messianic prophecy to describe His own experience in life and ministry (John 15:25). The wave of Christ's suffering billowed in the brutality of His last twenty-four hours of life, then crested and crashed down on Him at the Cross—the epitome of human hatred, demonic disdain, and divine rejection. His agony becomes the standard by which we must measure the "fairness" of all our suffering.

> The God who handed over Job to his torturer was no Olympian figure, content to win his victories through others [and at their expense]. He would say, in Christ, to his own more hideous tormentor, "This is your hour, and the power of darkness" (Luke 22:53). Any thinking about the sufferance of evil, and exposure of the innocent to grief, must take its bearings now from that crucial and seminal event.[9]

No one was more undeservedly exposed to the hostility of man and the fury of Satan than the Lamb of God. We correctly gauge our own suffering not by the experiences of others but by the experiences of Christ.

Satan dared God to set His hand against Job, and God relinquished Job into Satan's hand (1:11–12; 2:5–6). Now Job 2:3 brings us nose to nose with an unambiguous if uncomfortable, divine admission: He is responsible for what happened to Job.[10] We may as well get used to the discomfort; this is not the last time the book of Job will bulldoze our tidy theological formulas.

Physical Affliction (Job 2:4–8)

Nothing like barely surviving a flood only to hear that there's more rain on the way. Fire you can fight, but how do you stop more rain? God initiated attention on Job by bringing up his name in the first place (1:8). He did it again in 2:3. Knowing where all this would lead, God brought up the subject of Job not once but twice. God, not Satan, was initiating all this. God, not Satan, was in control. And ultimately it was not God in a corner with His back to the wall; it was Satan. Like the snake he is, he tries to writhe his way out of it.

"Skin for skin," scoffs Satan (2:4).[11] Man will gladly trade off the skins of others, even his children's, to save his own. Again projecting his own twisted traits onto others, Satan, the supreme narcissist, cannot imagine Job doing otherwise. Last time Satan confidently alleged that the sincerity of Job's faith was only as deep as his pockets. Now he is just as cocksure that the sincerity of Job's faith is only skin-deep, meaning his personal health and well-being.

A typical sore loser, Satan won't admit defeat but whines that the outcome was invalid. The parameters were too limiting even though they encompassed everything he had requested. But change the rules to include "his bone and his flesh, and he will curse thee to thy face" (2:5). God consents: "He is in thine hand; but save his life" (2:6). God grants Satan the necessary authorization but again sets the boundaries. Satan wastes no time. He went forth and "smote Job with sore boils" (2:7).

These exchanges between God and Satan in the book of Job echo in the gloomy cavern of Luke 22:31–32. On the eve of His crucifixion, Jesus warned His disciples that Satan had obtained permission to sift them like wheat.[12] If the disciples were not immune, neither are we.

We constantly need to recalibrate our thinking to God's thinking. The function of the Bible is to help us see things as God does. God does not entrust certain trials to just anyone.

> We may pause to note that the cause of Job's suffering was more than Satan's insinuation against him. He was suffering to vindicate more than himself. He was vindicating God's trust in him. He was not so much abandoned by God as supremely honored by God.[13]

This is not just a piously perverted way of minimizing hardship and heartache. Every adversity or calamity we face is a divine vote of confidence, backed by the guarantee of 1 Corinthians 10:13. Nothing you face is unique to you: "no temptation [testing] has overtaken you that is not common to man" (ESV). Nothing you face is sufficient to overwhelm you unless you allow it to: "God is faithful, and he will not let you be tempted [tested] beyond your ability, but with the temptation he will also provide the way of escape, that you may be able to endure it" (ESV). God knows your capacities and limitations. If God promises never to test or tempt you beyond your ability, then whatever He sends or allows you can handle by His grace.

Sometimes God uses trials to draw sinners to Himself. Like Francis Thompson's Hound of Heaven, He pursues and corners them so they have nowhere else to turn but to Him (Acts 9:5). Sometimes God uses trials to do the same thing for His children who have wandered from Him (Ps. 119:67). Odd as it may sound, sometimes such trials are reserved for God's choicest saints—to discipline their spirits, to refine their faith in Him, and to magnify His grace through their experience (Rev. 2:9–10).[14] If this is hard to accept, consider a biblical example from the life of our Lord.

God Sends Suffering Because He Loves?

John Piper has Job's wife voice what often remains buried in the heart amid suffering.

> I think you are a fool. How much
> From him will you endure till such
> A love as this from God, the Great,
> Is seen to be a form of hate?[15]

Those who do not know God well can easily misconstrue affliction as judgment. Naomi did (Ruth 1:20–21).[16] Minor inconveniences might be attributed to divine discipline, but serious suffering must be inconsistent with a truly loving God. That kind of pain and loss looks more like divine hate than love.

One of Christ's favorite haunts was the home of Martha, Mary, and Lazarus on the outskirts of Jerusalem. He visited them frequently and always received a warm welcome. We know that Jesus loved them (John 11:5). That is what makes the sentence that follows so startling. When word reached Jesus that Lazarus was seriously ill, He purposely delayed visiting them. To be sure we don't misread this gesture, John clarifies Jesus' posture toward this family: "Now Jesus *loved* Martha, and her sister, and Lazarus. When he had heard *therefore* that he was sick, *he abode two days still* in the same place where he was" (John 11:5–6). Not *nevertheless* but *therefore*. Jesus delayed intervening not *despite* His love but *because* He loved.

This is hard to understand in the throes of seemingly pointless suffering. "If God really loved me, He would do something for me right now!" Sometimes God does nothing for us immediately because He loves us and has a greater purpose for His glory and for our good. Seeing that takes time and maturity and faith. Read the rest of John 11.

This sounds good in theory. It is one thing to withhold help from your child because you want him to learn how to master some skill on his own. It is cruel not to intervene when he breaks a leg. We are talking about serious suffering, not merely learning to live with inconveniences. The analogy is flawed, however. We assume that personal comfort and physical health in this present life are the greatest good and highest priority. We place the highest premium on what we can see and feel here and now. The very idea that there are greater goods and higher priorities than physical welfare or personal happiness sounds like insulting, hyperpious nonsense. That is because we are shortsighted, self-centered sinners. "It is therefore possible to understand and correctly evaluate the sufferings of the innocent Job"—or our own sufferings—"only from the perspective of eternity. The real purpose of life is not to attain personal ambitions or desires, but to glorify God."[17]

Anyone who rejects that foundational biblical truth is out of the mainstream of God's purposes and priorities, trapped in a backwater eddy of bitterness, confusion, and frustration. Physical life and health are not the greatest good, and death is not the end.

What Does Suffering Say About God?

Job's suffering does not indicate that God has lost control. The Lord initiates, permits, governs, and limits Job's suffering. He alone claims ultimate control and responsibility for all that Job experiences.

Job's suffering does not mean that God is ignorant. The prologue communicates God's awareness and involvement at every stage of Job's experience. The Lord's final answer will emphasize that He knows even when wild animals need food or give birth.

Job's suffering does not suggest that God is unkind. The Lord will address that issue, too, in His answer to Job. James sums up Job's experiences this way: "The Lord is compassionate and merciful" (James 5:11, ESV). You hear it in Job 2:3. You hear it in Job 38–41. You see it in Job 42.

Jeremiah is called "the weeping prophet." Eyeing the wreckage of his beloved Jerusalem, *God's* Jerusalem, he pulls back the curtain of a window into the Lord's heart: "For He does not afflict from His heart" (Lam. 3:33, lit.).[18] Our pain and grief give God no pleasure. Sending suffering and causing pain are not what is in His heart. If that is true of the chastisement (deserved suffering) of rebellious Judah in Lamentations, it is doubly true of the adversity endured by a believer. God begrudges the sting that necessarily accompanies affliction but judges the intended benefits worth the pain.

Human Provocation (Job 2:9–10)

A human voice goads Job to do what Satan said he would. Whatever her motive, one can hear the echo of Satan's whisper in the words of Job's wife: *You're already as good as dead. God has obviously turned against you. You'd be better off to curse God and let him kill you.*

Debate swirls around Job's wife. "No details of her character are given, so commentators have had to guess what kind of woman she was."[19] And guess they have. Epithets range from compassionate consoler[20] to she-devil.[21] Some seek to rescue her from ignominy by assuming that she recovered from her foolishness.[22] With so little explanation in the text, the motivation for her counsel is difficult to discern.

Was she expressing a genuine, if misguided, compassion for her husband by advising the quickest way out of suffering (*Go ahead and curse God so He will finish you off*)? Possibly. But her question ("Dost thou still retain thine integrity?") suggests a less sympathetic spirit.

Was self-preservation a motive? Up to this point Job had lost everything *except* her. He was a human lightning rod. You can imagine her pondering, *Let's see. He's lost all his livestock, all his servants, all his children, and now his health. What else could he possibly . . . Let's go,*

Job! God obviously has it out for you. May as well give up and get it over with—before God takes me next!

Why *is* Job's wife still around? Why didn't he lose her, too? One commentator answers with wry severity:

> Job has lost his children, but this wife he has retained, for he needed not to be tried by losing her: he was sufficiently tested by having her. . . . Why, asks Chrysostom, did the devil leave him this wife? Because he thought her a good scourge by which to plague him more acutely than by any other means. Moreover the thought is not far distant, that *God* left her to him that when, in the glorious outcome of his sufferings, he receives everything doubled, he might not have this thorn in the flesh doubled.[23]

Her character is not the point of including her in the story. The incident simply underscores the pressure on Job to capitulate in the face of every conceivable reason to do so. He does not.

Job rebuked his wife, "You speak as one of the foolish women." The word *foolish* (*nabal*) does not denote a dolt but someone who knowingly rejects the words and ways of God. The rebuke implies that such language was out of character for her, but in this instance she is thinking like a fool. "It is not the first nor the only time that fond hearts and friendly hands have unknowingly leagued themselves with the destroyer, and ignorantly done the work of Satan."[24]

The apostle Peter once insisted that the death of Jesus in Jerusalem could not possibly be God's will and must be avoided at all costs. Christ's stinging reply was not overstatement: "Get thee behind me, Satan . . . for thou savourest not the things that be of God, but [those] that be of men" (Matt. 16:23). Anytime you counsel someone to do what you know in your heart is not right or what you know in your mind is not biblical, however prudent or necessary or reasonable it may seem to be under the circumstances, you act like the "foolish" who willfully reject the words of God and echo the whispers of Satan.

Is Job Beginning to Crumble?

Denial is often identified as the first stage of grieving, the initial instinct to disbelieve devastating news. The believer faces a different kind of denial. Because we believe His Word, we feel obligated to suppress sentiments that contradict what we believe from the Bible to be true. When feelings of bitterness or thoughts of God's apparent unfairness surface, we instinctively deny them. But suppression does not make those thoughts and feelings disappear. Sometimes we even feel (or are made to feel) unspiritual for hurting.

The narrative of Job 1–2 implies what the lament in Job 3 will articulate. Despite his initial acceptance of affliction, Job wrestled with this kind of denial, repressing the creeping encroachment of disturbing thoughts and feelings. Compare Job's response to the first wave of catastrophe ("in all this Job sinned not, nor charged God" with folly, 1:22) and Job's response to the second onslaught ("in all this did not Job sin *with his lips*," 2:10). What Job would *say* was the heart of Satan's charge. The delicate insinuation of 2:10 seems to be that just as there was more to Job's circumstances than met the eye, there was more to Job's response than met the ear. More was going on in the recesses of his soul than he admitted with his mouth. Job guarded his lips, but that he began to waver in his heart is clear from his initial lament and from the words later provoked by his friends. Who wouldn't begin to waver and wonder? Despite what he says later, he never curses or renounces God but clings to the Lord in his confusion over his circumstances and his frustration over God's silence.

The agony of Job is the stuff of martyrdom. He was not a dying martyr but a living martyr, suffering as a witness to the genuineness of human faith and to the integrity and worthiness of God. His witness was all the more eloquent and authentic because it was unwitting.

7

How to Help the Hurting (and How Not To)

Job 2:11–13

"Now when Job's three friends . . ." *Friends*? Familiarity can breed contempt, but so can false impressions founded on hearsay. Job eventually called them "miserable comforters," but not until 16:2.[1] Are these three "fair-weather friends"?[2] That certainly applies to Job's other acquaintances and relatives; disaster strikes Job and they are nowhere to be found (19:13–17). From all appearances God had forsaken Job, so they did too. But not these three.

Job sat alone in humiliation. His seat was no longer "in the gate" (29:7–8) but amid the reek and smolder of the town dump (2:8). Festering sores covered his body (2:7–8), oozed openly (7:5), and hardened into dark scabs (30:30) before cracking and breaking out afresh (7:5). Amid emaciation (17:7; 19:20), revolting physical disfigurement (2:12; 19:19), fetid breath (19:17), and fever spikes (30:30), Job's days dragged on in constant and unrelieved pain (30:17). Everyone deserted and avoided him (19:19)—except these three friends. They were willing to travel significant distances to meet with him (2:11).

Vultures will wing a long way to pick over a fresh kill. But these three men came with no relish or intention to point their fingers and wag their heads. The narrator tells us that they came on a mission of mercy: to *mourn* with him (2:11), to *comfort* him (2:11), to *weep* with him (2:12), and—this is perhaps the highest commendation of their character—simply to *sit* with him and say *nothing* for *seven days* out of sympathetic respect for his "great grief" (2:12). Even when the debate heats up, they stay, in spite of some scathing verbal abuse from the one they had come to console at considerable inconvenience to themselves. Whatever else they may be, "fair-weather friends" is hardly an appropriate description.

> It is possible to dismiss these friends of Job too lightly, for the book does not present them as hypocrites arriving to gloat, nor as heretics offering manifestly false doctrines, nor again as fools producing no serious arguments. . . . Their outlook chimes in very largely with the promises and warnings of the law, especially Deuteronomy, and with the wisdom of Proverbs and the moral standpoint of the Prophets.[3]

The narrator is the crucial link between the reader and the record of Job. His perspective is the inspired lens through which we are to view the characters and incidents of biblical narrative.

> The narrator is the one who controls the story. His is the voice through whom we hear about the action and the people of the narrative. The narrator's point of view is the perspective through which we observe and evaluate everything connected with the story. In short, the narrator is . . . to shape and guide how the reader responds to the characters and events of the story.[4]

Our understanding of Job is enhanced when we, like the friends, sit in sympathetic silence and *listen* to it.[5] The narrator's introduction to the friends requires that we initially give Job's companions every benefit of the doubt. Their example invites some counsel for how we respond to those who are suffering, so the chapter wanders from the text of Job here for some practical reflection.

Helping Those Who Are Hurting

Job's three friends stand out as positive (initially) and negative (eventually) role models for ministering to someone in affliction. How can you help—or hinder—those grappling with illness, loss, or injustice? Personal embarrassment prods us to avoid the sufferer. We wouldn't know what to say. Suffering alone compounds the suffering (Ps. 142:4). Here is some practical advice for how to help those who are hurting, and how not to.[6] Most of it originates from the observations of Christians, many of them personal friends, who have suffered not only the weight of affliction but also the added burden of well-intentioned but unhelpful "help." These are not merely sterile suggestions. They are pleas from sufferers as well as principles from Scripture.

Be inclusive. We focus all our attention on Job, but Job's wife lost everything, too. Be attentive to background sufferers. Affliction rarely affects isolated individuals. No sufferer is an island. Surrounding almost any primary sufferer are secondary sufferers—spouses, children, siblings, caretakers. Secondary suffering may be a different kind of suffering, but it can be every bit as acute.

When a couple lost their first child five hours after her premature birth, I regularly contacted the father to see how he was doing and to listen to anything he might have to say. He told me once that I was the only one who made an effort to talk with him about their loss. As the primary sufferer in this case, the mother was the natural focus of attention and consolation. He understood that his wife needed special support; but nobody really thought of the father in the same terms.

A woman whose husband was in the last stages of cancer shared a similar observation from the other side of the gender aisle. She was deeply grateful for the hospital visits her husband received from the men of the church. What she missed was their wives during those visits: "I would have appreciated a comforting hug from the wives. It made me think that this was a way that the wives could come alongside their husbands and minister too."

Especially in cases of serious or terminal illness, it is usually the secondary sufferers for whom we can and need to do the most. Family members require as much ministry as the one lying in the hospital bed, and caretakers may bear the brunt of the hardship in cases such as Alzheimer's disease. Extend the ministry of consolation as widely as the impact of the suffering.

Be sympathetic. "Weep with them that weep" (Rom. 12:15) is not fuzzy, feel-good advice or hyperbole. It is a command to sympathize, to "feel with" those who suffer (1 Cor. 12:15–26). Your calling is not to attach some explanation to their circumstances. You need not—and probably don't—have the answer to their affliction. There is a time for counsel, usually when the sufferer solicits it, and there is a time to lay your hand upon your mouth and just weep with them (Eccles. 3:7). The open ear of a sympathetic Christian brother or sister willing to listen without rushing to explain or advise or criticize can be more helpful in working through a difficult experience than you will ever know, until you are the sufferer. Our instinctive response to a suffering saint should be sympathy, not suspicion or censure or advice. Be willing just to sit with them. Even Job's friends could do that.

Be available. "Bear ye one another's burdens" (Gal. 6:2). When Paul says that everyone is to bear his own "burden" (Gal. 6:5), he uses the word for a backpack, something suitable and appropriate to an individual, the customary duties of our daily life and calling for which we are individually responsible. The "burden" we are to help others bear (Gal. 6:2) is the word for cargo, a great load too heavy for one person. Offer the sufferer a hand. Run errands; keep the children; help with chores; provide meals. Drop a note or card. Call periodically. Simply being present and available reminds them that they are not alone and that their difficulty is not being ignored or forgotten.

Be sensitive. Sometimes aloneness is necessary, preferable, or helpful (Jer. 15:15–18; Lam. 3:25–28). Balance availability with respect for privacy. Visits and calls are encouraging, but at times your presence may be intrusive. Ask ahead to avoid imposing your presence at a time when privacy, not company, is needed. Sometimes the most helpful thing you can be is absent. Do not take that personally and do not be offended. Ministering to others in times of affliction is about their needs, not about your feelings.

Be prayerful. "Remember . . . them which suffer adversity, as being yourselves . . . in the body" (Heb. 13:3). It is not a pious cliché to say that prayer is the most effectual ministry you can have to fellow believers in the furnace of affliction. Pray in their shoes. Pray for them as you would want to be prayed for if you were in their circumstances. Find a biblical request that matches their needs and pray it for them thoughtfully. Tell them that you are praying for them, and even what you are praying for them. God often instructs us through the trials of others and adjusts our own spirits as we pray for them.

Be patient. "Support the weak, be patient toward all men" (1 Thess. 5:14). Working through a trial of any magnitude takes time. Scripture exhorts the sufferer to "let patience have her perfect work" (James 1:4), so it is not too much to ask those around the sufferer to do the same. Suffering is not an inconvenient obstacle to "normal" life.

Affliction *is* "normal" life. For the duration of the trial, this *is* God's will for their life and ministry. Serving God is not about accomplishing tasks but waiting on Him in all His appointments. No one has expressed this truth more famously than John Milton, the Puritan poet who lost his eyesight by the age of forty-five. "God doth not need / Either man's work or His own gifts; who best / bear His mild yoke, they serve him best." Others may travel far and labor long at God's bidding, but "They also serve who only stand and wait."[7]

Be scriptural. By this I do *not* mean you should quote lots of Scripture. Though there is a large place for the Scriptures in consoling the afflicted, resist the temptation to be a surrogate Holy Spirit. Some passages are better left to Him to minister. Do not quote Romans 8:28 to a suffering saint. It is a wonderful verse, but the afflicted have thought of that verse long before you have. Some truths can be effectively ministered to the believer by God alone. Sufferers draw Spirit-ministered comfort from Romans 8:28, but it is not a verse to be doled out like spiritual aspirin, as though it instantly answers all questions, quiets all concerns, and heals all the hurts.

What I mean is, be scriptural in *your* approach to the sufferer and his or her suffering. Allow the full range of the Bible's teaching on suffering to inform your ministry to the sufferer. Think through the stories of those who suffer in the pages of Scripture—Joseph, Job, David, Jeremiah, Jesus, Paul. All suffering goes through God and He rarely forwards suffering to accomplish a single object. God typically orchestrates a symphony of purposes through any single experience of affliction.

Someone Always Knows How You Feel

When this book was in its early stages, one of the couples to whom it is dedicated was enduring the extended excruciation of watching their child fight a losing battle with neuroblastoma. I later asked the father to read over this chapter and make any suggestions he thought would be helpful. One of his insights was directed to fellow sufferers: *Beware of the "nobody-knows-how-I-feel" syndrome.* This can breed a twisted kind of pride, an unnecessary solitude that cuts you off from the valid help of others. You end up accepting counsel only from those who have suffered similarly and therefore seem to you to have credibility, while discounting the help of those who haven't. Besides, the assumption is dead wrong. There is always *someone* who knows how you feel. And Someone *always* knows how you feel.

One evening Jesus embarked with His disciples to cross the Sea of Galilee (Mark 4:35). Mark inserts a seemingly insignificant detail: "And there were also with him other little ships" (4:36). Soon "there arose a great storm of wind, and the waves beat into the ship,[8] so that it was now full" (4:37). Now insert that detail: "and there were also with him other little ships" caught in the same storm. The disciples, most of them seasoned seamen, feared for their lives (4:38). Now insert that detail: "and there were also with him other little ships" with crews who felt the same fear. Affliction is isolating. The disciples saw no one else. This was their storm and it was dark. But others were right there in the same storm.

Mark's key apostolic source for his Gospel was Peter. Peter almost certainly supplied Mark with the eyewitness detail about the "other little ships." Later, Peter encouraged his readers with what might almost be a subtle commentary on Mark's storm account (1 Pet. 5:6–9). The links to Job are uncanny.

> Humble yourselves, therefore, under the mighty hand of God [Job 40:3–5; 42:1–6], that he may exalt you in due time [Job 42:12–17]: casting all your care upon him; for he careth for you [Job 38–39]. Be sober, be vigilant, because your adversary, the devil, as a roaring lion, walketh about, seeking whom he may devour [Job 1:7; 2:2]; whom resist steadfast in the faith, *knowing that the same afflictions are accomplished in your brethren that are in the world* [Mark 4:36].

John Bunyan captured the kernel of this confidence in a scene in *The Pilgrim's Progress.* When Christian entered the Valley of the Shadow of Death, he was overwhelmed by its horrors. Alone amid the dreadful darkness, he suddenly heard a man's voice somewhere ahead of him saying, "Though I walk through the valley of the shadow of death, I will fear no evil, for thou art with me." That heartened Christian, "because he gathered from thence, that some who feared God were in this valley as well as himself."[9] He was not alone. Neither are you. There's always *someone* who knows exactly what you are going through. But that's not all.

There is Someone Who *always* knows how you feel—not by virtue of an antiseptic omniscience but by virtue of painful personal experience. Pour out to Him whatever you feel and think and fear and hope; your words enter a hearing ear and a sympathetic heart. "I can see how God might *know* my suffering," says someone, "but how can He really *understand* it? I know He's God, but . . . He's *God*." The implication is that He cannot really understand my pain because He is *only* God. But He is not *only* God; He also *became* man. One of the benevolent byproducts of the incarnation is that in Christ we have Someone Who is "touched with the feeling of our infirmities," Who was "in all points tempted [or tested] like as we are, yet without sin" (Heb. 4:15). One writer puts a poignant face on the relevance of Christ's suffering.

> Gloria fell into deep anguish over the dismal prognosis of her daughter's illness. Little Laura had already suffered enough from the degenerative nerve disorder she had been born with, and now the doctors' forecast included more suffering and impending death. One night after leaving her daughter's bedside, she spat, "God, it's not right. You've never had to watch one of your children die!" As soon as the words escaped, she clasped her hand over her mouth. He did watch his child die. His one and only Son.[10]

Any parent understands that personal pain is more endurable than helplessly watching one's own child suffer. More deeply than we know, God our Father understands that experience—not theoretically because He is an all-knowing God, but experientially because He sacrificed His Son for us. The difference was that God was not a helpless onlooker. The Father's own loss and the Son's own suffering *could* have been avoided, but it wasn't; it was voluntary. And it was for you.

> God suffered in Christ. He knows what it is like to experience pain. He has traveled down the road of pain, abandonment, suffering and death. . . . God is not like some alleged hero with feet of clay, who demands that others suffer, while remaining aloof from the world of pain himself. He has passed through the shadow of suffering himself . . . and, by doing so, transfigures the sufferings of his people.[11]

Job's companions sat with him in his devastation and shared in his disgrace. They came together for the express purpose of grieving with him. Granted, they came with the erroneous assumption that Job had brought this on himself by some grievous sin. That assumption does not diminish the genuineness of their sympathy but heightens it. Despite their belief that Job was in sin, they inconvenienced themselves and came to mourn, comfort, weep, and sit with him. The narrator's description of Job's friends compels us to give them the benefit of any doubt about the sincerity of their compassion.

The Cowardly Cur

Angus was one of the kindest, gentlest, most exuberant eighty-five pounds of dog you can imagine. Even at ten years old he acted like a puppy. One day my wife and I were walking him when a rottweiler escaped from a neighbor's fenced yard. He was interested in Angus, not us. I tried to keep them apart, but once the rottweiler lunged, I had to release Angus's leash to give him his best chance to fight back. After a noisy tussle that lasted less than thirty seconds, we watched the tail-tucked rottweiler make a mad dash back to his own yard with Angus in enthusiastic pursuit. Angus got extra food and attention that day.

The end of Job 2 brings us to a fascinating threshold in the story. Satan seems to have disappeared! Like an arrogant but cowardly cur that tangled with a dog too big for him, he has slunk away tail-tucked, half-growling to save face and half-whining over his injuries. Bullies are cowards at heart, and Satan is the consummate cosmic bully. As far as Satan's own terms are concerned, it would appear the test is over. Twice he promised that, given the opportunity, he could induce Job to curse God. Twice he was dead wrong. The narrative pays him no more attention.

Job 2:7 is the last glimpse we catch of Satan in the entire book. How active he may have remained behind the scenes no one knows.[12] As far as the narrative is concerned, he is irrelevant. He never surfaces in any of the discussions between Job and his friends. Neither God nor narrator stoop to a victory speech. Satan receives the ultimate insult—he is ignored. God is at the beginning and end and center of everything, after all.

Job has successfully passed the tests. He has not turned on God in his heart (1:21–22) nor sinned with his lips (2:10). Yet he is still suffering. His circumstances have not altered. His afflictions have not been alleviated. His pain and loss are not remedied. Job still knows nothing about what is going on or why. And the book is just beginning.

In our mental overview of the book of Job, it is easy to jump glibly from the initial triumph of chapter 2 to the "Romans 8:28" conclusion in chapter 42—ignoring what God Himself has purposefully belabored in the massive middle of the book. Job endured unparalleled suffering. Both his initial response (Job 1–2) and his final response (Job 40, 42) expressed profound faith and exemplary submission. It was the long in-between that caused him the most trouble. Nothing seemed to change. No explanation was forthcoming; no relief was in sight.

At the end of chapter 2, standing on the edge of the next forty chapters, Job is suspended in a limbo of static chaos. Suffering can seem like that, as if God pours your life into a blender that throws everything crazily out of alignment—disarranging all your plans and priorities and daily routines—and then suspends the awkward constellation of circumstances indefinitely. Job began to wrestle with questions and appearances that seemed to contradict everything he thought he knew about God. In chapter 3, Job opens his heart as well as his mouth. Opening up is the first step to the Physician's diagnosis and treatment.

III

Human Dialogue: Job and Three Friends

8
How to Read the Debate

"Where there are so many, all speech becomes a debate without end. But two alone may perhaps find wisdom."[1] The first statement fits Job's arguments with his friends, the second his encounter with God. Yet God has given us twelve thousand words of debate (Job 4–37) before we get to witness the "two alone." The Lord has good reasons for directing the construction and proportions of this book.

Many readers bog down in these debates. Mired in the Slough of Despond, Christian discovered "certain good and substantial steps, placed even through the midst of the slough" to help him get through. Several steppingstones help the reader negotiate these seemingly endless and circular debates with understanding and profit—which is why they were preserved in the first place (Rom. 15:4). By finding those steps, the weary reader can work his way through this slough of dispute and even enjoy it.

Chapter 1 recommended a broad reading strategy for the book of Job. The "Hints for a Profitable Reading of the Book of Job" become indispensable in the dialogue segment. In addition to those general suggestions, this chapter explores some specific guidelines to help you hear the words you read.

The Influence of Intonation

As readers of this extended dialogue, we are at a distinct disadvantage. Here we most miss what the audience of a play has in their favor: vocal tone and facial expression. We cannot see or hear the characters deliver their lines. We have minimal asides from the narrator to explain the implication or intent of what was said. Different readers form diverse impressions of what was spoken, how it was spoken, and what was meant. But the interpretational field is not as wide open as it might seem.

The impact of intonation in communication can hardly be overstated. In written communication, context is crucial. In spoken communication—or written dialogue like Job—intonation can be just as important.[2] The same words can be differently intoned to communicate various and sometimes opposite meanings. Even a single word can mean very different things.

(Agreement) "Right." [Trans.: "Yes, exactly."]

(Joking) "Right." [Trans.: "Ha! I get it."]

(Exasperated) "Right." [Trans.: "Yes, I know already!"]

(Sarcastic) "Right." [Trans.: "No way!"]

The dialogue line is identical, but the intended meaning varies significantly. A context for each example would be helpful but sometimes even a surrounding context is not determinative. That is why narrators insert verbal signposts to point the reader in the right interpretational direction ("Yeah, right!" he sneered). Such signposts are absent in Job. The narrator introduces each new speaker with the same formula: "Then Eliphaz (or Bildad, or Zophar, or Job) answered and said . . ." That is why discerning the "mood, or tone, of each of the speakers in each of their speeches" becomes "fundamental to interpretation."[3] The absence of tonal signposts does not mean the reader can intone the dialogue any way he wishes. There are some solid steppingstones for helping us determine mood and tone.

Interpretive Factors

Dramatic interpretation of fictional works allows a degree of subjectivity and flexibility for artistic license. But when it comes to Scripture, we are dealing with an inspired record of historical events. One intonation is not necessarily as valid as another, and some we can confidently rule out altogether. Though an element of subjectivity is unavoidable in interpreting written dialogue, the goal of any author is to be understood, not misunderstood. The skillful author furnishes enough interpretive tools and concrete clues in the text to govern our conclusions in this area.[4]

The Narrator's Inspired Commentary

The narrator's introduction of Job's three friends is the most objective indicator for how we should begin reading their words. Job 2:11–13 offers an inspired opinion of these men and the motives for their visit. They were not monsters or cardboard characters. They were not stereotypical bilge-spouting pompous hypocrites.[5] Like you, they were flesh and blood, complex and nuanced. The narrator introduces them as genuine friends attempting to engage Job meaningfully. Compassion motivated them to inconvenience themselves to minister to Job. We ought "not minimize the friendship of the three who came a long distance to comfort him. Although men of wealth and worth, they were not ashamed to associate with the outcast on the rubbish-mound."[6] Apparently, they were the only acquaintances of Job willing to do so. "These men were not frauds," another writer maintains. "The compassion of these three men was true. They were the real thing. No one can fault them for not caring."[7]

Obviously they arrived with erroneous assumptions. Who would not be inclined to the same assumptions without the revelatory benefit of the prologue, let alone the combined testimony of the Old and New Testaments? They became increasingly exasperated with Job. Who would not, given Job's genius for insult? They were determined to pound the square peg of Job's experience into the round hole of their theology. In the end, God expressed His displeasure directly to them, "because you have not spoken of me what is right, as My servant Job has" (42:7, NASB). But that is God's final analysis, just as 2:11–13 reflects the inspired initial assessment of them. It is a mistake to infer from God's final expression that everything they said was wrong, just as it is a mistake to infer that everything Job said was right, since God rebuked Job specifically for verbal indiscretions (40:2). It is equally mistaken to ignore the narrator's initial introduction of the friends to the readers (2:11–13). From the outset, we are meant to see their gestures of compassion and to hear the genuine sympathy in their voices. If we read into their words a tone that we have prejudged to be between the lines, we can misread them and the text. Moreover, we miss what is really going on. Cardboard characters are easy targets for scorn but how many of them do you meet in real life? The Bible deals in real people, not straw men and stereotypes. Dismissing unpleasant characters with simplistic labels is a convenient way to avoid pondering the reflections of our own fallenness in their behavior. Job's friends have much to teach us, negatively and positively.

Job's Reaction to the Friends

This second interpretive pointer is nearly as objective as the first. We cannot hear how the three friends intoned their words, but Job did. His responses, then, become a barometer of how we should interpret their words. The fact that Job says nothing personally combative until after Zophar's first speech (12:2–3) suggests that the opening speeches of Eliphaz and Bildad ought to be intoned with passion and honest incredulity. To them the diagnosis of Job's condition is a no-brainer; they cannot believe he is even questioning why this has happened.

Job's response also indicates that their attempts to reason with him are compelled by compassion not condemnation. That compassion is evident in their assurances that if he will just repent, God will certainly be gracious to him (5:8–27; 8:20–22). Once Zophar speaks, however, it is apparent to Job that they are all dismissing his credibility, ignoring his arguments, and decided in their diagnosis. That is when he finally breaks out in exasperation with all of them (12:2–3; 13:4–12).

Identifying Kernel Statements

In chapter 1, I suggested sifting through the dialogue for the kernel statements that summarize the central thrust of each speech. David Clines explains, "In most of the speeches there appear one or two sentences, usually addressed to Job directly, which further define the tonality of the speech as well as pinpointing the content of the speech's argument."[8] Once you identify them, they jut up like buoys and help you chart a course through the sea of words. These kernel statements map out the overall progression of the dialogue. Identifying kernel statements also furnishes more stable guidelines for identifying the tone of a speaker.

Comparing Alternative Translations

Poetry is one of the most complicated genres to interpret in English, let alone in Hebrew. Apart from the narrator's portions, the book of Job was composed in Hebrew poetry. The Hebrew text of Job is often notoriously difficult, sometimes at key points in the dialogue.[9] The Greek text (Septuagint) is no better.[10] Reading the dialogues in other translations informs you of other possible nuances.

On the other hand, if you are accustomed to reading a translation other than the KJV, you owe it to your understanding to consult that version as well. The KJV possesses one invaluable interpretive aid that all other modern versions have forsaken. Ironically, that aid is the very feature from which the modern versions sought to escape: the archaic *thee*'s and *thou*'s. In updating this obsolete phraseology, the modern versions have lost a grammatically precise hermeneutical aid for interpreting some texts. In the KJV, *thou* or *thee* or *thy* always reflects a second person *singular* pronoun in the Greek or Hebrew text. Likewise, *you* or *your* in the KJV always reflects a second person *plural* pronoun in the Greek or Hebrew text. You don't have to know Greek or Hebrew to derive the hermeneutical benefit of this translational device.

In modern English (and modern English versions) we use the word *you* interchangeably for both singular and plural. What does this mean in practical terms? Here's just one example. Job 9:30–31 in the NIV reads, "Even if I washed myself with soap and my hands with washing soda, you would plunge me into a slime pit so that even my clothes would detest me." To whom is Job referring when he says *you*? Some argue that Job is referring here to his friends, who refuse to believe that he is righteous. No matter how much he protests his innocence, they will plunge him right back into the muck of their accusations. But *you* is, in fact, a singular pronoun. The KJV reads: "If I wash myself with snow water, and make my hands never so clean; yet shalt thou plunge me in the ditch, and mine own clothes shall abhor me." The translation *thou*, along with the surrounding context, demonstrates that Job is referring to God, not to his friends.[11]

These textual indicators help the reader understand the dialogue in a way that is realistic, meaningful, and consistent with the narrator's presentation and intention.

9 Anguish Finds a Voice

Job 3

In Elizabeth Gaskell's 1866 novel *Wives and Daughters* Squire Hamley was devastated when he lost his cherished wife of many years. Now his eldest son, Osborne, whose precarious health was further weakened by the anxiety of an estrangement from his father, lay dead as well. His faults notwithstanding, the old squire is a good-hearted man. But his life is crumbling around him as age and death conspire to loosen his grip, little by little, on the things and people that mean the most to him. Sitting by his fireside, he reflects with rustic eloquence, "I do try to say, 'God's will be done' . . . but it is harder to be resigned than happy people think."[1] The chasm between sufferer and spectator is a broad one to span.

The longest portion of the book of Job is the tortuous debate between Job and his friends. God first brought up the subject of Job, not Satan. Now it is Job who first breaks the silence, not his three friends. Let the reader tread reverently in this "house of mourning" (Eccles. 7:2),

> for now the most pious man on earth is among the most wretched. It is irrelevant that 40 chapters later he will be restored to his wealth, for the bulk of the book revolves about what it signifies that a righteous person can be in such misery. What counts now is that in a world where it is believed and taught that actions have appropriate consequences (despite the many evidences to the contrary), heaven itself now has sabotaged that doctrine with a most shocking infringement.[2]

Breaking the Silence (Job 3:1–2)

Satan swore that Job would curse God. Instead, Job blessed God. But time has passed, and Job has had nothing to do but sit and think. He has no more distractions—no possessions to protect, no wealth to invest, no household to run, no children to visit. For seven days of voiceless grief questions have been fermenting in his soul. The wine-skin bursts. His anguish finds its voice. Job opened his mouth "and cursed his day."

Was Satan right, after all?

This is a different word for *curse* (*qalal*) than Satan promised, and a different object—not God, but the day of his birth. Still, cursing "his day" isn't Job indirectly cursing God for creating him? His lament is not an emotional revolt against God or a substitute for cursing God. Job vents a sentiment that echoes throughout the book: in light of his loss of God's blessing, he longs for death. It would be better never to have been born than to endure the (apparent) desertion of God. He is not saying, "I wish I was never born because this hurts so much," but "I wish I was never born if I have to live without God."

Doesn't suffering of such magnitude signify something? It is not merely the affliction itself that Job finds so hard to bear; it is the sudden and inexplicable change in God's posture toward him that circumstances seem to signal. How can anyone endure such disaster and *not* assume that God has turned against him? Even the most righteous of men, especially the most righteous of men, would have to wonder.

> The sufferer considers himself as forgotten, forsaken, and rejected of God . . . therefore he sinks into despair; and in this despair expression is given to a profound truth, that it is better never to have been born, or to be annihilated, than to be rejected of God. . . . In this condition of entire deprivation of every taste of divine goodness, Job breaks forth in curses.[3]

Job's lamentation ultimately *magnifies* God by articulating the immeasurable value of His favor and the irrelevance of life without it. If God means this much—that man is better off not to have lived at all than to live without Him—then this God must be supremely desirable above life itself. Securing His pleasure must be the single worthwhile ambition in life. Job's lament progresses through three stages.[4]

Why Was I Born? (Job 3:3–10)

Would that the day I was born could perish! Would that the day of my birth could be erased from the calendar for all time! History has no rewind. Pining over the past is illogical. But logic can't compete with instinct when it comes to raw pain.

> A man suffering the torment of physical and mental pain does not think logically and progressively. His thoughts are instinctive. They fly out like sparks struck from the iron as it lies between the hammer of God and the anvil of life.[5]

Passion—whether expressed openly or in the silent cry of the soul to God—is instinctive. A rabbit with its foot clamped in a steel-spring trap does not calmly consider its options. Frantic yelps and frenzied commotion give way to exhaustion and despair. That is instinct. We are not animals, but we can have equally instinctive reactions to pain.

Like Elijah, Job was "a man subject to like passions as we are" (James 5:17). He was made of the same stuff. If we imagine that Job's initial response places him on a pedestal of spirituality beyond our reach, his lament shows that his feet are rooted in the same clay as ours. Yet there is cathartic value in this lament.

Why Did I Live? (Job 3:11–19)

If I had to be born, Job thinks, *I could have at least died at birth* (3:11) *or been stillborn* (3:16). Then he would have been able to bypass all this suffering and "rest in peace" in good company. At least in the grave one is beyond the reach of the wicked; there the weary find rest, freedom from oppression, and no suffering. Robbery, murder, pain, and sickness may rage on the turf overhead, while the dead sleep in blissful immunity to all that goes on above them.[6]

Job introduces us to the interrogative that defines his dialogue for the next thirty chapters. Three times in two verses (3:11–12) he asks, "Why?" Nearly twenty times in Job's nine speeches he echoes that question.[7] It is a question with which we immediately connect, because it is *our* instinctive question. It is the involuntary reflex of every sufferer's mind.

Why Can't I Just Die? (Job 3:20–26)

Having been born and survived to endure such humiliating suffering, Job asks why he is not at least granted the mercy of a swift end. If God is this displeased with him, why won't He just finish him off? Job is not even permitted the dignity of death, though he begs God for it. Job's longing for death may seem morbid, almost suicidal. Job's words actually offer a compelling argument *against* suicide that we will consider at the end of this chapter.

One thing Job says is particularly intriguing: "For the thing which I greatly feared is come upon me, and that which I was afraid of is come unto me" (3:25).[8] Did Job suspect something like this might happen some day? Was he secretly plagued by anxiety? Was he haunted by a lingering apprehension of calamity that might suggest a guilty conscience after all? Such an interpretation would undercut God's own assessment of Job (1:1, 8), contradict God's admission that Job deserved none of this (2:3), and undermine the foundational proposition of the entire book. It also would render Job's dogged insistence of his innocence throughout the rest of the book schizophrenic.[9]

His words could indicate an inexplicable apprehension that things had just been going so well for so long that something was bound to happen. Some think that Job is reflecting back on his reaction to the relentless one-two punch of his calamities; he received news of one calamity only to fear another.[10] Others say Job is referring specifically to his physical suffering. After he had lost everything else (children, flocks, servants), he feared that calamity would next strike him personally—and sure enough, it did. In this case, verse 26 would mean, "I had no quiet, no repose, no rest, and trouble only increased."

Perhaps Job is saying that the one thing he dreaded ever happening—the loss of God's blessing and favor—and which he took pains to avert, even for his own children (1:5), has now happened; and what is worse, "he has no idea why."[11] His words may convey a perpetual sense of foreboding, a kind of "what next?" paranoia.[12] Some versions translate the verbs in the present tense: "For what I fear comes upon me, and what I dread befalls me" (NASB, ESV). Job seems to be saying, "I fear a fear, and it overtakes me! I think, 'What if this happens next?' and then it happens! I am not withheld from any calamity."

One writer suggests that Job's words in verse 25 simply foreshadow one of his key arguments throughout the rest of the book—that there *is* such a thing as innocent suffering, that it is not always only the wicked who suffer.

> Job had already thought about these matters. He was no amateur in the things of God. He had thought enough about them to know that, from his own observations, from his own knowledge of God, he could not consider himself exempt from the possibility of disastrous loss. Such loss was what he feared. To that extent, he was prepared for it; probably that prepared mind was also one of the reasons why his initial responses are so entirely noble.[13]

Why? Why? Why?

When God called Moses to a personally dangerous and humanly impossible mission, Moses scrambled for excuses. "I'm insufficient for such a task" (Exod. 3:11). "I don't know You like I should" (Exod. 3:13). "What if they won't believe me?" (Exod. 4:1). When Moses objected that he was insufficiently gifted for the task, God countered with a breathtaking claim: "Who hath made man's mouth? or who maketh the dumb, or deaf, or the seeing, or the blind? have not I, the Lord?" (Exod. 4:11).

Without embarrassment or explanation, God asserts that He is the Maker not only of the healthy and whole but also of the handicapped. To us, handicaps are genetic flaws or unfortunate accidents. God candidly corrects us, "No, *I* did that. I *make* them that way." We instinctively ask "why?"

Why He does so is beyond the scope of this discussion and, for the moment, beside the point.[14] To some, this sounds like convenient evasion, so I will offer the only honest and biblical answer I have: I don't know why. God rarely explains why. We are preoccupied with "why" for a number of reasons.[15] "Why?" is a "me-oriented" question.[16] It is not the question God is primarily concerned to answer. He never answered it for Job. Table your "why?" long enough to consider a different question: "Who? *Who* did this? Who *is* in charge?" Ponder the biblical answer to that question and knowing "why" loses its urgency. Once you settle the "who?" and submit to that answer, the next question you begin to ask is not "why?" but "how?" How do I respond rightly to this? How do I handle this situation and adapt to this circumstance in a way that honors God and contributes to accomplishing His purposes? "We cannot expect to find the [right] answer if we are asking the wrong question. Thus the question needs to be reframed from 'Why me?' to 'What now?'"[17]

Is Job a Good Example of Grieving?

By God's own standard, Job is a spiritual giant. His initial response in the face of personal devastation is heroic, exemplary (1:21; 2:10). Being the man he is reputed to be, we hardly expect any less. The lesson some carry away is that Job's is the response of any mature and truly spiritual believer, nobly accepting devastating losses immediately.

That is why Job's lament surprises and unnerves us. Suddenly Job no longer sounds like a super saint. He unleashes a spirit of anguish that threatens to contradict his earlier resolve. As the dialogue progresses, Job expresses both anger (18:4) and despair (6:26).[18] "Grief is an almost unavoidable consequence of bereavement, maltreatment, or pain."[19] Is Job, then, a positive or negative example of grieving? Neither, really. Job is a *realistic* example of grieving by one of the godliest men in Old Testament history. This is what grief looks like, sometimes even for spiritually mature saints, because even spiritually mature saints are human.

Some excuse Job's reaction as understandable for an Old Testament believer, given the sparsity of revelation he had to bolster his faith, but they insist that Job is not a model for how a New Testament believer should respond even to the severest trial.[20] I am not suggesting that believers "model" their grief after the pattern of Job or anyone else. I am suggesting that when believers find themselves grieving like Job, they are in good and godly company. The view that Job's grief is sub-Christian is unbiblical, unrealistic, and unhelpful for Christians who do suffer severely. Here are four reasons.

First, to excuse Job's grief only because he did not have access to scriptural truth *underestimates the enormous amount of truth that Job possessed about God and His ways.*[21] Granted, a great deal of enlightening and comforting truth was not yet revealed, penned, and preserved in Scripture. But if Job is to be excused only because he antedated the Scriptures, then what is Jeremiah's excuse? In terms of Old

Testament history, Jeremiah lived at the other end of the chronological spectrum from Job. Jeremiah had the Pentateuch, the Psalms, most of the Prophets, and even the book of Job. Yet Jeremiah cursed the day of his birth in terminology strikingly similar to Job's (see Jer. 20:14–18).[22]

The similarity between the language of Job and Jeremiah suggests a second reason that Job's reaction should not be construed as sub-Christian: *human nature remains fundamentally unchanged.* The weaknesses of our flesh are not eradicated by the possession, or even the persuasion, of more truth. When harsh realities bend belief to the breaking point, the thoughts and feelings that often result are intensely, entirely, and appropriately *human*. Being a modern Christian with the New Testament in our hands does not erase our humanity. Expressions of grief may not fit some people's sanitized ideas of what a Christian "ought" to think and feel. But when catastrophe strikes like lightning, ripping ragged holes in the lives of previously serene saints, God has preserved a record of the grief of godly saints for our consolation. Angst is not unbelief and questions are not sinful; they are human and shared by some of the best of God's people. That leads to another consideration.

Third, *the experiences of past saints are recorded to teach and encourage us in our times of suffering*. "For whatever was written in earlier times was written for our instruction, so that through perseverance and [through] the encouragement of the Scriptures we might have hope" (Rom. 15:4, NASB). The book of Job fleshes out the value of transparency before God. "Job is determined to be absolutely honest with God. Job tells God everything, every fear and every doubt. . . . God prefers we speak with him honestly, even in our moments of deepest gloom, than that we mouth innocuous clichés far removed from reality."[23] There is nothing spiritual about making yourself say and pray all the things that you are supposed to say while ignoring or pretending away the questions, doubts, confusion, and pain. But there is virtue and healing in honesty with God.[24]

> God does not blame us if in our suffering we frankly vent our despair and confess our loss of hope, our sense of futility, our lamentations about life itself. . . . Of course, it is possible in grief and misery to say the wrong things, to say blasphemous things. . . . But within certain boundaries, it is far better to be frank about our grief, candid in our

despair, honest with our questions, than to suppress them and wear a public front of puffy piety. Whatever "resolution" the Book of Job provides turns on Job's questions and God's responses. Without the questions, there would have been no responses.[25]

We have a word for saying one thing (whatever the right thing may be in any given situation) and thinking or feeling quite differently. We call it *hypocrisy*. "This people honoreth me with their lips, but their heart is far from me" (Mark 7:6). It was a recurring issue with the Israelites (Ps. 78:36–37; Isa. 29:13; Jer. 12:2; Ezek. 33:31), not because hypocrisy is a genetically Jewish problem but because it is a genetically human problem, a universal tendency of fallen human nature. Hypocrisy masquerades in many guises.[26] You may think it a noble thing not to want to offend God with your faltering faith, nagging doubts, or disturbing questions. So you put on a false bold front, say and pray all the right spiritual things, and teach your soul to bite its lip. But hypocrisy in any form is not noble or helpful.

There is relief and security in knowing that you can set aside all your pretenses and bare your whole soul to God. How absurd to do anything else! He has already read your MRIs. He *knows* every thought and doubt, every disgruntlement and question. Only when we are honest with ourselves and candid with the Lord can He minister to our diseased hearts and heal whatever He finds there, whether pain or bitterness, doubt or anger, confusion or lingering questions.[27] Imagine a patient with internal pain sitting on the physician's examination table, arms tightly crossed and insisting that everything is okay. The divine Physician cannot treat us if we pretend everything is fine and refuse to open up to Him.[28] Hypocrisy hinders healing and denial is therapy resistant.

A fourth reason for not attributing Job's lament to a lack of revelation (and therefore rejecting it as sub-Christian) is that *Job finally found peace and resolution not by receiving new truth but by understanding and appropriating truths he already knew.* Suffering tests and tempers our faith in what we already believe and transfers truth from impersonal theory to personal reality. The issue is not how much we know. The issue is how much and how deeply we really believe what we know, even when appearances argue to the contrary.

Adoniram Judson, pioneer missionary to Burma in the early 1800s, is called the father of modern missions. After the death of several children and then his wife, he withdrew from ministry and society and became reclusive. He grieved not only for his loss and loneliness but for the depravity it had brought to light in his own soul. The experience stripped him emotionally and spiritually, unmasking the pride that had motivated much of what he did even as a self-sacrificing Christian missionary. He sat for days beside an open grave, contemplating his inward corruption and hoping this meditation would somehow purify him. He lamented being unable to find God, to hear from Him, or to experience any deliverance from his inner corruption. When his close friend and missionary associate died, Judson offered the man's widow, Sarah Boardman, this bit of realism:

> You are now drinking the bitter cup whose dregs I am somewhat acquainted with. And though, for some time, you have been aware of its approach, I venture to say that it is far bitterer than you expected. It is common for persons in your situation to refuse all consolation, to cling to the dead, and to fear that they shall too soon forget the dear object of their affections. But don't be concerned. I can assure you that months and months of heart-rending anguish are before you, whether you will or not. You take the bitter cup with both hands, and sit down to your repast. You will soon learn a secret, that there is sweetness at the bottom. . . .[29]

Providence eventually brought them into each other's mind and life. Adoniram came to admire Sarah on several counts, not least of which was her resolute, contented, even cheerful continuation of life and ministry after her husband's death. "She had not tried to cut herself off from the world," in stark contrast to Adoniram. "She had not sat for days by an open grave. She had equably accepted what came as the will of God and kept on with His work."[30] Not everyone handles calamity the same way. God preserved the record of Job's grief "so that through . . . the encouragement of the Scriptures we might have hope."

Was Job Suicidal?

No one should conclude that Job 3 suggests or condones suicidal tendencies. Job was not suicidal. He never contemplated taking his own life. Suicide was not an option. The closest brush with suicide in the story was his wife's suggestion that he "curse God and die"—that is, commit a willful act of blasphemy to provoke God's instantaneous judgment. Job recoiled in horror at this suggestion from his would-be "enabler" (2:9–10).[31]

Even amid torturous grief and bodily pain, Job was not suicidal but submissive to the will and timing of a sovereign God. In despair over what he assumed was incurable misery, Job wanted God to kill him outright (see 6:8–10). As it turned out, his assumption was shortsighted and entirely mistaken. "Despair is only for those who see the end beyond all doubt."[32] Job did not, and neither do we. Yet even Job's "death wish" was just that—a wish, a request, a *prayer* ultimately resigned to the wishes and purposes of the Lord of life.

Throughout the Bible, other godly men under great duress also asked God for death. Such requests argue against suicide, not for it. None of them regarded taking his own life as an option. Those who longed for death included some of the Old Testament's most notable saints: Moses (Num. 11:14–15), Elijah (1 Kings 19:4), and Jonah (Jon. 4:3, 8). Only the treacherous ever took their own lives,[33] for suicide is an unauthorized taking of life from its Giver and Owner (Job 12:10). Your life belongs to God, spirit and body along with the breath that sustains it, whether you are a believer (1 Cor. 6:19–20) or an unbeliever (Dan. 5:23, where Daniel is speaking to pagan King Belshazzar).

John Bunyan shows remarkable relevance when he addresses a temptation to suicide in *The Pilgrim's Progress.* Christian and Hopeful fall into the hands of Giant Despair, who imprisons them in Doubting Castle. On Thursday he beats them mercilessly, "so all that day they spent their time in nothing but sighs and bitter lamentations." The next day he advises them "that since they were never like to come out of that place, their only way would be forthwith to make an end of themselves, either with knife, halter, or poison." As they confer in their misery whether they should take the Giant's advice, Christian (quoting Job 7:15!) seems inclined to do so: "My soul chooseth strangling rather than life, and the grave is more easy for me than this dungeon." Hopeful dissuades him, saying, "Let's be patient and endure a while, the time may come that may give us happy release." Friday night the Giant, seeing they had not taken his advice, threatens them again. Christian nearly capitulates again, but

Hopeful encourages him to persevere. Finally, it is on Sunday (significantly) that they are enabled by providence to make their escape from Giant Despair and Doubting Castle.[34]

The Loneliness of Suffering

Inexplicable suffering is difficult enough all by itself, but it is doubly difficult when it is in glaring contrast to the prosperity of others. This incongruity is the centerpiece in much of the debate between Job and his friends. Job keeps noticing the apparent prosperity of the wicked in particular—much to the chagrin of his friends, who keep insisting that *only* wicked people, and *all* wicked people, suffer like Job.

Personal suffering can be a lonely row to hoe. "Lord," asked Peter, pointing to John, "what shall be to this man?" That was Peter's reflex when Christ told him that he would suffer the indignities of persecution in his old age (John 21:18–19).[35] Christ punctuated that disturbing revelation with a command designed to realign Peter's perspective: "Follow me." Looking up and seeing John standing nearby, Peter asked Jesus, "What about him, Lord?" This may be a veiled form of "Why me? Why not him? Or, at least, why not him too?" Peter's words may imply an appeal for some explanation of why the Lord was singling him out for this unappealing future. Or it may simply reflect a human reflex to pain—comparing our lot with others'.

Jesus' response to Peter is the biblical tonic for this instinctive but incorrect view of suffering. "If I choose for him an entirely different path, what is that to you?" Peter's question reads literally, "Lord, but what to this one?" Jesus' answer reads literally, "What['s it] to you?" To drive the point home, the Lord gently but intensively repeats his previous command: "*You* follow *me*" (John 21:22).[36] That is all the sufferer need focus on. You cling to Christ. Follow the path He has laid out for *you*. Comparing your experience with either the plight or prosperity of others is fruitless because it accomplishes nothing, it is misleading because it is based purely on the appearances of the moment, and it is disorienting because it distorts your thinking and defocuses your view of God.

Andrée Seu is not a writer. She is a an artisan of the literary craft. Her prose is as tight and evocative as poetry. Prior to losing her husband in 1999, she wrote a "postcard" from the lengthening shadows of that valley of death. Her "grieving primer" concludes,

> If in your crisis you discover that you are much worse than you thought, go to Him anyway. What else can you do? He has the words of life. . . . You will fail. Then you will catch yourself and get up again. Till in due time you learn to walk. This is the dialectic of the Christian life. There are no larger battles. There are no other methods.[37]

Job personifies this counsel. Amid all his pain and frustration, Job's tenacious grip on God never loosens. The hard providences of God wean us from reliance on self, preoccupation with the visible, and contentment with the temporal.

He intends them to draw us, or if necessary to drive us, to Himself. Where else will you go?

10

Well-Meaning Friends, Misguided Counselors

Job 4–14

Job's three friends must have stared at him in disbelief. This was not what they expected to hear. "They were shocked by Job's words because from the start they took it for granted that he must deserve all he was getting."[1] Surely Job, an honorable man, would admit it. The empirical evidence was overwhelming. They came to comfort, but they assumed they were coming to comfort a *penitent*.[2] How could he possibly stand amid this wreckage and ignore the only obvious conclusion? This was an open-and-shut case of divine judgment for sin. Was Job in denial? Or rebellion?

Job's outburst set in motion the first of three cycles of patterned dialogue between him and his friends. The discussion runs for nearly the next thirty chapters like a river whose clear headwaters of consolation soon turn turbid with debate.

Eliphaz: Appreciate God's Correction and Return to Him (Job 4–5)

Eliphaz first ventures a word with Job. His opening speech reasons, warns, and appeals in compassionate tones.[3] Some see sarcasm and vitriol in his speech.[4] Job's reply (Job 6–7) gives no hint that he interpreted Eliphaz's words that way, so there is no reason that we should. All the contextual data indicate that we should give Eliphaz the benefit of the doubt in spirit, tone, and motive.[5]

> The real sympathy and affection of this first speech of Eliphaz ought to remind us that "Job's comforters" were not what they are often represented to be. They were not cold-hearted hypocrites; they were good and sincere men, whose chief defect was that suffering had not unlocked the door for them into the larger world of Job's thoughts.[6]

Sympathetic Reasoning (4:1–11)

Eliphaz opens tentatively: *Should one venture to speak to you while you are so upset? But who can withhold words under such circumstances* (4:2)?[7] *Remember how many you have counseled and encouraged* (4:3–4). *Now it has happened to you. It is time to follow your own counsel to others. Let your past devotion and integrity encourage you that all is not lost beyond recovery* (4:5–6). There is no mystery here; such calamity, he reminds Job, comes only upon those who have sinned (4:7–11).

Sober Warning (4:12–5:7)

Eliphaz recounts a dream-vision that has earned him the dubious distinction of being dubbed the "mystic" among the three friends (4:12–21).[8] But in this early stage of human history prior to written revelation, such dreams or visions were God's standard means for communicating revelation.[9] Sometimes these were theophanic, featuring a veiled manifestation of God Himself, as 4:15 may suggest.

There is nothing unorthodox in this dream-vision,[10] no reason to doubt Eliphaz's words, and no reason to suspect an ulterior motive in his relating it to Job.[11] Eliphaz describes being in a "deep sleep" (4:13), the same kind of divinely induced slumber when God revealed Himself to Abraham (Gen. 15:12).[12] The grammar may also suggest that this was not merely an angelic spirit, but the Spirit of God.[13] It is unclear exactly where the quotation from the vision concludes, but it seems to extend to the end of 4:21.[14]

What was this mysterious midnight message to Eliphaz? Many argue that the traditional rendering of the KJV ("Shall mortal man be *more* just than God? Shall a man be *more* pure than his maker?"), though grammatically possible, cannot be the intended meaning here.[15] As one writer remarks, man hardly needs divine revelation to tell him that he cannot be more righteous than God.[16] Rather, the suggested sense is "Can a mortal be righteous before God? Can a man be pure in the presence of his Maker?"[17] Job never "suggested that he is more just than God, and no awful oracle is needed to convince him of the folly and impiety of such an idea."[18] However, this is the very crux of the Lord's charge against Job (40:8). If Job justifies himself *at the expense* of God's righteousness (as God says he did), then he has virtually, if unintentionally, made himself more righteous than God. This sin is more common than we suppose.

Whenever we think that God is being unfair, or that we would never do some of the things God does, we make ourselves more righteous than God. Maybe we need this revelation more than we think we do. We are not above being reminded that God is always more righteous than we are.[19] The Lord's charge against Job in 40:8 dispels such self-flattery. Those who find fault with God's words, God's ways, God's judgments, God's dealings with people, imply that if they were God, they would be more reasonable, more compassionate, more righteous. One translation preserves both senses in 4:17 as equally valid and pertinent to the context of Job—"Can a human be more right than God? Can a person be pure before his maker?" (NCV).

If even God's angels sin and are not exempt from His judgment, how much more will fallible, fragile, fallen man be held to account (4:18–21)! One cannot sue for leniency in judgment by appealing even to those heavenly beings; they are held to the same standard (5:1). Sin has inescapable consequences (5:2–5). Affliction does not spring out of nowhere for no reason; every man generates whatever trouble comes to him (5:6–7).[20]

Impassioned Appeal (5:8–27)

Some may hear a note of self-righteous superiority in Eliphaz's voice here, but there is every contextual reason for reading his words as the compassionate counsel of a mistaken but true friend. "What-I-would-do-if-I-were-you" advice is usually only as valuable as the degree to which the advisor has faced comparable circumstances. Inexperience doesn't make the advice insincere or necessarily useless. Overall, Eliphaz's counsel is sound in all but the last two words—"What he should do is go straight to God and cast himself at his feet in penitence."[21] Apart from that one point, this is what Job does throughout the rest of the book. Job seems to spend nearly as much time talking to God as he spends answering his friends.

Eliphaz's poetic flight (5:9–16) stands out as "one of the most beautiful examples" of a creedal hymn to be found in the Bible.[22] Even Paul picks up on one line (5:13) and quotes it to his Corinthian audience (1 Cor. 3:19). Eliphaz closes with a graceful word of encouragement (5:17–27). That a portion of his exhortation is echoed in a surprising variety of passages (Ps. 94:12; Prov. 3:11–12; Heb. 12:5–6) testifies to its trustworthiness in principle. Eliphaz concludes on an optimistic note, confident that Job will find restoration because God is gracious. His final appeal

> is a beautiful tribute to the fatherly care of God, strict but kind. His apparent severity in sending sickness (verse 18), setbacks (19), famine and war (20), fire and flood (21), plagues and wild beasts (22)—there is not the slightest doubt that all these natural things come immediately from His sovereign hand—is more than outweighed by His goodness in sending remedies for all these disasters.[23]

Despite his erroneous assumption that such catastrophe can mean only that Job has obviously committed a series of wicked whoppers, Eliphaz's optimism for Job speaks eloquently of his high conception of God's gracious and forgiving nature. Eliphaz is no legalist.

Job: Waiting for Death, Looking for Loyalty (Job 6–7)

Job's initial reply comes almost in the form of a soliloquy. Things are far worse than they seem to realize.

It's Worse Than You Think (6:1–7)

This is not mere "correction" or "chastening" (cf. 5:17), he implies. This is grief and calamity heavier than all the sands of the sea (6:2–3). *God has pierced me through with poison-tipped arrows and set all His terrors in battle array against me* (6:4). *This is full-bore divine bombardment. If my words sound rough and reckless, that's why* (6:3*b*, 5). Like a wild ass deprived of grass or an ox left unfed (6:5), Job is denied any reasonable explanation and left to starve. He can't swallow what Eliphaz has offered him—flavorless food, tasteless as unsalted egg white that neither satisfies the palate nor feeds the soul (6:5–7).[24]

What Job Expects from God (6:8–13)

What does Job expect from God? Death. The sooner the better. He is convinced that these catastrophes signal the end and begs God to kill him and be done with it (6:8–10). Thank the Lord that He is wise and gracious enough not to give us everything we ask. *Look at me*, Job appeals to his friends. *What's left of me that I should hope for some kind of reversal? Why would I want to prolong my life? How much more of this do you think I can take* (6:11–13)?

What Job Expects from Friends (6:14–30)

Job's opening line here is riddled with interpretational uncertainties.[25] He seems to say that one in affliction has a right to expect loyalty[26] from his friend, that the disloyal friend has forsaken the fear of the Almighty. Job has been bitterly disappointed in this expectation. *My brothers have been unreliable, like a wadi* (6:15). I live near mountains where streams stay put and rarely dry up. Job's imagery reflects the seasonal streambeds of the Middle East. The wadi becomes a gushing torrent during a heavy rain or a spring thaw in the snowcapped mountains (6:16) but withers to a bone-dry bed in the hot season (6:17–18). The seasonal flow of water encourages plants to sprout along the wadi's course, raising the hopes of thirsty travelers looking for refreshment, then dashing their hopes when they find none (6:19–20). Those who should have showed their loyalty (6:14) by sticking with Job through this calamity have deserted him. Like dry wadis, they were not there when he needed them most.

Job personalizes his portrait of the thirsty caravaners in 6:20. When they come to the wadi—camouflaged with vegetation to look like a flowing stream—they are *ashamed* and *confused* because they had *trusted* that they would find refreshment there. Disappointment we expect, but *shame* and *confusion*? Job transitions from imagery back to reality. That's how he felt when, confident in the compassion of his companions, he turned to them and they turned away. "Disappointment" can't begin to describe it. This man of wealth and wisdom, of godliness and goodness, of fame and influence, this friend of every man and advocate for the underling, was *shamed* and *confused* at suddenly finding himself the community pariah, the friendless outcast of Uz. Those once proud to be seen with him now shut their doors in his disfigured face.

Lord, may we not be wadis. Make us streams whose flow is fed by the springs of Your own unfailing faithfulness to us, so that when others look to us for compassion to slake their thirst for acts of kindness in their need, we may readily offer the refreshing loyalty they deserve from us as brothers and sisters and friends.

Many think that Job has three particular friends in mind here (6:14–20). But these three are the only ones who have *not* deserted him. Job does not couch his complaint in 6:14–15 as though he is talking to them or about them, but about others. This is not the last time he will express his disillusionment with the abandonment of friends, neighbors, servants, and even relatives. Job uses similar terminology in 19:13–19 to describe the desertion of every conceivable companion. Everywhere he turned, people scattered from him. You wouldn't want to be caught comforting God's enemy. Only a fool could look at Job and not read the handwriting of divine judgment. It wasn't safe to be one of Job's children; they were all dead. It wasn't safe to be one of Job's servants; most of them were gone too. It wasn't even safe to be one of Job's *animals*. Whatever Job did to bring all this on, they're not having any part of it.[27] Only a fool stands near a tree in a storm. And to a man, they were no fools. Whatever else you may think of Eliphaz, Bildad, and Zophar, they were willing to take the risk.

Another indication that Job is not talking about them in 6:14–20 is that in 6:21 he clearly—and by implied comparison—*is* talking about them now. Job described the disloyal desertion of "friends" and "brothers" in the third person. Now he shifts to the second person to talk about them and to them: *But now you . . . !*[28] One translation captures the shift: "Now you too have proved to be of no help" (NIV). Job senses that they are at a loss to know how to deal with this: *You see a horror like this and fear* (6:21).[29] The reason they reject Job's defense and cling to their theory of Job's guilt will be explored in chapter 12.

No one knows quite what to make of Job's rhetorical questions in 6:22–23 or their link to 6:21. Perhaps they form a bridge between verses 14–21 and 24–30. *All my friends have dried up and disappeared like desert wadis* (6:14–20). *Now you are no more help than they; you behold my disaster and are bewildered* (6:21). *I am not asking for a bail-out to compensate my losses* (6:22–23). *All I am asking for is some explanation! Teach me, and I will be quiet; show me what I have done wrong* (6:24). *Upright words sound forceful, but what does your argument prove* (6:25)?[30] *Will you quarrel and treat the speeches of a despairing man like wind* (6:26)? *You might as well gamble for orphans and barter away your friend* (6:27). *Look at me! I will not lie to your face* (6:28).[31] *Desist, no more injustice! My integrity is at stake* (6:29).[32] *Is there perversity in my tongue? I am not speaking falsehood* (6:30).[33]

Resigned to God's Allotment (7:1–10)

In the presence of physicians he will later describe as "worthless," Job diagnoses his own condition as best he can. Rejecting any connection between his symptoms and their usual explanation, Job instinctively arrives at a sound conclusion: *This is simply God's inexplicable allotment for me* (7:1–3). His reference to "months of vanity" (7:3) may give a clue as to how long his suffering has lasted so far.[34] Or Job may be anticipating that this is going to draw out into a lingering slide into the grave. Job shows no sign that he expects any change; his only hope is that God might be merciful enough to finish him off quickly. Job describes his misery in pathetic, gruesome detail (7:4–5). He nurtures no optimism for any recovery from this calamity (7:6–7). He looks only for death (7:8–10).

I cannot read Job 7:3 without thinking of my mother. Her "months of vanity (lit., emptiness)" have multiplied under the slow erosion of Alzheimer's disease. She has lived with us for over twelve years. I know no more apt description of that thief of memory and mind than Job's expression "months of vanity and wearisome nights," and no more biblical resolution to this mystery than Job's conviction that "months of vanity and wearisome nights are *appointed*" to her. Job understood that there is Someone in charge. So must we.

"Months of vanity" may describe the experience of the one suffering from Alzheimer's disease or similar long-term, debilitating illnesses. It should not describe the experience of the caretaker who sees the larger picture. I once wondered why God would leave His child to linger so helplessly and uselessly. A friend who had been down the same road before us cleared it up. "There is a reason the Lord leaves them here," he said, "and it's not for *their* benefit." God appoints "months of vanity" to our loved ones to polish *us*. Such appointments are not obstacles or inconveniences but equally God's appointment for us. Parents or siblings or children who require our care become the Lord's tools to shape our character, to sculpt in us a likeness to Christ, to reorient our personal ambitions and even our service. All rests on our submission to the providences of God in the lives of those around us as well as in our own lives. It is easy to resent these appointments as obstructions to a "higher" calling, interruptions to our efforts to serve the Lord. My mother *is* God's will for us right now; she is our service, our ministry, our calling. If God calls you to that kind of situation, it is not a setback to fulfilling God's will; it is the means to living out God's will for you and in you. God arranges such circumstances because His primary purpose is not for us to accomplish great things for Him but for Him to accomplish great things in us.

Lord, Why? (7:11–21)

Job believes he is on a short dead-end street to death, with no egress and no U-turn. What, then, does he have to lose by cutting loose with his complaint and venting his frustration (7:11)? Where else does he have to go but to God? Oblivious to his friends, Job lapses into another prayer-soliloquy.[35] The second person singular (7:12, 14, 17–21) and clear references to deity (7:17–18, 20–21) indicate that Job is now talking to the Lord.[36]

> It is Job's remembered intimacy with God . . . that really hurts him. . . . So now there can be no question for him of merely suffering in silence, like an animal or a stoic. He must find out what has happened between himself and God, for it has all the marks of an estrangement—and silence is no remedy for that. Indeed God's attitude appears to go beyond coolness to a positive hostility, expressed in a ceaseless rain of blows. Chapter 7 in particular . . . has the added bitterness of a conviction that every throb and every terror comes immediately from God.[37]

"I have sinned" (7:20) might be better translated as a rhetorical question: "Have I sinned?" (NKJV, NASB).[38] Job knows he is a sinner but confident that there is no correlation between his sin and his circumstances. We know that he is right on this point (1:1, 8; 2:3). Why, then, has God set him up as a target to shoot at (7:20*b*)? Why won't God accept his confessional sacrifice and pardon his transgression (7:21)?

> If he seems defiant, it is the daring of faith. All Job has known about God he still believes. But God's inexplicable ways have his mind perplexed to the breaking point. Job is in the right; but he does not know that God is watching with silent compassion and admiration until the test is fully done and it is time to state His approval publicly (Job 42:8).[39]

Bildad: Conventional Wisdom (Job 8)

Listening to Job's "rant," Bildad grows bolder and more insistent than Eliphaz. Any suspicions aroused by Job's unrepentant lament have been confirmed. Job actually has the cheek to deny any responsibility for his own disasters! Bildad takes up Job's "wild and whirling words" (6:26), throws them back in his face (8:2), and "accuses Job bluntly of being a windbag, vehement but empty."[40] He unloads a double-barreled rhetorical question: "Does God pervert justice? Or does the Almighty pervert what is right?" (8:3, NASB).

Bildad strikes below the belt. God obviously destroyed Job's children because they sinned against Him (8:4). If Job were as "pure and upright" as he insists, God would surely awake for him, put an end to this suffering, and bless him even more than before (8:5–7). No question about it—that's just how He deals with the righteous.

Appealing to the collective wisdom of the ages (8:8–10), Bildad returns to one of Eliphaz's themes. These things don't just happen for no reason (8:11–12). This has all the earmarks of how God treats the wicked, who forget Him (8:13–19).[41] God will not forsake a man of integrity nor abet the wicked. If Job were truly in the right, He would stand up for him (8:20–22).

Job: Seeking a Mediator, Soliciting His Maker (Job 9–10)

Job concedes Bildad's argument. But the issue posed by Eliphaz's dream-revelation (4:17) is relevant here: "How can a man be justified before (lit., with) God" (9:2)?

In its context, this question does not ask how a mortal can be pure or holy before God, but how a mortal can be *vindicated* before God. "I know God is just," says Job. "But my problem is that in this case I too am just; I am suffering unfairly. But how can I prove it to God? How can I be vindicated before him?"[42]

Job 9:3–4 bears out that this is what Job means. Anyone who wants to challenge God does not stand a chance. He is wise and powerful; who has ever come out on top in a fight with God? Literally, "who has hardened himself against Him and remained in one piece?" A man facing a fight braces himself—sets his jaw, squints his eyes, clenches his fists, tenses his muscles. But the one who hardens himself for a fight with God won't finish; not only will he not come out on top, he won't even be left standing.[43]

I recall seeing a cocker spaniel disappear beneath the unforgiving wheel of a school bus. He was a small and ignorant dog but compensated by also being obnoxious and arrogant. He began chasing the bus as it pulled away, the lumbering vehicle obviously retreating in response to his ferocity. Then the animal lunged too close. What looks like "no fear" may be nothing more than brute stupidity. We might expect that from a dog. But what do we make of otherwise reasonable people who snap at the wheels of God's purposes and providences?

Job stands no more chance against God than a spaniel versus a school bus. He affirms that the Lord is sovereign and all-powerful (9:5–9), inscrutable (9:10–11), invincible (9:12–20),[44] indiscriminate and unpredictable (9:21–24), determined (9:25–31),[45] and most frustrating of all, unapproachable (9:32–35). Job will not fight against God. He sues instead—for peace, for some explanation, or failing all else, for a speedy execution of his sentence. Job's speeches brim with legal language. Yet he intuits that even in the safer environment of the law court, he has no recourse against his high-powered Prosecutor (9:14, 19, 30–31). All he can do is beg for mercy (9:15, 20). What he craves is an intermediary, an advocate and arbiter (9:32–33). If only a ceasefire could be arranged and he could be granted safe-conduct (9:34), then he would lay his case out in court. But, he sighs, "It is not so with me" (9:35).

So I will voice my complaint and vent the bitterness in my soul (10:1). What does he have to lose? "Job is fully aware of the difficulty" and hopelessness of bringing his case before God, "but he is undaunted by it."[46] Where else can he turn?

Job 10:2 opens the door to an impassioned prayer-complaint to God. Is that an oxymoron? Isn't complaint to God in prayer impertinent? Aren't we supposed to say only holy and righteous things to God in prayer? If all that is in your heart are holy thoughts and righteous reflections, by all means. But saying one thing while thinking or feeling another is hypocrisy (see chap. 9). Job complains to God in exasperation (10:2–7) and appeals to his Maker. God's creative care and kindness first fashioned him (10:8–12). Now He hunts him down like a beast (10:13–17). Why, then, did God make him in the first place (10:18–19)? *Please, Lord, just let me live out my last few days and die in peace* (10:20–22).

C. S. Lewis married Joy late in life. Not long after, he watched helplessly as cancer sunk its claws into his wife's life. He recounted much of his internal wrestling in *A Grief Observed.* The parallels between Lewis and Job are remarkable. Despair can drive us to perverse thoughts. One passage echoes Job's struggle in 10:3. Does God *enjoy* afflicting? Perhaps God was not like Job thought He was after all. Lewis wrestled with the same thoughts.

> I tried to put some of these thoughts to C. this afternoon. He reminded me that the same thing seems to have happened to Christ: "Why hast thou forsaken me?" I know. Does that make it easier to understand? Not that I am (I think) in much danger of ceasing to believe in God. The real danger is of coming to believe that God is far different than what I always thought. The question I am faced with is not, "So, there is no God after all?" Rather, it is, "So, this is what God is like?"[47]

That Lewis (like Job) later describes these doubts as "filth and nonsense" does not diminish the reality with which they press down upon the sufferer. Not every sufferer thinks such thoughts but many have, both in and out of the Bible. These are not thoughts to be pretended away but confronted head-on with Scriptures (a luxury Job apparently did not possess) that remind us of what God really is like despite all appearances to the contrary.

Run your eyes down the columns of Job 9 and 10. Notice all the pronouns, about seventy of them referring to God. Job mentions his suffering (9:17–18, 25–28; 10:15–16), but always in the context of his relationship to God. This is one more hint that the book of Job is less about Job's suffering than about God—His nature and character, His attitudes and actions, and above all, His relationship to man. Job's suffering is the catalyst that ignites all this talk about God and to God. He is the central issue of the book. He is at the eye of Job's storm and yours.

Zophar: God's Gone Easy on You (Job 11)

Apparently the youngest of the three, Zophar is downright annoyed with Job. He is not cowed by long-winded, pious-sounding ramblings (11:2). As far as Zophar is concerned, all this talk of Job's innocence and God's cruelty makes a mockery of God. Job's audacity cannot go unanswered (11:3). Job insists, says Zophar, that his words are pure and his life is clean in God's eyes (11:4).[48] *But, oh! that God would break His silence and answer your outrageous claims* (11:5)*! Know this, Job: God has been soft on you! He has punished you less than you deserve* (11:6)*!*[49] (One wonders what else Zophar imagined God could possibly have done to Job.) *How can you possibly pretend to know what God does and why* (11:7–9)*? If God has judged, you cannot fool or fight against Him; He knows whom He judges and why* (11:10–11). *But a hollow man* (like Job?) *will become wise when a wild donkey's colt is born a man* (11:12)*.*[50]

Zophar's stinging rebuke turns a corner and holds out hope in an appeal to Job. He echoes once more the pleas of Eliphaz and Bildad. If Job would turn his heart and stretch out his hands to God and put away whatever iniquity he has embraced, then he could lift up his face without the marks of God's judgment and be unafraid in God's presence. All this misery would evaporate from memory, and God would restore his security and reputation (11:13–19). But he ends with a barb. If Job persists in this foolish talk, there is no hope for him (11:20).

However wrong they are to press Job so relentlessly for repentance, what stands out about the theology of these men is their confidence that God is unfailingly forgiving. They do not call on Job to offer a mountain of sacrifices or to perform great works of penance to regain the divine favor. Even in the face of what looks to them like monumental judgment from God, they understand that a simple "broken and contrite heart" God will neither despise nor refuse. Their view of God is higher than many give them credit for.

Job: Go Soak Your Heads (Job 12–14)

At seventy-five verses, this is Job's longest rejoinder yet. It is also his severest yet.[51] His language is acerbic at points. An imaginative paraphrase of 12:2 might run something like this: *Truly you are world-class wise men! Whatever will mankind do when you die? For wisdom will vanish from the face of the earth with you! Go soak your heads!* As their vehemence intensifies, so does Job's impatience. They have told him nothing new or even relevant (12:3).

> Thus, as often happens in debate, *they* never come in sight of the question that racks *his* mind. They go on applying their argument with increasing severity to prove that he must be a sinner because he is a sufferer. But all the time he, knowing that he is innocent of any sin that can call for such suffering, is beating the wings of his spirit like some imprisoned bird against the narrow limits of their faith.[52]

They have now gone so far as to mock Job (12:4). Whether this is a reference to Zophar's tone of voice (perhaps in 11:4) or his insulting swipe at Job (11:12) is unclear. They are rapidly losing their sympathy for Job along with their patience. "He who is at ease," Job complains, "holds [the] calamity [of others] in contempt" (12:5, NASB). The NCV is looser but colorfully captures the sense: "Those who are comfortable don't care that others have trouble."

Each of Job's friends presses home to his conscience that God is the One Who has done this to him (cf. 4:9ff.; 5:17ff.; 8:4, 13; 11:6, 10–11). No one doubts that God is behind Job's calamity, least of all Job. Even the beasts of the earth understand that much, he says; and if they could speak, they would testify that "the hand of Yahweh[53] has done this, in whose hand is the life of everything living and the breath of all mankind" (12:7–10).[54] These verses have sometimes been misconstrued as a declaration of creationism.[55] As sympathetic as I am to that doctrine, it would be difficult to imagine anything further from Job's point in this context than arguing that Yahweh created all the animals.

After an apparent aside (12:11–12),[56] Job launches into another doxological hymn exalting God's sovereignty (12:13–25), a practical exposition of the providence of God. Job's theology is just as orthodox, his knowledge just as complete, his convictions just as sound as theirs (13:1–2). All their speeches have told him nothing new. Job wants a second opinion. *I want to speak to the Almighty; I want to reason with God. You whitewash everything with lies; you are all worthless physicians! Your comprehensive analysis is rivaled only by your ignorance. You would display more wisdom if you just kept your mouths closed* (13:3–5).[57] Their flawed diagnosis has only confirmed that they are incompetent doctors. They don't listen seriously to the patient's complaints or bother with time-consuming diagnostic tests. Instead, they just plaster over the problem with a routine diagnosis and the same simplistic prescription. "Stomach cramps? Obviously that bug that's been going around," they say, when a vigorous diagnostic examination would reveal colon cancer.

Job's next accusation is just as piercing. Can it be wrong to take "God's side" on an issue? Or can one take "God's side" incorrectly, or insincerely, or out of unworthy motives? If I tell a lie or side with a known or suspected falsehood, even if it magnifies God's truth and makes Him look better, I am still guilty of dishonesty (Rom. 3:7). Job knows that "God will have no truck with anything untrue."[58] God will call Job's three friends on the carpet for this (42:7–8). Job calls them on it now.

Job accuses his friends of speaking "wickedly," or unrighteously, for God and talking deceitfully for Him (13:7). They are taking "God's side" (13:8), but they are doing so out of cowardly, calculating, intellectually dishonest motives. They are defending not God but their view of God. To some degree, at least, they are siding with God out of panic. For if Job is right, then what has happened to him could happen to them as well—and what will they do then (13:9)? That option is unacceptable because it sabotages their theology and threatens their personal security and well-being. So they ignore the possibility and scurry over to the "right" side for their own protection—ironically, a dangerous move.[59] Job is confident that God will reprove those who disingenuously show partiality even toward God (13:10–11).[60] God desires truth in the inward parts (Ps. 51:6)—integrity that governs all we say because it has penetrated your innermost being.

All their fine speeches are nothing but ashes and clay (13:12). *If you have nothing more substantive to offer*, Job implies, *then be silent and let me speak and take whatever consequences come* (13:13). *Why risk my life by speaking my mind so freely* (13:14)*?*[61] *Because despite what He does to me—even if He slays me—I still trust in Him!*[62] *Nevertheless, honesty compels me to defend my own ways before Him, because I do not deserve what He has done to me* (13:15)*! That is my only hope for deliverance; I would not dare to come before Him or hope to stand if I were a hypocrite* (13:16)*!* There is Job's affidavit; his integrity compels him to swear it out. He is ready to present his case before God (13:17–19).

Turning again to God, Job pleads for two concessions (13:20). They are two conditions he has already requested (9:34): that God would call at least a temporary ceasefire for the sake of diplomacy and that God would not overwhelm Job with fear (13:21). Then Job would be ready for an actual *hearing* (13:22; cf. 9:35). Job will get what he has asked for, conditions and all (38:3; 42:4). Like many answered prayers, it will be more than he intended. For now, in God's apparent absence and deafening silence, Job rehearses his case passionately and pleadingly (13:23–27).

A sympathetic reading of Job senses the fluctuations of his spirit, even within a single speech. Anyone who has wrestled through pain or puzzlement on his knees, reasoning with God and with his own soul, understands this experience. "Job's utterances seem to oscillate between hope and despair. A uniform mood cannot be imposed on them, nor can a steady trend be found."[63] Job turns from passionate self-defense to a nearly melancholy musing on the brevity of man. This next segment seems to begin in 13:28 and proceed into chapter 14.[64]

Man is so brittle, life so brief and turbulent (13:28–14:2). Why does the eternal God even bother to add to the grief of so pathetic a creature? Since God has set such brief boundaries for man's life, can't He wait till man has run his fleeting course and put in his few hours of labor before calling him to account (14:3–6)? Even the stump of a felled tree may spring to life again (14:7–9), but not man. Once man expires and lies down in the grave, he will not rise from his sleep "till the heavens be no more" (14:10–12). Job is not denying but confirming a resurrection, however cloudy it may be on the fine eschatological details (cf. Ps. 6:5; 88:9–11; 115:17; Eccles. 9:10). Job speaks of God's *hiding* him in the grave *until* His wrath is withdrawn (14:13), of *waiting* until his *change*[65] comes (14:14), of God one day summoning the work of His hands and Job's response to that call (14:15). If the answer to Job's central question—"If a man dies, shall he live again?" (14:14*a*)—is to be construed as "no," it is only because he is reiterating the point expressed in 14:12. Death terminates man's earthly life, not his spiritual—or bodily—existence.[66] The confidences Job expresses in this passage militate against the notion that he knows nothing of resurrection.[67] Nor is this Job's last word on the subject.

Future certainty is one thing. Present reality is another. Just as the elements gradually erode mountain and rock, stone and earth, so Job's God-sent sufferings eat away at his hope (14:18–19).[68] The claw's slash, the whip's lash, though excruciating, is more bearable than the deathly silence that follows, where nothing changes, nothing heals, and no one answers or explains. The storm has moved on. Nothing remains in the aftermath but an eerie stillness punctuated only by the distant rumble of thunder, a faint reminder of its fury. The elements resume their relentless feast—the ceaseless drip and flow of water, the whisper of wind that wears away rock, and the trickle of time that saps the hope of the suffering spirit left dangling amid the strewn wreckage of life. Job, like a sick man exhausted by a sudden exertion of faith, sinks back again into a settled despondency. God and death, it seems from where he now lies, are life's only winners (14:20–22).

11

Waves Crashing Against a Rock

Job 15–21

One of my favorite magazines is *Country.* The byline reads, "For those who live in or long for the country." I'm one of the latter. Stunning photography, good-hearted humor, neighborly ambiance, and absence of advertisements make it a special treat to thumb through whenever I find it nestled in our mailbox. Each issue includes pithy sayings printed along the pages' side margins. *Quarrels would not last long, if the fault was only on one side. It's better to have people wonder why you don't talk than why you do. Eagles may soar, but turtles don't get sucked into jet engines.*

Proverbs are born of human experience and observation. Every culture has its own wealth of traditional folk wisdom. A proverb is a truth in capsule form, general validity combined with portability. Compactness is what defines a proverb and makes it memorable. But compactness also defines a proverb's limitations—no room for variables and exceptions. That's by design. We understand instinctively that proverbs are universals but not absolutes. "We need no telling that a maxim like 'many hands make light work' is not the last word on the subject, since 'too many cooks spoil the broth.'"[1] They are *proverbs,* after all.

Weigh these biblical proverbs in light of what you know about the book of Job.

"There shall no evil happen to the just: but the wicked shall be filled with mischief" (Prov. 12:21). Is this an absolute promise without exception? What about Job?

"Behold, the righteous shall be recompensed in the earth: much more the wicked and the sinner" (Prov. 11:31). Is this always true? Job was recompensed in the earth (Job 42), but others, both righteous and wicked, are not. That is one of Job's recurring arguments.[2]

"The fear of the LORD prolongeth days: but the years of the wicked shall be shortened" (Prov. 10:27). Is this generally true? Absolutely. But is it *absolutely* true? History is full of exceptions to both sides of this equation.

These proverbs voice the kinds of principles that Job's friends sought to press on his conscience.[3] *Job, look around you! Everyone knows that this kind of calamity always happens to the wicked alone.* Yet this is the very argument Job turns on its head: *Look around you! Haven't you noticed that the wicked often escape this kind of calamity? Instead, now it has happened to me, and I'm not wicked.* Exceptions do not prove that a proverb is wrong; they prove that a proverb is a proverb. The problem is not proverbs, but proverbs translated into absolutes.[4]

Is Job arguing *against* what would later become part of God's inspired revelation of reality? Are the friends arguing biblical orthodoxy, which Job wrongly disputes? Even God comes down on Job's side. Does that mean that, in the book of Job, God contradicts His own orthodoxy?

H. Wheeler Robinson ventures in this direction when he writes that the friends' arguments form "the background of conventional religion, which throws [Job] into relief as a daring pioneer, who values truth more than orthodoxy."[5] But this proves too much. How can you pit "truth" against "straight teaching" (orthodoxy)? They are cut from the same cloth, or words don't mean anything. Robinson clarifies that the problem is not orthodoxy, but orthodoxy misapplied.

> The doctrine for which they stand is that of moral retribution.... They are sure that God is righteous and all-powerful; they believe that He is directly concerned with the individual lives of men. It follows that God must punish evil and reward good. So far there is nothing in their argument to which we can object. But they go on to commit a logical fallacy. They say, in effect: All evil-doers are sufferers; Job is a sufferer; therefore Job is an evil-doer. The fallacy lies in supposing that the class of sufferers is exhausted by the class of evil-doers, and that suffering can spring from no other purpose of God than the will to punish evil.[6]

If we are too quick to censure Job's friends, we discredit the validity of the biblical principles they argue.

> It is possible to dismiss these friends of Job too lightly, for the book does not present them as hypocrites arriving to gloat (see 2:11–13), nor as heretics offering manifestly false doctrines, nor again as fools producing no serious arguments. . . . Their outlook chimes in very largely with the promises and warnings of the Law, especially Deuteronomy, and with the wisdom of Proverbs and the moral standpoint of the Prophets.[7]

Seeing Job's friends as purveyors—and Job as the dismantler—of traditional, biblical religion is perilous since much of what they say is affirmed elsewhere in the Bible. Because the book so thoroughly disowns their arguments against Job, it is easy to misconstrue the message of Job as a disavowal of orthodoxy.

> This, however, is too sweeping. A closer look at the material shows that the basic error of Job's friends is that they overestimate their grasp of the truth [ironically, God will say the same thing about Job], misapply the truth they know, and close their minds to any facts that contradict what they assume. . . . Rather, [the book] attacks the arrogance of pontificating about the *application* of these truths, and of thereby misrepresenting God and misjudging one's fellow men.[8]

The problem is not that reality and experience contradict revelation and faith, but that revelation is limited (a factor explored in the final chapter). God has told us enough, but He has not told us everything. When we assume we know everything there is to know, we nourish a superficial knowledge of divine realities and a surface understanding of how eternal things work. Both Job and his friends wrestle with these deficiencies. So do we.

Eliphaz: Taking Off the Gloves (Job 15)

Try reading in succession all the speeches of each of Job's three friends. Read everything Eliphaz says (Job 4–5, 15, 22) without reading any of the intervening material. Read all Bildad's speeches together (Job 8, 18, 25) and both of Zophar's (Job 11, 20). Despite its weaknesses, that exercise gives you a sense of the thought and personality of each of Job's three friends.[9]

Reading Eliphaz's speeches successively uncovers some fascinating patterns. In his first speech, Eliphaz opened with sympathetic reasoning (4:2–11). There is no parallel to 4:1–6, no reference to Job's past ministry to others, anywhere in chapter 15. Instead, he opens with an impatient and undiplomatic depiction of Job as an audacious blowhard (15:2–6), an arrogant and insolent know-it-all (15:7–10). *Do you despise the comfort and remedy God offers to you? Will you turn on God and allow such perversity to pour out of your mouth* (15:11–13)*?*

Eliphaz knows what he knows. He returns to the sober warning of the vision he related earlier. He means to press home to Job's conscience its message that no one is pure or righteous in God's sight (15:14–16; cf. 4:12–19). Eliphaz also knows what other wise men have told him. So he confronts Job with the wisdom of the ancients (15:17–19) by expanding on another earlier theme—the constant misery and certain fate of the wicked (15:20–35; cf. 4:7–11; 5:3–7). "Eliphaz cannot even admit the fact—the frequent fact—of the untrammeled prosperity of the bad and the unrelieved misery of the good, let alone reconcile it with the justice of God."[10] Denial is the first line of defense against an uncomfortable reality. It is debate technique. If you have no answer to your opponent's argument, ignore the argument and simply restate your original assertion more vigorously. It may win debates, but it doesn't resolve valid objections.

Eliphaz's thrust at the wicked who "stretcheth out his hand against God" (15:25) is a feint; his real target is Job, who has turned his spirit against God (15:13).[11] In his final speech in Job 22, Eliphaz is even more direct, turning his verbal blade fully on Job. For now, Eliphaz details the fate of the wicked hoping that Job will look around him and notice the similarities. Conspicuously missing from this speech, however, is the impassioned plea that dominated his first appeal to Job. He is growing impatient.

Job: Despair over Divine Decimation (Job 16–17)

"O spare me now, my friends, your packages of God!"[12] Eliphaz had warned Job not to disdain "the consolations of God" that they offered him (15:11). Job picks up on that word: *Miserable consolers you are! Is this your idea of consolation* (16:2)?[13] *Miserable comforters* are literally *comforters of trouble* who "increase trouble rather than ministering comfort."[14] *Vain words* are literally *windy words*. "Blowhard" or "windbag" seems to be a favorite Semitic insult (16:3; cf. 8:2; 15:2).[15] Job could find it just as easy to berate them if he were in their shoes (16:4).[16] Instead, he would *strengthen* them with his words (16:5), just as he had always done for others in need. He retrieves the same word that Eliphaz had used (4:4) to commend Job for having "strengthened the feeble knees" of sufferers.

Once more, with an occasional sideward glance to his friends (16:20; 17:2, 4–5, 10), Job lapses into soliloquy to and about God (16:7–17:16). He cannot help himself. His orbit has swept him into a barrage of verbal meteors from his friends that threaten to knock him off course, but the overpowering gravitational pull on his soul maintains his orbit around the Center of his universe. He has nowhere else to turn. Though God seems to have become inexplicably cruel to him, he is not letting go. He is now moving on the long arc of his elliptical orbit away from his Center but God will keep his soul in orbit and pull him back to Himself.

Job's language adopts even darker tones of despair. God has exhausted him and decimated his whole circle of companionship (16:7).[17] Job's experience defines loneliness. The change from third person ("He") to second person ("You") in the middle of 16:7 disturbs scholars who prefer grammar to be nice and neat.[18] But grief is messy. Anguish is spontaneous and unscripted. Nothing could be more natural and lifelike here. Job's propensity for soliloquy bounces back and forth between talking to himself and talking to God. The scene is not hard to imagine. Read it like a dramatic script.

> **Job** (*forlornly to his friends, dropping his gaze to the ground*): ". . . But now He has worn me out . . . (*then, pausing to look up, he speaks again to God*) . . . You have desolated all my company. . . ."[19]

Job's perception of God's posture toward him is as graphic as it is sad. "Only literal translation can do justice to the savagery of Job's description of God's vicious attack."[20] God has "shriveled up" Job with a disfiguring disease (16:8), torn him in pieces[21] like a beast bent on revenge,[22] and gnashed on him with His teeth, His eyes shooting daggers at him (16:9).[23] Others have joined in the abuse (16:10) as

God turned him over to be victimized by the wicked (16:11).[24] Job was at ease, but now he is a shattered man. Lionlike, God has taken him by the back of the neck and shaken him (16:12).[25] Then God set him up for His archery practice (16:12*c*–14). Job's is a pathetic case, all the more pathetic being undeserved (16:15–22).

Job believes his days to be numbered (17:1). God has withheld understanding from his "mockers." They are as opinionated as they are ignorant of what is happening to Job (17:2–5, 10). Despite his humiliation and emaciation (17:6–8), he clings to his righteous ways (17:9) and looks forward only to the release of death (17:11–16).

Job's words teach us that our perception of God's posture toward us—based on circumstances alone—can be so far wrong as to impugn His own character.[26] "Judge not the Lord by feeble sense," wrote William Cowper. If anyone had an excuse for misinterpreting God's posture toward him it was Job, given his limited revelation. If anyone does not, it is you or me.

Bildad: This Sure Looks to Me Like the Address of the Wicked (Job 18)

After the customary retaliatory insults, Bildad's second speech develops a single theme with a double-entendre: *Thus* is the dwelling place of the wicked, and *this* is the dwelling place of the wicked (18:21).

Bildad's double meaning is first apparent in his curious way of addressing Job in the second person *plural*: "How long will it be before *ye* (plural) make an end of words? Mark [*ye*] (plural), and afterward we will speak. Why are we counted as beasts, and reputed as vile in *your* (plural) sight?" It appears that he is grouping Job with the wicked and addressing him as one of them: *How long will it be before you (wicked people) end your speeches?*[27]

Indignant at Job's dismissal of all their studied wisdom, Bildad displays the impatience of wounded pride. By this time, our antipathy is aimed entirely at the three friends and our sympathies naturally lie with Job. Still, probably "Job has asked for this [abuse] with his [own] derogatory remarks" (12:2; 13:4–5; 16:2–3; 17:10).[28] Bildad picks up Job's words and hurls them back (18:4).[29] God is not the

One "tearing" Job; his wounds are self-inflicted (cf. 16:9). Does the world revolve around Job? Must heaven and earth move for him (cf. 14:18–19)?

Man once supposed that the earth was the center of everything—a myth nurtured by the man-centered theology of the religious establishment and defended long after it was proven false. Life and reality are God-centered. Everyone's life revolves around some consistent center of gravity. If He is not at the center of your orbit, your life is seriously out of alignment and perhaps in the wrong galaxy. Bildad accuses Job of being so self-absorbed in his suffering that he made life and the world egocentric, putting himself and his experience at the center.

Is this a valid charge? Job's speeches are (almost without exception) nearly twice as long as his friends' speeches. At the end of the third cycle after Job has answered the final rejoinder of his friends, the narrator notes, "Moreover, Job continued his discourse, and said . . ." (27:1, NKJV). Job proceeds unabated and uninterrupted for four more chapters (145 verses) before "the words of Job are ended" (31:40). Even God implies that Job is so centered on defending his own righteousness that he has displaced the centrality of God's character and rights and place in the world (40:8).

Egocentricity is endemic to suffering. I do not mean arrogance but a mindset that places oneself and one's suffering at the center and weights the value of everything and everyone else as it relates to the present experiences and needs of self. Such egocentricity is a temptation to any sufferer. A natural and understandable temptation but a *temptation* nonetheless, a self-perpetuating pull that sucks you inward. Cancer in a spouse, leukemia in a child, the victimization of a loved one, the devastation of a career, loss of investments, resources, or health—these are necessarily time-consuming and often all-consuming experiences to work through. But it is possible—it is essential—even surrounded by such attention-demanding circumstances, to resist the atrophy of a theocentric life, a theocentric worldview, your own theocentric soul, into an unbiblical egocentricity. Unchecked, an egocentricity that pulls everything inward becomes a black hole.

Like Eliphaz, Bildad withdraws the compassionate appeals he made to Job the first time around (cf. 8:5–7, 20–22). He is preoccupied with impressing on Job the unmixed and inescapable misery of all the wicked.[30] "Bildad's concern was to establish in Job's mind the absolute certainty that every wicked man gets paid in full, in this life, for his wiçked deeds."[31]

Job stands as a man at a mark, the unwilling assistant of a knife thrower. Chosen with care and honed to a personal edge, Bildad's blades continually strike within a hair's breadth of Job. By the end of his speech, the silhouette outlined by the daggers is unmistakably Job's.

For example, when Bildad sketches the snuffing out of the light of the wicked (18:5–6, 18), he is not merely mimicking Eliphaz (15:22–23, 30); he is exploiting Job's own words (10:21–22; 12:25; 17:12–13). Is Job terrified (7:14; 9:34)? Well, says Bildad, that's exactly what happens to the wicked (18:11, 14).[32] These insinuations are relatively subtle. Some are much more pointed. Bildad notes that the wicked suffer from skin-devouring diseases (18:13), just like Job. And this is not the first time Bildad has callously rubbed salt in Job's chief wound, his dead children (18:19; cf. 8:4).[33]

Imagine Bildad sweeping his extended arms around him and drawing attention to their surroundings, as he closes with a double-entendre: "Surely *such* are the dwellings of the wicked,[34] and *this* is the place of him that knoweth not God" (18:21). Bildad's catalog of the plight of the wicked "is too similar to Job 1 and 2 for the point to be missed. But the sermon is wide of the mark. It might take effect in a man with a bad conscience; but this, for all their efforts to develop one, is what Job does not have."[35]

Job: From the Pit to the Pinnacle (Job 19)

Job is not indignant. He is crushed (19:2–3). If he has committed some sin worthy of all this suffering, it remains a secret; they certainly haven't produced any evidence of transgression (19:4). *You keep pressing your case and insisting that my calamity proves that I have wronged God. If you want to argue circumstantial evidence, then I submit that* God *has wronged* me (19:5–6).

The friends have succeeded only in goading out of him his most disturbing assertion yet. Their relentless pursuit of his conscience has cornered Job into retaliating with their logic. "His language is audacious, but on the old theory of retribution it was the only logical conclusion from the given premises."[36] If they are going to insist that God does this kind of thing only to the wicked, then God *has* perverted justice (cf. 8:3) and "*made* me crooked."[37]

Job's friends hound him into extreme accusations about God that he might not otherwise have made. Thinking that their grasp on theology is complete, they feel competent to evaluate not only the meaning of Job's circumstances but also the condition of Job's heart. They force him into their own theological box and badger him to answer according to their terms. So he does.

Job says God has trapped him in His net (19:6).[38] Trappers after African antelopes camouflage a large net with branches, string it between two trees, and stampede the animals in that direction. Panicked and running at high speeds, the antelopes become helplessly entangled in the net and are easily captured (cf. 19:8–9).

Job understands that his calamity comes from God (19:10–11).[39] It is hardly a fair fight; God's troops surround him, build up their ramparts, and lay siege to Job's *tent* (19:12)![40] Job stresses the absurdity of this divine overkill. Does God feel threatened by Job as if he were some giant sea monster (7:12)? Why would God bother frightening a leaf or hunting down chaff (13:25)?

He has already mentioned God's desolation of all his company (cf. 16:7 and comments). Here he catalogs it (19:13–20).[41] He is utterly alone, ostracized, forsaken by man and (it seems) by God. Out of that isolation drifts a pathetic cry to his friends for pity (19:21).[42] God Himself is on his trail, chasing him; why must they also hound him (19:22)?[43]

Suddenly and inexplicably, out of this dismal pit of isolation Job's soul momentarily soars in a "magnificent burst of faith."[44] The transition from his slough of despond to this summit of confident expectation is occasioned by a request remarkably granted: "Oh that my words were written . . . inscribed . . . engraved . . . forever!" (19:23–24, NKJV).

Virtually everyone agrees that 19:25–27 is not only "notoriously difficult"[45] to translate (let alone interpret) but also "of crucial importance."[46] Some scholars carry into these verses the baggage of their unbelief, determined to find nothing that suggests any anticipation of resurrection.[47] On the other hand, Christians hearing echoes of Handel's *Messiah* may be eager to read more into Job's words than the text can reasonably be expected to bear out. We must be content to enter the passage with no prejudgment as to what we will bring out of it. That's the only way to insure that we derive our theology *out of* the text (exegesis) rather than read our theology *into* a text (eisegesis). In view of the difficulties, it is best "to find the firm ground first, and use this as a foothold for venturing into less certain places."[48]

The transition (19:23–24) that leads into this bolt out of the blue plainly points to Job's anticipation of future vindication.[49] He wants it all written down permanently. There is no mistaking his expectation that he will see God for himself; he repeats this three distinct times (19:26–27).[50] His initial assertion in 19:26 is admittedly ambiguous if it is isolated from the context. Literally "from my flesh," it could be translated either "*apart from* my flesh I will see God" or "*in* my flesh I will see God."[51] The former is unlikely; he can hardly be speaking spiritually or metaphorically, otherwise the emphatic specificity of 19:27 is misleading: "whom *I* shall see *for myself*, and [whom] *mine eyes* shall behold" (19:27).[52] Job's ardent expectation of seeing God with his own eyes is so clear in 19:26–27, and 19:25 is "so tightly knit" with 19:26–27, that "there should be no doubt that the *Redeemer* is *God*."[53] This agrees with what he has already said in chapters 9 and 16.[54]

But when will this vision of his Redeemer-God take place? To insist that Job expects to experience this vindicating vision prior to his death counters everything he has said up to this point and everything he says after it. He anticipates no reversal or restoration or vindication in this life. He waits only for death, and "there would be no need for Job to deposit a written testimony [19:23–24], if he expects to be vindicated before he dies."[55] Moreover, he specifies that he will see God *after* his skin has been destroyed.[56] His emphatic insistence that he himself will see God with his own eyes leaves only one other option: he is, indeed, speaking of a resurrection.[57]

One question remains. It is clear that Job's Redeemer is none other than God Himself. Is this a reference to the Messiah? Did Job possess a conscious conception of God incarnate as a messianic figure who would become his Redeemer from sin? If so, the clues are so sparse and tenuous as to demand considerable speculation.[58] Nevertheless the New Testament's explanation is that Job's words foreshadowed more than he himself understood (1 Pet. 1:10–12).

While the term *redeemer* (*go'el*) is not strictly a title of deity, it becomes a significant title for God.[59] It is a word with a specific and unique connotation: *kinsman-redeemer*. Several sources spell out the significance of this title,[60] but Old Testament scholar Michael Barrett pinpoints the spiritual pertinence.

> This word assumes a relationship between the redeemer and the redeemed. The word assumes that the *goel* will perform the appropriate action to alleviate the need of those with whom he has a relationship. In fact, the *goel* is under obligation because of the relationship to do whatever is necessary to do. . . . The point is that whether paying a debt, freeing from slavery, reclaiming property for the family inheritance, or avenging a death, the *goel* did whatever was necessary to meet the need of his relatives. All of this reaches its zenith when applied to the Messiah. Christ is for His people the Ideal *Goel;* He never fails to fulfill His obligation—we may say His covenant duty—in behalf of those with whom He is related by virtue of that covenant. . . . Man needs to be delivered from sin; Christ delivers from sin; He does so on the basis of a covenant relationship. That is *Goel* work. . . . [But] Christ's being our Kinsman Redeemer is not limited to His redeeming us from sin. That is a wonderful part of it, but that He is our Redeemer means that He will always without fail be there for us. He does not save us to leave us. Whatever our need or crisis, the fact that we have a saving and personal relationship with Jesus Christ guarantees that He will meet our every need.[61]

The Old Testament applies this title to God, but in contexts that future revelation clarifies as references to Christ (e.g., Isa. 59:20; cf. Rom. 11:26–27). Barrett ties Job 19:25 to 16:19, where Job expresses his confidence that his Witness is in heaven—again, clearly referring not to a mere mortal but to a divine being. "Although Job does not call this Advocate the Messiah, what Job expected that Advocate to do is exactly what Christ does for His people."[62]

To credit Job with a clear and conscious messianic understanding of a God-sent God-Man is probably anachronistic, reading too much back into his mouth and mind. But to recognize in such statements prophetic shadows of realities later revealed more fully is progressive revelation in action. Peter informs us that the prophets did not comprehend the full import of some of their own prophecies because much of the revelation God gave to them was not for their own contemporaries so much as it was for later generations (1 Pet. 1:10–12).[63] Was Job a "prophet"? James implies that he was (James 5:10–11).[64] It should not be surprising that such men spoke more about Christ than they knew, since it was the "spirit of Christ that was in them" (1 Pet. 1:11).

The confidence of Job's spirit ebbs and flows and ebbs again. This passage is the fourth wave of faith that has surged and tumbled out of Job's sea of despair (13:15–16; 14:13–15; 16:18–21; 19:23–27). Each successive wave climbs a little higher, before receding again into the dejection of a man who *knows* (19:25) but *sees* no hope.[65]

In the end, Job's burst of confident faith emboldens him to conclude with a warning to his friends. If they continue hounding him (19:28), they'd better watch their own backs (cf. 15:22); God's sword flashes against all who deal falsely (19:29). If we didn't know better, we would be tempted to think that Job's brave face is just that—disingenuous bravado or, worse, impudence. But we do know better (1:1, 8; 2:3).

How could Job maintain such unintimidated conviction of his innocence amid the driving rain of circumstances and the endless bluster of accusations? "The righteous are as bold as a lion" (Prov. 28:1).[66] Job was not just a really nice guy, but neither was he some quasi-human super-saint. He was a mortal man—molded from the same clay we are, laboring with the same longings and leanings we have—who feared God (1:1), kept short accounts with Him (1:5), and devoted his life to a studied pursuit of moral excellence and purity (31:1–40). Granted, there are not many like him. But that is our fault, not God's.

Zophar: A Parting Shot (Job 20)

This is Zophar's last shot at Job. He will give it everything he has. Their discussion has not gone where it was supposed to. Zophar earlier suggested that God had obviously punished Job even less than he deserved (11:6). That was gentle. Now he moves in with both barrels blazing. He may have "nothing new to say to Job, but he says it with passion."[67] Strahan's description of Zophar's final tirade flickers with insight.

> Zophar is the hottest and most violent of the three, and his impassioned harangue is marked at once by a fanatical fierceness and unmitigated coarseness that are unequalled in other parts of the drama. . . . The innuendo that Job is perishing in his sin, cut down as an evil-doer in the midst of his days [20:6–11]; the suggestion that he has been a gourmet in wickedness, rolling it as a dainty morsel under his tongue [20:12–13]; the assumption that . . . [Job] is being compelled to disgorge his ill-gotten wealth and deserves the fierceness of God's wrath [20:14–19]—all of this would be incredible if it were not the natural outcome of the dogmatic rabies which devours the innocent with the guilty, the fanatical perversity which changes the truth of God into a lie. Zophar's rhetorical diatribe is well worth studying as the utterance of a partisan who . . . magnifies God's strictness with a zeal [with what Strahan elsewhere calls "an indecent enthusiasm"] He will not own. . . . And his haste explains his theology; for, making God, as every zealot does, in his own image, he conceives Him, like an impatient judge, blazing out wrath against evil-doers, exulting in the doom which He pronounces upon them. . . . According to the zealot, the wheels of God grind quickly. . . . When the zealot makes his own opinions and sentiment as the standard of divinity, there is a magnified Zophar on the throne of the universe.[68]

An electrical tension pulsates beneath the surface of Zophar's subdued preface. Though offended by Job's effrontery, he dispenses with the introductory banter as economically as possible (20:2–3).[69] A hint of either condescension or contempt laces his opening question: *Are you stubborn or stupid? You talk about what you "know"* [19:25]. *Do you know this elemental truth that dates back to the time when man was first placed on the earth* (20:4)*?*[70] *The triumph of the wicked is transitory, his merriment momentary* (20:5).

Zophar is annoyed by Job's penchant for poking holes in their arguments by pointing at the wicked who seem to be doing just fine (9:24; 12:6). Crudely but confidently he affirms that the wicked, be his success ever so lofty, will perish like his own refuse (20:6–7). Every trace of him suddenly vanishes (20:7–11). The sin he secretly relishes will turn to cobra venom and cause him to vomit up all his swindled wealth (20:12–18). Because—and here Zophar slyly accuses Job indirectly—he has crushed and forsaken the poor, and seized the property of another (20:19). Nothing he loves will be left when God rains His wrath on him in the middle of his pleasures (20:20–23). God's judgment will shadow him and gut him (20:24–25). Nothing awaits him but consuming fire, shameful exposure, and total loss (20:26–28). That's what God gives the wicked without fail (20:29).

It is tempting to read too much into Zophar's personal theology on the basis of this speech. Andersen, for instance, sees it "as a sign of the narrowness of Zophar's beliefs, that his speech contains no hint that the wicked might repent, make amends and regain the favor of God. Zophar has no compassion and his god has no mercy."[71] But this misses Zophar's point. In this case, "the wicked"—namely, Job—is *refusing* to repent. In fact, he won't even admit that he has done anything to warrant repentance! That explains, even if it doesn't justify, Zophar's vehemence.

Besides, Zophar has a point.[72] God *does* judge the wicked, often ferociously. When we rail on the three friends overmuch, we threaten to undermine the legitimate orthodoxy that underlies their arguments (along with those who would like to see it undermined). It is the *inferences* and *applications* of a basically correct theological posture that bedevil their arguments. They have hammered general principles into an invariable, iron-clad, one-size-fits-all modus operandi.

In the absence of any written revelation about Himself, and as a means of communicating a general revelation about what He approves and disapproves, God's frequent practice was to judge the wicked swiftly and to bless the righteous.[73] This may well have reflected God's standard mode of governing early human history. It is assumed in Abraham's plea for Lot (Gen. 18:25). Nevertheless, there was enough empirical evidence around them to modify not their theology but their certainty that their theology answered every question, explained every incident, and applied to every instance.

One of the humbling messages of Job explored in the final chapter of this book is that man does not know nearly so much about God and His ways as he thinks he does. The point for now is, when theology clearly conflicts with reality, one need not abandon theology nor ignore reality.[74] Acknowledge reality, cling to the theology we do know, and be willing to admit that just *maybe* there are a few things we don't yet know about an infinite God (Deut. 29:29).

Job: Let's Go Over This Once More (Job 21)

I do not imagine these four men at each other's throats, shouting back and forth in shrill voices. When I listen to Job in 21:2, I hear a pause and a sigh. Then Job enunciates his words s-l-o-w-l-y in an audibly restrained voice of labored patience: *Okay . . . let's go through this one more time. Listen carefully to my words.*[75] *You offer me consolation* (cf. 15:11)*? Let this be your consolation to me: try actually listening to what I say for a change. Hear me out, and when I am done, proceed with your scorn* (20:2–3). I imagine this last remark ("mock on") not so much as bitter defiance[76] or sarcasm,[77] but a flick of the wrist with a sigh of resignation. Appalled silence is the only appropriate response to Job (21:5–6).[78] His friends insist on haranguing him, so he will answer their argument point for point.[79]

Chapter 21 is markedly different from all Job's prior speeches. "It is the only one in which he confines his remarks to his friends and does not fall into either soliloquy or prayer."[80] So far "the friends' thesis is that sin produces suffering. Their inference is that suffering proves sin. Job denies both."[81] Up to this point, Job has largely ignored the fallacy of their argument, popping their theological balloons only occasionally (9:24; 12:6) Now he is going to butcher and barbecue their sacred cow.[82]

Zophar! You say that the triumph of the wicked is short, their joy momentary [20:5–7]*? Why, then, do the wicked live to a healthy old age and enjoy their posterity* (21:7–8)*? God does not chasten them—their houses are safe* (21:9), *their animals breed and multiply* (21:10), *their children are numerous and happy* (21:11–12), *they live out all their days in prosperity and die "peacefully—in a moment"*[83] (21:13). *Yet these are the very ones who will have nothing to do with God* (21:14–15). *But that's not me* (21:16). Job does not argue for his point; he merely makes observations that are apparent to all. "Job does not consider the facts to be open to question. It is the reason for them he seeks."[84]

Bildad! You say that the light of the wicked is snuffed out [18:5–6], *and calamity crouches beside him ready to pounce* [18:12]*? But how often is it, really, that the lamp of the wicked is extinguished and calamity actually ambushes him* (21:17)[85] *so that he becomes like chaff driven before the storm of divine wrath* (21:18)*?*[86] If the friends counter that sometimes God waits to judge the children of the wicked instead, Job's reply is indignant: *What kind of retribution is that? Let God recompense* him [the wicked man himself, not his children] *that* he *may know God's judgment! What does he care what happens once he is gone* (21:19–21)*?*[87] But who can presume to teach God what He should do and how He should deal with His own creatures (21:22)? The fortunes of life over which God rules seem, from this earthly vantage point, indiscriminate (21:23–26).[88]

Job could read from their countenances that they remained unconvinced and intended to renew their same old sarcastic arguments (21:27–33). What further "consolation" (cf. 21:2; 15:11) could the empty words of these nattering nabobs possibly provide, since their answers remained riddled with willful infidelity to the truth (21:34)?[89]

The Error of Job's Friends

One cannot read through the debates between Job and his friends without being struck by their dogged persistence in seeking to persuade Job of their viewpoint: Job has sinned and needs to repent. They seem scarcely to listen to his arguments and never address them when they answer him. That failure is so obvious that it is noted both by the narrator (32:3) and by Elihu (32:11–12)—none of them answered his words, yet they were bent on condemning him. Why were the friends so persistent? Gleason Archer offers an intriguing answer to that question.

> An adequate psychological motive for their persistence in carrying on the controversy with Job over so many chapters is to be found in the dilemma which his catastrophic disaster had placed them. If a man of such high reputation could suffer so devastating a misfortune, their own security was imperiled by the possibility that the same thing could happen to them. Their basic motive in attempting to elicit from Job a confession of sin was to establish their own sense of security. If in point of fact Job had been guilty of some grievous sin of which the public had no knowledge, his overwhelming disaster could be easily understood as the retribution of the righteous God. Failing to

> secure from him any such confession despite all their diligent efforts to compel from him an admission of guilt, they felt unable to return home relieved and reassured that calamity would be kept from their door if they only lived a good life.[90]

Several passages suggest that this is more than Archer's psychological speculation (6:21; 13:9; 19:29).

Fleeing from God to God

Amid despair, desolation, and hopeless isolation, Job's faith has been supremely "tried" (James 1:3; 1 Pet. 1:7). Like a caged bird that catches a glimpse of blue sky beyond its bars, his faith drives him to hope in what he knows but cannot attain. From Job's limited vantage point, God is his aggressor—but also his only defender. His loss of God has made him hopeless, yet God remains his only hope.

Satan's charge of insincere piety out of self-interest might have stood against many a lesser man or woman. Satan's most vicious assaults could not drive Job away from God. But the view from where Job sits is even more astonishing. He perceives correctly (though he interprets it wrongly) that all his misery is from the "hand" of *God* (1:11–12; 2:3; 2:5–6). Yet even *God* cannot drive him away from God! Job looks around him and seems to hear only hard words from God; yet still he says, "Lord, to whom shall [I] go?" (John 6:68). Job already understands what God later reiterates in His Word—there is nowhere else to go, because there is no one else to go to, because there is no one else.[91] So Job will cling to God, even if he slays him.

> Therefore though You slay me, I will trust You.
> For if You pursue my iniquity,
> I will flee from You to Yourself,
> And I will shelter myself from Your wrath in Your shadow,
> And to the skirts of Your mercies I will lay hold
> Until You have mercy on me.
> And I will not let You go till You bless me.[92]

God has answered that prayer before (Gen. 32:26). He answered it for Job (Job 38–42). He will answer it for you.

12 Looking for God

Job 22–26

Trial and error have given medical advances a checkered history. Take, for instance, the early diagnostic use of x-rays. Initially, x-ray pictures were often taken with the patient standing. After all, who lies down for a picture? A lady might complain of abdominal discomfort and, sure enough, the x-ray revealed a "fallen" stomach. This was diagnosed as ptosis of the stomach, and sophisticated surgical procedures were developed to string up the organs back where they belonged. When someone finally suggested the possible effects of gravity on the internal organs of standing patients, the "advanced" diagnosis and its accompanying surgical procedure disappeared. Medical history illustrates the fallibility of human judgment—of diagnosis and therapy—when we assume that we have all the facts in hand and are interpreting them correctly; conventional wisdom is not the most reliable guide.

Job's friends are convinced that their patient has a radical sin disorder. Job has asked them more than once to be specific, to tell him what he possibly could have done to merit all this pain and loss. So far, they have stuck to their general but inflexible diagnosis, talking about Job's sin by inference, hoping that he will take their medicine. He won't. Now it is time for more invasive procedures.

Eliphaz is the chief surgical resident, but he lacks the surgeon's delicate touch and his bedside manner has deteriorated considerably. He probes Job's conscience with a machete, slashing his way through the jungles of Job's mind and memory. What is he looking for? *Anything.* Anything that will touch a raw nerve, jolt a hardened conscience, awaken some sleeping sense of shame. He is determined to mallet every reflex nerve in hopes of jarring a response, justifying their diagnosis and salvaging their theology.

The problem is, he is still misreading the symptoms. He has examined the patient, but he hasn't really *listened* to him. He assumes that what he learned in medical school (he attended a long time ago) covers every conceivable malady known to man and that there is no room for advancement. Because he has seriously misdiagnosed Job's condition, his recommended remedy is not only useless but also dangerous. For Job to be browbeaten into "confessing" uncommitted sin with the assurance that his fortunes will be restored is to trifle with his soul, to confuse his conscience, and to redirect everyone's attention to materialism as the motivation and demonstration of one's spiritual condition. The danger of this type of "internal medicine" is still with us. The health-and-wealth gospel and the belief that chronic illness signals a failure of faith operate on the assumption that physical comfort is always God's will for all His people.[1]

Machete in hand and convinced that Job is concealing a massive malignant tumor, Eliphaz insists on immediate, invasive, exploratory surgery. The "incompetent physician" (13:4) goes to work without benefit of anesthesia and with only circumstantial evidence to suggest that there is anything to find. If ever there was a case for malpractice, this is it.

Eliphaz: Getting Personal (Job 22)

One cannot help noticing a striking change of tone in Eliphaz's final "sermon." The time for subtlety is over.[2] He no longer describes the sins and miseries of the wicked in terms of *he* and *him,* but *you* and *your.* Bildad skillfully silhouetted Job with his knives (Job 18), but Eliphaz aims to draw blood. He "speaks poniards, and every word stabs."[3] The friends' approach has evolved from implication (round one), to insinuation (round two), to accusation (round three).[4]

Job's "Sins" (22:2–11)

In chapter 21, Job bulldozed the false premise on which their whole case was built. Eliphaz can't refute Job's argument because the facts are on Job's side. He can't admit Job's argument because . . . well, why not? Why not at least acknowledge that Job has a point, that their theology may need a little adjustment, that honest observation confronts them with an anomaly that is worth trying to think through together? Good question. But it's not one that Eliphaz pauses to consider. "The idea of a good man suffering never enters their thoughts. It would demolish their theology, or, as Eliphaz has already said, undermine religion (15:4)."[5]

Eliphaz plunges in. God does not need man. *Do you think God is impressed by your professed righteousness* (22:2–3*)?* According to 1:8 and 2:3, He was. *I suppose God is doing this to you because you fear Him* (22:4)*!*[6] According to 1:9–12, He is. The reference to Job's "fear" of God links 1:9 and 22:4.

Eliphaz assumes a direct proportion between retribution suffered and sin committed (22:5). Job has asked for specifics (cf. 6:24; 19:3–4). Eliphaz obliges with a vengeance, picking up where Zophar (20:19) left off. *You want me to "teach" you how you have sinned and "show" you what you have done? You want specific charges? Try these.*

Eliphaz files three allegations against Job. Surprisingly, none of them are sins against God directly. All are sins of social oppression or humanitarian neglect arising from an abuse of power.[7] First, Job has ruthlessly demanded and retained people's garments as a pledge for financial loans (22:6).[8] This was an evil later addressed and prohibited in the Law (Exod. 22:25–27; Deut. 24:10–13). Job will repudiate this accusation (31:19–22). Second, Job has heartlessly withheld the basic necessities of life from those in need, water from the faint and food from the hungry (22:7).[9] This evil was also addressed in the Law (Deut. 15:7–11) and condemned (Deut. 23:3–4). Again, Job will expressly rebut this allegation (31:17–22). Third, Job has mercilessly refused to assist the most vulnerable in society, widows and orphans (22:9).[10] This, too, was an evil prohibited by the Law (Exod. 22:22–24; Deut. 27:19). Once more, Job will explicitly deny the charge (31:16–22).

That, Eliphaz concludes, is why Job is surrounded by snares and terrors, darkness and flood (22:10–11). All these trumped-up charges are unsubstantiated. Eliphaz is bluffing. This is his final, all-or-nothing throw of the dice. All his chips are out on the table. The image fits because Eliphaz's last gamble is a huge risk. If this fails, he has nothing left. It is not just about the personal satisfaction of winning. At stake is the danger of being proved wrong. If he is wrong, the repercussions are serious enough to threaten his entire theological structure, his intellectual comfort, and even his personal security.

Job's "Thoughts" (22:12–20)

Eliphaz charges Job with crimes against man, not God. Behind any mistreatment of the *imago Dei* (the image of God in man), however, lurks impious attitudes and assumptions toward the *Deus* Who fashioned us in His image. So Eliphaz confidently proceeds to expound the thoughts of Job's own heart—the kind of irreligious reasoning that could have allowed Job to commit such crimes against his fellow creatures in the first place. The surgeon turns psychoanalyst. Eliphaz's insight into how wicked people think about a God they cannot see is right on the mark, but Job is the wrong target.

Eliphaz gestures skyward in 22:12. God dwells in the height of heaven out of man's sight, but man is not out of God's sight. Does Job suppose that God cannot see everything he does from way up there (22:13–14)? That is how the wicked have always reasoned; that is why they are cut down prematurely and swept away by flood (22:15–20).[11]

Job's "Need" (22:21–30)

For all his faults, Eliphaz's heart is instinctively pastoral. He seems to display it once more even here. Yet one cannot help wondering if his earnestness is aimed at helping Job or winning an argument. It is necessary for the triumph of their theology to secure Job's admission of *anything.* "The only thing wrong with Eliphaz's exhortation is that it is completely irrelevant to Job's case."[12] Nevertheless, it is a passionate, beautifully crafted, even God-centered appeal that "could not be improved upon by prophet or evangelist."[13]

Eliphaz calls Job to reconcile with God (22:21),[14] to submit to God's words (22:22),[15] to return[16] to the Almighty and abandon iniquity in his lifestyle (22:23), and to find his delight and his wealth in God alone (22:24–26). Then God will hear his prayer (22:27) and once again bless all his ways (22:28–30).[17] Eliphaz's assurance that God will again hear Job's prayers once he is restored is laced with "exquisite irony."[18] In the end, God's acceptance of Job's prayer will rescue Eliphaz (42:7–10).[19]

Job: Where Is God? (Job 23–24)

Eliphaz exhorted Job to return to God. Job's reply bursts like a dam. *Return to God? I can't even find Him* (23:3)*! I wish I could present my case before Him and hear His explanation of all this* (23:4–7). *I may not be able to find Him* (23:8–9), *but He knows my ways and when my case is finally tried I will be vindicated* (23:10), *because I have followed His ways and obeyed His words* (23:11–12). *For now, I am a prisoner to His power and purposes* (23:13–17). Believers sometimes find themselves in terrain where they feel abandoned and God seems to be absent. It is not virgin territory. Job pioneered it for us long ago.

God's Silence (23:1–9)

Job's opening soliloquy runs rich with pathos. He longs to find God, to appear before Him, to present his case, and to hear God's answers (23:2–7). But *finding* Him is the problem. In 23:8–9, Job vents a sentiment diametrically opposite to David's in Psalm 139:8–10. Psalm 139 affirms, *God is everywhere and I cannot get away from Him*; Job 23 complains, *God is nowhere to be seen and I cannot find Him.* Psalm 139 expresses what the believer knows; Job 23 expresses what the believer sometimes feels. Why *is* God sometimes so hard to find and silent when we need Him most? Or is He? This is a massive question for any suffering person.

C. S. Lewis kept a spiritual diary while his wife was battling cancer—a battle that she ultimately lost. We explored some of *A Grief Observed* in chapter 10. Another passage bears an uncanny resemblance to Job's experience in Job 23. Both are frank confessions of what goes on in the dark closet of the hurting human soul.

> Meanwhile, where is God? This is one of the most disquieting symptoms. When you are happy, so happy that you have no sense of needing Him, so happy that you are tempted to feel His claims upon you as an interruption, if you remember yourself and turn to Him with gratitude and praise, you will be—or so it feels—welcomed with open arms. But go to Him when your need is desperate, when all other help is vain, and what do you find? A door slammed in your face,

and a sound of bolting and double bolting on the inside. After that, silence. You may as well turn away. The longer you wait, the more emphatic the silence will become. There are no lights in the windows. It might be an empty house. Was it ever inhabited? It seemed so once. And that seeming was as strong as this. What can this mean? Why is He so present a commander in our time of prosperity and so very absent a help in time of trouble? . . .

Sooner or later I must face the question in plain language. What reason have we, except our own desperate wishes, to believe that God is, by any standard we can conceive, "good"? Doesn't all the *prima facie* evidence suggest exactly the opposite?

What chokes every prayer and every hope is the memory of all the prayers H. and I offered and all the false hopes we had. Not hopes raised merely by our own wishful thinking; hopes encouraged, even forced upon us, by false diagnoses, by X-ray photographs, by strange remissions, by one temporary recovery that might have ranked as a miracle. Step by step we were "led up the garden path." Time after time, when He seemed most gracious He was really preparing the next torture.

I wrote that last night. It was a yell rather than a thought. Let me try it over again. Is it rational to believe in a bad God? Anyway, in a God so bad as all that? The Cosmic sadist, the spiteful imbecile?

Or could one seriously introduce the idea of a bad God, as it were by the back door, through a sort of extreme Calvinism? You could say we are fallen and depraved. We are so depraved that our ideas of goodness count for nothing; or worse than nothing—the very fact that we think something is good is presumptive evidence that it is really bad. Now God has in fact—our worse fears are true—all the characteristics we regard as bad: unreasonableness, vanity, vindictiveness, injustice, cruelty. But all these blacks (as they seem to us) are really whites. It's only our depravity makes them look black to us.

Why do I make room in my mind for such filth and nonsense? Do I hope that if feeling disguises itself as thought I shall feel less? Aren't all these notes the senseless writhings of a man who won't accept the fact that there is nothing we can do with suffering except to suffer it? Who still thinks there is some device (if only he could find it) which will make pain not to be pain? It doesn't really matter whether you grip the arms of the dentist's chair or let your hands lie in your lap. The drill drills on.[20]

Adoniram Judson also echoed the pathos of Job in 23:1–9. When war broke out between Burma and England in 1824, English foreigners became espionage suspects. Execution of spies was routine. Judson and a fellow missionary were imprisoned. Nightly, their shackled ankles were raised over their heads until only their shoulders touched the ground. Daily, the executions continued. At one point, Judson contemplated suicide. After more than a year in prison, he was summoned to assist as an interpreter in peace negotiations. Near the end of a long absence from his wife, he received word that she had succumbed to fever and died. His baby girl followed a few months later.

Judson's instinctive reaction was to throw himself relentlessly into translation work. Inwardly he wrestled with loneliness, guilt, and grief for over a year. Guilt and grief gave way to despair and doubt. He left mission work, built a hut in the jungle, and dug a grave where he perched for long periods of morbid meditation. Lost in a desolate wasteland of mind and soul, this veteran missionary penned a pathetic plea to his dead wife's parents: "Have either of you learned the art of real communion with God, and can you teach me the first principles? God is to me the Great Unknown. *I believe in him, but I find him not.*"[21] This may not sound very spiritual. But it sounds very human, and remarkably like Job in chapter 23.

When and why does God hide Himself? Two verses in the same neighborhood articulate the paradox between promises of God's presence and experiences of God's absence. Psalm 46:1 exults that "God is our refuge and strength, a very present help in trouble." Psalm 44:24 asks, "Wherefore hidest thou thy face, and forgettest our affliction and oppression?" They are within twenty verses of each other but express opposite sentiments about the accessibility of God in times of trouble. If God is a very findable help in trouble, then why does He seem to be unfindable and unaware in our times of need? Isaiah famously sums up this spiritual anomaly: "Verily, thou art a God that *hidest thyself*, O God of Israel, the *Saviour*" (45:15). He is our *Savior* and yet *hides Himself* when we need Him?

Sometimes God is silent and hidden because of our sin (Deut. 32:20; Isa. 8:17; 57:11; Jer.14:8; Ps. 50:21). But sometimes He hides Himself from His people even when they cry to Him in distress

(Job 13:24; 34:29; Pss. 10:1; 13:1; 22:1; 30:7; 44:24; 88:14; 89:46), prompting them to implore Him to manifest His presence and intervene (Pss. 27:9; 69:17; 143:7).

Citing all these passages makes a point: when you feel like that, you are not alone. God's saints throughout history have known this experience. To find yourself in the company of Job is no small consolation. Start here: open your heart and examine yourself to see if the reason for His withdrawal is in you. Then wrap one of these biblical cries around your pain and frustration. Pray back to God some of these inspired prayers. Using these passages in prayer is an act of faith. Like Job's, these cries insist that the world be experienced as it is and not in a pretended way. God includes them in His Word as prayer templates, to sanctify such feelings and experiences as a proper subject of discourse with God.

The advantage we have over Job is a reservoir of written revelation. Access amplifies accountability. However silent He seems to us, God *has* spoken. If you want a word from God, go to the Scriptures and immerse your soul until you recognize His voice to you there. If you are looking for God amid your suffering, you will not find Him apart from His Word. Sometimes God seems silent only because we are not listening to what He has already said.

How do we respond to the silence of God? The answer lies in returning to the broader context of Psalms 44 and 46. Psalm 42 actually begins Book 2 of the Psalms (42–49 were composed by the sons of Korah).[22] While each psalm is a distinct unit, there is a providential progression to their arrangement. The psalmist craves God's presence while his enemies mock, "Where is your God?" (42:1–3, 9–10). Though God is veiled, the psalmist encourages his soul to dwell on (42:6) and to hope in God (42:5, 11). These same thoughts resurface in Psalm 43 (see vv. 2 and 5).[23]

In Psalm 44, the psalmist is emotionally fatigued. He has no heart to encourage himself, and cries out for God to answer and intervene (44:9–26). He is weary of waiting, confused by God's delay, and wonders if God will ever hear and act. Psalm 45 does not seem to fit this larger context, until you realize that the psalmist is losing himself in God, meditating on the King's control over everything. That focus facilitates the transition to Psalm 46.

Psalm 46 resolves the quest for God that began in Psalm 42. The psalmist exults that God has answered at last. He also comes to recognize that God was actually present, aware, concerned, and active in the plight of His people all along. He closes with an admonition to fellow waiters: "Be still, and know that I am God; I will be exalted among the heathen, I will be exalted in the earth" (46:10).

The biblical response to calamity and divine silence is threefold: (1) Hope in God. Who else is there? Biblical hope is confident expectation based on the fact that God has given His word. (2) Dwell on God. Remember all His past acts for you. Meditate on His character in Scripture. (3) Be still and know that He is God. Cultivate a patient, quiet acceptance of His sovereign purposes and timing.[24] God always answers . . . eventually, just as He does for Job. Whoever *goes on knocking*, to him it will be opened; whoever *goes on seeking*, he will find (Luke 11:9–13). The knocking and seeking imply the occasional hiddenness of God. The opening and finding imply that the hiddenness of God is only temporary.[25]

Alchemy or Innocence? (23:10)

Job longs to find God (23:3–7) but cannot (23:8–9). Even though he cannot find God, Job *knows* God *knows* (23:10). Knows what? That question deserves some extended exploration into this celebrated verse: "But he knoweth the way that I take: when he hath tried me, I shall come forth as gold."

This verse appears to embody a scriptural truth that has comforted and encouraged countless believers. God knows everything we are going through and intends it to strengthen and purify us. One writer cites this passage as proof that "for the Christian, affliction is gold in the making. If we will cooperate in the process, we will come forth as gold."[26]

I would love to write about God, the divine Alchemist, using the heat of adversity and the pressure of affliction to purify our lives and to refine our faith and character. Before this chapter is over, I will. But not from this verse. For one thing, there is little left to say that hasn't already been squeezed out of it. For another, while the Bible does teach that God knows all our troubles and that trials have a refining effect on believers, Job 23:10 does not.

Job 23:10 has joined the ranks of verses whose familiar words have taken on a hallowed life of their own—verses used to teach truths that are wholesome and biblical, but truths that are foreign to the verse's context.

It is a mistake to read any verse as a devotional island isolated from its context. Once a verse's familiar language finds its way into poems and hymns, devotionals and sermons, no one bothers to investigate its context or question its meaning anymore. That's when we turn traditional translations and interpretations of men into commandments of God, nullifying God's original intent in that passage (cf. Mark 7:13). Every time we derive an interpretation and application from a text that is not consistent with its contextual sense—no matter how biblical the truth itself may be—we rob that text of the meaning and application that God intended when He gave it. In the process, we rob ourselves and others of that text's truth from God. Worst of all, we rob God of His voice in that verse.

Some are suspicious of the suggestion that we may have misread the context of such a well-known text. It smacks of intellectual sophistry, spiritual snobbery. But context is a text's only safeguard against misunderstanding and misuse. The failure to insist on a contextual reading of any text is to leave that text bound and gagged while the language of the verse is commandeered to a noble but erroneous use. The instant you drop 23:10 back into its local and larger context the meaning is unmistakable.

Job 23:10 is often seen to mark the moment when Job finally rises to the assurance that God knows all he is going through, and realizes that when God is done testing him he will come out refined and strengthened. But this is not at all what Job meant. Job 23:10 reads literally, "But He knows (the) way (that is) with me;[27] if He should test me, I would come forth as gold."[28] Job is certain of two things: he is innocent, and God knows it. God knows his way of life—actions, words, and thoughts. If He would only put Job to the test, he would come through like gold. How does this fit into the larger context of what Job has been saying? Six contextual observations clarify what Job means in 23:10.

First, Job has just declared his certainty that if only he could come before God's court and present his case, he would be vindicated

(23:4–7). One of Job's recurring themes is his confident assertion of innocence and final vindication (9:32–35; 13:3, 18–24; 16:18–19; 19:23–27). But he cannot be vindicated as long as God is nowhere to be found (23:3, 8–9). He searches for Him everywhere, but God is silent and seemingly absent. Job sees himself in the frustrating position of having been accused, tried, found guilty, and sentenced to affliction without ever getting his day in court to hear the charges and make his defense.

Second, Job is sure that though he cannot see God (23:3, 8–9), God sees him and knows his way of life (23:10*a*). Job's star witness is God Himself. That being the case, he reiterates his confidence in the outcome when his case is adjudicated. Convinced of his innocence and certain of exoneration, Job can state with conviction that he would pass through God's law court like gold. Not sinless—that is not his point. He has admitted he is a sinner like everyone else. But he also knows he is a righteous man innocent of anything deserving of this magnitude of suffering—that is the book's underlying admission.

Third, Job is responding in chapter 23 to Eliphaz's allegations in chapter 22. Eliphaz had just maligned Job's "way" with false accusations (22:5–14). But Job doesn't want to stand before Eliphaz and be judged by fallible men who don't know the truth about him and won't believe it when he tells them. He wants a perfect Judge who knows his heart: *How I wish I could find God and come before His seat* (23:3ff.). Eliphaz may think Job's way has been wicked, but God knows better: *God knows my way. God knows I am not guilty of those charges.* Job's words are neither a testimony to the refining effects of suffering nor an expression of arrogance. They are one more bold declaration to his friends that God knows his innocence, even if they don't.[29] How can he be this confident? That leads to another contextual argument based on what follows 23:10.

Fourth, Job's words after 23:10 explain why he expects to be found innocent whenever his case does come before God. He has closely followed in God's steps, kept to His way, and not turned aside from it (23:11). Eliphaz's last appeal insinuated that Job had rejected God's law and devalued His words (22:22). But Job protests that he had *not* departed from God's commands; he *had* treasured God's words as supremely valuable (23:12; see discussion below). Nevertheless, Job is resigned to the fact that God is inscrutable and sovereign—He does whatever He wants. Job just does not understand why God has done *this* to *him* (23:13–17). What follows 23:10 simply does not make sense unless Job is once again asserting in 23:10 his confidence that he will be vindicated when God finally tests him.

Fifth, Job never expresses any expectation of surviving his affliction. Far from seeing his sufferings as a temporary "test" designed to make him a better man, Job has consistently anticipated only one outcome: death. He is not a man patiently enduring to be made better; he is a man waiting to die (3:20–22; 6:8–11; 7:16, 21; 9:25–26; 10:1, 18–22; 14:5–6, 13; 16:22; 17:1, 11, 13–16; 30:20–23). If you take the time to retrace these passages and listen to what Job has been saying all the way through the book, an unmistakable impression emerges. Job maintained an unshakable faith in God, a confidence in His sovereign control over all his experiences, and a belief that he would someday see and hear God for himself. But nowhere does Job express any inkling that his circumstances are only a temporary hardship through which he will pass perfected and purified. To take 23:10 in that way is to make it a schizophrenic exception to Job's unwavering attitude throughout the book. As Job reads his circumstances, God has simply turned against him for unknown reasons (7:20–21; 9:17–18; 10:2–7; 13:23–24; 16:7–17; 19:6–22). He anticipates no end in this life to this mysterious desertion by God.

Sixth, a parallel passage settles what Job means in 23:10. Job asserts the same confidence in nearly the same words in 31:4–6. *Does He not see my ways* [same word as 23:10*a*] *and count all my steps? If I have walked in falsehood or if my foot has hastened after deceit, let Him weigh me in a just scale,* [synonymous with 23:10*b*] *and He will know* [same word as 23:10*a*] *my integrity.* Job's meaning here is unambiguous. Here he draws the same link between God's knowledge of him and the vindication of his integrity that he makes in 23:10.

Job is not saying, "God knows what I am going through, and when He is done testing me, I will be the better for it, purified like gold."[30] He is saying, *God sees me and knows me.*[31] *He knows I am innocent. When he tests me*—for Job is confident that one day God will certainly hear his case—*I will come through like gold.* Not because the process will purify him but because he is already "gold"—innocent, blameless, righteous—as he has been claiming throughout the book.[32]

What about all the sermons and songs and Sunday school lessons and devotionals that have taken this verse in the popular sense? In a way, Job spoke truer than he knew. He had no idea that all his adversity was a test of the integrity of his faith, and no anticipation of release from (let alone victory over) his circumstances. But we know better. Job was waiting for God to finish him off, but He didn't. What Job thought was the desertion of God was, in fact, a temporary test through which he was humbled and his view of God refined. In that sense, then, there is even more comfort for the suffering saint in a contextual reading of Job's words in 23:10. What we, like Job, may be convinced is dark and mysterious with no way out is not God's desertion but only a "trial of our faith." As long as we are clear that what we mean by 23:10 is not what Job meant, there seems little harm in borrowing his language. The sentiment that this verse has traditionally been used to express is more accurately reflected in other passages (cf. Ps. 66:8–12; 119:67, 71; Zech. 13:9; James 1:12; 1 Pet. 1:7). God, the divine Alchemist, *can* transform our afflictions into priceless experiences that purify us. But we do better to teach that truth from verses that teach it, not just sound like it.

Job's Priorities (23:11–17)

Satan accused Job of worshiping God only because of what God gave him and valuing his wealth and comfort more than God. Strip all that away, sneered Satan, and Job's true priorities would surface. It didn't happen. Job is still clinging to God in the face of a similar charge brought now by his friend.

Eliphaz had insinuated that Job needed to heed God's law and find his wealth in God rather than in gold (22:22–26). Job protests, "There was no need to tell me so; I have done so already."[33] He has conscientiously kept his feet in God's path (23:11). He has not departed from God's commandment and has treasured God's words more than his wealth (23:12).[34] Job's use of a verb meaning to "treasure" seems to be answering Eliphaz's exhortation in 22:22 to "lay up" God's words in his heart. The word translated "my necessary *food*" (KJV)[35] means "my portion, allotment" or "my statute, law, rule." The same term frequently describes God's Word as a "boundary."[36] No word for "food" or "bread" appears in the text.

The contextual link to the preceding speech of Eliphaz seems to be the best indicator of what Job is really saying in 23:12. Eliphaz zeroed in on what he guessed to be Job's presumption—that "gain is godliness." He fabricated a list of probable sins (22:5–11), all depicting Job as a tightfisted scrooge defrauding or withholding from those in need. Eliphaz implored Job not to be like the wealthy wicked who sin in spite of God's goodness to them (22:17–18) but to reconcile with God, heed His words, and find his wealth in God (22:21–26). It is this insinuation to which Job objects so strenuously. In his final defense he will detail his integrity and marshal evidence of his generosity against any such spirit of greed. But here in chapter 23 he simply counters that he has always had the highest regard for God's word and has scrupulously ordered his life in accordance with God's commands (23:10–12). Job contends that he has valued God's word far more than his God-given "allotment." His allotment was enormous wealth, but he did not let that blur his vision of Who gave it nor steal his affections from God's law. He gave God's words priority in his life above all else.

Job uses allotment again in 23:14. "For he performeth the thing that is appointed for me: and many such things are with him" (23:14). In other words, Job confesses, *When God allotted me great fortune, I valued His words more highly than my God-given prosperity. Now that God, in His sovereignty, has allotted loss and suffering to me, I will cling to Him still.* Job's conviction that both conditions—prosperity and penury, woe and weal—come by the Lord's allotment is clear all the way back at the beginning: "The Lord gave, and the Lord hath taken away" (1:21). "Shall we receive good at the hand of God, and shall we not receive evil" from His hand as well (2:10)?[37] The difference in 23:12 is Job's conclusion in 23:15–17. This passage proves that his initial response was not just shallow surface reaction. Time has passed and things have not changed. Friends have accused him. The community has shunned him. Worst of all, God has remained aloof and silent, raising questions in Job's mind that feed his frustration. He cannot fathom the rationale behind his circumstances. He will wrestle with these questions until God finally breaks the silence. But he remains confidently resigned to this fact: *God has performed what is appointed for me. He alone knows why. He is in control.*

All this talk about God's words—"the words of His mouth," no less—raises a larger question. What "words"? Where did these words come from, and in what form? We have already noted that the book of Job conveys a massive amount of truth about God corroborated elsewhere in Scripture. Where did they get this knowledge? How did they get these "words" from God? We know from the Genesis record of the prepatriarchal and patriarchal period (from Creation to the time of Moses)—during which the story of Job occurred—that God regularly communicated truth about Himself to man through a variety of media: dreams, visions, and at times (apparently) even direct speech.[38] This revelation included more than individual directives (e.g., Gen. 22:1ff.). God's revelation in this era is described as "the way of the Lord" in which Abraham would rear his children (Gen. 18:19), and even as the "charge . . . commandments . . . statutes and . . . laws" that God gave to Abraham (Gen. 26:5), five centuries before Moses ever wrote anything. Whether such revelations were ever written down we have no way of knowing. What is clear is that in every generation God has not left Himself without witness (Acts 14:17). And every generation is accountable according to the degree of witness God has left them.

Frustrations of the Righteous (24:1–25)

Job returns once more to the burning interrogative: Why? "Since times are not hidden from the Almighty, Why do those who know Him see not His days?" (24:1, NKJV). This is the UPS (Un-Pulled Speeder) syndrome. Anyone who has been stopped for speeding knows the frustration of watching speeders zip down the highway and thinking, "Where is the highway patrol *now*!" It's not that you enjoy seeing people get in trouble; but our sense of fairness is satisfied when we witness the punishment of those determined to do wrong. The general impression that crime has no consequences (or at least a good chance of going undetected) encourages presumption in fence-straddlers and frustration in those who at least try to abide by the law.

> In this chapter Job presented a picture of a world that was still a deep enigma to him. His courageous honesty led him to expound on the mystery of how the wicked get by unpunished while they perform

> their evil deeds against the innocent. The touching pathos of these word-pictures should be felt by the reader, for they give us some insight into Job's contempt for wickedness and his ability to empathize with those in distress.[39]

Chapter 24 opens with this frustration, then launches into a litany of the kinds of crime that so often seem to go unnoticed and unpunished by God (24:2–17).[40] Job 24:13–17 illustrate the practical side of the spiritual diagnosis of humanity in John 3:19 ("Men loved darkness rather than light, because their deeds were evil").

A difficulty arrives with 24:18–25. In some translations (KJV, NASB, NIV), it sounds as if Job has completely reversed himself and is now arguing that the wicked *are* cursed in the earth (24:18), that their prosperity *is* only momentary (24:24). Those two statements (24:18, 24) are the only ones that seem to be directly at odds with Job's previous arguments.[41] Several solutions (and some nonsolutions) have been offered.[42]

It seems most likely that Job is pronouncing an extended curse on the wicked.[43] *May their portion be cursed in the earth. . . . May the womb forget him. . . .*[44] If this is the case, Job is expressing his disdain for wickedness and his wish that God would judge it. He even weaves into this extended imprecation his confidence that though the wicked presume upon the life and security God grants them, "His eyes *are* upon their ways" (24:23). Though Job is frustrated with the ubiquity of unjudged wickedness, he is confident that wickedness *will* one day be judged (24:24–25). God's temporary inaction against the wicked does not indicate His complicity with sinners any more than God's destruction of Job (2:3) indicates His displeasure with him.

Bildad: What's Left to Say? (Job 25)

Bildad offers an abortive last-ditch effort. No more sardonic swipes at Job's sophistry and sanctimony. No more cocky declamations on the destiny of the wicked. Bildad's final speech—its brevity hardly merits that word[45]—has the feel of a disputant who has been beaten but not convinced and wants to get in a last word to prove it.

This is the eighth speech from Job's friends. What new argument can they offer that has not been made with escalating passion seven times over already? The friends' speeches, with the exception of Zophar's second, have progressively shrunk.[46] The implication of that pattern, along with the remark of the narrator (32:3) and Elihu (32:11–12) that the friends had failed to answer and convince Job, confirms that they had run out of material arguments.[47]

Bildad concludes with a two-pronged rejoinder: the transcendence of God and the unworthy insignificance of Job. God is immeasurably mighty and majestic (25:2–3). How, then, can any man make the kind of claim on God that Job has made? If even the moon and stars pale in comparison to God's purity, how much less is man, a maggot, a worm (25:4–6)?

Eight times Job has referred to himself as *tsadiq*—righteous (6:29; 9:2, 15, 20; 10:15; 12:4; 13:18; 17:9).[48] He will claim it again four more times before the end (27:6, 17; 29:14; 31:6). Bildad returns to that claim in the form of a question that will not go away. The Spirit of God directed the narrator to include it three times in three different mouths (4:17; 9:2; 25:4). It frames the dialogue of the friends, occurring in the first speech by Eliphaz and in the final speech by Bildad, and once in between by Job. Apparently, Bildad hopes to arouse a final pang of self-doubt by ending on a note Job himself sounded. *You said it yourself, Job! How can a man like you—a mere maggot, a worm—claim to be righteous before God?* The question is a theological crux in the book, encouraging the reader to ponder the larger theological issue that the Scripture will answer in great detail elsewhere (e.g., Rom. 3).

Job and his friends are arguing on two different planes. Neither can fathom any other scenario. From their perspective, Job has committed some heinous sin(s) that he refuses to admit and is, instead, impiously insisting on his innocence. For his part, Job cannot get them to acknowledge the disconnect between the surrounding evidence of reality and their theological assumptions and, consequently, the utter irrelevance of their arguments.

Job: Thanks a Lot, You've Been a Big Help! (Job 26)

Job's initial reply is aimed specifically at Bildad (note "thou" in 26:2–4).[49] The NASB captures the cutting tone:

> What a help you are to the weak!
> How you have saved the arm without strength!
> What counsel you have given to one without wisdom!
> What helpful insight you have abundantly provided!

Bildad championed the obvious. Who can dispute the magnificence of God and the unworthiness and uncleanness of man?

> Job has no quarrel with such assertions. But how different the inference! According to Bildad, puny man counts for nothing in the infinite space of God's mind. But Job thinks that God, precisely because of His boundless capacity for knowledge, can give to each individual the most complete personal attention.[50]

Job soars into his own meditation on the glory of God as reflected in creation (26:5–14). His expressions are, unsurprisingly, consistent with modern astronomy and meteorology.[51] He ends on a note as theologically insightful as it is harmonious to the ear. "Indeed these are the mere edges of His ways, And how small a whisper we hear of Him! But the thunder of His power who can understand?" (26:14, NKJV).

"These are the mere edges of His ways." The word *edges* (KJV, "parts") denotes a termination, a boundary line or coastline, an edge or corner. What we can discern of the infinite God from His works in nature and history are the mere coastlines of the continent of the mind and character of God. Imagine landing for the first time on the seventeenth-century American continent. You have no idea that the sand onto which you step is the fringe of a continuous landmass over 3,000 miles wide and 9,500 miles long. Imagine formulating views of what this whole continent is like based on what you can see from the bay where you drop anchor. Suppose you forge your way five miles inland, or even fifty miles, to get a better idea of what this new country is like. As tangible and verifiable as what you see is, you are experiencing a minuscule fraction of an unimaginable stretch of vast and varied terrain yet to be explored—massive and multiple mountain ranges, trackless prairies, impenetrable forests, mammoth lakes and mighty rivers with deafening waterfalls, swamps and deserts, flora and fauna yet unknown. How much more there is to know about our magnificently infinite God than what we can see from where we are, only eternity can tell.

"And how small a whisper we hear of Him." The word *whisper* (KJV, "portion") is a major term for *speech* or *word* (*dabar*). Job is speaking from the other side of written revelation, so far as we know.[52] But even on this side of biblical revelation, God has disclosed in the Bible a tantalizingly tiny percentage of what there is to know about Him and His ways. How can it possibly be otherwise? How can the moderately small book we call the Bible (even my copy of Shakespeare's works dwarfs my Bible) be anything but a fractional revelation of an infinite and eternal Being? (How can we even speak of a "fraction" of infinity or eternity?)

God is the infinite and unexplored continent, His Word the map that outlines—accurately, yet finitely—the mere coastlines of His character, the boundaries of His being, the edges of His ways. The final chapter will return to the implications of the book of Job for our pursuit of theology in general.

13
The Defense Rests
Job 27–31

My former pastor used to say that two kinds of preaching stirred him up and made him want to preach: good preaching and sorry preaching. Good preaching inspired him to affirm truth well presented. Sorry preaching provoked him to rescue mangled truth. The preaching of Job's friends has not exactly been sorry preaching. Most of it has been truth eloquently and forcefully presented but badly misapplied, a finite theological system pressed into service to answer questions it was not equipped to address. Three exhausted men have tried their hardest to force a bronco into a stall much too small. They've pled and pulled, coaxed and shoved, frightened, smacked, and called him names; and they've got bruises to show for it. Job bucks free and cuts loose on his longest discourse by far.

"Moreover Job continued his parable and said, . . ." (27:1). This is new language for the narrator in the book of Job. This phrase in 27:1 and 29:1 unites Job's protracted final defense (27–31) and sets it off from the preceding dialogue (Job 4–26).[1] The word *parable* (*mashal*) translates a versatile Hebrew noun. It describes speech designed to cause someone to reflect and come to a verdict about the subject under discussion.[2]

Eliphaz's last attempt to turn up the heat and make something stick to the Teflon prophet short-circuited. Bildad's parting shot from the hip, aimed at Job's conscience, went wide of the mark. Zophar was speechless. So Job proceeded with a discourse that contrasts theological fantasy with existential reality and compels his hearers to practice sober self-assessment.

Job Affirms His Righteousness and God's (Job 27)

Job employs "the most extreme measure available in [his] society for a condemned person to plead innocent," namely, "an oath based on the existence of God."[3] He solemnly denies all the charges laid against him, reaffirms his innocence of any sin warranting his suffering, and avows his integrity and clear conscience (27:2–6). Job frequently cries out directly to God. Curiously, the friends never do.[4]

Embedded in the oath is a subtle irony. Job swears to his own righteousness by the same God Whose character he has impugned for denying him justice. It is impossible to know whether his initial lamentation (Job 3) would have mutated into such daring insinuations against God without the needling of his friends. Nevertheless, before the end Job will be called to account for impeaching God's justice, not only by Elihu (34:5–6, 10, 12, 17; 35:2) but by God Himself (40:2, 8).

Job's follows his oath of innocence with an imprecation upon his enemies, which certainly included Eliphaz, Bildad, and Zophar (27:7–10). If this sounds spiteful, remember the severity of the crimes that they labored to pin on him. What began as an assumption of some nameless sin grew in innuendo and erupted in Eliphaz's libelous and "malicious prosecution of the innocent."[5] But bitterness is damaging. The remedy for resentment against others is to pray for them. In the end, that will be God's prescription for Job (42:7–10).

Job teaches them things they should have known already had they only opened their eyes (27:11–12). Job 27:13 is an obvious echo of Zophar's conclusion in 20:29, only Job now sounds as if he is agreeing with what the friends have been saying all along.[6] The paradox here is even trickier than the similar difficulty of Job's words in 24:18–24.

Many are content to let 27:13–23 stand as Job's agreement with the friends' general principle of the just judgment of God on the wicked. Job never disagreed with that principle in the first place, only with their determination to apply it to his circumstances.[7] What Job denies is that God always judges the wicked swiftly, He always does so in this life, and all severe suffering necessarily signals divine judgment for sin since God's justice would never allow such things to happen to the innocent. Still, Job seems to use language here that not only agrees with the absolutist views of his friends but contradicts his own previous arguments against their views.

For example, Eliphaz insisted that the children of the wicked are "far from safety" and never have anyone to deliver them (5:4); Zophar added that they are forced to cater to the poor defrauded by their father (20:10); Bildad even suggested—in an indelicate dig at Job's loss—that the wicked would leave behind no offspring (18:19). But Job has already argued that the wicked often enjoy a prolific posterity that live in security and happiness (21:8–9, 11–12). He anticipated his friends' retort to the prosperity of the wicked and scornfully rejected the "solution" that God was just waiting to punish the next generation (21:17–21). Yet now he seems to admit, *If the children of the wicked are multiplied, it is for the sword, and his offspring will be hungry* (27:14). Has Job changed his mind?

Again, Bildad called the house of the wicked unstable and insecure (8:15, 22), Eliphaz said that fire would consume their tents (15:34), and Zophar added that all the amassed wealth of the wicked evaporates so that he cannot enjoy it (20:15–23, 28). Job rebutted that often the wicked wax powerful and enjoy their wealth all their days (21:7, 13), while "their houses are safe from fear" (21:9). But now Job seems to agree that the wicked will, indeed, forfeit the enjoyment of all his wealth to the innocent (27:16–17) and that his house is fragile as a cocoon, unstable as a shack (27:18).

Once more, Bildad and Zophar said the wicked were constantly besieged with "terrors" (18:11, 14; 20:25). Job demolished that fantasy with an idyllic portrait of the security and prosperity of many of the wicked (21:7–13). Yet now he appears to agree that "terrors" (the same word Bildad used) will overtake the wicked like a sudden flood and a tempest will sweep him away in a night (27:20–21).

Commentators assure us that Job is merely affirming, with the friends, his persuasion that God is just and that judgment will certainly come on the wicked. But this fails to explain a careful comparison with what the friends and Job have said previously.[8] Job's language and imagery, combined with the unqualified assertion that "this is the portion" and "heritage" of the wicked, seem to contradict his whole argument in 21:7–26. Only one other explanation seems feasible, and it is hinted at in Job's words in 27:11–12 as well as his virtual quotation of Zophar in 27:13. He is mimicking his friends' oversimplified doctrine of retribution one last time.

In 27:11–12, Job proposes to teach his friends the truth about God, realities they have seen but have stubbornly refused to admit. They have shut their eyes and folded their arms and stood pat on their strict theory that God *always* sends calamity on the wicked and *only* on the wicked.[9] Would Job (27:12) call their position "altogether vain" (KJV), "foolish" (NASB), "nonsense" (NKJV), "meaningless" (NIV), then paint *his* depiction of "the hand of God" (27:11) in exactly the same language as his friends?

Just as he did in 24:18–24, Job is quoting his friends to make his point.[10] It looks like this: *I will teach you what is in the hand of God, and what is with the Almighty I will not conceal. Surely you all have seen it; why then do you talk such nonsense as this: "This is the portion of a wicked man with God (says Zophar), and the heritage given by the Almighty to oppressors"?* Job recounts their view one last time, quoting them and borrowing their imagery extensively—not in agreement but in demonstration of its experiential bankruptcy. Perhaps nowhere is it more hermeneutically necessary, for the textual reasons I have cited above, to recognize the probable presence of this rhetorical device of unannounced quotation than in 27:13–23.[11]

At this point (27:23), Job's tone shifts noticeably for the remainder of his defense. He makes no further reference or address to his friends in chapters 28–31. It is pure soliloquy and prayer. The friends may exchange glances or comments with each other, but they do not exit the stage yet. We will see them again.

Finding the Wisdom of God (Job 28)

The calm, reflective mood of this chapter seems distantly removed from the rancorous debate that has now climaxed and stalled. The subject of wisdom is a new one. No one disputes that Job 28 is a masterpiece of poetic brilliance and a delight to read aloud. The question is, who is speaking, Job or the narrator?[12]

Many regard this chapter as an interlude inserted by the narrator.[13] Some see it as a breather for the reading audience, a narrative transition from Job's heated debate with his friends to his more introspective final defense.[14] Others argue that it performs an artistic function as well, providing symmetry to the overall structure of the book.[15] Some have compared its role to the "commentary supplied by a Chorus between the acts of a play."[16]

The view that the narrator is the speaker in Job 28 is not particularly problematic, but it seems both unnatural and unnecessary. The theory is prompted, in part, by the dramatic change in Job 28; for Job to shift his tone and topic so suddenly seems unrealistic to some. We should not suppose, however, that the narrator penned *everything* that each of these men spoke, just as the Gospel writers did not record everything Jesus said and did. The narrator has selected, edited, and arranged his material under the direction of the Holy Spirit. It is unnecessary to assume that Job proceeded directly from 27:23 to 28:1 with nothing between but a single breath.[17] Any apparent shift in mood or tone makes sense if we grant the author the same privileges of selection and arrangement of material that we accord to other writers of Scripture.[18]

The view that chapter 28 is an insertion by the narrator is also inconsistent with his unfailing habit of alerting us to his presence. He always announces his input, not only in the prologue and epilogue but also between the speeches, including a lengthy summary and introduction to Elihu in 32:1–6. By sandwiching chapter 28 between two identical narrative markers that note the continuation of Job's extended discourse (27:1 and 29:1), the narrator gives the reader the clear impression that chapter 28 is part of Job's speech, not his own composition.[19] In addition, the narrator consistently expresses himself in prose, not poetry. The unannounced insertion of a lengthy poem conflicts with the narrator's pattern throughout the rest of the book. Any argument against reading chapter 28 as the words of Job can be surmounted with an appeal to narrative consistency, authorial selectivity, and minimal imagination.[20] Even the content links Job 28 to what precedes and what follows.

Job just announced that he would teach his three friends things about God that they should know, instead of the clichéd claptrap and tired platitudes they have been parroting (27:11–12). Having just summarized their view (27:3–23), which he earlier trounced (21:7–26), he takes a step back and sets the stage more broadly.

The poem revolves around the central question posed in 28:12 and its refrain in 28:20—where can one find wisdom (*chokmah*) and understanding (*biynah*)? It is perfectly natural that Job would address this subject at this point. The others have repeatedly referred to "wisdom" and "understanding" without evidencing much of either. This was particularly true of belligerent Zophar. Job had just cited the friends' view of the wicked by quoting Zophar's words especially (27:13). Now Job turns to another topic raised by Zophar; for it was Zophar who longed for God to show Job "the secrets of wisdom [*chokmah*]" (11:6) and who claimed that he was compelled to answer Job out of a spirit of "understanding [*biynah*]" (20:3). Job has thrashed the arguments of Zophar and the others. Now he pauses, masters his spirit, shifts emotional and topical gears, and embarks on a course that is both poetic and pointed, reflective and instructive.

The poem is in three movements. Man knows where and how to find earthly wealth. He drops a shaft into the blackness of the earth and dangles from swaying ropes to fetch its treasures (28:1–11). But where is the mine for *wisdom*, the shaft from which man can retrieve *understanding*? Those are incomparably more valuable than anything man can dig out of the dirt (28:12–19).

Where, then, does wisdom come from, and where can one find understanding? Neither man nor beast can discover it unaided. It is hidden with God. He alone knows its source because He alone *is* its source (28:23–28).[21]

God is the only mine for wisdom and the bottomless shaft from which understanding may be quarried. Here is the entrance: "Behold, the fear of the Lord,[22] that is wisdom; and to depart from evil, is understanding" (28:23–28).[23] The verbs that define wisdom and understanding—*fearing* God and *departing* from evil—should be familiar to us as readers of Job. These actions have been characteristic of Job's lifestyle from the very beginning. They are the same verbs used in the prologue to describe Job as one who "feared God" and "eschewed [departed from] evil" (1:1, 8; 2:3).

Chapter 28 is not just an interlude in an otherwise lengthy discourse or a reply to the friends' claim to wisdom. This speech subtly introduces thematic threads to which Job will return in his defense to follow. He here directs attention to the God Who sees everything and knows the truth about everyone (28:23–24; cf. 31:4), to the Lord's prescription for wisdom that had been Job's own testimony all his days (28:28; cf. 1:1, 8; 2:3), to the Judge Who measures out his life in a scale (28:25; cf. 31:6). Job is about to submit his formal and final affidavit to Him in the next three chapters.

Reflecting on Past and Present (Job 29–30)

A comparison of 29:2 ("Oh, that I were as in months past . . .") and 30:1 ("But now . . .") shows the connection between these two chapters.[24] Job's final lament consists of two major movements: reminiscing over the blessings of the past and reflecting on the ignominy of the present. "The contrast could hardly be more extreme. Present loss made worse by past achievement; both complete."[25] Job the defendant sums up his lawsuit, beginning with an account of the losses he has suffered. Nothing kindles belated gratitude for what you have like losing it.

One feature of Job's longing for the "good old days" is particularly striking. What Job laments first and most is the loss of God's presence and blessing (29:2–5). He mentions his recently lost prosperity only in passing (29:6). He recalls his honor and esteem among all the men of his community (29:7–11), but not because he craved fame and popularity. Men held him in high regard, he says, because he fought for the oppressed, gave generously of himself to the orphan and widow, and provided selflessly for the poor (29:12–17). Here was a genuine altruist who loved doing righteousness for righteousness' sake. He delighted in the fruit of his autumn years, his God-given security and well-being (29:18–20), and was highly esteemed by all for his measured words and wise counsel (29:21–25).

"But *now*" (30:1) he finds himself just as widely mocked. Having enjoyed the respect of the most respectable, he now endures the contempt of the most contemptible (30:1–8). "And *now*" (30:9) he has become the subject of insulting proverbs ("Who hides his sin under wealth's fine robe, Belongs on the dunghill with old man Job!") and men think nothing of spitting at him (30:9–15). "And *now*" (30:16) day and night torment him with disfiguring disease and gnawing pain (30:16–19). Worse than all human humiliation is the cruelty of God's desertion (30:20–23).[26] Hasn't Job done everything that could be expected of him and more (30:24–25)? His hopes are dashed, his expectations smothered in darkness, his mourning unrelieved, and his suffering unexplained (30:26–31).

> There is no one source of Job's misery. Several causes converge and reinforce each other. No remedy can be found in identifying "the" explanation and dealing with that. Yet there is one Source, Cause and Explanation, and He alone can be the Remedy.[27]

A Catalog of Righteousness (Job 31)

Job concludes his case with a solemn, detailed, formal oath of innocence.[28] His affidavit is marked by a consistent pattern ("If . . . then . . ."). He protests his scrupulous attention to righteousness in every corner of his life. This inventory of righteous living catalogs more than the mere avoidance of evil or the absence of blasphemy. Job's life has been characterized by the positive pursuit of internal integrity as well as external morality. Job's preaffliction testimony as one who feared God and avoided evil (1:1, 8; 2:3) is fleshed out in daily living in chapter 31. If you want to know what it looks like for someone to live a God-fearing, evil-eschewing lifestyle, here it is, spelled out in every sphere of life.

Moral Propriety (31:1–4). Job begins with a man's primary vulnerability. He understands (1) that sexual sin does not begin with an act but with a look, not with a deed done but with a desire nourished; (2) that such sin surfaces first as an internal betrayal (covenant-breaking) before it ever becomes an external behavior; and (3) that God sees man's every step and reserves judgment for such sin (cf. Heb. 13:4).

Financial Probity (31:5–8). The reference to being weighed in a balance, coupled with the curse of losing his crops, suggests that Job has more than general honesty in mind. He is defending his integrity not only in his external business dealings (31:5) but also in his internal disposition, including his defiance of covetousness (31:7; cf. Heb. 13:5). This was not a man who attained his wealth through greed, but who did so in spite of its absence.

Marital Purity (31:9–12).[29] In 31:1–4, Job renounces entertaining the thought of fornication by severing it at its root. Here, however, Job directly denounces adultery (hence the reference to "my neighbor's door").[30] To solemnize his protestation of innocence in this area, Job's imprecation calls for a just retaliation against himself. If he ever took another man's wife, may his own wife be taken by another man and become another man's wife or slave or concubine (31:10).[31] Some are offended that Job's curse would unjustly victimize his wife rather than him.[32] But this criticism misses the whole point. Job is not wishing any evil on his wife; he is asserting his innocence in this area in the strongest possible terms. His wife is completely safe because he has never met the condition.

Domestic Equity (31:13–15). In a society where slaves were second-class at best and their rights were minimal or nonexistent, Job went above the call of duty as a master and employer. He was always willing to hear any grievances and amend any abuses. Job displayed an egalitarian attitude toward slaves, regarding them as his brothers before the God Who fashioned them both in the womb. If Job were to mistreat his fellow man, even a slave, how could he possibly stand when God called him to account?[33] The KJV "visiteth" in verse 14 translates a Hebrew verb that means to inspect, evaluate, and reward according to one's deeds.

Social Generosity (31:16–23). Absence of mistreatment and abuse is good. But proactive provision for the poor and needy, for widows and orphans, is a rare and noble virtue. His was not a life of wealth selfishly hoarded. No poor Lazarus ever perished at his gate (cf. Luke 16:19ff.) but went away well-fed and warmly clothed. Conscientious openhandedness toward the less fortunate had been Job's lifelong lifestyle, providing for the underprivileged as for his own children and clothing them with the wool from his own sheep. Job was a philanthropist par excellence. Once again, the imprecation for divine judgment so matches the offense that the retribution would be manifestly from God. *If I have ever lifted up my hand against the defenseless, may the offending appendage fall off from the shoulder or be broken in half.*

Material Detachment (31:24–28). The rich man's chief temptation is to trust in his riches rather than in God (Prov. 11:28; Jer. 9:23; Mark 10:23–24; 1 Tim. 6:17). Job never rested his confidence in his wealth or rooted his security in his riches. He was under no idolatrous delusions as to the source of his prosperity. Worship of the sun and moon as the supposed givers of life and fecundity was prevalent in ancient society, but Job denies ever being enticed by such folly or secretly expressing any reverence toward the heavenly bodies (such as kissing his hand and extending it in reverence to the sun or moon).[34] Job admits that such iniquity would warrant divine judgment from the one true God above.

Relational Sympathy (31:29–30). Job has not been vindictive, nor delighted in the calamity of his enemy, nor prayed for a curse to befall his foe. "Not even in his heart did Job wish the most wicked men harm. To claim this is a most daring invitation for God to search him to the depths for wicked ways (Ps. 139:23f.). Here then is either a very clean conscience or a very calloused one."[35]

Communal Hospitality (31:31–32). Job disavows parsimony. He had a reputation for hospitality that included exceptional bed and board. His provisions were never grudging or tightfisted.

Personal Integrity (31:33–37). Job is well aware that he is a fallen creature. The reference to "Adam" (31:33) might refer to men in general, since *'adam* means "man(kind)" (hence NIV, "If I have concealed my sin as men do"). But that thought seems stilted and unnatural here. It is more likely that Job is alluding to Adam and the Fall. The historical tradition would have been well known to Job and passed along from generation to generation before Moses' written record of the event in Genesis 3.[36] Job makes no pretense of sinlessness; he protests only the accusation that he has played the hypocrite by concealing his sin. He has been open and frank with both God and man about his "transgressions." He has conscientiously kept short accounts with God and redressed his transgressions through the requisite sacrifices.

Nevertheless, perhaps nowhere does Job step over the line more blatantly than in 31:35–37. He has made some daring, even shocking, assertions (cf. 19:5ff.). He has grown increasingly confident of his innocence and of the apparent unfairness of his suffering. He is fairly full of himself in these closing moments of his final defense.[37] That Job does step over the line at some point(s) is beyond dispute; God Himself rebukes Job for doing so (38:2 ff.; 40:2, 8).

Job reiterates his longing for a hearing, figuratively appends his signature ("my mark") to the suit he has just laid out, and calls on God to answer him and write out a list of the charges against him (31:35). He is confident that he could clear himself of any divine indictment laid against him and rebut all insinuations against his integrity. Audaciously sure of himself, he even says he would parade such an arraignment in public view as a badge of honor, or even a crown (31:36).[38] He would approach God as a prince wrongfully accused and give a full account of all his ways before God (31:37).

Agricultural Sensitivity (31:38–40). Job appends a final amendment to his testimony.[39] He has not abused even the land itself or exploited those whom he hired to work his crops. If he has, he calls down one last curse upon himself: "May thistles grow up instead of wheat and weeds instead of barley." With that, "the words of Job are ended." Case closed.

> Here the debate ends. After this noble speech of the sufferer the friends are silent. To the end they have maintained his guilt and he his innocence. With all the eloquence of the disputants the theological aspect of the problem is not advanced, but the poet has made his point. . . . Virtue is not necessarily co-extensive with prosperity; calamity is no sure sign of misdeeds.[40]

Summary

Job 31 is "not a handbook on personal ethics."[41] It is the affidavit of a suffering saint struggling to answer the human accusations brought against him and to comprehend the divine sentence that seems already to have been passed. More than that, this passage is a page out of Job's journal, "a moving recital of all the godly things that made up Job's life in the days before he was afflicted. They bear the most careful reading: would to God I could claim half so much."[42]

Is this extended focus on *his* righteousness unnerving? Is he naturally boastful? Before all this happened, did he enjoy talking about how good he was? Is Job displaying pride in talking so much, and so confidently, about his integrity? Job's self-attestations of righteousness are nearly incredible, and his account of the unparalleled high regard in which he was held sounds almost boastful.[43] An underlying reality that goes unmentioned in this self-focus—and one element of Job's speech to which Elihu will react—is the absence of God. Only God could grace a man to be this genuinely righteous.

It is tempting "to interpret [this chapter] as a prime example of self-righteousness, but to do so would fly in the face of Job's just call for vindication."[44] Indeed, it would undermine the book's depiction of Job as a genuinely righteous and blameless man. It is suggestive that God never directly rebukes Job for pride. Nor does He correct Job for self-righteousness, per se. He censures Job for defending his own righteousness *over against* and *at the expense of* God's righteousness (40:8). "If it is a question of *one* of us being righteous," Job says in essence, "I *know* I am. And God does, too." The insinuation is every bit as offensive to God as the friends' insinuations were to Job.

IV

Human Monologue:
Job and Elihu

14

The Character and Function of Elihu

Job 32:1–5

Ornate oration was the trademark of William Gladstone, prime minister of Great Britain in the late nineteenth century. It was also his liability. His political opponent, Benjamin Disraeli, once lampooned him as "a sophistical rhetorician, inebriated with the exuberance of his own verbosity, and gifted with an egotistical imagination that can at all times command an interminable and inconsistent series of arguments to malign an opponent and to glorify himself."[1] Some feel the same way about Elihu.

No one knows when Elihu arrived, or whether the others even knew him. He is apparently a descendant of Abraham and an ancestor of David (32:2).[2] His occasional quotations from earlier parts of the debate suggest that he has been a silent listener throughout much of Job's dialogue with his three friends.[3] Once Job and his accusers fall silent, he feels compelled to speak. But first, the narrator introduces Elihu to us. As with any personal introduction, the object of this one is to shape our opinion of Elihu. First impressions are important. The narrator wants to condition our attitude toward Elihu and create the context in which we hear his words.

What Are We to Make of Elihu?

To many, Elihu is egotism personified, arrogance on two legs, Elihu the Bombastic, a cocky upstart with nothing to offer to the debate but a wordy rehash of worn-out arguments. There seem to be at least two reasons for this opinion of Elihu.

The first is a perpetuated prejudice against Elihu. The great London Baptist preacher (and contemporary of Gladstone and Disraeli) Charles Haddon Spurgeon nurtured a deep love and respect for the value of commentaries. But commentators, he once observed, are often like sheep; they follow one another and they all go astray. Once we are introduced to Elihu as a swaggering know-it-all—first impressions, I say, are important—it is easy to read that intonation into his words. But where does this notion come from in the first place? That question suggests a more systemic cause for an anti-Elihu bias.

The second reason Elihu's reputation suffers is the failure to take our interpretive cues from the text itself, and from the text alone. Elihu's speech is often misread on three levels: (1) reading "between the lines" an attitude and tone into Elihu's speech that is not necessary or native to the text; (2) ignoring the narrator's inspired portrayal of Elihu; and (3) overlooking significant parallels between Elihu's speech and God's final answer to Job.

Before you dismiss Job 32–37 as just so much recycled hot air, consider the evidence for an alternative view of Elihu. He is not the divine spokesman; he is human and, therefore, fallible. His assessment of Job may not be flawless,[4] but he transitions our attention from the errors of Job's friends to the answers of Job's God.[5] Along the way, he refocuses the lens of the debate. All that the friends can see is that Job's calamities must mean that he sinned. Elihu sees something quite different.

Elihu breaks the logjam and leverages a significant shift in the debate. Eliphaz, Bildad, and Zophar have argued that *Job is suffering because of his sin*. Elihu observes that *Job is sinning because of his suffering*. More on that later. First, let's examine the variety of opinions on Elihu, and try to establish a textually rooted approach to this character to whom the Holy Spirit devotes so much space.

Views of Elihu

Few characters in Scripture elicit more contempt than Elihu. He is among the bête noires of the Bible. Elihu has endured withering derision at the hands of Bible interpreters. David Noel Freedman's comments embody a common disdain for Elihu as

> a comparative youngster, brash at that, who speaks to and at everybody, criticizing the friends for inferior debating but at the same time attacking Job for his behavior. He argues vigorously, brooking neither interruption nor rejoinder. . . . While Elihu is highly critical of all who have preceded him and very scornful in his excessively polite and prolix fashion, he does not add much to the sum of human knowledge. In spite of his insistence on being heard, and his rapid fire, non-stop loquaciousness, he earns the ultimate reward: He is totally ignored.[6]

Others have echoed these same arguments for Elihu's irrelevance: (1) his allegedly pompous self-introduction, (2) his supposed failure to contribute anything new to the debate, and (3) "the most unkindest cut of all"—his total disregard by his peers and by God.[7] Liberals suggest these as evidence that Elihu's character and speeches are not part of the original book of Job but later fabrications interpolated into the text.[8] (Data from the Dead Sea Scrolls erodes this liberal reconstruction of the text of Job.[9]) But this derogatory assessment of Elihu is not limited to liberals. Henry Morris sees Elihu as a braggart spoiling for a theological fight, a tool of Satan, even a false Messiah.[10] Others are equally hard on Elihu.[11]

On the other hand, many are just as convinced that Elihu's personality and message have been completely misunderstood. William Brown calls such attacks on Elihu "nothing less than character assassinations done under the guise of scholarly objectivity."[12] Matthew Henry sees Elihu as "a man of great modesty and humility . . . of great sense and courage."[13] Another writer thinks Elihu's "is the most courteous speech of the debate, and undoubtedly surpasses all the preceding speeches in spiritual grasp."[14] In Elihu, says Elmer Smick, "we find a more balanced theology than that of the [three] counselors" and "a warmer personal response to the greatness of God."[15] Then there are some who seem to have a hard time making up their mind.[16]

What accounts for such diverse opinions of Elihu? In his nineteenth-century classic, *The Argument of the Book of Job Unfolded*, Princeton professor William Henry Green put his finger on the source of the misunderstanding and its solution—the degree of attention and weight we give to the inspired introduction of Elihu's person and to the actual content of Elihu's speech.[17]

KEYS FOR INTERPRETING ELIHU

The Significance of Spirit-Inspired Narrative

The first line of evidence intended to mold our impression of Elihu is the Spirit-inspired introduction of him to the reader through the narrator.

> The narrator's point of view is the perspective through which we observe and evaluate everything connected with the story. . . . In short, the narrator is a device used by authors to shape and guide how the reader responds to the characters and events of the story.

The narrator's presentation includes at least six features that incline the reader to be favorably disposed toward Elihu.[18]

Elihu's introduction by the narrator contains no hint of censure (32:1–5). The narrator reports the reason the three friends had ceased answering Job (32:1), the reason for Elihu's anger with Job (32:2), the reason for Elihu's anger against the three friends (32:3), the reason Elihu had not spoken previously, and why he is compelled to speak now (32:4–5). The narrator's focus on Elihu's *wrath* is addressed below. For now, nothing in the narrative compels us to view Elihu's wrath negatively—as either bluster or annoyance—any more than we should interpret God's wrath negatively (42:7). Nor does wrath preclude other equally motivating concerns and emotions.[19]

The narrator implies that Elihu possesses a correct perception of Job's real problem (32:2). The narrator does not editorialize; he simply explains. He could have conveyed that this was merely Elihu's opinion. He could have written that Elihu "supposed" or "thought" or even "said" that Job "justified himself rather than God." Instead we have a straightforward observation: Elihu was angry with Job "because he justified himself rather than God." The unadorned report carries the authoritative weight of the narrator's "omniscient" and inspired viewpoint.[20] In other words, this is the narrator's reflection of objective reality[21] and not merely Elihu's subjective opinion. The primary confirmation that this diagnosis of Job's problem is correct, however, is the fact that God levels the same charge against Job

(40:8). On this point the narrator and the Lord agree: Elihu was right. Intentionally or not, Job was justifying himself at the expense of God's righteousness.

The narrator describes Elihu's appropriate dissatisfaction with the failure of the other friends (32:3). Elihu was also angry with the three friends for continuing to condemn Job even though they could neither produce a case against him nor answer his arguments. Any sensitive reader shares Elihu's frustration with the three friends on this point. Like the preceding diagnosis, this assessment also bears the stamp of divine corroboration. God, too, was angry with the three friends and their arguments (42:7).

Elihu's introduction by the narrator highlights a unique emotional parallel between Elihu and God (32:2, 3, 5). The narrator accentuates Elihu's anger. Four times he says Elihu's "wrath was kindled." God uses this identical expression to describe His own anger (42:7). This expression is connected to only two persons in the book of Job: Elihu and God. In view of the agreement between God and Elihu on the previous two points, it is arbitrary to assume that Elihu's wrath is a blustering and pretentious caricature of God's wrath. Rather, Elihu's wrath foreshadows God's.

The narrator credits Elihu with an authentic respect for his elders (32:4). It is one thing for Elihu to profess his own respectful reticence (32:6–7, 11–12). Many interpret this self-professed deference as pragmatic and insincere. But the narrator credits him with genuine motives when he explains that Elihu waited to speak "*because* they were elder than he" (32:4). There is no trace of sarcasm when the narrator describes Elihu's deference, and no reason to suspect Elihu's sincerity when he expresses it (32:6–9).

Finally, *Elihu's exemption from God's displeasure (42:7)* has been the subject of imaginative speculation. Some think that God did rebuke Elihu immediately and severely: "Who is this that darkeneth counsel by words without wisdom?" (38:2). If Elihu has merely regurgitated the same arguments as the three friends, why not, "Who are *these* that darken counsel by words without wisdom"? But this exclamatory question (like every other question in the divine interrogation of Job 38–41) is not addressed to Elihu or aimed at any of the friends. "The

Lord answered *Job*" (38:1), not Elihu. Job understands that he alone is the target of the initial rebuke in 38:2 (see 42:3).[22]

Others interpret God's silence regarding Elihu as the ultimate slap in the face. Elihu is not even worth the trouble of a rebuke, let alone a reply. But if Elihu is as arrogant and out-of-line as some believe, is it reasonable that God would so conspicuously exclude him when He rebukes the others (42:7–9)—especially since Elihu's lengthy speeches are the last words ringing in our ears when God appears? In the narrative, Elihu comes out of nowhere and disappears into thin air. But then, so does the theologically significant Melchizedek (Gen. 14:18–20). To extrapolate from Elihu's sudden disappearance that his arguments don't even deserve the breath it would take to correct them is the ultimate argument from silence, and ignores the narrator's candid presentation of him outlined above. "If he is not praised, it is because his contribution is eclipsed by what God himself says; if he is not criticized, it is because he says nothing amiss."[23]

The Significance of Intonation

Earlier in this book, we explored the impact of intonation on interpreting written dialogue. The issue resurfaces in dealing with Elihu. His words (32:6–12, for example) *can* be intoned as the pontifications of a sophist.[24] But do the words themselves demand such an intonation? If we allow our reading of Elihu to be shaped by the narrator and colored by the contextual markers within the text, Elihu's words can be just as believably intoned as the genuine, passionate, righteously indignant words of a respectful but perceptive young man. How do we decide which way to read them?

In chapter 8, we discovered that the answer to that question lies in some objectively verifiable indicators. One of those is the narrator's inspired introduction of the speaker. What picture does the narrator himself paint of the speaker? Another key indicator is the reaction of those who were there. How they respond to the speaker gives us important clues to how they understood him and, therefore, how *we* should intone and interpret his words. In the case of Elihu, however, no one answers him. Job and the three friends are silent. The next speaker is God and echoes some of Elihu's own words. The narrator's description of Elihu's character and the Lord's reiteration of Elihu's words, combined with the content of Elihu's arguments, all support intoning and interpreting Elihu in a far more positive tenor than is often credited to him.[25]

In addition, unless explicit textual evidence suggests otherwise, we must regard Elihu as psychologically sound. Some see Elihu as evasive, disingenuous, even pathologically loquacious. To others he is bizarre and bipolar—saying one thing only to contradict himself later. A few regard him as a megalomaniac who applies terminology to himself that he also applies to God.

Elihu's is a normal, complex, multilayered personality, not a cardboard character. Read Elihu holistically and contextually. Do not assume the face value of any isolated statement, especially not on the basis of how it sounds in a particular English translation. When his words are viewed in the broader light of everything he says, and under the influence of everything the narrator has objectively told us about him, the pompous, plagiarizing, cardboard Elihu collapses. Whatever his weaknesses, Elihu's passion for God is obvious, and his concern to defend God's reputation deserves every benefit of doubt for which there is any textual justification.

The Significance of Elihu's Words

The next chapter unfolds Elihu's discourse in detail. This chapter concentrates on 32:1–5. However, an introduction to Elihu is incomplete without some attention to his speech in Job 32–37. The significance of Elihu's argument lies in its dissimilarity to what the friends argued before him and in its parallels to what God says after him.

Dissimilarities Between Elihu and the Friends. "Except for chapter 33," opines one scholar, Elihu's "speeches merely reiterate the trite dogmas of the friends."[26] To those unsympathetic to Elihu, he is not only pompous but also banal and unoriginal, plagiarizing earlier arguments as his own innovations. One wonders why the Holy Spirit would waste so much coverage on someone so unnecessary. On the contrary, an attentive reading of Elihu's argument reveals conspicuous differences from that of the other three.[27]

First, *Elihu's spirit is markedly different from the others.* If we allow the narrator's depiction of Elihu to govern our opinion, and if we permit Elihu's words to speak for themselves without coloring them in arrogant tones, a distinctive Elihu surfaces.[28] He has *listened* to Job. He is less censorious, less harsh, and more sensitive to Job's difficulties. Dismissing Elihu's compassion for Job (33:1, 5, 32) as disingenuous is unjust and contrary to the textual and contextual indicators. Elihu sustains a level of sympathy with Job that is absent in the later speeches of the other three.

Second, *Elihu's focus is unique*. The three friends were committed to coercing a confession from Job. Not Elihu. In fact, that is why he was angry with the others—they kept condemning Job without being able to convict him on any charges (32:3). Instead, Elihu focuses not on Job's alleged *sins* as the *cause* of his suffering but on Job's *words* in *response* to his suffering (32:12; 33:8ff.; 34:5ff.; 35:2ff.).[29] The friends have their figurative fingers in their ears, ignoring Job's words and insisting that he was suffering because of sinning. Elihu had listened to Job's words and concluded that Job was sinning because of his suffering.[30] Job was no longer responding rightly to his circumstances or to God. Whether or not sin is the cause of Job's suffering, Elihu reasons, it is certainly a result of Job's suffering.[31] This emphasis is evident in several passages of Elihu's speech (33:8–13; 34:5–6; 35:2–3, 14–16; 36:21).

Job and his friends have been at loggerheads. The three friends argue that Job's suffering is consistent with God's justice because he has (obviously) sinned. Job argues that his suffering is contrary to God's justice because he has not sinned. Elihu offers a revolutionary third perspective: *suffering is not necessarily linked to God's justice at all*.[32] God's justice remains intact, therefore, and may not be impugned (34:12).[33] The issue is *man's* justice in responding to inexplicable suffering sent or allowed by a just God. That suffering may not be explicitly "deserved" does not render the suffering itself unjust, nor does it imply that God is unjust for permitting it. These were the errors of Eliphaz, Bildad, Zophar, *and* Job. Elihu is the first one to put his finger on this miscomprehension, redirecting their attention to the immediate problem of Job—not his supposed precalamity sins but his postcalamity words.[34]

Unlike the three friends, Elihu repeatedly quotes, summarizes, and analyzes Job's words—then answers those words directly. His citations of Job can be tracked and charted.[35] He progresses through his speech in a logical, orderly fashion that answers Job point by point.

Elihu's Answers to Job's Complaints[36]

Job's Complaint	Elihu's Citation	Elihu's Answer
23:3–12; 30:25–26 I do not deserve this.	33:8–11	33:12–13 God is the Sovereign.
19:6–7; 27:2 God is treating me unjustly.	34:5–9	34:10–12, 17–20; 35:14–16 Impossible. God is always just.
27:3–6; 31:1–40 I *know* that *I* am righteous.	35:2–3	35:4–8, 13–16; 36:2–3; 37:23 *God* is the righteous one.
19:8ff.; 30:20–23 God has become inexplicably cruel to me.	33:10–11	36:1–12, 22–23; 37:1–24 God is great and always good.

Third, *Elihu speaks with a confidence and passion that distinguish him from the others.* His is not the power of personal opinion. Nor does he reason that "everybody knows this because this is just the way it has always been"—like Eliphaz (4:7–8; 15:17–18), Bildad (8:8–10), and Zophar (20:4–5). Elihu claims an insight and understanding arising from the presence of God's Spirit in him (32:8).[37] Some take this as a claim to direct inspiration—that he is functioning consciously as the divine mouthpiece speaking God's own words.[38] Even if that were the case, why should the suggestion scandalize us? Was David presumptuous when he asserted, "The Spirit of the Lord spake by me, and his word was in my tongue" (2 Sam. 23:2)? Was Solomon guilty of arrogant overconfidence when he claimed that the words he penned in Ecclesiastes were entirely trustworthy and given by God (Eccles. 12:10–11)?[39] Elihu is, after all, an indirect contributor to Scripture. Why should a claim to insight borne of divine inspiration offend anyone who takes seriously the narrator's depiction of him, coupled with the remarkable similarities between his speech and God's? Still, this is probably reading more into Elihu's words than he meant.

Four of Elihu's statements need to be addressed briefly here (32:8, 18; 33:4; 36:2–4); the next chapter revisits them in more detail. (1) In 32:8, Elihu merely notes that wisdom is not the sole possession of the elderly; insight ultimately comes from God alone, and He is no respecter of persons or age. (2) The reference to "the spirit within me" in 32:18 might be a reference either to the Holy Spirit or (more naturally) to his own spirit compelling him to speak. (3) In 33:4, Elihu asserts, confidently and correctly, a direct relationship with the Spirit of God, Who created him and was currently sustaining his life. (4) His words in 36:2–4 appear to come closest to a claim of divine inspiration. He voices his conviction that he is speaking on God's behalf, securing his knowledge "from afar" (that is, from God—something that Eliphaz claimed in relating his vision in Job 4).

The words of 36:4 are the most alarming initially: "one who is perfect in knowledge is with thee." If one carries into this passage a bias against Elihu and assumes that he is describing himself here in virtually the same words he uses to describe God in 37:16, one might conclude that Elihu is a megalomaniac of monumental proportions, if not outright blasphemous.[40] But this is not a realistic reading of human nature generally, nor is it consistent with everything else we know about Elihu from the narrator. If Elihu is *this* theologically schizophrenic, this unstable and audacious, how could we possibly take seriously *anything* that he says?

An alternative understanding of Elihu's words in 36:4 fits the wider data more realistically. If Elihu is describing himself, the words need imply nothing more than his ability as a reliable communicator of divine truth—"a claim to accuracy, not omniscience."[41] It may be that the "one" Elihu is describing in 36:4 is not himself at all, but God—reminding Job that God is present in spite of His silence. That Elihu is referring to God here is supported by the fact that he immediately turns Job's attention to God's character and activity in the next verse, and further reinforced by Elihu's later use of a nearly verbatim phrase to describe God as "perfect in knowledge" (37:16). In his exquisite climax (36:24–37:24), Elihu calls attention to the tangible presence and activity of God in the approaching storm—the storm out of which the silent God finally answers Job.

Similarities Between Elihu and God. Several thematic parallels connect the speeches of Elihu and God. These similarities demonstrate that Elihu is much closer to the divine answer and emphasis than anyone else.[42] Elihu integrates at least five significant motifs that God echoes and expands in His answer to Job (Job 38–41).[43]

Elihu addresses Job's words rather than his alleged actions (32:12–14; 33:8–13; 34:5–9, 31–37; 35:1–4, 13–16). So does God. This emphasis distinguishes Elihu's approach from the answers of the three friends. It also links Elihu's speech with God's answer to Job. God repeatedly calls attention not to Job's actions but to Job's words (38:2–5, 18; 40:2, 7–8). Job gets the message. His confession references the folly of his *words* at least seven times (40:4–5; 42:3).

Elihu criticizes Job's defense of his own righteousness at the expense of God's righteousness (33:8–13; 34:5–12, 17–19, 31–37; 35:2–7). So does God. The three friends initially regarded Job's claims to innocence as a massive oversight on his part; but in the face of Job's firm resolve, they became convinced of a cover-up. Elihu plays no such games. He alone underscores the sober implications of Job's insistence that if *he* is in the right, God must be in the wrong. The Lord, with conspicuous displeasure, levels this very indictment against Job (40:2, 8).

Elihu stresses the glory and incomprehensibility of God in creation (36:22–37:24). So does God. Everyone acknowledges this truth throughout the book, in theory and in passing. But godly as he was, even Job later confesses that his declaration of these truths was little more than creed without comprehension (42:3–6). Yet Elihu dwells on this as a perspective-altering truth to be pondered, a radically relevant reality to which man must submit his spirit if he is to find both wisdom and peace. The last thirty-six verses of Elihu's speech dwell on this theme (see especially 36:22, 24–26, 29; 37:4–5, 14, 22–23). This, again, is a major thrust of God's discourse (e.g., 40:9–14).

Elihu questions Job's knowledge of God's ways in creation (37:14–18). So does God. This is the driving force propelling the Lord's interrogation of Job. God peppers him with some eighty questions on this very point. Elihu's preliminary interrogation is a miniature version of the full-scale interrogative assault Job is about to encounter, the first drops of rain before the hurricane hits. Elihu's charge that Job is speaking "words without knowledge" (34:35; 35:16) becomes God's own opening keynote when He addresses Job (38:2).

Finally, *Elihu hints at the condescending kindness of this sovereign and inscrutable God.* So does God. Because Elihu accents the sobering facets of God's character—His purity and justice, glory and majesty, omniscience and omnipotence—his references to God's benevolence are easily overlooked. He tucks in several gentle reminders that God is not all austere infinitude and unapproachable splendor. He is also compassionate and merciful (36:28, 31; 37:13), correcting and forgiving (33:17–18, 29–30), gracious (33:24–26) and attentive to the needy (34:28; 36:15). God likewise underscores His more intimidating attributes. Yet He, too, sprinkles His verbal offensive with subtle tokens of His tender mercy and compassionate nature (e.g., 38:25–27, 39–41; 39:1–4).

Thematic Similarities Between Elihu and God

Thematic Emphasis	Elihu	God
Emphasizes Job's postsuffering words (response to suffering), not Job's presuffering actions (cause of suffering)	32:12–14 33:8–13 34:5–9, 31–37 35:1–4, 13–16	38:2–5, 18 40:2, 7–8
Rebukes Job's defense of his own righteousness at the expense of God's righteousness	33:8–13 34:5–12, 17–19, 31–37 35:2–7	40:2, 8
Stresses the glory and incomprehensibility of God	36:22–37:24	38:4–38 40:9–14
Questions Job's knowledge of God's ways	37:14–18	38:4–39:30
Underscores God's benevolent awareness and condescending kindness toward His creation	33:17–18, 24–26, 29–30 33:24–26 34:24–26, 28 36:15, 28, 31 37:12–13*	38:25–27,* 39–41 39:1–4

The Literary Function of Elihu

The parallels between the speeches of Elihu and God are not minor or incidental, but determinative for an accurate appraisal of Elihu. He emphasizes the very themes that color God's arguments in correcting Job. His "main themes prepare the way for the central thrusts of the answer that God himself ultimately gives."[44] Taken together with the narrator's Spirit-inspired introduction of Elihu, the striking resemblances between Elihu's speech and Yahweh's answer (38:1) command a respect for Elihu that is too often denied him.

The history of Job is related in the form of a story. Stories have protagonists (God and Job) and antagonists (Satan and Job's three friends). Where does Elihu fit? He really does not qualify as either a protagonist or an antagonist. Elihu occupies a middle ground, sharpening our focus on Job's real problem and transitioning us from the off-base accusations of the friends to the on-target assessment of the Lord.

A third kind of character in stories is called a *foil.* Protagonists are "central characters . . . most indispensable to the plot." Antagonists are "the main adversaries or forces arrayed against central characters." Foils are "characters who heighten the central character by providing a contrast or occasionally a parallel."[45] Who is "the central character" in the book of Job? Job is certainly the central *human* character. God, however, is the One Who began this story. He raises the name of Job to Satan in the first place, setting the chain of events in motion. God is the One Who dominates the discussion between Job and his friends. God is the One Who will end the story. He has the first and last word. The story of God has relevance with or without Job; but the "story of Job" has relevance only as it relates to God. The Lord is the ultimate central character.

Elihu functions as a foil to heighten the central character of God, not primarily by way of contrast but of *parallel*—in the precision of his diagnosis and the perceptiveness of what he emphasizes as most important. Both of these elements of Elihu's speech—diagnosis and emphasis—prepare the way for what God will say with infallible accuracy and unimpeachable authority.[46]

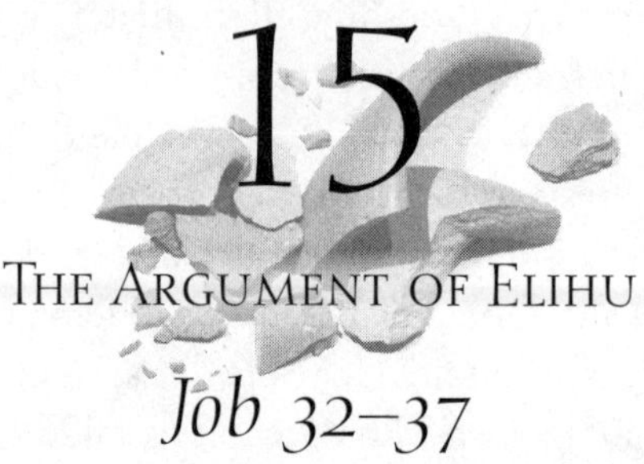

15
The Argument of Elihu
Job 32–37

Have you ever studied the facial expression on Michelangelo's *David*? Only in his late twenties when he sculpted the massive fourteen-foot figure, the master captured in marble "the tense moment of resolution and apprehensiveness as the young David poised his sling for the triumphant blow."[1] Francis Andersen creates an equally evocative verbal snapshot when he notes that the literary image of Elihu in Job 32–37 portrays a "combination of deference and cocksureness that captures the pose of youth that sees a little, but sees it clearly."[2]

After introducing Elihu to the reader (32:1–6), the narrator steps in to note the progression of Elihu's speech on three occasions (34:1; 35:1; 36:1). I have adopted the narrator's division of Elihu's speech into four segments (Job 32–33, 34, 35, 36–37). The first three speeches display a consistent structure: (1) *allegation*—an account of Job's own words or implications, (2) *rebuttal*—a defense of God that answers the implications of Job's words, and (3a) *appeal*—an offer to Job to defend himself, or (3b) *diagnosis*—an assessment of Job's condition based on his words and what they imply about God. The structure of the fourth speech diverges from the first three. (See chart on page 177.)

Along the way, folded into Elihu's speeches, four contextual indicators signal that Elihu's evaluation of Job's problem at key points is correct. These occur in 33:13; 34:17; 34:35; and 35:2. In each case, the Lord Himself will echo Elihu's verdict.

Overview of Elihu's Rhetorical Structure

First Speech: *God Is the Sovereign* (32–33)

Introduction (32:6–33:7)

Allegation: *Job claims to be the victim of unjustifiable affliction from God* (33:8–11).

Rebuttal: *God is sovereign and unaccountable to you and has His own methods and purposes* (33:12–33).

Appeal to Job: *Prosecution rests for any statement from the defendant* (33:31–33).

Second Speech: *God Is Always Just* (34)

Allegation: *Job claims God has denied him justice and fair treatment* (34:1–9).

Rebuttal: *God is unfailingly just and can never pervert justice* (34:10–30).

Diagnosis: *Job wants to dictate his terms to God and multiplies ignorant words against God* (34:31–37).

Third Speech: God Is Transcendently and Infinitely Righteous (35)

Allegation: *Job implies that he is more righteous than God* (35:1–3).

Rebuttal: *God's righteousness is unaffected by human actions and accusations* (35:4–8).

Diagnosis: *Job is speaking empty words without knowledge* (35:9–16).

Fourth Speech: God Is Great and God Is Good (36–37)

Theodicy: *Ascribing righteousness to my Maker* (36:1–12).

Diagnosis: *Job's reaction to God's dealings puts him in danger of the judgment due the wicked* (36:13–21).

Doxology: *Behold how great and majestic and incomprehensible and faithful God is* (36:22–37:18)*!*

Deferral: *The approaching presence of God* (37:19–24).

First Speech: God Is the Sovereign (Job 32–33)

Introduction: Apology and Application (32:6–33:7)

Elihu's opening apology (32:6–14) explains why he is butting in at this point. There is good reason for these protracted formalities.[3] He has clearly heard most of the dialogue but has refrained from speaking in deference to his elders (32:6–7). Meanwhile, his thoughts have been percolating. What compels him to speak is not pride but a persuasion: it is the Spirit of God that imparts insight and understanding, not age or experience alone. Though age ought to be heard and revered, it does not guarantee wisdom (32:8–9).

He offers to fill the role that Job had requested (16:21) and that the friends had failed to supply—that of an arbiter (32:12–14; also 33:5–7).[4] The three friends have not only failed to make their case (32:12*a*, 13) but also neglected to address Job's arguments (32:12*b*). Elihu is removed from the personal rancor of the debate (32:14*a*). For these reasons, he proposes to adopt a fresh approach and different arguments (32:14*b*). Despite some overlap (he shares their basic theology, after all), he achieves his purpose.[5] In what sounds almost like a momentary prayer (32:21), Elihu turns his attention from the three friends in 32:10–14 to Job in 32:15–22 (a shift clearly signaled in 33:1). He desires that his words may not be swayed by intimidation or blunted by flattery (32:21–22). He wants to be fair and frank.

Elihu assures Job that he is speaking sincerely and from an upright heart (33:3).[6] Despite his youth, he is confident that his words have value because he, like his elders, is a fellow creature of the same God that Job serves (33:4). Job has longed for an intermediary whom he need not dread (9:32–35; 13:20–21). Elihu qualifies, for he is flesh like Job (33:5–7). His strategy is sensible yet revolutionary: he interacts thoughtfully with Job's words.

Allegation: Job claims to be the victim of unjustifiable affliction from God (33:8–11).

Elihu rarely quotes Job verbatim. Rather, he cites the gist or summarizes the implications of Job's words from various statements in the dialogue.[7] (For cross-references to Job's own words, see the chart on page 171.) Elihu first exposes an incongruity in Job's position (33:8–11). Job has claimed that, in spite of his innocence (cf. 9:21; 10:7), God has inexplicably found fault with him anyway and treated him as though he were guilty (cf. 13:24–27; 16:9). NASB captures it nicely: "Behold, He invents pretexts against me" (33:10). For all Job's declarations of innocence, Elihu rebuts that on this point at least Job is *not* righteous.

Rebuttal: God is sovereign and unaccountable to you and has His own methods and purposes (33:12–30).

God is the indisputable Sovereign. He does not make such "mistakes" and is not answerable to us even if we think He has (33:12–13). "By this Elihu does not mean to say that greatness provides an excuse for wrongdoing"—might makes right—"but that God may well have some purposes and perspectives in mind of which Job knows nothing."[8]

The first contextual indicator that Elihu's reading of Job's problem is on target appears in 33:13. Elihu interprets Job's words as *contending* (accusing, quarreling) with God. God, too, will rebuke Job for *contending* with Him (40:2).[9] Elihu is the first person in the book to diagnose Job's indiscretion in these terms; the only other is God. If Elihu is wrong, then God is too.

Though God owes man nothing, including accountability, He nevertheless graciously communicates His purposes to man in various ways (33:14). What follows is a glimpse into God's method of self-revelation in pre-Bible days. Remember the remarkable level of theological knowledge displayed by the characters in the book of Job. Knowledge of God can come only by revelation from God. But by what means? In terminology almost identical with Eliphaz's earlier account (compare 33:15 with 4:13), Elihu confirms that in this patriarchal era prior to written revelation, one of the "divers manners" (Heb. 1:1) in which God characteristically revealed Himself and His will was through dreams and visions (33:15–16).[10] This was one means God used to dissuade men from evil and to protect them from judgment (33:17–18). God did this in the case of Abimelech (Gen. 20:1–10) and Laban (Gen. 31:29). Others received divine revelation in this manner as well.[11]

God speaks through revelation (33:15–18), but "God may also speak in the language of pain."[12] Such experiences are designed to correct and discipline people toward purity[13] and save them from judgment ("the pit"). "No trial is so hard to bear as a sense of sin," a Puritan prayer reflects. "If thou shouldst give me choice to live in pleasure and keep my sins, or to have them burnt away with trial, give me sanctified affliction."[14]

In addition to dream-visions and providence, a third means of divine revelation was the sending of a mediator with a message from God, a messenger whom God could use to rescue the submissive man from sin, error, and "the pit" (33:23–28).[15] There seems to be a delicate hint (33:23) of Elihu's mediatorial role here (cf. 32:12; 33:6–7) and a faint echo of 33:27 in Job's confession (42:1–6).

The Pilgrim's Progress alludes to this passage in Job. While at the house of Interpreter, Christian tours a gallery of spiritual images. The first portrait depicts a man with "eyes lifted up to heaven, the best of Books in his hand, the Law of Truth . . . written upon his lips, the World . . . behind his back" who "stood as if he pleaded with men, and a crown of gold did hang over [his] head." When Christian inquires who this is, Interpreter replies: "The man whose picture this is, *is one of a thousand*" (cf. 33:23). Bunyan knew his Bible and understood it. He lifts an inconspicuous phrase out of an obscure passage to paint a picture of the godly preacher as the tool of God's grace (33:24), a messenger and mediator sent by God to turn men away from destruction and the pit (33:26–28). The image should sober and inspire any minister of the gospel.

Note the repeated reference to "the pit" (33:18, 22, 24, 28, 30). God's revelation is gracious and protective in intent (33:17–18, 24–28). He patiently deals with erring men and women over and over again, rather than judging them outright (33:29–30).

Appeal: Prosecution rests for any statement from the defendant (33:31–33).

Elihu invites Job's feedback and pauses for any reply (33:31–33). Job's silence is noteworthy. He has never yet been at a loss for words; he has been by far the most loquacious of the company. The absurdity of an argument never failed to provoke some (often sarcastic) response from Job. If Elihu were merely trotting out old arguments in new garb, as many commentators insist, Job would have been just the one to point that out. Never before has he missed an opportunity like this! It is implausible to suppose that Job is rolling his eyes in silent disdain because Elihu is *so* irrelevant.[16] Twenty-nine chapters of precedent argue that if Job had any impatience, annoyance, or dispute with Elihu's words, he would have spoken up.[17] Elihu has gotten Job's attention.

Second Speech: God Is Always Just (Job 34)

The narrator's note (34:1) marks a second phase in Elihu's argument. After appealing to the others to evaluate what he says (34:2–4), he proceeds to the second stage of his case against Job.

Allegation: Job claims God has denied him justice and fair treatment (34:5–9).

Laying Job's statements of self-defense side by side with his inferences about God makes the contrast starker and more blatant (34:5–6). Some suggest that Elihu is being unfairly selective, citing only those statements that incriminate Job and suit Elihu's purpose.[18] Of course he is! Elihu's objective is to address and correct the *errors* in Job's response to God's dealings with him. Naturally he is going to focus on those statements that cross the line.

The reader understands that Job's statements of righteousness have been couched amid admissions that he is a sinner like everyone else. So does Elihu. Job never claimed sinless perfection, and Elihu is not accusing him of such a claim. Job's assertion of innocence argues only for the absence of any sin that would trigger this kind of retaliation from God. Elihu understands this as well. But Job's insistence that *he* is just insinuates that God is not.

The latter half of Elihu's allegation alarms the attentive reader (34:7–9). This is the first of a trio of potentially problematic charges against Job in Elihu's speech.[19] On the surface it appears that Elihu is accusing Job of companying with the wicked and mocking delight in God as a fruitless endeavor. Either Elihu is seriously misunderstanding Job or *we* are seriously misunderstanding Elihu.[20] I suspect the latter.

Job would never allow such a gross mischaracterization of his position to stand unchallenged and uncorrected. It seems clear that Elihu is not quoting Job but summarizing his words and then analyzing their implications. Elihu finds Job's insistence on his righteousness and insinuation of God's unfairness shockingly *un*righteous. Job has, at points, implied that if the three friends' strict retribution theology is correct, he and God cannot *both* be right. To Elihu, this is equivalent to scorning God (34:7), to walking and talking like the wicked (34:8), and to insinuating that following God is fruitless (34:9).

Elihu may also have in mind a seeming implication of Job's words in 9:27–31—that no matter what Job did to keep his life clean, God was seemingly determined to plunge him into the mire and find him dirty anyway. At least that's how it looked to Job through the retributionist spectacles of his friends' assumption that his suffering was linked to his sinfulness. But Elihu is not lumping Job in with the wicked in the same way that the three did. They argued that Job obviously had *become* one of the wicked and was now suffering the consequences. Elihu argues that Job is *becoming* like the wicked by what he is implying about God.[21]

Rebuttal: God is unfailingly just and can never pervert justice (34:10–30).

To Job's complaint that God has denied him justice, Elihu replies in a word, "Impossible!" God could never condone robbing a man of justice (34:10–11). The Almighty is incapable of injustice (34:12). To suppose that the Sovereign of the world is capricious when it comes to justice would implode the moral structure of the world (34:13–17). How, then, could Job dare even to imply such a thing (34:18)? God rules over all His creatures righteously (34:19–20). God rules over all men omnisciently; He sees (34:21–24), knows (34:25–27), and hears (34:28) all that transpires in His kingdom. And God rules sovereignly; no one can thwart His intentions (34:29–30).

A second contextual indicator that Elihu's interpretation of Job's words and their implications are correct surfaces in 34:17. Elihu challenges Job: *Will you condemn* the *Righteous One*? God echoes this challenge to Job: *Will you condemn* [same word] *Me that you may be righteous* (40:8)?[22] Standing resolutely on his innocence, Job left the issue of God's justice open to question.[23] Elihu is the first to infer that Job's words, however inadvertently, condemn God; the only other to draw this inference is God.

Diagnosis: Job wants to dictate his terms to God and multiplies ignorant words against God (34:31–37).

Elihu interprets Job's words as symptomatic of a desire to get control over his suffering circumstances by dictating his own terms to God (34:31–32). The citation is reminiscent of Job's words in 10:2 and 13:21, 23—language that Elihu interprets as Job's attempt to call for a divine ceasefire. But God is not obliged to order His providences according to our dictates just because we insist that we have learned our lesson (34:33).

Job has spoken out of ignorance and uttered unwise words (34:35). Elihu sounds almost like Zophar (34:36–37; cf. 11:5–6), but there is a crucial distinction. Zophar mocks Job's early assertions that his sin is not responsible for his sufferings; he wants Job ransacked, prosecuted to the fullest extent of the law because he is certain Job is hiding his sin. That is not Elihu's argument. Elihu wants Job "tried to the limit because he answers like wicked men" (NASB)—that is, he implies the kinds of things about God that the wicked say outright. Job's irreverent insinuations add rebellion to his sins by defiantly multiplying his words against God. Elihu has "advanced the discussion by suggesting that Job's greatest sin may not be something he said or did *before* the suffering started, but the rebellion he is displaying *in* the suffering."[24]

A third contextual indicator that Elihu's evaluation is correct appears in 34:35. In language that he will repeat once more (35:16), Elihu charges Job with speaking "words without knowledge." Harsh, perhaps. But this is the very charge with which God opens His interrogation of Job (38:2).[25] God is not throwing those words back at Elihu. Job himself will not allow that reading; he hears 38:2 directed at him alone (42:3). So should we. Elihu is the first to diagnose Job's language in these terms; the only other one who does so is God.

Third Speech: God Is Transcendently and Infinitely Righteous (Job 35)

Allegation: Job implies that he is more righteous than God (35:2–3).

Job has talked a great deal about what is just (*mishpat*).[26] Elihu takes Job on his own terms and challenges him on his own turf.

Does this seem just to you,[27] *that you say, "My righteousness is more than God's"?* (35:2). Job, of course, has never uttered those words; nor would he be likely to. Elihu is again pointing out Job's juxtaposition between his actions and God's actions—leaving the observer to draw his own conclusions.[28] Job's uncompromising insistence on his innocence, Elihu infers, implies that he is more righteous than God.[29] Is this a valid inference for Elihu to draw? The narrator seems to think so, when he relates in nearly identical language that Elihu was incensed with Job "because he *justified* himself *rather* than God" (32:2).[30]

A fourth contextual indicator that Elihu's instincts are on the mark emerges in 35:2. God's identical accusation against Job signals that He heard the same implication in Job's words: "Wilt thou condemn me, that thou mayest be righteous?" (40:8).

The linkage between 35:2 and 3 is a bit problematic.[31] Part of the solution lies in seeing 35:3 as a combination of both indirect and direct discourse—that is, a summary of Job's position (35:3*a*), followed by a summary quotation of Job's words (35:3*b*): *For you ask what advantage it will be to you, when you say things like, "What do I gain from having avoided sin?"*

How does this relate to Job's insinuation of superior righteousness in 35:2? Job's words imply that his righteousness exceeds God's because he has fulfilled his obligations, but God has not. How, then, has it profited Job to avoid sin and fulfill his obligations if God is not going to fulfill *His* obligations by governing the world in a consistently just and moral way? It is not that Job regrets his righteousness or begrudges what he missed by avoiding sin. He loves and prefers and does righteousness because he *is* righteous—not because he assumes he will get more by being righteous. That was the ulterior motive of which Satan accused him. Nevertheless, the expectation in a moral universe that behaviors have consequences is frustrated when those consequences frequently fail to materialize.

Job has wrestled with the inequities of life in a world he honestly believes to be morally governed by a just and all-knowing God. This is especially clear in Job 21.[32] But how *does* one believe in a righteous God, Who judges evil and rewards righteousness, and at the same time explain the surrounding anomaly of suffering saints and successful sinners? Whatever the answer to that question is, Elihu suggests, the implication that God may not be as righteous or as powerful as we thought is not a valid option.

Rebuttal: God's righteousness is unaffected by human actions and accusations (35:4–8).

Elihu has an instant illustration at hand in the height of the clouds over the earth (35:4–5).[33] Man's sin cannot harm God, nor does our righteousness help Him in any way—as though He were dependent upon us for His completeness (35:6–7).[34] That is not to say that God does not care what you do one way or the other; your actions, wicked and righteous, do harm or help others (35:8). God is neither diminished nor enhanced by our actions. But man is. And God responds to that (35:9ff.).

Elihu's answers sound irrelevant only to those for whom such theological truths have become "commonplace."[35] Our deepest problems are not caused by our ignorance of some profound new truth but by our failure to take seriously the most obvious and elemental realities of God. Searching for some as yet undiscovered answer is too often a substitute for not believing and submitting to what we already know. Job does not discover anything "new" in God's answer to him. The fresh impact of the most basic attributes of God—His omnipotence and sovereignty, omniscience and wisdom, justice and benevolence—revitalized his faith and revolutionized his life.

Diagnosis: Job is speaking empty words without knowledge (35:9–16).

Elihu draws a comparison between Job and those who cry out because of oppression. "Job had devoted an entire speech to the subject of God's apparent indifference to his plight (ch. 23) and the plight of all who suffer and are oppressed (ch. 24)."[36] Elihu's clear allusion in 35:14 to Job's frustration with his inability to find God (sentiments Job expressed in 23:2–3, 8–10) confirms that this is the angle of Job's thought that he is addressing.

God, says Elihu, does not answer such cries when they are purely self-centered, suffering-focused, and relief-oriented (35:9); not God-centered, wisdom-focused, and fellowship-oriented (35:10–11);[37] and rooted in presumption or pride (35:12).[38] God is under no obligation to answer such prayers, despite the oppression suffered by those who offer them (35:13).[39] How much less, then, will God regard it when Job complains that he cannot find Him anywhere or see evidence of His presence (35:14*a*)?[40] God may *appear* absent and inactive, but He is just; Job must simply wait on the Sovereign's timetable (35:14*b*). Because God does not deal with sinners according to Job's expectations, and seems to ignore their transgressions (35:15), Job mouths nothings[41] and multiplies words without knowledge (35:16). Again, God will affirm this assessment (38:2).

It speaks highly of Elihu that, in gently chiding the oppressed for seeking comfort rather than the Comforter, he could contribute to the vocabulary of God's people one of the warmest expressions of the benevolence of God: "Where is God my Maker, Who gives songs in the night" (35:10, NKJV).

Fourth Speech: God Is Great and God Is Good (Job 36–37)

The fourth and final movement in Elihu's discourse is marked by 36:1. This speech takes a distinctive turn in structure marked by four divisions: a defense of God, a final diagnosis of Job, a doxology, and a closing deferral to God. Some hear an entirely new tone in Elihu's voice when he comes to the end of this speech.[42] Only those with a low view of Elihu are "pleasantly surprised" by his concluding speech. In reality, it harmonizes seamlessly with the Elihu we have come to know through the content of his earlier speeches.

Defense of God: Ascribe righteousness to my Maker (36:1–15).
Elihu cannot say enough about God (36:2). His passion is to "ascribe righteousness (*tsedeq*) to my Maker" (36:3).[43] He is confident of what he knows (36:4).

Elihu's words here have raised some eyebrows, particularly the assurance that "one perfect in knowledge" was in their midst. But even a jaded critic of Elihu can argue that his words here are "a claim to accuracy, not omniscience."[44] If Elihu is referring to himself in this phrase, the words denote merely his ability as an accurate communicator of divine truth.

It is more likely, however, that the "one" to whom Elihu is referring is not himself but God, reminding Job that God is present even if He is silent. Several factors commend this interpretation. First, Elihu immediately focuses Job's attention on God's character and activity beginning in the next verse (36:5). Second, Elihu later uses a nearly verbatim phrase to describe God as "perfect in knowledge" (37:16). Third, in the colorful climax of his speech (36:24–37:24), Elihu repeatedly calls attention to the immanent presence and tangible activity of God in the approaching storm—the storm out of which God Himself will answer Job. Finally, titles for deity that surface in other ancient texts also support reading 36:4 (like 37:16) as a reference not to Elihu but to God.[45]

The job of the preacher is to direct his hearers' attention away from man and toward God. Elihu models good preaching in this respect. In the next eleven verses, he highlights fifteen verbal or adjectival descriptions of God's activity and character (36:5–15). Then he demonstrates the other task of the preacher—personal application (36:16–21).

God is mighty but merciful, powerful but compassionate (36:5; cf. Isa. 57:15). He does not preserve the wicked but gives justice to the oppressed (36:6).[46] That Elihu nourishes a far-sighted conception of God's justice (in contrast to the three friends' earthbound and shortsighted view) is evident in what follows. God never ignores or overlooks the righteous but exalts them to kingly thrones forever (36:7). If, in the meantime, the righteous (like Job) find themselves fettered by affliction, "or if trouble, like rope, ties them up" (NCV), God unfolds to them what they have done and corrects their pride (36:8–9).[47] He opens their ears (36:15, cf. 33:16) to be instructed by His discipline and commands them to turn (*shub,* "repent") from iniquity.[48] If they respond positively to God's discipline, all will be well; but if not, God will ratchet up the discipline and turn them over to affliction (36:11–12).[49]

The difference between the inwardly righteous and the "impious at heart"[50] is whether they cry out not just *to* God but *for* God in their affliction (36:13). The wicked are abandoned to ignominy but God delivers and instructs the righteous who are poor and oppressed (36:14–15).

Diagnosis: Job's reaction to God's dealings puts him in danger of the judgment due the wicked (36:16–21).

Elihu transitions skillfully from his defense of God to his application to Job. If Job had maintained the humble submission that characterized his initial reaction to his calamity (1:21; 2:10) and had not gotten so caught up in defending his righteousness and diminishing God's by implication, God might already have acted in his behalf (36:16). Even now God is willing to do so, if Job will respond humbly to God's sovereign discipline.[51]

But Job's condition is now virtually indistinguishable from that of the wicked—chastisement looks like judgment to the outsider (36:17).[52] Job is on precarious ground by virtue of his developing reaction to his circumstances (36:18–19). *Be careful what you wish,* warns Elihu, *for you may get it* (36:20). *Beware, do not turn to iniquity, for you have chosen this reaction instead of submitting to God in your affliction* (36:21).[53]

Elihu's final warning and appeal underscore one last time his core concern—not what Job *did* but what Job is *doing*. Elihu refuses to focus on Job's supposed past wickedness and zeroes in on his present iniquity—casting aspersions that undermine the integrity, justice, and goodness of God. The issue is not Job's *ways* but Job's *words*. God will press home to Job's conscience this very point. By then, Job will be ready to respond.

Doxology: Behold how great and majestic and incomprehensible and faithful God is (36:22–37:18)!

Elihu's transition from diagnosis to doxology is seamless. There is no one like God (36:22). Who, then, could dare to insinuate that He has done wrong or ever could (36:23)? At this point Elihu "rises to a more exalted plane, and soars on the wings of doxology."[54]

Remember to magnify God's work (36:24–25). Here is an invitation worth rehearsing regularly, a subject that ought to prompt the saint's soul to sing. Take the time to observe and contemplate the manifestations of God's power and kindness that surround you in creation. Power that He has created such a massive and complex world. Kindness that He has invested so much of His infinite imagination in it, so much beauty and variety to delight the senses, and so much evidence of His wisdom and watch care in sustaining it. All these are thoughts to which Elihu introduces us, and on which God will concentrate Job's attention. God is not only greater than we know; He is greater than we can comprehend (36:26).

Suddenly, "as Elihu speaks, the signs of a gathering storm are seen in the sky, and he breaks into a paean of praise to the greatness of the Creator, whose mysterious ways are manifest in nature" (36:27ff.).[55] It takes little imagination to see the tempest approach while Elihu speaks—a gray sheet of rain falling in the distance (36:27–28), billowing thunderheads (36:29*a*), the grumble of distant thunder mixed with the flash and flicker of lightning (36:29*b*–30). These phenomena of nature, beautiful and awe-inspiring as they are, possess a potential for destruction that becomes a metaphor for God's sovereign control of calamity for discipline and provision (36:31–33). "The one act of God can be destructive and beneficent."[56]

Lightning strikes unexpectedly close and the abrupt explosion startles Elihu (37:1–4).[57] Again, he draws a metaphor from the belly of the storm. The purposes of God are as indecipherable to us as the meaning of God's majestic thundering voice (37:5). God displays not only His power in the storm but also His wise management through the seasons. Take winter, for example (37:6–10).

God demonstrates His sovereignty by the multiplicity of purposes for which He controls the weather (37:11–13). Here Elihu reflects an understanding of the wise and warm-hearted nature of God. These insights are tenderly expressed, not mechanically fabricated from an arrogant or artificial theology; they rise effortlessly and involuntarily from a soul that has contemplated the ways of the Almighty. God fills the clouds with moisture, then dispatches them to perform His pleasure throughout the earth. He may use storms for correction (lit. "a rod"), as he has on many occasions (Gen. 6; Josh. 10:11; Judg. 4–5; 1 Sam. 7:10). Or He may use it simply to water "His world" (NASB) when it needs it (Ps. 104:10–13). Or He may send it purely as a specific expression of his kindness (*chesed*). The NCV is colloquially to the point: "He uses the clouds to punish people or to water his earth and show his love."

God validates Elihu's meditation once again by returning in His monologue to the very points Elihu underscores here. He employs His weather as a "rod" by reserving snow and hail for the time of trouble and the day of battle (38:22–23). And He describes His use of weather for merciful maintenance, causing it to rain even in the unpopulated wilderness where no man will benefit from it (38:25–27).

Once more, Elihu unwittingly sets the stage for God (37:14–18). He launches into a miniature examination (37:14–18) that serves as a prototype for the full-scale interrogation God will launch momentarily (38:3ff.).

Deferral: The presence of God approaches (37:19–24).

How quickly the storm blew in no one can say. Elihu seems to notice it as far back as 36:27. The rest of his speech takes three minutes. That's about how much warning onlookers had in 1888. A roaring noise prompted an instinctive glance northwest where "the sky was suddenly filling and bulging and ripping open. . . . There was scarcely time to exclaim at the unusual appearance" when the most famous blizzard in American history pounced.[58]

The fact that 38:1 refers to "*the* whirlwind" rather than *a* whirlwind implies that the Lord speaks from the same storm they have been watching with growing apprehension. Of the last thirty-four verses of Elihu's speech (36:24–37:24), twenty-four verses are preoccupied with weather—wind and rain, sky and clouds, lightning and thunder.

As this storm roils overhead, Elihu can no longer concentrate to say anything. He is being blown, bowed, pressed into silence (37:19–20). In what appears to be a sudden explosion of lightning or a momentary burst of blinding sun from behind a cloud, God announces His approach (37:21–22).[59] Elihu responds with a similarly spontaneous burst of worship for God's awe-inspiring majesty, incomprehensibility, unparalleled power, and infinite abundance of justice (*mishpat*) and righteousness (*tsedeqah*) (37:23). Men rightly fear Him, for He is perfectly impartial in His treatment of all (37:24).

Several elements of Elihu's storm description parallel the appearance of God in Ezekiel 1:4. Both passages feature an approach from the north, the same Hebrew word for *whirlwind*, massive storm clouds, brightness, a golden hue, and a theophany. "Then the Lord answered Job out of the whirlwind" (38:1). The immediate progression from the end of Elihu's speech to the beginning of God's "suggests that Elihu prepared the way for God, and the voice of God followed in natural sequence with the voice of Elihu."[60]

The Transitional Role of Elihu

Visualize clipping out Elihu altogether from the book of Job. Imagine jumping directly from Job's final, lengthy self-defense into God's dramatic and corrective confrontation with Job. What would we lose? Absolutely nothing, some would have us believe. Is it reasonable that God would waste 165 verses on the hackneyed banalities of an unoriginal blowhard? That's five-and-a-half pages of my wide-margin, straight-text Bible. Elihu's speech occupies the amount of space given to Joel or Micah, Galatians or both Thessalonian Epistles.

Even if Elihu's contributions are minimal, that seems an excessive amount of scriptural real estate to surrender. Nor is it sensible to argue that the narrator was bound to record these "blustering speeches" just "because they happened."[61] The biblical authors were necessarily selective under the direction of the Holy Spirit about what they recorded. What, then, do we gain from the arguments of Elihu? What purpose do they serve? What is their function?

When Job finishes his defense and "ends his words" (31:40), we sense that things are not quite right with Job. But no one has been able to put his finger on Job's problem. The three friends are not even addressing Job's problem; they are fabricating a nonissue. Stuck in their retributionist rut, they will not engage his words and evaluate his arguments.

Elihu shatters the impasse. Job's problem is not what he did before he suffered but what he has been saying since. Elihu's preliminary diagnosis prepares the way for God's infallible diagnosis of Job's disorder and its treatment. Elihu transitions us from the false accusations and flawed arguments of Job's friends to the final word from God.[62] He *might*, like the others, also incorrectly assume that Job is suffering the consequences of his sin (34:11, 31–37). But unlike the others, he concentrates on Job's reaction to what has happened, not on what Job did to deserve it. This is the issue to which the suffering of Job has shifted—not "why has God done this to me?" but "how do I respond to what God has allowed?"

Elihu is on the right track. On at least four occasions God echoes Elihu, using the same language and indicating that Elihu's assessment of Job is on-target. The evidence argues that Elihu deserves to be treated with the dignity accorded him by the biblical text.

Agreement Between Elihu and God on Job

Elihu	God
Why dost thou **strive** against him? (33:13)	Shall he that **contendeth** with the Almighty instruct him? (40:2)
And wilt thou **condemn** him that is most just? (34:17)	Wilt thou **condemn** me . . . ? (40:8)
Job hath **spoken without knowledge**, and his words were without wisdom. (34:35) Therefore doth Job open his mouth in vain; he multiplieth **words without knowledge**. (35:16)	Who is this that darkeneth counsel by **words without knowledge**? (38:2) Who is he that hideth counsel **without knowledge**? Therefore have I uttered that I understood not. . . . (42:3)
Thinkest thou this to be right, that thou saidst, My **righteousness** is more than God's? (35:2)	Wilt thou condemn me that thou mayest be **righteous**? (40:8)

*Bold indicates identical Hebrew terms.

Gleason Archer summarizes Elihu's contribution with high praise:

> His insights prove to be valuable as a critique of both sides of the controversy and as a theological preparation for the speeches of Yahweh. . . . But his most important contribution is that of an advocate for the wise and loving providence of God. In some ways he can be considered as the most acute theologian of them all, and he throws more light upon the central problem of undeserved suffering than any other speaker in the book (except for God Himself, of course).[63]

The central problem of undeserved suffering is not why it happens but what to do with it.

Do You Enjoy Thunderstorms?

I have loved thunderstorms as far back as I can remember. I used to climb a forty-foot pine tree on the edge of a lowcountry marsh to watch the lightning of a summer squall dance over Charleston Harbor in the distance. It was only fitting that my wedding, held in an outdoor chapel perched on the side of a mountain, featured a magnificent electrical storm that struck just minutes before the ceremony was to start. A good thunderstorm always reminds me of my wedding—not my *marriage,* but my wedding.

Not everyone feels that way about storms, though. Nothing so petrified the young Jonathan Edwards as a thunderstorm. After his conversion to Christ, however, he could write that

> scarce any thing, among all the works of nature, was so sweet to me as thunder and lightning; formerly nothing had been so terrible to me. Before, I used to be uncommonly terrified with thunder, and to be struck with terror when I saw a thunderstorm rising; but now, on the contrary, it rejoiced me. I felt God, so to speak, at the first appearance of a thunderstorm; and used to take the opportunity at such times to fix myself in order to view the clouds, and see the lightnings play, and hear the majestic and awful voice of God's thunder, which oftentimes was exceedingly entertaining, leading me to sweet contemplations of my great and glorious God.[64]

Knowing the One Who creates and controls such potentially devastating natural forces makes all the difference in the world. For Edwards, something as simple as watching a storm was transformed into an experience of spontaneous worship. "While thus engaged" in storm watching, "it always seemed natural to me to sing, or chant for my meditations; or, to speak my thoughts in soliloquies with a singing voice."[65]

The next time a thunderstorm rolls in, pull out your Bible and read Job 36:24–37:24. Read it aloud. Read it slowly. If you have children, read it with them. And pause to ponder the storm for what it is intended to be—a part of God's natural revelation of Himself. Like Edwards—like Elihu and Job and his three friends—watch His lightnings play and listen to His majestic voice in the thunder (37:2–4). When you can no more decipher the "meaning" in a roll of thunder than you can deny its rumble, remember the parallel truth that you can no more decipher all the purposes of an infinite God than you can deny His promise that He is in control (37:5ff.). Think about His wise and gracious uses of weather (37:13). Rehearse your ignorance of the workings of natural wonders that are daily deeds for the Almighty (37:14–18). And bow in loving reverence before this tangible display of God's "awesome majesty" (37:19–24). This is not flowery pantheistic imagination. These are not commonplaces. They are biblical realities. And their enjoyment is the birthright of all who know God in truth.

V

Divine Monologue: Job and God

16

Cleaving the Clamor

Job 38–39

When Meriwether Lewis and William Clark embarked on their legendary exploratory journey in 1804, they carried only vague notions of what they would encounter. Their aim was to locate a water route linking East and West, Atlantic and Pacific. Their maps were sketchy. New discoveries beckoned beyond every sunset as they threaded their way west and north along the Missouri River. Then they hit the Rocky Mountains. No waterway would part those peaks. Their bewildering size and scope forced the explorers to reevaluate their plans and revise their maps to reflect reality.

Job 38–41 is the divine continental divide that looms imposingly near the end of the journey of Job and his friends. In the prologue, God initiated the experiences of Job. Throughout the dialogue, God is the central subject of discussion. Now this mountain range of a monologue by the Lord overshadows all that has been said. God started this whole affair, and God will finish it. The monologue reminds us that the book of Job is not ultimately about Job or suffering after all; it is about God and our relationship to Him.

The divine speech divides into two movements, each punctuated by a response from Job. In the first movement (Job 38–39), God challenges Job's knowledge of, control over, and ability to care for creation. The second movement (Job 40–41) rivets Job's attention on just two of God's more impressive creatures, behemoth and leviathan.

God's First Speech (Job 38–39)

Introductory Issues (38:1–3)

The first movement of God's speech is panoramic in scope. Its topics range over the wide world and beyond, from the depths of the sea (38:16) to the stars above (38:31–33), from dawn (38:12–13) to darkness (38:19–20), from the denizens of the earth (39:1–25) to those that aviate overhead (39:26–30), from tending the most vulnerable creatures (38:41–39:4) to equipping the horse for battle (39:19–25) to creating animals stubborn (39:5–8), strong (39:9–12), or stupid (39:13–18).

Behold, He Cometh with Clouds. The Lord answered Job "out of the whirlwind" (38:1; 40:6).

> The clouds, to which Elihu had pointed as covering the light, had grown darker and more threatening, until they overspread the sky. The lightning, the thunder and the tempest, in which the Lord had veiled His awful majesty, had been steadily approaching, and filled all hearts with solemn dread. And now from the bosom of the rushing storm comes forth a voice, the voice of Jehovah . . . speaking unto Job.[1]

Overwhelmed by the approaching storm, Elihu personifies it in terms of God's glorious presence and activity. The thunder is God's majestic voice; shafts of lightning are His servants; weather is a tool in His hand to deal with man and land. This was more than metaphor. It was a theophany and perhaps a Christophany.[2]

Whirlwind is the same term used to recount Elijah's departure into heaven (2 Kings 2:1, 11) and Ezekiel's experience when he saw the Lord (Ezek. 1:4). Job used a form of this word to complain that God was crushing him with a *tempest* (9:17). The same form occurs in Nahum 1:3, "The Lord hath his way in the *whirlwind* and in the storm, and the clouds are the dust of his feet."

I used to think Nahum 1:3 was saying that God *gets* His way in whirlwind and storm—that He is always in control and accomplishes His purposes even when things seem most out of control. The idea of His sovereignty over chaotic circumstances is certainly latent. But an even greater assurance than God's control over chaos is God's personal presence in the midst of chaos.

The word *way* (*derek*) means "road" or "path" and parallels the next phrase, which poeticizes the clouds as God's dust-raising footsteps. The verse reads literally: "In whirlwind and in storm is His way, and clouds are the dust from His feet." The Lord's path is *in* the whirlwind and the storm; and those dark clouds you see surrounding you are merely the dust from His footsteps on that path. The storm is not a sign of God's absence but a sign of His presence. The tempest marks the path He is treading; the dark clouds prove that He is nearby. The dust rising from His footsteps as He paces the path of whirlwind and storm can mean only one thing: He is there. God "gets" His way even in seemingly random circumstances as chaotic and destructive as hurricanes and tornadoes. But this verse goes beyond God's aloof control over the stormy events of our lives; it insures His personal presence in the very midst of them (cf. John 10:4).

Job was not suffering for his sin. But even when believers suffer under the chastening hand of our Father, He tenderly offers Himself as a refuge for His people in the midst of their suffering. "Thus says the Lord God, 'Although I have cast them far off among the Gentiles, and although I have scattered them among the countries, *yet I shall be a little sanctuary for them* in the countries where they have gone'" (Ezek. 11:16, NKJV). If the Lord is that gracious in the midst of disciplining us for our sin, how much more may we count on this in unmerited affliction.

Comfort in distress comes not from principles, but from a Person. The reality of an authentic relationship to a personal God is at the heart of the sufferings and message of Job. Amid tempest and even humiliation, what matters to Job is that God is there and no longer silent.

He Is There and He Is Not Silent. "The Lord answered Job" (38:1). Job had lots of questions for the Lord (e.g., 7:17–21; 10:1–22). An answer from God is exactly what he has been after: "My desire is, that the Almighty would answer me" (31:35) and "I would know [what] he would answer me" (23:5). He has expressed his frustration with God's silence: "I cry unto thee, and thou dost not hear [lit. *answer*] me" (30:20). He even specifically requested that God would arrange a hearing: "Then call thou, and I will answer: or let me speak, and answer thou me" (13:22).[3] That is why every word of 38:1 is pregnant.

The friends have taken their shot at answering Job, but now it is God's turn—"the *Lord* answered Job." For the moment God is concerned with no one else—"the Lord answered *Job*." But in light of all Job's questions, the verb is the most meaningful—"the Lord *answered* Job." He has been silent but not absent. The quotations of Job and Elihu that surface in God's answer show that He has been present and listening all along. Now He answers.[4] He may not explain, but He does answer. And it is enough for Job.

What Do You Know? "Who is this that darkeneth counsel by words without knowledge?" (38:2). The Lord's opening salvo is aimed squarely at Job.[5] God later credits Job with words that are "right" in contrast to those of his three friends (42:7–8), but "this does not mean that all of Job's speeches have been entirely without fault."[6] God explicitly censures Job's speech sins (40:2, 8) and Job confesses them (40:5; 42:3). It should not be surprising, then, that at the outset "God charges Job with darkening His counsel 'with words[7] without knowledge' (38:2)."[8] One writer offers a more "lucid rendering": "Who is this that clouds up my divine plan with ignorant verbiage?"[9]

> Job has spoken as if his innocence gives him direct access to the mind of God and as if his wisdom earns him an explanation from God. His greatest fault, however, is to presume that his own finite mind can comprehend the infinite mind of God. With such presumption, Job has been staggering along the border between limiting God's power and denying His justice. Notably, God does not condemn him for sin. Instead He chides him for throwing up a barrage of empty words about a subject beyond his knowledge.[10]

Job wanted to discuss ethics—issues of right and wrong, innocence and guilt, justice and unfairness—but God has something more basic in mind.

This first movement of God's answer tests what Job knows. The opening verses (38:2–5) reiterate the Hebrew word for *knowledge*. Though camouflaged by translational variety, the noun or verb form occurs in every verse. A more literal rendering of the word bears this out:

- 38:2, "Who is this that darkeneth counsel by words without *knowledge*?"

- 38:3, "Gird up now thy loins like a man; for I will demand of thee, and thou shalt make me *know*."
- 38:4, "Where wast thou when I laid the foundations of the earth? Declare if thou *knowest* understanding."[11]
- 38:5, "Who hath laid the measures thereof, if thou *knowest*, or who hath stretched the line upon it?"

Again, 38:18 makes the point bluntly: "Declare if thou *knowest* it all!" The Hebrew words *knowledge* and *know* appear fifteen times in God's speech.[12] The synonym *understand(ing)* occurs an additional seven times.[13] Job uses both terms to admit that even when he said what was right, he didn't really know what he was talking about (42:2, 3, 4). The Lord's first point is to rebuke Job for speaking on the presumption of knowing all about God's works and ways, of having all the facts at his disposal.

The Question Is Not "Why" but "Who." "Why" is an instinctive question when we are faced with the inexplicable. It is the mark of a thinking soul to ask why, rather than to sit lifelessly on the ash heap of disinterest, feeling nothing, caring nothing. It has been Job's chronic question throughout the book. We are not alone when we ask "why."[14] But answering our "why" is never God's primary concern, nor our chief need.

When God finally speaks, He answers but does not explain to Job why all this happened to him. The irony is, He could have explained. It is not that complicated. We got the explanation in the prologue. But Job never finds out even that much. Those who are frustrated by God's nonexplanatory answer have a fundamental flaw in their thinking:

> They assume that everything that takes place in God's universe *ought* to be explained to us. They assume that God owes us an explanation, that there cannot possibly be any good reason for God not to tell us everything we want to know immediately.[15]

That is the very attitude that God aims to humble out of Job.

Innocent and instinctive as it seems, Job's "why" has become infected like one of his boils. Under the pressure of his friends' persistent accusations and the ferment of time, Job's question ("*Why would* You do *this* to me, God?") festers into a complaint ("*How could* You do this to *me*, God?"). The Hebrew noun (*siach*), consistently translated *complaint* in the King James Version, along with its verb form occurs seven times in the book—always in the mouth of Job.[16]

The Creator's countersuit comes whirling out of the wind in response to the creature's innuendos of injustice. Job complained (23:2) that he could order his case before God and prove his own righteousness, but God would not come to court.[17] The implication is that God is doubly unfair, first for bringing undeserved suffering upon Job and second for avoiding the plaintiff and not allowing Job to present his case. This complaint indicts God's justice. For this complaint Elihu faulted Job. And it is principally this complaint and its implications that provoked God to "answer" Job. This is clearest when God's rebukes are most direct (40:2, 8). Job is not rebuked for asking why. He is rebuked for an honest question that has soured into a complaint laced with insinuation. God reprimands Job for sins of speech and attitude subsequent to his sufferings—speech and attitudes that reflect wrongly on the character of God.

God's answer to Job's question is a counterquestion. Job asks "why." God asks "who." "Who are you" to question God's actions and attributes? "Who am I?"—that is, do you realize just Whom you have been challenging?[18] The juxtaposition between "why" and "who" is echoed by Paul in Romans 9:20. "Shall the thing formed say to him that formed it, '*Why* have you made me like this?' Nay, O man, *who* are you to reply against God? Does not the potter have power [i.e., freedom] over the clay?"[19] God's answer to Job is not an explanation nor a question seeking information. It is a rhetorical question. In reality, it is a declaration.[20]

If God could have explained, and if the reader already knows the explanation, then why did He not let Job in on it? Several feasible reasons suggest themselves. (1) To avert pride. What temptations lie coiled to strike in the heady knowledge that God esteemed him as the most righteous man on earth! Even Paul was prohibited from relating his unique visionary experience to curb his own pride and to prevent others from exalting him too highly (2 Cor. 12:1–9). (2) To negate the assumption that the prologue explains all *our* suffering as well. It is necessary for the reader to know that Job's suffering was undeserved; that is why we have the prologue. But the fact that God did not tell Job what we know preserves the larger issue at stake—submissive trust in what we know the character of God to be even when life looks otherwise.[21] (3) To preclude the presumption that God owes every sufferer an explanation. He did not explain everything to Job in order to make the point that He does not have to explain everything to us. The only appropriate response to our sovereign Savior is submission—not blind, servile submission but trusting, loving submission because He has earned our trust and love by a thousand mercies. "Job needs to learn that the issue is not ethical, the question is not *why*, and the need is not understanding. The issue is spiritual, the question is *who*, and the need is trust."[22]

Is It Science or Poetry? To some, the divine speeches are brilliant poetry uttered "from the ancient point of view, and with the ancient limitations of knowledge."[23] In other words, we must overlook all the scientific blunders in these chapters because it is poetry couched in an antiquated worldview. The doubter argues too much here. Poetry speaks in figures and pictures. No one accuses Joyce Kilmer of scientific ignorance when he described "A tree that looks at God all day, and lifts her leafy arms to pray." If it is poetry, then one is not obligated to take it (or defend it) as a scientifically precise narrative. Those who belittle its alleged scientific inaccuracies must first dismiss its poetic dimensions.

The criticism, therefore, that Job 38:4–6 betrays a prescientific misapprehension of the earth as "a fixed, immovable building, which rests on solid foundations"[24] or that Job's contemporaries thought that lightning bolts reported to God for their striking instructions (38:35),[25] forgets that this is poetry.

Puritan preacher and poet Edward Taylor (1642–1729) was born in England and emigrated to America in 1688. His poetic imagery is unmistakably reminiscent of Job 38.

> Infinity, when all things it beheld
> In nothing, and of nothing all did build,
> Upon what base was fixed the lathe, wherein
> He turned this globe, and riggaled [carved] it so
> trim?
> Who blew the bellows of his furnace vast?
> Or held the mold wherein the world was cast?
> Who laid its corner stone? Or whose command?
> Where stand the pillars upon which it stands?

Who laced and filleted the earth so fine,
With rivers like green rivers smaragdine [emerald]?
. . . .
Who spread its canopy? Or its curtains spun?
Who in this bowling alley bowled the sun?
Who made it always when it rises set
To go at once both down, and up to get?
. . . .
Who? Who did this? Or who is he? Why, know
It's only might almighty this did do.
. . . .
Who spoke all things from nothing, and with ease
Can speak all things to nothing, if he please.[26]

Is it science or poetry? As with Job 38–39, the two are entirely compatible. Taylor clothes a scientifically accurate awareness of cosmological realities in evocative poetic imagery. So does God.

The Divine Examination (38:4–39:30)

Part One: Physical Science (38:4–38). Part one of Job's examination is in the area of geophysics and astrophysics. The Lord questions Job's grasp on cosmology and geology (38:4–7), oceanography (38:8–11), sub-oceanic hydrology (38:16–18), meteorology (38:12–15, 22–30, 34–35, 37–38), spectroscopy (38:19–21, 24*a*), and astronomy (38:31–33). God also poses His questions in a variety of forms. He probes Job's antiquity ("Were you there?"), his knowledge ("Do you know?"), his experience ("Have you?"), and his control ("Can you?").

Into the discussion of such "sterile" scientific topics God folds a tender subtheme. The warmth and intimacy of God's acquaintance even with inanimate aspects of His creation is remarkable. He mentions the musical ecstasy of angelic delight when they witnessed His creation of matter and earth (38:7). He describes the ocean in birth language (38:8–9) and aspects of the weather in terms of conception and delivery (38:28–29). He uses storms to nurture uninhabited areas of His creation, "to cause it to rain on the earth, where no man is; on the wilderness, wherein there is no man; to satisfy the desolate and waste ground; and to cause the bud of the tender herb to spring forth" (38:26–27). Running beneath the surface of this exercise in teaching Job humility is a sweet undercurrent of compassion and benevolence. It is a theme to which He will return.

Part Two: Life Science (38:39–39:30). Part two of Job's examination turns to zoology. The Lord takes Job on a verbal safari—a term well-suited to the original setting of Job, since it derives from the Arabic word for *journey*. The transition is sudden and unannounced, and the previously muted motif of God's compassion now becomes a dominant theme. Note God's emphasis on the young and the helpless. God supplies prey for lions and satisfies their cubs with food (38:39–40). The Creator provides for the raven "when its young cry to God and wander about without food" (38:41, NASB). In one of the most intimate images of the entire passage, the Lord implies that He is aware whenever wild mountain goats labor to give birth and whenever a deer calves (39:1).

God's awareness of His animal creation is not about His technical omniscience of the various gestational cycles that He built into different animals (38:2). Nor is the point that these events are mysteries that Job has never seen. He was a rancher. He knew what it was to manage over eleven thousand head of stock (1:3). He knew all about gestational periods and the birthing process, at least when it came to domesticated animals. Maybe God was making a point about how much went on in the wild world beyond Job's personal experience. Clearly something even more personal is going on here in terms of God's *self*-revelation. The question "do you know?" (39:1) implies that Job doesn't but that God does. He is attentive to such details.

The Lord *takes note* of the labor pains ("they bow themselves"), the birthing process ("they bring forth their young ones"), and the postpartum relief ("they get rid of their labor pains," NASB) of His creatures (39:3). He delights in the healthy growth ("their offspring become strong," NASB), maturity ("they grow up in the open field," NASB), and independence ("they go forth, and return not unto them") of their young (39:4). A major thrust of God's argument lies in the obvious: *these are animals*.

Haven't you ever read all of the emphasis in these chapters on the minute aspects of God's creation and wondered, "What does this have to do with Job's problems? How does this answer Job's questions?" The "seemingly magnificent irrelevance of Yahweh's speeches"[27] radiates a magnificent relevance. By belaboring this point with Job, God unveils one of His divine qualities. The Lord is powerful and majestic and wise beyond man's comprehension, but He is also compassionate . . . *even toward beasts*. He talks as if He has an intimate knowledge of their nature and their needs because He *does*. That's the point.[28]

The Creator cares when wild animals give birth and provides food for lion cubs and raven hatchlings. Don't you think He is intimately aware of your circumstances and compassionate toward you in your need? You are the only creature He has fashioned in His own image (Gen. 1:26–27). You are the only creature qualified to be called the *child* of God. You are infinitely more valuable to God than lions or ravens or goats or deer—or sparrows. Christ makes that very point to His disciples (Matt. 10:29–31).[29] Just how many sparrows do you suppose you are worth? A hundred? A thousand? God didn't suffer and die for sparrows or even angels; but He did for you. We may not always see the signs of God's goodness in our immediate circumstances, but what we see is not all there is. That is a significant part of God's answer to Job.[30]

The Lord proceeds to test Job's knowledge—or display his ignorance—of a series of wild creatures. God paints evocative vignettes of each animal, mixing straightforward description with striking metaphors.[31] In each case, He highlights a unique feature that brings His sovereignty and man's impotence into view. God—not Job—gave the wild donkey the wilderness domain to match its solitary nature (39:5–8),[32] the wild ox its untamable power (39:9–12),[33] the ostrich its comical combination of speed and stupidity (39:13–18),[34] the horse its capacity for fearlessness even in the face of battle (39:19–25),[35] the hawk and eagle their migratory instinct, nesting habits, and keen-sightedness (39:26–30).[36]

God's questions are pointed and purposeful. "*Can you supply* food to feed all the lions? *And who provides* food for the ravens? *Do you know* when deer and mountain goats bear their young? *Who made* wild asses the way they are? Will the wild ox serve *you* or plow *your* furrows? *Have you* given the horse strength? *Has your wisdom* encoded the migratory and nesting instincts in birds or equipped them with such phenomenal eyesight?" The interrogatives are declaratives designed to make several points about God.

- God's generative power implies sustaining power. He providentially sustains and cares for that which He has created.
- God's providential care for creation implies awareness and compassion. He tenderly minds the needs of His creatures.
- God's creative sovereignty implies the rights of ownership. He creates as He sees fit and retains, therefore, absolute rights over His creatures.
- God's inventive diversity implies imagination and skill. He has invested His creatures (both man and beast) with individuality of abilities and circumstances according to His wisdom.

John Piper appeals to Job 38–39, among other passages, to make the point that "God rejoices in the works of creation because they praise him." In

> distant deserts millions of flowers [will] bloom, blush with vivid colors, give off a sweet fragrance and never be touched or seen or smelled by anybody but God! God, it seems, wanted Job to think about this very thing. . . . Creation praises God by simply being what it was created to be in all its incredible variety. And since most of the creation is beyond the awareness of mankind (in the reaches of space, and in the heights of mountains and at the bottom of the sea) it wasn't created merely to serve purposes that have to do with us. It was created for the enjoyment of God. . . . One of the tragedies of growing up is that we get used to things. . . . What a wonderful experience it is when God grants us a moment in which we don't take anything for granted, but see the world as though it was invented yesterday. . . . We should pray for the eyes of children again, when they saw everything for the first time. . . . These are the eyes we need to see the unending wisdom of God running through all the world.[37]

God's verbal safari made a profound impact on Job.[38] But the journey is not over yet.

17

Behemoth and Leviathan

Job 40–41

In a celebrated segment of *The Chronicles of Narnia*, C. S. Lewis has bequeathed to Christian readers one of his most insightful depictions of the nature of God. For any who have not had the pleasure of visiting Narnia, I need only mention that Aslan is the symbolic Christ-figure in a parallel "spiritual" world (populated by animals and mythical creatures) that is, for the moment, under the thumb of a White Witch, who calls herself the Queen of Narnia. Four children unwittingly led into Narnia are seated at supper in the home of Mr. and Mrs. Beaver.

> "Who is Aslan?" asked Susan.
>
> "Aslan?" said Mr. Beaver, "Why don't you know? He's the King. He's the Lord of the whole wood, but not often here, you understand. . . . But the word has reached us that he has come back. He is in Narnia at this moment. He'll settle the White Queen all right. . . ."
>
> "Is—is he a man?" asked Lucy.
>
> "Aslan a man!" said Mr. Beaver sternly. "Certainly not. I tell you he's the King of the wood and the son of the great Emperor-Beyond-the-Sea. Don't you know who is the King of Beasts? Aslan is a lion—*the* Lion, the great Lion."
>
> "Ooh!" said Susan, "I'd thought he was a man. Is he—quite safe? I shall feel rather nervous about meeting a lion."
>
> "That you will, dearie, and no mistake," said Mrs. Beaver, "if there's anyone who can appear before Aslan without their knees knocking, they're either braver than most or else just silly."
>
> "Then he isn't safe?" said Lucy.

> "Safe?" said Mr. Beaver. "Don't you hear what Mrs. Beaver tells you? Who said anything about safe? 'Course he isn't safe. But he's good. He's the King, I tell you."[1]

Not "safe" but good. Job is discovering this firsthand. God is imprinting it deeply on his soul.

Recess (Job 40:1–5)

Restating the Challenge (40:1–2)

In 40:1, the narrator signals a momentary pause.[2] God clarifies the issue at hand. *Will the one contending with the Almighty correct Him Who creates and sustains all these wonders? Let the one who has taken it upon himself to rebuke God answer* (40:2)![3]

> All proves the power of God and the helplessness of man. All proves the wisdom of God and the ignorance of man. The lesson is clear and it is left to Job to take it to heart. If man is so impotent and so ignorant in regard to the world of things he can see and touch, how can he imagine himself fit to sit in judgment on God's moral government of the universe. Here the issues are far more complex and far more difficult to understand.[4]

God uses strong language to characterize Job's behavior. The One Who knows even our unspoken words (Ps. 139:4) interpreted Job's protests to His actions as disputing, faultfinding, correcting, instructing, even rebuking, of all persons, the Almighty!

We need to be careful about intonation. "The question is ironical, of course; but . . . not at all snide."[5] The Sovereign is never insecure or threatened. Supreme authority can afford to express itself quietly (1 Kings 19:11–12).[6] And His original estimation of Job stands (1:8; 2:3; cf. 42:7–10). It is appropriate, therefore, to hear in His words a tone of earnestness bordering on incredulity—*Do you understand what you have been implying and to Whom you have been speaking?*[7]

Job viewed God as his Prosecutor, Who would not explain the reason for His lawsuit against Job. Legal language saturates the book. Confronted by divine silence and provoked by three false witnesses, Job countersues, making God the defendant. But Job has seriously underestimated the firepower—and the terrible benevolence—of this Litigant.

> Job had set himself up arbitrarily as God's accuser. How could Job assume such a lofty position in the light of who God is? After . . . surveying the marvels and mysteries of God's created universe, was Job still ready to make his proud insinuations and accusations about the nature of God's lordship over all things? It was Job's turn to speak again. But there would be no long speeches, no more rage, no more challenging his Creator.[8]

Job Responds (40:3–5)

"Behold, I am vile" (40:4). We use *vile* to describe what is disgusting. The Hebrew term (*qalal*) means to be light, small, of little account. "Insignificant" (NASB) is technically accurate but seems a touch too refined for the occasion. Job's emotion suggests something a little more colorful: *puny, pathetic, worthless, nothing*. The same Hebrew word is frequently translated "curse" (3:1; 24:18) and describes that which deserves to be accursed, that which is *despicable, contemptible*. That is how Job sees himself.[9] He senses how puny he is before God, how despicable his behavior, how contemptible his words. He loathes himself and dares not pollute the air with any more of his talk.[10] "What shall I answer thee? I will lay mine hand upon my mouth" (40:4). He has nothing else to say (40:5), which is a good sign at this point.

> Job had come almost full circle—from hesitation to confront God ("*How then can I answer Him?*" [9:14]) through confidence ("*I will answer*" [13:22*a*]) and a final sweep of assertiveness ("*Like a prince I would approach Him*" [31:37]) to humbled inability to respond.[11]

There is "a time to keep silence and a time to speak" (Eccles. 3:7). In saying little to nothing, Job is saying the right thing for the moment.

Silence is the first stage of true contrition deeply felt. One who gets a glimpse in God's mirror is not inclined to be loquacious. The comfort and courage of the contrite comes from God's assurance that He delights in them (Ps. 51:17) and dwells with them (Isa. 57:15). God is slow to anger and quick to forgive when we respond rightly to His correction. But the Lord is not quite finished.[12] He has made one point; now He will drive it home by making another. It is good that Job says nothing here. But that's not enough. There are still some things that Job *needs* to say.

God's Second Speech (Job 40:6–41:34)

Job 38–39 was a creation-wide panorama of God's power and sovereignty, from planetarium to safari. In Job 40–41, God parks the safari jeep for some close-up observation of two curious creatures. But first, God rehearses His case against Job.

Restating the Case (40:6–14)

God's first indictment against Job was this: *presuming to have sufficient knowledge of the facts to bring God's ways and character into question.* Job concedes—no rebuttal, no self-defense. The Lord now tacks and introduces a new argument against Job: *defending his own righteousness at the expense of God's righteousness.*

"Will you even put me in the wrong? Will you condemn me that you may be in the right?" (40:8, ESV).[13] Elihu introduced this accusation (34:17*b*; 35:2). Here the charge carries the weight of infallible authority. However inadvertently, Job's defense of his righteousness and sense of justice diminished God's by comparison. "But any mortal's alleged superiority to God's justice must be accompanied by a similar superiority of power."[14] So the Lord offers Job a proposition.

If Job feels he is up to it (40:9), then let him array himself in majesty and splendor, put on his glory and beauty (40:10), and express his indignation by humbling the proud and judging the wicked (40:11–13). Then Job will be on a level with the Lord to lend credence to his critique of God's government of the world (40:14).[15] Like the previous rhetorical questions, this is not so much a divine challenge ("If you think you can do better, give it a go!" as my New Zealand friends would say). Still less is it a complaint ("This is harder than you think!") or anything else that would compromise the dignity of God. It is irony designed to remind Job that he is infinitely out of his depth.[16]

Resuming with the Evidence (40:15–41:34)

The Lord directs Job's attention to two created colleagues. There is a divine strategy in this approach. God had just issued a

> challenge to Job to try his hand at world government (40:10–14). . . . Then, to bring home to him, not crushingly but provocatively, vividly, his unfitness to call God to order, he is invited to try his hand on two of his fellow creatures, "which I made as I made you" (40:15).[17]

The Lord takes a distinctive approach in presenting each creature to Job. Introducing behemoth, He says simply, "Observe!" God never asks Job a single question about the behemoth. His introduction of leviathan, however, reopens the interrogation format with some sixteen questions in 41:1–14, before returning to the observation mode of a skilled guide (41:15–34).

Exhibit A: Look at Behemoth! (40:15–24). What was "behemoth"? We don't know. The word behemoth is a Hebrew plural (lit., "beasts"), though the pronouns and verbs that describe this beast are singular. The plural name may have an intensive effect, signaling the animal's mammoth proportions—"a designation of majesty, the brute beast par excellence."[18] The description of behemoth contains a few puzzling features, but nothing especially problematical. This creature is essentially a land animal (it eats grass like an ox, 40:15), but it possesses aquatic features as well (it dwells both by and in the water, 40:21–23). It was a creature with which Job must have been familiar or the point would be drained of impact. The details match what we would expect of a denizen of the river regions from Palestine down to Egypt and into Africa. Numerous suggestions of its identity have been offered: brontosaurus, water buffalo, rhinoceros, hippopotamus, and elephant are among the chief proposals,[19] the last two generally being the most widely preferred.[20]

What it was is not nearly so important as *why* the Lord talks about it. What is the point of God's discussion of this animal? Is He just trying to wow Job with an impressive brute? One point is tucked into 40:15. Like the behemoth, Job is a mere creature. A sense of creative pride and artistic delight pervades God's description of this beast as well. It is a powerful specimen, an impressive marvel of biological engineering. Man is a scrawny weakling by comparison (40:19). In the immediate wake of God's challenge to Job in 40:9–14, it is almost as if God hints that even this brute beast is better equipped to abase the proud and send the wicked fleeing in fear than Job is.

The chief relevance of behemoth, however, is compressed into 40:19.[21] "He is the first [or chief] of the ways of God; only He who made him can bring near His sword" (NKJV). This suggests that behemoth was the largest or most impressive land animal within the circle of Job's knowledge and experience.[22] Whatever it is, behemoth is a massive creature far beyond man's strength and capacities to contain; and yet, powerful and fearful as it is, even this mammoth beast is under the control of the infinitely stronger God Who created him.

Exhibit B: Can You Tame Leviathan? (41:1–34). As with behemoth, curiosity centers immediately on the identity of this denizen of the deep. Difficulties swirl around leviathan like eddies around a submerging alligator. Also like behemoth, leviathan's identity does not suffer from a shortage of suggestions: a marine dinosaur, a whale, a dolphin, a crocodile, and even a mythical seven-headed sea monster named Lotan.[23] The crocodile is far and away the most widely accepted hypothesis. (Problems attached to its description require extended discussion that would be unduly distracting here. Readers interested in an expedition into interpretation will want to see the discussion in the appendix.)

Some of the same observations regarding behemoth apply to leviathan. It must have been a creature known to Job or the impact of the image would be lost on him. Most of the details match a creature of the Palestine-Egypt-Africa rift. The significant literary difference is the extensive attention devoted to leviathan—thirty-four verses as opposed to only ten for behemoth. God intends this impressive creature to furnish a dramatic climax to His speech.[24]

The Lord suspended His interrogation when He drew Job's attention to behemoth but now returns to peppering Job with questions about leviathan. Each question brims with irony as God proposes obviously outrageous scenarios. The preposterous progresses toward sheer lunacy: from capturing this creature with a hook like a fish (41:1–2), to the animal begging Job for mercy (41:3) or becoming Job's servant (41:4), to playing with this beast as though it were a little bird or putting it on a leash as a playmate for little girls (41:5), to divvying it up for dinner with its cooperation (41:6), to taking it single-handedly with multiple spears (41:7).[25]

Of course, a group of men could gang up on leviathan, overcome it with many spears, drag it away with a hook, and carve it up. But that's not the issue. The pronouns in 41:1–8 are not plural but singular (reflected in the KJV as *thou, thee, thy*). This is not about men; this is about a man. This is about Job, and confronting him with just one fellow creature that would make his knees knock. The concluding caution

(41:8) confirms the point: Just try laying your hand on leviathan—you'll remember the battle, and you'll never do it again!

As with behemoth, the primary point is not what this creature is but why God brings it into the discussion. And once again, the significance of this segment of God's speech is folded into the description of the creature. The point surfaces like leviathan—suddenly, without warning, and seemingly out of nowhere (41:9–11). Leviathan is a terrifying animal; the very thought of coming face to face with this beast in the wild is a petrifying prospect (41:9). No man in his right mind would dare disturb or pick a fight with one of these creatures of God (41:10*a*). Who, then, could be so foolish as to think that he could challenge God and stand up against Him (41:10*b*)? Who in his right mind would pick a fight with the Almighty and expect to win? But that's not all. *Who has first given anything to Me that I should be obliged to repay him? Everything under the whole heaven is Mine!* (41:11).

The Lord's declaration drives us back full circle to a truth we confronted early in the book. Job had done nothing to deserve the loss of everything he possessed (2:3). What we often forget is the opposite side of that truth: Job had done absolutely nothing to deserve anything he possessed in the first place. This is so obvious that it is forgettable. Job affirmed it in the face of all his losses (1:21; 2:10). But the Lord takes pains to underscore it dramatically here. Your possessions, your position, your ministry, your children, your health, your breath—*none* of it is yours. You have given God nothing that obligates Him to repay to you anything that you presently possess. What He gives without cause He may remove without cause. "Everything under heaven is Mine," He interjects into His discussion of leviathan. This is so basic, but have we made it even this far in our understanding? We confess it with our mouths. So did Job. Do we grasp it in our souls and live it? That is what affliction tests.

The Lord has made His point. He now proceeds with the description to make the abstract concrete, to clothe the conceptual with flesh and sinew (41:12). Leviathan is unapproachable (41:13), his teeth terrible (41:14), his scales virtually impenetrable (41:15–17), his appearance unearthly and terrifying (41:18–21),[26] his build powerful (41:22–23), his temperament cruel and merciless (41:24), and his sudden presence terrorizing to even the mightiest of men (41:25). You may throw a sword or spear at him from a distance (no one dares approach too near), but it won't do any good (41:26–29). He leaves a deep trail in the mud (41:30), makes the water turbid with his twistings (41:31), and swims so swiftly that his wake looks like white hair (41:32).[27] For personifying fearlessness and instilling fearfulness, he has no match on earth; "he knows no fear, but inspires it" (41:33).[28] He stares down the high and mighty; he is king of all the proud (41:34)![29]

The Defense Rests Its Case

God concludes His case abruptly. No homily. No moral. No final lesson or application. Job doesn't need any. Remember the divine invitation that opened this second speech? If Job has a mighty arm and a thunderous voice like God's, then let him display his majesty and splendor and righteous wrath by humbling the proud and judging the wicked (40:9–14). As it turned out, even behemoth was better equipped than Job to run the world and deal with the wicked. But leviathan is even more so.

God had invited Job, "Deck thyself with *majesty* and *excellency*," (40:10). But leviathan is already decked with these qualities! His scales are his *pride* [same root as *majesty*] (41:15), and he is superior to those who are *high* [same root as *excellency*]" (41:34).[30] The final image of leviathan staring down the high and mighty—"He looks on everything that is high; He is king over all the sons of pride" (41:34, NASB)—echoes God's earlier challenge to Job: "Look on everyone who is proud, and make him low. Look on everyone who is proud, and humble him" (40:11–12, NASB). Leviathan, too, is better equipped than Job to deal with the wicked. Job can't even measure up to two of God's animals, and he wants to challenge God's management of the world?

God closes with words to humble humans who are inclined to file grievances against God. Even this *animal* is stronger than Job and looks down on all those who are proud and demanding. Job cannot stand up to one of God's *beasts*. How can he even dream about standing up to God? Who is Job to critique God's ways and advise God on how He should run things?

> That a discourse which began with the cosmos should end in praise of two aquatic monsters, however fearsome, may strike us as eccentric; and that it should ignore our burning questions altogether may be a bitter disappointment. But there is no mistaking the thrust of it, congenial or not. It cuts us down to size, treating us not as philosophers but as children—limited in mind, puny in body—whose first and fundamental grasp of truth must be to know the difference between our place and God's, and to accept it. We may reflect that if, instead of this, we were offered a defense of our Creator's ways for our approval, it would imply that he was accountable to us, not we to him.[31]

Some have complained that God's reply to Job, though artistically beautiful and poetic, is so irrelevant to Job's problem as to border on absurdity. Oddly enough, it didn't strike Job that way at all. The problem is not with the Lord's answer. Job gets it. Do we?

18

Bowing Before God

Job 42:1–6

"As I look back on that time," writes Elisabeth Elliot, "I think it was Lesson One for me in the school of faith. That is, it was my first experience of having to bow down before that which I could not possibly explain." That lesson came in the Ecuadorian rain forest, but it was not the now-famous story of her husband's murder. It was the murder of her sole translator, Marcario, while she was a young, single missionary. "Usually we need not bow. We can simply ignore the unexplainable because we have other things to occupy our minds. We sweep it under the rug. We evade the questions." Now there were no rugs left, no "other things" to occupy the mind, nothing to distract. Nothing *but* questions, and leisure to turn them over and over. For Elisabeth Elliot, for Job, and for many of God's people since, life slammed to a stop.

> Faith's most severe tests come not when we see nothing, but when we see a stunning array of evidence that seems to prove our faith vain. If God were God, if He were omnipotent, if He had cared, would this have happened? Is this that I face now . . . the reward of my obedience? One turns in disbelief again from the circumstances and looks into the abyss. But in the abyss there is only blackness, no glimmer of light, no answering echo. . . . It was a long time before I came to the realization that it is in our acceptance of what is given [whatever that may be], that God gives Himself. This grief, this sorrow, this total loss that empties my hands and breaks my heart, I may, if I will, accept, and by accepting it, I find in my hands something to offer. And so I give it back to Him, who in mysterious exchange gives Himself to me.[1]

Four thousand years before Elisabeth Elliot, Job bowed before the same God and found that same mysterious exchange.

Drama climbs to a climax, a defining event that opens the door to resolving the story. Job 38:1 announces the arrival of the climax: "Then the Lord answered Job out of the whirlwind." A climax triggers a crisis, a decisive moment that determines the outcome of the story. In athletic contests, unchoreographed and unrehearsed, the outcome frequently pivots on key moments measured in tenths or hundredths of seconds. Job 42:1 announces the arrival of the crisis: "Then Job answered the Lord." Knowing the end of the story needn't dull its impact or our interest. We always relish the endings of our favorite stories. Sometimes new discoveries delight us even in familiar endings. Literature, like history and life itself, is less about events and more about people. Likewise, the book of Job is less about what happened to Job—and why—than it is about Job himself—and God—in the theater of what happened.

Coming face to face with God's might and insight, antiquity and awareness, majesty, sovereignty, and freedom is more than enough to humble Job into the dust, literally (42:6). Any stranger to that dust has not yet seen God for Who He is, however much he may know about Him (42:5). Beneath the Lord's attributes that arouse Job's awe runs an undercurrent of compassion and benevolence—qualities that, once recognized and experienced, awaken love and submission. "For the first time, he sees the God of grace, who is not only just but loving and caring. Job is reconciled with God and ready for healing."[2] This is evident in what he says and in how he says it.

Job's Reponse: Retraction and Repentance

God Is Sovereign and Free (Job 42:2)

Job may sound as if he is admitting God's omnipotence ("I know that thou canst do every thing"). The second line clarifies what he means, however: "no thought can be withholden from thee." Job is not acknowledging God's *power*; no one ever doubted that, least of all Job. Job is finally confessing not God's omnipotence to do anything, but God's sovereignty to do anything He *chooses*, His freedom to do everything He purposes.[3] *I know that You can do all things* (i.e., anything You want); *Your thoughts cannot be thwarted, Your purposes impeded, Your decisions hindered.*[4] Obviously nothing Job says denies God's omnipotence. But it implies God's omnipotence only secondarily. What it spotlights is a truth far greater and even more personal and practical. God not only *can* do anything He chooses (theoretically); He *does* do anything He chooses (actually). God purposes what He pleases and performs what He purposes.

How is Job's confession of God's sovereignty an "answer" to what God has been saying? Three segments of God's second speech constitute the core of His message to Job, where He makes His point most directly and unambiguously. (1) Job is infinitely underequipped to do God's job of dealing with the wicked; a couple of God's *animals*, behemoth and leviathan, are better equipped for this than Job is (40:9–14)! (2) Job cannot control or overcome even a fellow creature, a beast no less; only God can (40:19). Finally, (3) if Job is no match for a mere beast, how can he possibly hope to stand against God (41:10*b*); and with what claim does Job suppose he can obligate God when everything under heaven, including everything Job lost, belongs to Him in the first place (41:11)? "Anyone who cannot undertake God's works has no right to undermine God's ways. And anyone who trembles at the sight of fierce beasts is unwise in boldly contending with the beasts' Maker."[5] That is why Job acknowledges God's undiluted right and ability to do *whatever* He purposes or pleases.

"I know," says Job. Ironic words, since God began by challenging Job's *knowledge* (38:1–5). But they are also theologically weighty words. For Amy Carmichael, missionary to India, "1912 was a year of stripping. The power allotted to the enemy seemed at times far beyond the limits the love of God might set." The first blow came when Amy's spiritual mother in India passed away. Four days after that Lulla, a precious convert saved out of unspeakable horrors as a "temple girl," also died. Just one week later came "the master stroke," the death of stalwart fellow missionary Thomas Walker. In less than two weeks, far from home, Amy Carmichael was stripped of three of her most treasured earthly relations.

> Kind people, wanting to console, made the usual observation: "It is very hard to see how this can be for the best." "We are not asked to

> SEE," said Amy. "Why need we when we KNOW." We know—not the answer to the inevitable Why, but the incontestable fact that it *is* for the best. . . . Others, with a sigh and a shake of the head, observed that it is difficult for us human beings to escape bitterness, even dumb rage, when such things happen. "It is indeed not only difficult, it is impossible," Amy wrote. "There is only one way of victory over the bitterness and rage that come naturally to us—*To will what God wills brings peace.*"[6]

When we *know* God's sovereignty is not only absolute but also benevolent, we no longer need to trouble ourselves with *seeing* why God does what He does. We may ask why as many times as Job asked, but we are not likely to get any more of an explanation than he got. "The only course for man is humbly to acknowledge his own incompetence, to put absolute trust in God knowing that his dispositions, whatever they may be, are wise and just and good."[7]

Listen to Job now and you no longer hear The Question that tumbled time after time from his tongue. "Knowing the answer to the question *who,* Job no longer needs to ask the question *why.*"[8] The answer of God to Job—and Job's response to it—instructs us in the art of reacting to the inexplicable.

> [Job's] suffering is as mysterious as ever, but plain or mysterious, why should it vex him any longer? He has seen God, and has entered into rest. . . . [Once] we know God we can trust Him to the uttermost; we know, incredible though it may seem, that the world's misery does not contradict the love of God.[9]

To *believe* God with or without evidence simply because He has spoken, to *submit* to God with or without understanding because He is both sovereign and good, and to *worship* God with or without reward because He is worthy delivers to the believer a peace that surpasses understanding and baffles unbelievers, instructs angels and glorifies God.

I Spoke in Ignorance, but Now I Know Better (42:3–5)

Job's words here are among the most evocative in the book. God's opening challenge still reverberates in his ears. Job seems to be rehearsing the scene in his mind. He cannot believe what the Lord had to say to him and echoes those words aloud: *You asked,*[10] *"Who is he that hides counsel without knowledge?" Indeed,*[11] *I have spoken what I did not understand, things utterly beyond me of which I had no knowledge* (42:3).

Job does not confess his ignorance but his *speaking* in ignorance. Beware that the authority of your opinions does not exceed your knowledge of the facts. Initially Job was stricken dumb (40:3–5). He was unwilling and unable to say anything. His heart *and* his foot were in his mouth. But he left important things unsaid. Now he is ready to speak and begs permission to do so (42:4*a*).

Again, he reflectively echoes God's words to him: "I will demand of thee and declare thou unto me!" (42:4*b*; cf. 38:3; 40:7). Job's previous theological proclamations sprang from a partial and flawed view of God (42:5). Job contrasts hearing about the Lord secondhand and experiencing the Lord firsthand.[12] The theoretical truth of his own words in 26:14 has come home to him with fresh force.

I Repent and Submit (42:6)

The undercurrent of humility in 42:3–5 finds articulation in 42:6. The verb *abhor* ("despise," NIV, ESV, NKJV mar.) has no object. Most translations supply "myself" (KJV, NKJV, NIV) to give the sense of self-abnegation. That is a possible reading, but not the most likely. The verb (*ma'as*) means "refuse, reject"; but the omission of an object is curious. Both the immediate and larger context (emphasizing Job's uninformed and ill-advised *words*) suggests a meaning that brings closure to the legal battle that began with Job's challenge and culminated in God's answer. Job is "abhorring" his rash and inappropriate *words*. A better rendering would be simply "Therefore I retract [my words]" (NASB).[13] Job is recanting, withdrawing all charges, dropping his case. But that is not all.

"I repent in dust and ashes." This is no admission that the three friends were right after all. The emphatic, nonnegotiable plot of the story remains intact and unaffected: Job was not suffering because of sin. Job's words do, however, convey a tacit admission that God (and, therefore, Elihu) was right: Job had sinned in his response to his suffering. He had contended with God as though He were the One at fault—just like Elihu (33:14) and God (40:2) said. He had condemned God—just like Elihu (34:17) and God (40:8) said. And he had spoken excessively and ignorantly about God—just like Elihu (34:35; 35:16) and God (38:2; 42:3) said.

Job's repentance is coupled with no request. True repentance strikes no bargains and poses no suggestions. Yet Job's restoration does not come at this point (contingent on repenting to his offended God) but in 42:10 (contingent on forgiving his offending friends).

In repentance Job finds resolution and peace. This is remarkable. Nothing has changed, yet Job is content.

> He does not simply resign himself passively to the impossibility of a solution, but yields himself in active reverence to find peace in the living presence of the God he thought he had lost. His restless spirit found rest when he rested in God.[14]

Job's Sin: Retrospect and Review

Folded into God's humbling interrogation is a rebuke for Job's sins of speech subsequent to his suffering. The emphasis on Job's speech punctuates the interrogation, from God's initial confrontation (38:2–3) to God's summary charge (40:2, 8), to Job's response (40:3–5; 42:1–6).

- Job is rebuked for uttering "*words* without knowledge" (38:2).
- Job is challenged to *tell* God what he knows since he has so much understanding (38:4, 18).
- Job is charged with *contending* with the Almighty, *correcting* Him, and *rebuking* God (40:2)—all verbal actions.
- Job is accused of effectively *condemning* God in order to justify himself (40:8)—a verbal action.
- Job confesses, "Behold, I am vile; what shall I *answer* thee? I will *lay mine hand upon my mouth*. Once have I *spoken*; but I will not *answer*: yea, twice [I have spoken]; but I will *proceed* [to speak] no further" (40:3–4).
- Job repents, "Therefore have I *uttered* that I understood not [and *spoken*] things too wonderful for me, which I knew not" (42:3).
- Job retracts his words (42:6*a*).

The fact that God answers Job but does not explain his suffering is what makes "Job's answer so appropriate. He does not say, 'Ah, at last I understand!' but rather, 'I repent.'"[15] Job is not repenting of any sin(s) that provoked his sufferings, for that would undermine the book's thesis. He is repenting for what both Elihu and God accused him—his wrong verbal response to his suffering by calling God's justice into question.

"Wait a minute!" someone objects. "You're telling me that God afflicted Job with all this suffering, without cause (as God Himself admitted in 2:3), and *Job* is the one who has to apologize?" If that is your reaction at this point, you still have not gotten the point. "To those who do not know God, to those who insist on being God, this outcome will never suffice. Those who do know God come in time to recognize that it is better to know God and to trust God than to claim the rights of God."[16]

A Word to the Unconverted . . . and the Converted

For a man of Job's character (remember 1:1, 8; 2:2) to admit the kinds of things he says is stunning. His words humble the holiest among us. They should inspire hope and confidence in the unbelieving sinner as well.

> "*Behold, I am vile*" (Job 40:4). One cheering word, poor lost sinner, for you! You think that you must not come to God because you are vile. Now, there is not a saint living on earth who has not been made to feel that he is vile. If Job, and Isaiah, and Paul were all obliged to say, I am vile, oh, poor sinner, will you be ashamed to join in the same confession? If divine grace does not eradicate all sin from the believer, how do you hope to do it yourself? And if God loves His people while they are yet vile, do you think your vileness will prevent His loving you? Believe on Jesus, outcast of the world's society! Jesus calls *you*, such as you are. . . . Even now say, "You have died for sinners; I am a sinner. Lord Jesus, sprinkle your blood on me"; if you will confess your sin, you shall find pardon. If now, with all your heart, you will say, "I am vile; wash me," you shall be washed *now*. . . . Oh! may the Holy Spirit give you saving faith in Him who receives the vilest.[17]

Who could have a closer relationship to Christ, a firmer or more acceptable standing before God, than His original apostles? But *you* can enjoy the same standing and relationship to God as any of the apostles. And you don't have to become an apostle to have it!

Peter wrote some remarkable things to unremarkable Christians. He addressed them as those who possess an apostolic faith, those who "have obtained like precious faith with us" (2 Pet. 1:1). Literally, they have "obtained a faith of equal value with us," a faith that gives them *equal standing* with the apostles themselves!

Peter chose his words with deliberate care. He did not say that we have "attained" faith. Even in English these two words carry distinctive connotations: *obtain* (to come into possession of) and *attain* (to achieve, accomplish). In Greek, the distinction is even more marked. The verb used here indicates "the receiving of something by lot."[18] When you receive something by lot, you haven't done anything to deserve it or achieve it. In the biblical teaching on lots, you don't even get it by luck, but by providence (Prov. 16:33). It has been granted to you. Faith, therefore, can be obtained but not attained. The Bible teaches that faith is something we are responsible to exercise and yet, at the same time, a capacity graciously granted by God. "Faith, which is necessary for salvation, is a gift . . . from God himself."[19]

The faith that believers "obtain" to believe the gospel that the apostles preached is of equal value with the apostles' own faith. Why? Because the apostles received *their* faith the same way as you! They obtained it too, just like you did. There is nothing "super spiritual" about being an apostle that makes their faith any more valuable or efficacious or saving than your faith. In God's sight, your faith is fully as valuable as Peter's or Paul's or James's or John's—it gives you the same standing before God, a standing equal to that of any apostle, because all of it comes from God in the first place.

By what means have we obtained it? Not through our own righteous works, Peter says, but "through the righteousness of God and our Saviour Jesus Christ." No personal merit is attached to the faith itself or to our having obtained it. This gives the believer incredible comfort and confidence. Indeed, it is our only hope.

Whether a child has intimate and unlimited access to me has nothing to do with how good he is; it depends entirely on whether he is *my* child. And whether *my* child has intimate and unlimited access to me has nothing to do with how good he has been. I do not refuse to see him if he has not faithfully performed all his duties. I may be disappointed with him at the moment, but my *love* and *acceptance* of him is unconditional. He can come to me at any time and find my arms open, not folded, because he is *my* child.

Your standing before God—and therefore your access to Him at any time—never rests on anything you have done; it is neither obtained nor maintained by your personal holiness. Your faithfulness is not what assures God's acceptance of you. Your standing and access rest solely and wholly on the righteousness of God and Christ in your behalf. That is meat and drink for sinner and saint alike.

"Now Mine Eye Seeth Thee": An Afterthought

In his final retraction and repentance, Job acknowledged the sovereignty and freedom of God. In doing so, Job was

> conceding that he did not and could not know the full mystery of the moral universe. Suffering is sometimes a mystery. We must affirm both the mystery and God Himself. The paradox remained, but now, at least, Job knew that it belonged there—that it is built into the moral and physical orders and into the very nature of God as He has permitted humans to perceive Him. . . . The God speeches remind us that *a Person, not a principle*, is Lord.[20]

We have returned to the central issue of *relationship*.[21]

In the previous chapter, I cited John Piper's reflections on the function of creation as an expression of the glory of God. Job has certainly been confronted with this reality. But Piper concludes his discussion with the most important function of the works of creation: "they point us beyond themselves to God himself."

> God means for us to be stunned and awed by his work of creation [as Job was]. But not for its own sake. . . . These are but the backside of his glory, as it were, darkly seen through a glass. What will it be to see the Creator himself! Not his works! A billion galaxies will not satisfy the human soul. God and God alone is the soul's end. Jonathan Edwards expressed it like this:
>
>> The enjoyment of God is the only happiness with which our souls can be satisfied. To go to heaven, fully to enjoy God, is infinitely better than the most pleasant accommodations here. . . . [These] are but shadows; but God is the substance. These are but scattered beams; but God is the sun. These are but streams; but God is the ocean.[22]

The book of Job is not really about suffering after all, is it? At its core, it is about God and you.[23] It is about the relationship between a man, or a woman, or a child, and God—in spite of solace or suffering, on earth and beyond.

The Job in chapter 42 is not the same man we met in chapters 1 and 2. Job grew exponentially that day. We grow the most when we become the smallest. We understand ourselves best and deepest not when we peer within but when we gaze on God and come to see Him more fully as He is. And we can see God as He is only if and when He reveals Himself to us. We possess a divine self-revelation to which Job apparently had no access. God has revealed Himself as He is, to a limited degree but accurately, in the Scriptures. Job 38–41 is one of those self-revelations. The degree to which we will respond as Job did depends upon the degree to which we see and submit to what Job saw. John Newton captured the believer's frustrated experience and its ultimate solution:

> Weak is the effort of my heart,
> And cold my warmest thought;
> But when I see Thee as Thou art,
> I'll praise Thee as I ought.[24]

VI
Epilogue

19 The End of Job

Job 42:7–17

Literature brims with tales that take dark turns yet turn out well. That is no accident. Such tales echo a worldview rooted (consciously or unconsciously) in a biblical truth—the grace of God operating in a fallen world, turning evil to good and bringing life out of death. J. R. R. Tolkien had a word for this: *eucatastrophe* ("good catastrophe"). Tolkien was no armchair philosopher speculating on catastrophe in the abstract. He served in the Somme offensive of World War I, where he contracted trench fever.[1] His later writings note the eucatastrophic thread running through literature, stories that spiral toward defeat and despair before dawn breaks. His own classic tale, *The Lord of the Rings,* epitomizes eucatastrophe. But that is literature. What about life? The experience of Christ is the supreme paradigm of undeserved suffering and, according to Tolkien, "the greatest and most complete conceivable eucatastrophe."[2]

Almost everyone appreciates a happy ending. For some, however, the happy ending of Job "reads like a child's tale," too predictable. The double restoration of all of Job's possessions sounds unrealistic, idealistic, too good to be literally true. The conclusion confirms their suspicions of the author's fabrication for moralistic purposes.[3] Real life simply doesn't turn out this neatly.

Others complain that the ending reinforces the very retribution theology the story has labored to discredit. Job is blessed materially for being good by responding rightly. This complaint is deaf to the very truth that Job voices so loudly: "God does what He pleases

[42:2]. It would be absurd to say that He must keep Job in miserable poverty in order to safeguard the theology."[4] Moreover, Job's final blessings are not "rewards that he has earned by his faithfulness under suffering. The epilogue simply describes the blessings as the Lord's free gift"—*without cause,* you might say, just like everything the Lord had given to Job in the first place.[5]

For still others, the ending engenders false hopes and bad theology. It is a cruel mockery of all the pain and suffering that does *not* end in this life. Those who read the story this way, however, miss its most rudimentary lesson. Still preoccupied with the physical and material, still fixated on the here and now, they fail to connect with Job's preoccupation with the spiritual, the relational, and the eternal.

It is a mistake to suppose that Job is happy now because things have finally changed; they have not, and yet he is. The curtain rises on this final scene to reveal a man still sitting in dust and ashes (42:6)—his wealth has not returned, his body is still racked, his children are still dead. But he is at peace. The Job of chapter 42 does not return to being the Job of chapter 1. He is not the good man, the best of men, that he was. He is better.

Reconciliation (Job 42:7–9)

Following his own repentance and reconciliation, Job is called to one more exercise in self-denial. This also comes before any change in his circumstances. But once you have heard the words of God, really *heard* them, circumstances are not an ultimate concern anymore.

Foreshadowing shades much of the dialogue in the book of Job. Earlier, Job had warned his three friends, "Will it be well with you when he searches you out?" (13:9*a*, ESV). The Lord has examined Job for the last four chapters. Now He turns His attention to Eliphaz, Bildad, and Zophar. Job is reconciled to God, but the friends are not. Nor are they reconciled to Job. Both of those breaches must be mended.

Reconciliation with God

Speaking to Eliphaz (probably the oldest), the Lord describes Himself in language used only of one other person in the book. Like

Elihu, God's "wrath is kindled against" Eliphaz, Bildad, and Zophar (cf. 32:2, 3, 5). Then, God describes Job in language that is as musical to the reader's ear as it was to Job's. "*My servant Job*" has not been heard for forty chapters, since 1:8 and 2:3. Even there it was uttered only in the divine council out of the hearing of men. Now it echoes four times in two verses in the ears of Job's friends. Returning to the label of divine commendation with which the book began makes the point: *God's posture toward Job, and Job's relationship to His Lord, never changed.* Some truths must be believed to be felt.

God's grievance against the three friends focuses on what they have said about Him: "Ye have not *spoken of me* the thing [that] is right, [as] my servant Job hath." This divine evaluation of their speech raises several questions.

We might have expected God to rebuke the friends for speaking falsely against Job, for they certainly did. But that is not the primary concern. It never is with sin. All sin is principally an offense against God (Ps. 51:4).[6]

Even more perplexing is the comparison of their speech with Job's. The Lord had just corrected Job for sins of speech. How can He now turn around and assert that what Job has said about God was right? After all, "was not Job the one who had arraigned His justice? How could God lead Job to repentance and then say that he had spoken the truth?"[7]

The word *right* comes from a verb (*kon*) that means to be firm or reliable. An adjective from this root means "upright" or "honest."[8] Twice God applies this term to Job's words (42:7, 8). By contrast, the Lord describes the friends' speech with the word "folly" (42:8). The term "emphasizes being ignoble, disgraceful, a downright boor"—someone who mouths off when he does not know what he is talking about. Saying things about God that are not true, even if they make God seem "greater," is still wicked in God's eyes (Rom. 3:7). This is part of the offense of Job's friends.

But what does God mean when He says that Job has spoken what is *right* while the friends have engaged in *folly*? Some suggest that Job's speech magnified God more eloquently or sincerely than the three friends,[9] while others credit Job with a higher view of God.[10] These explanations fail to fit the categories God uses. The contrast is not between who exalted God more eloquently, or between a high view of God and a higher view of God. The contrast is absolute: one has said what is *right* while the other is guilty of verbal *folly*. God's correction of Job specifically for his sins of speech creates the difficulty, and the unqualified contrast with his friends' speech amplifies the problem.

Commentators nearly unanimously assume that in labeling Job's speech as right, God is referring to Job's speech at large throughout the dialogues. This requires explaining right in terms of honest or sincere. Some of what Job said was inappropriate, but it was at least a sincere and honest reflection of what was in his heart.[11] Job's friends spoke their speculations with authority, and in so doing had to defy Job's testimony, honest observations about the world around them, and possibly their own consciences. They took up what they presumed to be God's side against Job and ended up misrepresenting both Job and God.[12] Many see in 42:8 a contrast between Job's sincere search (marred by some verbal indiscretions) and the friends' insincere retreat into the supposed security of an unquestioning orthodoxy.[13]

Explaining Job's right speech as his frank sincerity and his friends' verbal folly as intellectual dishonesty or insincerity has much to commend it. Still, God's rebuke and Job's repentance center so explicitly on Job's words and their erroneous depiction of God. That seems hard to reconcile with the blanket commendation that all he spoke of God was right.

The grammar in 42:7–8 may offer an alternative understanding of this puzzling statement. The most natural and grammatically consistent translation of God's rebuke to the friends is that they "have not spoken to Me what is right, as My servant Job has."[14] When did Job finally speak to God what was entirely right and reliable? In 42:1–6. A successive contextual reading suggests that this is the natural implication of God's words.

Frustrated by God's silence and provoked by his friends, Job says some shocking things about God. The Lord rebukes Job extensively for his ignorance and explicitly for his sins of speech against Him and Job repents, confessing and submitting to God's right to do whatever He pleases. When God turns to express his displeasure with the friends' foolish speech in contrast to Job's right speech to Him, the natural contextual conclusion is that He is referring to what Job has just said to and about Him in his repentance and confession. In other words, Job is right with God because he has said what is right to God. The friends are not yet right with God because they haven't.[15]

When God credits Job with speaking what was right, the immediate and obvious reference is to Job's confession in the previous six verses. There Job voices to God "right" truths about Him that his friends' theology had denied. God is free to do whatever He purposes. He is not obligated to answer Job's questions (or ours) without being accused of injustice. He is not obligated to operate according to the friends' theological expectations (or ours). "Their insistence that suffering must always be God's judgment on sin boxed God in; it said, 'God can act only in this way.' And that was not right!"[16] Their tidy theological system provided answers that were as sensible and logical as they were wrong because they were operating on the assumption that they had all the facts about God and His ways at their disposal. They didn't.

The Lord's stipulations for the friends in order to be right with Him push irony to new heights. They would be accepted by God only through the priestly intercession of Job (42:8).[17] This is poetic justice par excellence. The very one whom they were certain was guilty of blatant wickedness (cf. 22:5–11) now becomes their sole link to reconciliation with God. The one they condemned as a sinner whose prayers God could not hear is the only one whose intercession can bring them back into right relationship with God (cf. 22:27).

Job prefigures the reconciling role of Jesus Christ. The One men scorned and rejected as "stricken, smitten of God, and afflicted" (Isa. 53:4) is our sole, God-appointed means of being reconciled to God (1 Tim. 2:5; cf. Job 9:32–33) and has "made intercession for the transgressors" (Isa. 53:12). Like Job's friends, our only hope for reconciliation with God is rooted in our reliance on God's appointed Intercessor for us (John 14:6; Acts 4:10–12). Christ alone is able to save completely and forever those who come to God through Him because He lives on to make intercession for them (Heb. 7:25).

Reconciliation with Man

The Lord directed Job to pray for his friends (42:8). It wasn't an imprecatory prayer either, but an intercessory prayer for God to accept and bless them. There is no better therapy for a wounded or bitter spirit toward those who have wronged you than praying for them. I do not mean praying for God to chasten them, rebuke them, or make them miserable. That is not what Jesus means when He commands to "pray for those who persecute you" (Matt. 5:44) and "for those who mistreat you" (Luke 6:28, NASB). I mean praying *for* them, as Job did, for God to forgive, accept, heal, and bless. Pray through Bible prayers for them (Phil. 1:9–11; Col. 1:9–12; 2 Thess. 1:11–12).

God knew Job needed to pray for his friends as much as they needed him to pray for them. So do we. This command from God "led Job out of the imprisonment of self-preoccupation, and out of the deadlock of invective. Here was no arbitrary demand."[18]

Take a peek at the next verse: "And the Lord turned the captivity of Job, *when he prayed for his friends*" (42:10). Job's restoration came not after getting right with God in 42:6 but after getting right with his friends in 42:10.[19] If Job forgave those who had wronged him, and if God "accepted Job" and forgave them as well, so must we.

God expects no less from us than He did from Job. Pray for those who have wronged you particularly in the context of your suffering. It is the mark of humility, maturity, and Christlikeness.

The first circle of reconciliation is complete: God with Job (signaled by His commendation of Job), Job with friends (signaled by his intercession for them), friends with God (signaled by His acceptance of Job's intercession for them).

Restoration (Job 42:10–17)

"And the Lord turned the captivity of Job" (42:10).[20] Job's family and friends assumed God had deserted him, so they did too (Job 19:13–14). Now they return to celebrate with him, console him, and comfort him concerning all the calamity that God had brought upon him (42:11). We are tempted to despise these fair-weather friends. The final phrase of 42:11 arrests that instinct. They, too, understand now that the Lord had brought all this on Job not because of his sin but because of God's sovereignty and freedom. Each one brought a token of prosperity and well-being, "a tangible expression of their love and support."[21] Now the second circle of reconciliation is complete: Job with God (signaled by his restoration), Job with family (signaled by their mutual reception), family with God (signaled by their new understanding of Him).

"Now the Lord blessed the latter end of Job more than his beginning" (42:12, NKJV). He doubled Job's prosperity (42:10*b*).[22] God wanted no one to miss the fact that He was clearing and vindicating Job.[23] Job's children were not doubled. They are not commodities whose loss can be repaid by any amount of overcompensation. Neither can they be replaced. Anyone who has lost one knows that. They are *succeeded,* in order to increase Job's joy.[24] Blessing is always multiplied by someone else to enjoy it with you. He had again not only the "perfect" number of sons but also three daughters of unparalleled beauty[25] who received the unusual privilege of inheritance (42:15). The book ends (42:16–17) with "an epitaph reserved for the choicest or most favored of God's servants"—"So Job died, old and full of days."[26]

Job-like Suffering Is Christlike Suffering

Francis Andersen describes Job as "an early sketch of the greatest Sufferer." Christ is

> the chief Pilgrim and Pioneer of this way, "a man of sorrows and acquainted with grief" (Is. 53:3).... All the "meanings" of suffering converge on Christ. He entered a domain of suffering reserved for Him alone. No man can bear the sin of another, but Jesus carried the sins of all. As the substitute for all sinners, His sufferings were penal, a bearing of the death penalty for sin. They were also a full and authentic sharing of our human condition.... That the Lord Himself has embraced and absorbed the undeserved consequences of all evil is the final answer to Job and to all the Jobs of humanity. As an innocent sufferer, Job is the companion of God.[27]

So are you when you suffer inexplicably. The furnace of affliction may be transformed into a holy of holies, a sanctuary filled with the presence of the God Whose path is in the storm. Nothing so sanctifies suffering as the knowledge that you are "a partaker of Christ's sufferings" (1 Pet. 4:13) entering into "the fellowship of his sufferings" (Phil. 3:10) to "fill up that which is [lacking] of the sufferings of Christ" (Col. 1:24).

This does not mean that we see ourselves as miniature messianic martyrs. It will be helpful here to return to a point made much earlier in the book. God admitted that Job was suffering "without cause" (2:3). That phrase resurfaces in a poignant messianic prophecy (Ps. 69:4) that Jesus cites in John 15:25—"They hated me *without a cause*." This reference to Christ's suffering focuses on the one event in history that puts our severest suffering into proper perspective—the crucifixion of Christ. "Any thinking about the sufferance of evil, and exposure of the innocent to grief, must take its bearings now from that crucial and seminal event."[28]

The Lord asks no one to suffer more than He has. God did not do to Job—and does not do to us—anything He did not do to Himself in the person of His own Son. He has not made anyone more vulnerable to the unleashed hostility of Satan than the Lamb of God. As devastating as it was, even Job's experience is not the standard by which we gauge the severity of our suffering. As undeserved as it was, Job's experience is not the standard by which we gauge the fairness of our circumstances, either.

But remember, too, that Christ's sufferings had an end and, at the risk of monumental understatement, a *good* end (Heb. 2:9; 1 Pet. 1:11). This good end is more than just a happy ending. The passion (a word that means literally *suffering*) and death of Jesus was the central event in human history, where sin and suffering, evil and catastrophe, are the offsetting dark threads woven into a divine tapestry of astonishing beauty and brightness. Christ's suffering and death were as Tolkien observed, the supreme eucatastrophe.

The End of Job

There is a danger of misconstruing the happy ending of Job. It offers no guarantee that suffering will certainly end in this life as it did for Job (contrary to all his expectations). That misapprehension only salts the wounds of those who endure a life of unrelieved affliction, holding out hope that one day God *must* reverse their suffering because that's what He did for Job.[29] The point of Job 42 is not that there is an end in this life; the point is that *there is an end.*[30]

Satan's whole case, against man and against God, had crashed and burned. Job had clung to God and refused to abandon Him, let alone curse Him. The suffering had served its purpose. Since the accusations that initiated Job's calamities had been demolished, the affliction need not continue.[31] Job's suffering ended when its mission was accomplished.[32]

That thought invites a glance back to the book's beginning. God acknowledged that Job's suffering was without cause, but without *cause* is not the same as without *purpose.* Nothing Job had done caused his suffering, but that does not mean that his suffering was pointless or capricious.[33] Inexplicable is not the same as irrational. Job's suffering was excruciating. Satan's motive was evil. But the Sovereign's initiative and intention behind Job's suffering—and therefore its ultimate outcome—was *good*, in the highest possible sense of that word.

We are back to Tolkien's concept of eucatastrophe. The Bible reverberates with the music of eucatastrophe, modulating from major to minor to major key. God created everything good but the fall of Adam plunged the human race into ruin; yet from the cursed soil of Eden sprouted the Seed of promise (Gen. 1–3). The promising birth of Noah is followed by a flood that engulfed a rebellious world in a watery grave but washed away its sin for a fresh start under the rainbow reminder of God's faithfulness (Gen. 5–9). Joseph, the apple of Jacob's eye and the object of God's great plans, was betrayed by his brothers and sold into slavery but rose as ruler of Egypt to rescue his own betrayers and save the embryo of Israel (Gen. 37–50). A godly man named Job, blessed with unparalleled prosperity by the hand of God, stripped of everything without cause or explanation, lives to hear from the God he would never let go and receives back more than he lost. But the crescendo of the eucatastrophic strain is the Son of God, hanged on a cross, then sealed in a tomb as His followers huddled in hopeless dismay, before the mother of all dawns broke that black night of despair.

Plunged into the blackness of inexplicable catastrophe until the whirlwind of the Almighty blew it all away, Job has his own stanza in the eucatastrophic hymn. What good came out of Job's catastrophe? In the language of Job's confession, God had purposed what He pleased, and performed what He purposed. Job was changed. What he valued more than wealth or health or life itself, his relationship to his God, was exponentially deepened; his understanding of the Lord soared and what he now knew about God was intensely personalized. His friends' aberrant theology, still with us today, was debunked. Satan was not merely defeated but humiliated. Human faith was validated, human worship dignified. The angels were instructed and edified. God was magnified, made large in the eyes of all creation. And the story was preserved for the enlightenment and encouragement of countless generations of readers.

All this good could have grown to such fruition in no other conditions but the providential soil of suffering. "Such providences do not make evil any less evil. But as Tolkien put it in the Silmarillion, 'Evil may yet be good to have been . . . and yet remain evil.'"[34] If this baffles you, that is a good sign. You are learning lessons from the book of Job that we will explore more broadly in the final chapter.

Still, as one writer noted a year after 9/11, "it is hard to speak of the positive results of catastrophic events when people we have loved are dead and landmarks we have known are destroyed."[35] Surely Job felt this keenly. For anyone reading this in the midst of personal pain and loss, the very suggestion of good sprouting from such inexplicably evil soil may sound cruelly trite—as banal as Romans 8:28 from the spectator of another's troubles. But even in the mouth of a moron truth is still truth; the message is reliable in spite of the messenger because it is revelation from God Himself. It is the only reality. You come to see it gradually as you are willing to allow God's viewpoint, reinforced throughout Scripture, to shape your own.

Theology professor Robert Lewis Dabney wrote a classic biography of Stonewall Jackson, a vibrant and unashamed Christian under whose Confederate command Dabney served for a time. In *The Life and Campaigns of Lieutenant General Thomas J. Stonewall Jackson,* Dabney recounts a chaplain's visit after Jackson was severely wounded by friendly fire.

> As he entered and saw the stump where the left arm had lately been, he exclaimed in distress, "Oh, General! What a calamity!" Jackson first thanked him, with his usual courtesy, for his sympathy, and then proceeded, with marked deliberation and emphasis, as though delivering his Christian testimony touching God's dealing with him. . . : "You see me severely wounded, but not depressed; not unhappy. I believe that it has been done according to God's holy will, and I acquiesce entirely in it. You may think it strange; but you never saw me more perfectly contented than I am today; for I am sure that my Heavenly Father designs this affliction for my good. I am perfectly satisfied that either in this life or in that which is to come, I shall discover that what is now regarded as a great calamity, is a blessing. And if it appears a great calamity (as it surely will be a great inconvenience to be deprived of my arm), it will result in a great blessing. I can wait, until God, in his own time, shall make known to me the object he has in thus afflicting me. But why should I not rather rejoice in it as a blessing, and not look on it as a calamity at all? If it were in my power to replace my arm, I would not dare to do it, unless I could know it was the will of my Heavenly Father."[36]

Coming under fire from a brief Northern offensive, the soldiers who first attempted to remove the wounded Jackson from the field dropped the litter carrying him. Jackson later recounted that he assumed at that moment that he would die upon the field of battle:

> It has been a precious experience to me, that I was brought face to face with death, and found all was well. I then learned an important lesson, that one who has been the subject of converting grace and is the child of God can, in the midst of the severest sufferings, fix the thoughts upon God and heavenly things, and derive great comfort and peace; but that one who had never made his peace with God would be unable to control his mind, under such sufferings, so as to understand properly the way of salvation, and repent and believe on Christ. I felt that if I had neglected the salvation of my soul before, it would have been too late then.[37]

On Sunday morning, May 10, 1863, Mrs. Jackson woke her weakened husband. No kin to Job's wife, Mrs. Jackson told him,

> "Do you know the Doctors say you must very soon be in heaven? Do you not feel willing to acquiesce in God's allotment, if he wills you to go today?"
>
> Twice, with difficulty but distinctly, he replied, "I *prefer it.*"

"Well, before this day closes, you will be with the blessed Savior in his glory."

"I will be an infinite gainer to be translated."[38]

Not long after, Jackson "seemed attempting to speak; and at length said audibly: 'Let us pass over the river, and rest under the shade of the trees.' These were the last words he uttered."[39]

Beyond all our suffering there is a sovereign, just, and good God. There is a purpose. There is an end. And there is a reward. Job's voice swells the ancient chorus,

> Finding, following, keeping, struggling,
> Is He sure to bless?
> Saints, apostles, prophets, martyrs
> Answer, "Yes."[40]

20
The End of the Lord

James alludes to the story of Job to illustrate patience amid delay and affliction: "Behold, we count them happy [who] endure. Ye have heard of the patience of Job, and have seen the end of the Lord; that the Lord is very pitiful, and of tender mercy" (James 5:11). Taking for granted that we have seen "the end of the Lord" at the end of Job, James urges us to Job-like perseverance in the face of our own afflictions and delays.[1] His leverage is the character of God, His compassion and mercy especially toward His suffering children.

I have summarized the message of Job regarding our relationship to God in terms of verbs. Believe Him implicitly, with or without proof, because He has spoken. Trust Him submissively, with or without understanding, because He is sovereign and good. Worship Him reverently, with or without reward, because He is worthy. To these James adds one more dimension that blends with the other lessons Job learned: Wait for Him patiently, with or without reprieve, because He will come (see James 5:7–11).[2]

James's reference to "the end of the Lord" invites us to look at the message of Job from the other end. What does "the end of the Lord" at the end of Job teach us about God?

God's Sovereignty

The first great comfort the book of Job offers to steady the child of God even in the worst of inexplicable affliction is this: God is always the One in control of all your circumstances. He Himself claims this role and responsibility for Himself from the outset of the book (2:3). You may experience serious or extended illness, financial devastation, or the loss of loved ones. You may even have been victimized by the sins of others. Heap on top of all that the accusations of acquaintances, the misunderstanding of friends, the desertion of family, and, worst of all, the unresponsive silence of God. Job suffered all of these.

The message of Job is that you are never abandoned to the hand of man or the clutches of Satan. You are in the hand that holds the scepter of the world (Eph. 1:11). He alone grants permission for whatever He does not directly send. What Job understood instinctively and theoretically in the short term (1:21; 2:10) he had to relearn and submit to personally for the long haul (42:1–6). But when God sends what even the Bible calls "evil" ("bad" things in a non-moral sense) or permits us to suffer as the victims of others' evil deeds, doesn't that raise questions about another attribute? Job understood and acknowledged God's sovereignty. But how do we know He is really good?

God's Benevolence

The second great comfort the book of Job offers to sustain us in the midst of devastating circumstances is this: God is always good and benevolent in all He sends or allows. It was here that Job's confidence began to erode most visibly under the relentless drip of accusation and the logical but erroneous assertions of his friends.[3]

Job acknowledged that God was free to do as He pleased (Job 9, for example), but he wanted to know why God was pleased to act this way toward him (Job 10, for example). The silence of God only amplified the verbosity of his friends. Their arguments finally pressed Job into a logical corner. If what they said was true, that God does this kind of thing only to wicked people, then Job was forced to conclude that God had wronged him (19:2–6). Because he could not understand why God would exercise His sovereignty in this way in his life, Job was left questioning God's goodness and, indeed, His justice. That is the very issue on which God later rebuked Job most pointedly (40:2, 8).

We are prone to be governed more by our senses than by our sense, by what we see and hear and feel than by what we know. When what we know (by faith) doesn't match what we see, we tend to gauge reality on the basis of what we see. The repeated testimony of God Himself is that He is not only sovereign and free to do as He pleases but also always good in all that He sends or allows. James echoes these qualities in God's dealings with Job (James 5:11). It takes faith to believe in God's compassion when, to our shortsighted vision and low-altitude vantage point, all the signs indicate otherwise. As John Piper's Job tells his little daughter:

> Beware, Jemimah, God is kind,
> In ways that will not fit your mind.[4]

That kind of faith is not imagined into existence. It is cultivated and nurtured by two activities: reading His words—believing exposure to His revelation, saturation in His self-disclosure, hearing His assurances of Who He is and what He is like (Rom. 10:17); and remembering His works—purposeful reflection on His past actions both in the Bible and in your life where He has proved Himself true to His word (Ps. 105:1–2, 5; 143:5).

As we saw in Job 38–39, God highlights His kindness and compassion in His response to Job. Why does the Lord emphasize His intimate attentiveness to the needs of His animal creation? Is it primarily to make the point that He really cares about animals, or is there a larger intent? Paul raises a similar question in the New Testament. Citing an Old Testament law that cattle used to thresh grain were not to be muzzled while they worked, he asks, "Is it for oxen that God is concerned?" (1 Cor. 9:9, ESV). Or was there a higher design in giving that law? "Surely he says this for us, doesn't he? Yes," Paul concludes, "this was written for us" (1 Cor. 9:10, NIV). Paul's point is not to deny that God cares for animals but to emphasize that He cares for man even more.[5]

God's laws protecting animals and the descriptions of His intimate awareness of their ways and needs (cf. Ps. 104) accentuates His primary concern for man. If He really is this attentive to animals (and He is), how much more He cares for men and women, the only creatures fashioned in His own image! Not even angels are described in those terms. As the only creature made in God's image, you are of infinitely more value to Him than ravens (Job 38:41; Luke 12:24) or goats (Job 39:1–4) or oxen (1 Cor. 9:9–10) or sparrows (Matt. 10:29–31). We may not always see the signs of God's goodness in our immediate circumstances, but what we see is not all there is. Trials are, after all, tests of our *faith* not our sight (James 1). And what we experience in this life is not the end of the story.

God's Reward

That leads to the third great comfort the book of Job offers to support the suffering saint. God will reward the one who perseveres. Job had no clue why he was suffering, but he would not let go of God. He had no hint of the blessing at the end of the tunnel or that the tunnel even had an end, but that only magnifies the tenacity of his faith. The earthly blessings restored to Job were a visible expression of the Lord's invisible approval and spiritual blessings on him. Just as "the Lord blessed the latter end of Job more than his beginning," Scripture assures us that God will bless our latter end infinitely more than our beginning, beyond all experience or power of imagination: "But as it is written, Eye hath not seen, nor ear heard, neither have entered into the heart of man, the things which God hath prepared for them that love Him" (1 Cor. 2:9). To the one who perseveres the Lord promises an abundant entrance into an enduring inheritance (2 Pet. 1:11; 1 Pet. 1:3–5). It has nothing to do with what we deserve. God has bound Himself with an oath.

Job's restored wealth dazzles the imagination. But compared to what awaits the believer in heaven, God's earthly reward to Job was a pale shadow on the walls of this world. That's why we do not lose heart. Our light and momentary pressures produce for us an incomparable and eternal weight of glory. So we focus not on the things that we can see but on the things we cannot see because the things we can see are only temporary, but the things we cannot see are unending (2 Cor. 4:16–18; cf. 1 Pet. 5:10).

Granted, this is all easy enough to peck out in theory on a keyboard. But it is right theory, and right response to troubling circumstances begins with right theory. Biblical actions and reactions begin with biblical thinking.

These truths about God are the theological pillars that support the message of Job. They appear together in microcosm in a careful rendering of James 5:11. "We count those blessed who endured. You have heard of the endurance of Job and have seen the outcome of the Lord's dealings, that the Lord is full of compassion and merciful" (NASB). Perseverance is powered by a settled persuasion of God's sovereignty over all we experience (they are "the Lord's dealings"), God's goodness in all He allows us to experience (He is "full of compassion and merciful"), and God's reward after all He graces us to persevere ("the outcome" points to Job's restoration). The succinct, Spirit-inspired summary of James 5:11

> is the last word on the matter, both in the book of Job and in the New Testament's reflection on it. And that will be the last word in the bigger drama: not that man will demand and get his answers or his imagined rights, but that God will give . . . "such good things as pass man's understanding."[6]

God has not answered in the Bible all our questions about suffering. But there He has said all He needs to say and all we need to hear. One overarching reality He has revealed unambiguously is that this life is not "the end."

To those who believe (2 Pet. 1:1–2) and cultivate the evidences of an authentic faith in their lives (2 Pet. 1:3–10), God promises to furnish an extravagant entrance into His everlasting kingdom (2 Pet. 1:11). Now that's "the end"! And yet, it's not.

Students think of graduation day as an "end," but it takes the more mature perspective of adulthood to understand that it is really only a "commencement," a beginning. We think of death as "the end" of life. It takes the infinite perspective of God Himself to properly designate death for the believer not only as a "falling asleep" (1 Thess. 4:13) but an awakening to an "entrance" ceremony that is, itself, the commencement of real life as we have never known or imagined it. The fabulous entrance extravagantly staged by God will usher us into "the end of the Lord," which is only the beginning. C. S. Lewis captured this image of heaven at the end of *The Last Battle.*

> Aslan turned to them and said: "You do not yet look so happy as I mean you to be."
>
> Lucy said, "We're so afraid of being sent away, Aslan. And you have sent us back into our own world so often."

> "No fear of that," said Aslan. "Have you not guessed?"
> Their hearts leaped and a wild hope rose within them.
> "There was a real railway accident," said Aslan softly. "Your father and mother and all of you are—as you used to call it in the Shadow-Lands—dead. The term is over: the holidays have begun. The dream is ended: this is the morning."
> . . . [B]ut the things that began to happen after that were so great and beautiful that I cannot write them.[7]

Turning Tragedy to Testimony: A Parable

In the meantime, what do we do with our suffering? What use can we make of it? Robert Fulghum relates a true story pregnant with imagery and application for that question.

> Near the village of Gonia on a rocky bay of the island of Crete, sits a Greek Orthodox monastery. Alongside it, on land donated by the monastery, is an institute dedicated to human understanding and peace, and especially rapprochement between Germans and Cretans. An improbable task, given the bitter residue of wartime.
>
> This site is important, because it overlooks the small airstrip at Maleme where Nazi paratroopers invaded Crete and were attacked by peasants wielding kitchen knives and hay scythes. The retribution was terrible. The populations of whole villages were lined up and shot for assaulting Hitler's finest troops. High above the institute is a cemetery with a single cross marking the mass grave of Cretan partisans. And across the bay on yet another hill is the regimented burial ground of the Nazi paratroopers. The mementos are so placed that all might see and never forget. Hate was the only weapon the Cretans had at the end, and it was a weapon many vowed never to give up. Never ever.
>
> Against this heavy curtain of history, in this place where the stone of hatred is hard and thick, the existence of an institute devoted to healing the wounds of war is a fragile paradox. How has it come to be here? The answer is a man. Alexander Papaderos.
>
> A doctor of philosophy, teacher, politician, resident of Athens but a son of this soil. At war's end he came to believe that the Germans and the Cretans had much to give to one another—much to learn from one another. That they had an example to set. For if they could forgive each other and construct a creative relationship, then any people could.

To make a lovely story short, Papaderos succeeded. The institute became a reality—a conference ground on the site of horror—and it was in fact a source of productive interaction between the two countries. . . .

By the time I came to the institute for a summer session, Alexander Papaderos had become a living legend. . . . At the last session on the last morning of a two-week seminar on Greek culture, led by intellectuals and experts in their fields who were recruited by Papaderos from across Greece, Papaderos rose from his chair at the back of the room and walked to the front, where he stood in the bright Greek sunlight of an open window and looked out. We followed his gaze across the bay to the iron cross marking the German cemetery.

He turned. And made the ritual gesture: "Are there any questions?"

Quiet quilted the room. These two weeks had generated enough questions for a lifetime, but for now there was only silence.

"No questions?" Papaderos swept the room with his eyes.

So. I asked.

"Dr. Papaderos, what is the meaning of life?"

The usual laughter followed, and people stirred to go.

Papaderos held up his hand and stilled the room and looked at me for a long time, asking with his eyes if I was serious and seeing from my eyes that I was.

"I will answer your question."

Taking his wallet out of his hip pocket, he fished into a leather billfold and brought out a very small round mirror, about the size of a quarter.

And what he said went like this:

"When I was a small child, during the war, we were very poor and we lived in a remote village. One day, on the road, I found the broken pieces of a mirror. A German motorcycle had been wrecked in that place.

"I tried to find all the pieces and put them together, but it was not possible, so I kept only the largest piece. This one. And by scratching it on a stone I made it round. I began to play with it as a toy and became fascinated by the fact that I could reflect light into dark places where the sun would never shine—in deep holes and crevices and dark closets. It became a game for me to get light into the most inaccessible places I could find.

"I kept the little mirror, and as I went about my growing up, I would take it out in idle moments and continue the challenge of the game.

> As I became a man, I grew to understand that this was not just a child's game but a metaphor for what I might do with my life. I came to understand that I am not the light or the source of light. But light—truth, understanding, knowledge—is there, and it will only shine in many dark places if I reflect it.
>
> "I am a fragment of a mirror whose whole design and shape I do not know. Nevertheless, with what I have I can reflect light into the dark places of this world—into black places in the hearts of men—and change some things in some people. Perhaps others may see and do likewise. This is what I am about. This is the meaning of my life."
>
> And then he took his small mirror and, holding it carefully, caught the bright rays of daylight streaming through the window and reflected them onto my face and onto my hands folded on the desk. . . . [I]n the wallet of my mind I carry a small round mirror still.[8]

To a perceptive summary of truth once offered by a scribe Jesus replied, "Thou art not far from the kingdom of God" (Mark 12:34). The applications of the story above are multiple. I want to focus on one in particular—the mirror fragment salvaged from a disaster that occurred in the midst of nightmarish chaos and turned into a reflector of the light of truth for the help of others in darkness. That is what Job became for his generation. That is what the book of Job has become for uncounted generations after him who read with thought and sympathy. That is what we may, and must, become in our temporary suffering, "our light affliction," for those in our generation—living mirrors, reflecting the enlightening truth of the word, the promise, the presence, the goodness, and the glory of God.

21

Learning Theology with Job

> Everyone has warned me not to tell you what I am going to tell you in this last [chapter]. They all say 'the ordinary reader does not want Theology; give him plain practical religion.' I have rejected their advice. I do not think the ordinary reader is such a fool. . . . Theology is practical (C. S. Lewis, *Mere Christianity*).[1]

Because everyone thinks *something* about God, "everyone is a theologian." That is not to say that everyone reads theology but that everyone should.[2]

> Everyone reads, everyone hears things discussed. Consequently if you do not listen to Theology, that will not mean that you have no ideas about God. It will mean that you have a lot of wrong ones—bad, muddled, out-of-date ideas. For a great many of the ideas about God which are trotted out as novelties today are simply the ones which real Theologians tried centuries ago and rejected.[3]

Postmodernism makes it passé to say, but not all theology is equally valid. Reliable theology is predicated on revelation. It is crucial for our theology to be firmly rooted in the soil of that revelation. To whatever degree our thoughts about God are formulated apart from or in contradiction to an objective source of ideas about God, they are random, subjective, unreliable, and speculative. To the degree that we calibrate our thoughts about God to His self-revelation in the Bible, they will be orderly and consistent, objective and trustworthy. Our habitual speech and actions put our theology, our thoughts about God, on display.

The mistake of some theologians—professional or otherwise—is the assumption that we know, or can know, all there is to know about God. It is a massive misapprehension to suppose that to master God's revelation is to master God. Theology is not about mastering God; it is about being mastered by Him. If Job teaches us anything about theology it is that. But he has a great deal more to teach us. As a theology professor, I am convinced that the book of Job has a unique message for our approach to the knowledge and study of God that we call theology. That is what this final chapter is about.

The Theme of Job: Theology

The book of Job contains a great deal about suffering, spotlighting Job in the context of calamity. But we have discovered that suffering is not the central subject of the book. The dominating theme at every stage of the story is not a principle, a truth, an experience, or even a doctrine, but a Person. God overshadows the prologue—initiating, orchestrating, permitting, restricting. Throughout the dialogue the Almighty is the conversational topic of choice. The divine monologue is the purest self-revelation of the Sovereign. And the Lord dominates the epilogue—rebuking, commanding, accepting, restoring. God is the center of gravity around which every part of the book orbits.

Suffering is merely the catalyst poured into the crucible of life to demonstrate the chemistry of the divine-human relationship. That catalyst generates a spiritual reaction as the suffering percolates and saturates the soul. Questions and thoughts and attitudes—all revolving around God's character and ways and relationship to man and to the world—bubble up to the surface. By definition, a catalyst is not altered by the reaction it initiates. Nothing so clearly demonstrates suffering's catalytic quality as the distinction between the relational reconciliation and the removal of the suffering that takes place at the end of the story.

The Lesson of Job: Theological Humility

If the book of Job is the story of Job, it stands to reason that whatever he comes out understanding in the end, whatever ideas survive and surface at the last, these are the lessons that Job was intended to learn and, in turn, to teach us. How did this process of catalysis change Job? What does he come out confessing that he has learned about himself, about God, and thus about their relationship? Whatever he learned is what we are meant to learn.

- Man's littleness and the contemptibility of speaking rashly to God and about God (40:4)
- God's freedom and sovereignty to purpose what He pleases and to perform what He purposes (42:2)
- Man's ignorance of the vastness of God's ways and works, and the imprudence of advertising that ignorance by unwarranted theological confidence[4] (42:3)
- The supremacy of personal familiarity with God over second-hand hearsay and academic knowledge (42:5)
- The realization that correct theology expresses itself practically in personal humility and submission before God (42:6)
- The importance of forgiving those with well-intentioned but erroneous or ill-applied theology (42:7–11)

All of these lessons are predicated on four chapters of direct verbal revelation from God. And all of them share a common core of theological humility. What impact do Job's insights, and their part in the overall message of Job, have on our personal pursuit of theology?

The Tools of Theology: Revelation and Logic

I have written elsewhere about the healthy tension between revelation and logic.[5] Logic is a tool, a capacity that arises from the image of God in us. All tools have their uses as well as their limits. Logic can lead you into cul-de-sacs or down the wrong roads and still be logical, particularly if logic operates on the assumption that one possesses all the facts. You may know the frustration of watching or reading a whodunit, certain that you have solved the mystery, only to discover that the writer withheld some vital piece of evidence that changes the whole complexion of the case. Your confident deduction, under the circumstances, may be perfectly logical yet dead wrong, simply because you assumed you had all the data when you didn't. This miscalculation surfaces regularly in theology. The dialogues of Job and his friends illustrate the same phenomenon.

H. Wheeler Robinson describes the friends' thinking.

> They are sure that God is righteous and all-powerful; they believe that He is directly concerned with the individual lives of men. It follows that God must punish evil and reward good. So far there is nothing in their argument to which we can object. But they go on to commit a logical fallacy. They say, in effect: All evil-doers are sufferers; Job is a sufferer; therefore Job is an evil-doer. The fallacy lies in supposing that the class of sufferers is exhausted by the class of evil-doers, and that suffering can spring from no other purpose of God than the will to punish evil.[6]

The last phrase pinpoints the larger problem in their thinking—supposing "that suffering can spring from no other purpose of God than the will to punish evil." Their orthodoxy is factual, but the error arises in presuming that their orthodoxy is also comprehensive, that it incorporates *all* the facts—in this case, that because punishment involves suffering, suffering is always indicative of punishment. "God punishes sin with suffering" is an informed orthodoxy. "Suffering means God is punishing sin" is orthodoxy operating logically without adequate data.

Our access to revelation that they did not possess makes it easy to be critical. It may well be that in this early period of human history, apparently prior to written revelation, one of God's means of communicating His opinions and revealing His values was a tighter exercise of judgment on evil and reward for righteousness. Zophar suggests as much (20:4–5). That divine modus operandi was the very handle that Satan latched onto in leveling his charges against Job and God in the first place.

We know through revelation (including the book of Job) that God employs suffering for purposes other than punishment. Apparently their limited revelation did not include that datum. They were judging experience in the light of the revelation they possessed, forcing the square peg of Job's experience into the round hole of their theology. The result was serious friction and frustration on both sides. Their deduction was flawed by a false premise arising from incomplete data. Not all suffering indicates punishment, and not all evildoers suffer God's punishment in time and on earth. In fact, many of them do quite well all their lives—a point of reality that Job was inclined to point out to the annoyance of his friends.

At the same time, Job's efforts to explain his circumstances logically were also marred. The righteous are supposed to be blessed. Isn't that the way it had always worked in Job's experience? Job knows he is righteous yet he is suffering. The only logical conclusion is that God is failing. The assumption that God is *supposed* to bless the righteous fails at the very point at which Job would later be corrected; God is *supposed* to be free to do whatever He pleases. In any case, Job's conclusion may have been logical, given his inaccurate understanding of the nature of God's justice or the extent of His obligations and his inadequate grasp of the facts based on all his previous experience. But it was wrong. This was the essence of God's reprimand of Job: defending his own righteousness *at the expense* of God's justice (40:6–14) and speaking on the presumption of having all the facts at his disposal and knowing all there was to know about God (38:2–4).

It seems likely that in this early pre-Bible era, God communicated His value system by generally blessing the righteous and frequently punishing the wicked. Job's experience shatters the pattern, and he and his friends have diametrically opposite approaches to dealing with it. Though both are logical, both are flawed. And though both come to radically different conclusions ("God is punishing Job for sin" versus "God is mistreating me") they bear certain similarities. One is based on an erroneous assumption regarding God's works; the other is based on an erroneous assumption regarding God's character. Both are paradigms of various theological errors through the centuries. Their debate displays the timeless tension placed on a faith that stands between experience and theology, logic and revelation.

The Nature of Theology: Simplicity *versus* Complexity

Theology in general, and each field in particular (e.g., Christology, soteriology, eschatology), is simultaneously simple and complex—*impossibly* complex, if we speak of resolving issues in a way that is biblical, comprehensive, and universally satisfying. How can something be both simple and complex? By "simple," I mean "user-friendly."

The doctrines of salvation work even for a child, though he hasn't a clue exactly how it works. There is a world of difference between the *simplicity* of gospel truth and the *complexity* of gospel theology.

Modern toy stores market high-tech playthings that a child can use without difficulty, though he has no idea how they work. Adults depend on a host of simple-complex items every day that they rarely understand. (Try explaining to your child, or your spouse, exactly how your microwave works.) When one of these items breaks, we are helpless. We rely on the fact that there *are* people who *do* understand them and can fix them for us when they don't work properly. Most people do not concern themselves with *how* a thing works, only *that* it works.

C. S. Lewis admitted he was not a theologian, but he was an observant thinker. His classic *Mere Christianity* offers the following apologetic for those who dismiss Christianity as too complicated:

> It is no good asking for a simple religion. After all, real things are not simple. They look simple, but they are not. The table I am sitting at looks simple: but ask a scientist to tell you what it is really made of—all about the atoms and how the light waves rebound from them and hit my eye and what they do to the optic nerve and what it does to my brain—and, of course, you find that what we call "seeing a table" lands you in mysteries and complications which you can hardly get to the end of. A child saying a child's prayer looks simple. And if you are content to stop there, well and good. But if you are not—and the modern world usually is not—if you want to go on and ask what is really happening—then you must be prepared for something difficult. If we ask for something more than simplicity, it is silly then to complain that the something more is not simple. . . . When you try to explain the Christian doctrine as it is really held by an instructed adult, they then complain that you are making their heads turn round and that it is all too complicated and that if there really were a God they are sure He would have made religion simple . . . as if "religion" were something God invented, and not His statement to us of certain quite unalterable facts about His own nature.[7]

We are creatures that crave logic, order, symmetry. We like to arrange our knowledge in a logical, orderly, symmetrical fashion. After all, doesn't the fact that we are created in God's image suggest that God, too, is logical and orderly and symmetrical? But Lewis continues: "Besides being complicated, reality, in my experience, is usually odd. It is not neat, not obvious, not what you expect." Once you grasp the basic concept of planetary orbits in a heliocentric system, you might expect the planets to match in size, or in relative distances from each other, or rate of rotation, or number of moons. In fact, "you find no rhyme or reason (that we can see)" in these kinds of details. "Reality, in fact, is usually something you could not have guessed. . . . The problem is not simple and the answer is not going to be simple either."[8] It is worth considering the possibility, especially in the absence of explicit revelation in some areas of theology, that there is a bigger picture of logic and orderliness, a sense and symmetry that is "above" ours or our fallen conceptions.

According to Paul, even "the foolishness of God is wiser than men" (1 Cor. 1:25). Ponder that. What, exactly, is the "foolishness of God"? Does God engage in "foolishness" that is, nevertheless, still wiser than men's way of thinking? What Paul is arguing, of course, is that what men may regard as a "foolish" God, or deem to be "foolishness" on the part of God, is in reality wiser than what men would have God to be or do. Ancient Greeks applauded and approved eloquence and wit, taste and beauty. A plainspoken Jew who came from nowhere and preached that the all-powerful God became mortal and died a criminal's death in order to save wicked men from their sins was as nonsensical to ancient Greeks as it is to most modern Westerners. But the language that Paul uses and the contrast he draws suggest a fundamental disjoint between God's ways and man's, God's thinking and man's, what makes sense to God versus what makes sense to fallen man. It is Paul's echo of Isaiah 55—a New Covenant gospel passage (55:1–7) that asserts the same disjoint between God's ways and man's (55:8) and guarantees the certainty of what He has promised to do, however unlikely it may sound (55:9–13).

The Source of Theology: A Finite Revelation

My understanding of auto mechanics is nearly as limited as my patience with it. I can repair a respectable number of relatively uncomplicated malfunctions. I have changed headlight and blinker bulbs, plugs and wires, belts and hoses, transmission fluid and filters, alternators, water pumps, radiators, brake pads, flat tires, and oil. But when something major malfunctions that I cannot diagnose or that is too complicated for my modest assortment of tools and knowledge, I rely on professionals who are supposed to understand these things.

Preachers and teachers are supposed to be the theological "professionals."[9] My seminary students are training to become the next generation of professionals. God forbid that such a calling should fill any of them with pride or smugness. The calling ought to engender awe, apprehension, and a helpless dependence upon the sole Authority in our field.

The difference between technology and theology is that men have devised the former and therefore possess a nearly complete knowledge of how it works. But man did not invent theology. We are dealing with eternal truths about an infinite Person. Consequently, we are just as limited and finite as everyone else for whom we serve as the "professionals." Scripture is our authoritative "manual" but it is, after all, a limited resource.

Scripture a limited resource? Of course. Your Bible has covers and fits into a relatively modest slot on your bookshelf. I sometimes tell my students that they are certain to ask me questions I cannot answer. "But even if I don't have the answer," I say, setting them up, "the *Bible* has an answer for any question you have, right?" Not necessarily. That may preach well and draw an enthusiastic "amen" but it simply is not true. It's not even biblical. God has put eternity in man's heart (Eccles. 3:11), and you will think of questions that a *finite* revelation *cannot* provide and that a *wise* revelation *has not* provided. Acclimating yourself to that reality will remind you of your limitations and teach you humility, both personally and theologically.

God's revelation furnishes ample evidence to justify faith but also ample opportunity to exercise faith. He has designed it that way. He has not revealed everything there is to know, or everything we'd like to know to answer all our curiosities and iron out all our systems. There is a sense in which part of my goal is to see to it that some students "know" less going out than coming into my courses. I want them to understand enough to temper their cocksureness that they have everything figured out. That is how the Lord sent Job out of His seminary course.

The Subject of Theology: An Infinite God

In our discussion of the Lord's opening speech to Job (38:1–5), I pointed out the emphasis God places on knowledge, Job's lack of it, and the folly of advertising his ignorance by speaking. Though masked by translational variety, some form of the word *know(ledge)* appears in 38:2, 3, 4, and 5. This theme of knowledge and ignorance resurfaces regularly throughout God's speech to Job, both explicitly (38:12, 18, 20, 21, 33; 39:1, 2) as well as implicitly. Job's confession leaves no question as to whether he got the point (42:2, 3, 4). The question I am pursuing in this chapter is, do we?

The interrogation of Job dramatizes the deficiency of our knowledge of God and His ways. Our cornucopia of commentaries, translations, and theologies may lure us into believing that we can systematize God, explain all His past actions, pigeonhole His present doings, and predict His future plans in minute detail. To be sure, the Scriptures embody an essential core of unequivocal truth. Nevertheless, even when we speak truth that is corroborated by clear revelation, we must confess with Job (42:3) that we are speaking about things bigger than we understand, truths beyond our capacity to fully comprehend. We do not know as much as we may think we know, and only an infinitesimal fraction of what there is to know. We would be foolish to suppose that we have at our disposal all the facts about an infinite and eternal God. In fact, it would be unbiblical to suppose that we do.

Chapter 12 introduced us to one of my favorite verses in the book of Job. There Job observes that the things we know about God are "the mere edges of His ways, and how small a whisper we hear of Him! But the thunder of His power who can understand?" (26:14, NKJV). The word *edges* is sometimes used of a coastline. Let me expand on the illustration suggested earlier by this image—exploring the seventeenth-century American continent. Surveying the coastline from your ship would give you only the scantiest conception of what this country was like, and no sense of its vastness or diversity.

Suppose you landed at Charles Towne in 1670 and plowed a mile or two, or ten or twenty, into this country to get a better sense of what it was like. Even after penetrating a hundred miles inland—a task that took decades to accomplish—you would not even have reached as far as the midpoint and current capital of South Carolina, you would have covered only 3 percent of the distance it would take to get to the other edge of this continent, and you would have experienced only a single linear route that would leave you entirely ignorant of the first one hundred miles into Florida or Virginia or Maryland or Maine. Allowing your survey route a one-mile-wide swath, giving you at least some visual experience of one hundred square miles, we could calculate your total "knowledge" of the North American continent (which covers 9,394,000 square miles) at .00001 percent. Impressive.

Let's say, for the sake of argument, that you made it all the way across the three thousand miles to the opposite edge of the continent. Now you *know* America, shore to shore, right? Again, allowing one mile as an average "breadth of experience" for your survey route, you would have gained some degree of familiarity with a grand total of .0003 percent. How exhaustive would your botanical, biological, geological, and meteorological research be along the way? Just how well would you know even that .0003 percent? How many lives would you need to begin to exhaust all there is to know and experience of this fragment of the earth's surface called North America?

Here's the point. Even though you would see and experience and learn a vast amount of valid and verifiable truth about this continent, even though you would know far more about America than the guy who stayed in Charles Towne, your technical diagnosis would still be "massive ignorance." By the way, we are talking about only half of one of seven major continents in a single small world within a universe too big to measure. How much do you think there is to know about the ways and works of the infinite God, Who spoke all this into existence? Even what we know of Him are the mere edges of infinity, the bare boundaries of eternity. God is the infinite and unexplored Continent—Paul would say the "unsearchable" continent (Rom. 11:33). His Word is the map that only outlines—accurately, yet finitely—the mere coastlines of His character, the boundaries of His being, the edges of His ways. Sometime run your finger around the smooth, gold-edged pages of your closed Bible. The truths recorded on those pages, their record of God's doings, their revelation of God's character and works and ways—even "these" are merely "the edges of His ways."

"And how small a whisper we hear of Him!" exclaims Job. The expression *whisper* (KJV, "portion") is the primary Hebrew term for *speech* or *word* (*dabar*). But Job was speaking prior to written revelation. We have the Bible now. Surely that's more than a "whisper," isn't it? Is it? Even the New Testament confirms that God is a great deal bigger and more complex and more glorious than our Bibles can possibly communicate.

The apostle John makes an extraordinary claim in the final words of his Gospel. If everything Jesus ever did were written down, he says, "I suppose that even the world itself could not contain the books that should be written" (John 21:25). Many regard this statement as hyperbole—an accepted and common device in any language for emphasis. Others argue that John meant to be taken quite literally. Two significant factors favor understanding it literally. First, this statement comes immediately on the heels of a solemn assertion that everything the writer has testified is absolutely trustworthy: "This is the disciple that testifieth of these things, and wrote these things; and we know that his testimony is true" (John 21:24). To follow such a serious assertion of reliability with a hyperbole—however acceptable a literary device—seems inconsistent, to say the least. More importantly, John's express purpose has been to convince his readers that this Jesus of Nazareth is the eternal Word and Son of God (John 20:30–31), beginning with a description of His preincarnate deity and role in creation (John 1:1–4). That being the case, how could a world of writers record all the works throughout all eternity of an infinite Person *without* supposing that the world itself could not contain the volumes that would be written? What we possess in the Scriptures—as wonderful and adequate as it is—is a fragment of what there is to know about the nature, personality, works, and ways of God.

The apostle Paul confirms this same truth in Romans 11:33—"O the depth of the riches both of the wisdom and knowledge of God! How unsearchable are his judgments, and his ways past finding out!"

Savor the full force of those words. Don't diminish them by an iota. His decisions are ***un**searchable*. His ways are ***beyond*** figuring out. Paul does not suggest that comprehending all God's ways is extremely demanding even for the brilliant. He does not speak of complexity or difficulty. He speaks of *impossibility, impenetrability, incomprehensibility.* The language admits no exceptions. God is as much beyond the brilliant as the brainless. The dignified Washington Monument dwarfs the Vietnam Memorial, but does it really matter which is closer to the sun? The advantage is less than negligible. It does not matter how brainy you are. When it comes to God, you are as infinitely out of your depth as the rest of us.

Paul or John or Job would never deny our access to absolutes or our possession of objective truth. But all agree that God has revealed a tantalizingly tiny percentage of what there is to know about Him and His ways. How can it possibly be otherwise? The current edition of the *Oxford English Dictionary* consists of twenty volumes; each volume averages 1100–1200 pages. That is a total of 22,000–24,000 *pages* of words. The *OED* represents the most exhaustive presentation of the vocabulary of the English language. By comparison, my wide-margin Bible is a single volume of nearly 1400 pages. Are we prepared to assume that this represents an exhaustive presentation of the inexhaustible? How can the moderately small book we call the Bible be anything *but* a fractional revelation of an infinite and eternal God? Yet we construct minutely detailed theological systems—and *we* must construct them, for the Bible does not do so for us—confidently covering every contingency of God's actions, explaining every nuance of God's character, and supposing our systems to be impregnable fortresses of truth. We forget that we have built them out of a single load of stone delivered to us from a bottomless rock quarry.

One of the nearly eighty interrogatives with which God riddles Job is this: "Hast thou entered into the springs of the sea?" (38:16). Charles Spurgeon saw such mysteries of nature as a parallel to our theological curiosities.

> Some things in nature must remain a mystery to the most intelligent and enterprising investigators. Human knowledge has bounds beyond which it cannot pass. Universal knowledge is for God alone. If this be so in the things which are seen and temporal, I may rest assured that it is even moreso in matters spiritual and eternal. Why then have I

> been torturing my brain with speculations as to destiny and will, fixed fate, and human responsibility? These deep and dark truths I am no more able to comprehend than to find out the depth which coucheth beneath, from which old ocean draws her watery stores. Why am I so curious to know the reason of my Lord's providences, the motive of His actions, the design of His visitations? Shall I ever be able to clasp the sun in my fist, and hold the universe in my palm? Yet these are as a drop of a bucket compared with the Lord my God. Let me not strive to understand the infinite, but spend my strength in love. What I cannot gain by intellect I can possess by affection; and let that suffice me. I cannot penetrate the heart of the sea, but I can enjoy the healthful breezes which sweep over its bosom, and I can sail over its blue waves with propitious winds.[10]

Elsewhere Spurgeon expands on this lesson in theological humility:

> We are but beginners now in spiritual education; for although we have learned the first letters of the alphabet, we cannot read words yet, much less can we put sentences together; but, as one says, "He that has been in heaven but five minutes, knows more than the general assembly of the divines on earth."[11]

In the difficult questions of theology debated for centuries by wise and godly men our attitude must mirror the response of Job to the answer of God: to acknowledge God's undiluted sovereignty to do what He chooses, when He chooses, and how He chooses (42:2) and to remember our smallness and ignorance (42:3–4). That is the heartbeat of theological humility (42:5–6).

What does Job's response have to do with *theological* humility? As we have seen, the major topic of discussion throughout the book of Job is *God*. Proper names and titles for Him appear nearly 180 times in the book, and most of those are followed by dozens of pronominal references to Him. If the divine interrogation of Job teaches us anything, it should teach us what it taught Job: to anchor our minds and condition our spirits to the truth that *has* been revealed rather than strutting confidently into areas that have *not* been revealed.

One of my favorite spots to visit is a place called Craggy Gardens on the Blue Ridge Parkway. A brief hike through rhododendron, mountain laurel, and wild blueberry leads to the top of a spur and a spectacular view of the surrounding mountains. Posted signs mark areas that are off-limits due to fragile habitat. Some theological terrain is fragile habitat where a lumbering lummox of a know-it-all can do serious damage to the truth, the cause of Christ, and the consciences of others. Other signs warn you to stay within the borders of the viewing area not because the habitat is fragile but because *you* are. Get overly curious or cocksure and climb outside the boundaries on top of the cliff and you risk a long fall with a nasty landing.

God's interrogation intentionally emphasizes the limitations of our knowledge even of the natural world that we live in and can see. If that is the case in observable fields of knowledge, how foolish it is for us to suppose that we can fathom the depths of *invisible* (and therefore unobservable) and *revealed* (and therefore nonintuitive) truth.

> The lesson is clear and it is left to Job to take it to heart. *If man is so impotent and so ignorant in regard to the world of things he can see and touch, how can he imagine himself fit to sit in judgment on God's moral government of the universe. Here the issues are far more complex and far more difficult to understand.* The only course for man is humbly to acknowledge his own incompetence, to put absolute trust in God knowing that his dispositions, whatever they may be, are wise and just and good.[12]

Job's humility was keenest when he came to know God most directly and deeply. Yet he is least inclined to speak dogmatically when he has the most reason to do so—namely, a direct revelation of God.

The Problem of Theology: An Infinite God Partially Disclosed

I am not advocating a reductionist theology that insists we return to the revelatory era of Job. Most, if not all, of the revelation we have from God has come to us since Job's time. But even a work as ancient as Job, being a part of that divine revelation, conveys timeless truth intended to inform the most modern theological posture and pursuit.

I am also not advocating a kind of theological agnosticism. What is clearly revealed we may and must affirm absolutely. "Those things which are revealed belong unto us and to our children" (Deut. 29:29*b*). It is the duty of faith to embrace confidently what God has said. But it is not faith to pretend that we know "the secret things" of Deuteronomy 29:29*a*, that we have figured out what God has not explained, that we may pronounce with confidence what He has not revealed with clarity. Because reality, as Lewis observed, is often "not neat, not obvious, not what you expect," we should be guarded about systems of theology that deduce dogmatically, on the basis of reason rather than revelation, issues that remain unrevealed. The axiomatic starting point of all theology is that we know *nothing* of God apart from His revealing it.

The thesis of Deuteronomy 29:29 is that revelation is a matter of divine discretion. God chooses what to reveal and what to withhold. The corollary embedded in that thesis is that revelation is partial. Revelation is reliable disclosure but not full disclosure. The same word *secret* occurs several times in Deuteronomy (31:17, 18; 32:20) and throughout the Old Testament when God *hid* His face from Israel because of their sin. *Secret* doesn't refer to what is nonexistent, but to something that exists yet remains *concealed* or *withheld* and is, therefore, *unknown* and *unknowable*. The verse posits only two categories of truth or reality: what is revealed and therefore may be known with certainty and what is concealed and therefore may not be known with certainty. Revelation is all about divine self-disclosure, but only partial self-disclosure.

Scripture repeatedly drops reminders of the partial nature of divine revelation. One of the clearest examples occurs, ironically, in the book of Revelation when John tells us that he was not allowed to tell us something that he could have told us (Rev. 10:1–4). If God did not intend for us to know what the seven thunders said, why did He let John hear them in the first place? More to the point, why have John tell us that he was about to tell us but that God told him not to tell us? The curiosity is not just that he was forbidden to record a revelation he had received from God but that he *records* that he was given a revelation that he was forbidden to share with us. It is a not-so-subtle reminder that God has not given us all the revelation that He could have, and sometimes almost did. We possess all the data He means for us to have, but significant pieces of the puzzle are missing. If we are able and expected to deduce with confidence exactly what those pieces look like, why keep them secret in the first place and make a point of saying that they belong to Him alone?

Like his friends, Job drew logical inferences about God that were dead wrong, largely because he did not have all the facts. Four thousand years later, neither do we. Some, whose official theological position prohibits speculating on what lies behind the curtain that shrouds divine mysteries, try the hardest to explain and systematize what they would most certainly find there. Supposing that we possess all the truth we need to propound theories with confidence and authority, we become Eliphazes, Bildads, and Zophars. We share even in the folly of Job whom God rebuked for obscuring His counsel by words without knowledge, clouding what God has said by presenting as fact what we do not really know for sure.

Neither the Calvinists nor the Arminians hold a monopoly on this error.[13] No one who is flesh is immune. What is most intriguing is that disciples on both ends of the theological spectrum make the same mistake: overexplaining a God Whom both sides admit (theoretically) is ultimately inexplicable.

An example of this error on the Calvinist side surfaces in Iain Murray's *Spurgeon v. Hyper-Calvinism,* a detailed account of the debate between Spurgeon and other Calvinist preachers in London. According to Murray, "Hyper-Calvinism argues that sinners cannot be required to do what they are not able to do, namely, to believe in Christ for salvation." Ironically, Arminianism agrees. The two sides simply offer opposite but equally unbiblical explanations. The logically consistent Arminian concludes that since the Bible clearly requires man to believe, he must be inherently able to do so. The logically consistent Calvinist[14] concludes that since the Bible clearly teaches man's inherent inability to believe, we must not make him think that he can by requiring or exhorting him to do so. That is what Spurgeon was doing. The Hyper-Calvinist, says Murray, believes that

> the ability to believe belongs only to the elect, and that at the time determined by the Spirit of God. So for a preacher to call all his hearers to immediate repentance and faith is to deny both human depravity and the sovereignty of grace. Spurgeon did not reply to this argument, as many have done, by weakening the biblical teaching on human depravity and inability. . . . But his response to the Hyper-Calvinist argument was to assert another equally biblical truth, namely, that man is wholly responsible for his own sin. . . . Asked to explain such a mystery, Spurgeon constantly replied that it was not his business to do so. His duty was to deal with the whole range of scriptural truth and to declare it in its true proportions.[15]

Murray's diagnosis of Hyper-Calvinism is that it tends to "neglect one side of the Word of God because it does not know how to explain both." I think there is a different dynamic at work. The error is to *over*explain one or both sides in order to make them fit logically—to deduce what is unrevealed in order to reduce the mystery and relieve a paradox.[16] Murray devotes a separate chapter to Spurgeon's priceless remarks on 1 Timothy 2:3*b*–4 ("God our Savior; who will have all men to be saved, and to come unto the knowledge of the truth").

> What then? Shall we try to put another meaning into the text than that which it fairly bears? I trow not. You must, most of you, be acquainted with the general method in which our older Calvinistic friends deal with this text.... I was reading just now the exposition of a very able doctor who explains the text so as to explain it away [you can hear the echo of *over*explaining here]; he applies grammatical gunpowder to it, and explodes it by way of expounding it. I thought when I read his exposition that it would have been a very capital comment upon the text if it had read, "Who *will not* have all men to be saved, nor come to a knowledge of the truth." Had such been the inspired language every remark of the learned doctor would have been exactly in keeping.... *My love of consistency with my own doctrinal views is not great enough to allow me knowingly to alter a single text of Scripture. I have great respect for orthodoxy, but my reverence for inspiration is far greater. I would sooner a hundred times over appear to be inconsistent with myself than inconsistent with the word of God.... God forbid that I should cut or shape, even in the least degree, any divine expression.... I thank God for a thousand things I cannot understand. When I cannot get to know the reason why, I say to myself, "Why should I know the reason why? Who am I, and what am I, that I should demand explanations of my God?" I am a most unreasonable being when I am most reasonable, and when my judgment is most accurate, I dare not trust it. I had rather trust my God.*[17]

There is a man who has imbibed the post-whirlwind spirit of Job.[18]

The same flaw of overexplaining and demystifying God occurs at the other end of the theological spectrum. In his critique of openness theology, Arminian Jon Tal Murphree acknowledges the necessity of systematic theology. "But studying God systematically entails a sobering danger. A lurking liability crouches behind our attempts to analyze God, to categorize His attributes, to pigeonhole our propositions about Him. When we think we have explained Him, He loses mystery [and] ceases to be awesome" in our eyes.[19] Rather than discouraging theological exploration of an infinite and unsearchable God as a futile venture, the persuasion of His mystery lures us onward:

> What we do know about God is so enthralling that we long to explore the mystery further. The exploration may employ our energies throughout eternities to come. Each unfolding vista will open panoramic scenes in a colorful display of divine personality. With each discovery will come a deeper perception of areas yet unexplored. The process becomes one of unending gratification because the One we worship is inexhaustible![20]

Job discovered that God is "more mysterious when He is known than when He is but dimly discerned."[21] The more we know the Lord, and know of Him, the bigger and more *un*searchable we find Him to be.

Theology that presumes to explain all the mysteries and fill in all the gaps of revelation divests God of His sovereignty to reveal and to withhold according to His wisdom and will. He will not be divested. "It is the glory of God to conceal a thing" (Prov. 25:2). Duane Garrett perceptively comments, "God is glorious in concealing matters in that a certain level of mystery about the divine increases the sense of wonder and awe. Those who assume they have full comprehension of theological truth, however 'religious' they may be, lose true piety."[22]

The Danger of Theological Drift

A remarkable transition takes place in Job's thinking throughout the book. His initial, instinctive reaction to his calamities is as theologically correct as it is genuinely submissive. He does not understand his circumstances but concludes that God is free to do as He wishes without explanation. He had given to Job everything he possessed and was therefore free to remove it when and how He wished.

As time went on, however, his convictions on this point wavered. This process can be outlined in several steps. (1) A temporary setback is one thing, but this went on and on with no end in sight and, worse, no explanation from God. In other words, *it made less and less sense the more he thought about it.* (2) The persistent arguments and accusations of his friends goaded him into coming to conclusions he might not otherwise have ventured. (3) Along the way his thinking wavers between what he *knows* and what he *sees,* what he *believes* and what *seems to make sense.* (4) The vacillation leads to some frightful implications, which Elihu rebukes and God adjusts with revelation. (5) Finally, Job returns to his original conviction, but wiser, humbler, and more deeply convinced of the truth he already knew.

Job's pattern of thinking is repeated in many forms of contemporary theology. Unfortunately, some of those who start on Job's quest fail to return and end where Job ended.[23] They do not make it all the way through the book of Job in their theological pilgrimage. Job wandered from the theologically sound position with which he began, confused by circumstances and goaded by well-intentioned theology badly applied, into theologically dubious directions in quest of a position that made sense. Elihu alone penetrated Job's problem and pointed out the dangerous implications of some of his assertions. But it was hearing from God that rescued Job. It was not anything *new* Job learned that turned him around—no doctrinal discovery, no novel theological idea, no innovative philosophical insight. Direct confrontation with the words of God forcefully affirmed the truths he already knew about the nature of God, truths sincerely held but superficially held because his faith in them had never been put to the test. His trials, you see, were designed to test his faith and show its genuineness, and to produce endurance just like James says (James 1:2–3; 5:7–11).

A Psalm for Theologians

Psalm 131 expresses in three simple verses a noble ambition for anyone engaged in theological pursuits at any level—professional or armchair, teacher or student, pastor or layman.

"Lord, my heart is not haughty, nor mine eyes lofty: neither do I exercise myself in great matters, or in things too high for me" (Ps. 131:1). The word *exercise* is the common verb "to go, walk" (*halak*). Different contexts, however, may imply different kinds of walking. In this context of a proud heart and haughty eyes, a more communicative and appropriate translation here would be to "parade" or to "strut"—*neither do I strut around in great matters or in things too high for me.*

The phrase "things too high" echoes Job's words in 42:3—"therefore have I uttered that I understood not; things *too wonderful* for me, which I knew not." Even Job had to admit to mouthing off ignorantly about things of which he had little understanding or personal acquaintance, things too high for him. David refused to pontificate on matters beyond his depth, to play the authority on an issue outside his atmosphere. He would not even tolerate the presence of such people: "Whoever has a haughty look and an arrogant heart I will not endure" (Ps. 101:5, ESV).

Spurgeon likens these high-minded theological endeavors to a child who climbs a ladder to peer into his father's upper-story study window in order to find out what he cannot discover in a legitimate and direct way.

> Then we go on speculating, climbing the ladders of reasoning, guessing, speculating, to reach the lofty windows of eternal truth. Once up there we do not know where we are, our heads reel, and we are in all kinds of uncertainty and spiritual peril. *If we mind things too high for us we run great risks. I do not intend meddling with such lofty matters.*[24]

But isn't it true that *all* theology is too high, too wonderful, for us? Isn't that the essence of what Job confesses? In the sense that we deserve no such privilege and possess no capacity in ourselves to fathom such issues, yes. Nevertheless, God says that what He *has revealed* belongs to us and to our children (Deut. 29:29*b*). Delitzsch helpfully points out that "the opposite of 'things too wonderful for me' is not that which is trivial, but that which is attainable."[25] What is "attainable" is defined by what God has revealed in the Word (Deut. 30:11–14).

"Surely I have behaved and quieted myself, as a child that is weaned of his mother: my soul is even as a weaned child" (Ps. 131:2). David paints a picture of Job-like meekness and contentment, signaling a measure of maturity beyond the intellectually infantile stage of verse 1. A weaned child no longer cries for instant gratification or demands to have his cravings met immediately. He has learned to be satisfied with his mother's presence and to await her provision.

"Let Israel hope in the Lord from henceforth and for ever" (Ps. 131:3). "Hope in the Lord" is confident trust that waits expectantly for Him. That brings us back to the foundational issue of all authentic theology which is not merely knowledge but relationship.

Appendix

Leviathan: A Case Study in Literal Interpretation

What is important about Job 41 is not identifying what leviathan is but understanding why the Lord talks about him to Job. That is discussed in chapter 17. As readers, however, we are understandably curious to know the identity of this creature. In addition, reasoning through the data and the interpretive alternatives becomes a valuable study in hermeneutics—what literal interpretation does and does not mean.

What was, or is, leviathan? Suggestions have ranged from the prosaic (dolphin, whale, killer whale, great white shark, crocodile) to the primeval (a marine dinosaur that survived the Flood to the time of Job) to the esoteric (a mythological creature or metaphorical symbol for cosmic powers). Job 41 is not the only passage in the Bible where this creature, or one like it, appears. But it is the most detailed and furnishes its most extended description.

The Biblical Data

Besides Job 41, *leviathan* appears in Psalm 74:14 and 104:26, Isaiah 27:1, and Job 3:8 (where the KJV translates it "mourning"). It would be a mistake, however, to insist that whatever "leviathan" is, it must possess all the characteristics attributed to it in every given passage. Diverse literary factors come into play in different contexts. Suppose we adopt a similar methodology in a biblical study of "man" to discover more accurately and thoroughly what this creature is like. We might be shocked to find that at least *some* men possess two hearts (Ps. 12:2) or two brains (James 1:8) and have a terrifying facial appearance including spears for teeth and a sword for a tongue (Ps. 57:4)!

Many descriptions of "man" are laced with literary features common even in customarily literal speech; the same is true of leviathan. It would be absurd to insist, based on Psalm 74:14 ("thou brakest the heads of leviathan in pieces"), that the leviathan of Psalm 104 or Job 41 must be some now-unknown species of multiheaded beast. Psalm 74:14 is unquestionably a figurative reference to Egypt.[1] Leviathan in Isaiah 27:1 glistens with the metaphorical seawater out of which it rears its head and takes on additional serpentine and perhaps satanic imagery.[2] To superimpose these details upon less symbolically loaded (though still poetic) passages such as Job 41 and Psalm 104:26 is not sound hermeneutics. In fact, even these last two passages do not necessarily have the same creature in view.

The term translated "leviathan" seems to derive from a verb meaning "twist" or "wind." Some have suggested that the word does not identify a single species of animal but functions as a flexible, generic designation for large water creatures whose specific identity varies with the context. That may explain why the fearsome beast of Job 41 takes on the playful, ocean-frolicking, whalelike features of a marine creature in Psalm 104:26.

If *leviathan* functions as a nonspecific reference to a class of large aquatic animals rather than to a single species, it is unnecessary to insist that the animal described in Job 41 is the same as the marine creature of Psalm 104. Dismissing the crocodile out of hand on the grounds that "crocodiles are not sea creatures and this one clearly was (v. 31)"[3] is premature and factually mistaken on two counts. In the first place, Job 41:31 does not require that leviathan be a marine creature. The Hebrew word translated "sea" does not mean "ocean" but simply "depths." In Zechariah 10:11, the same term describes the depths of the Nile River. In the second place, even today a large (eighteen to twenty feet), man-eating species of saltwater crocodile (*Crocodylus porosus*) inhabits marshes from southern India to northern Australia and often swims far out to sea.[4]

Interpretational Options

While most of the descriptive details in Job 41 initially seem to suggest a massive crocodile, elements of the literary sketch tax the imagination. His snorts project "flashes of light" (41:18), his mouth emits sparks and flames (41:19, 21), and smoke issues from his nostrils (41:20). It is significant that these extraordinary details are limited to a single segment (41:18–21) in the middle of an impressive poetic description brimming with simile and metaphor. A survey of the literature reveals four major interpretational options: a mythological monster, a dinosaur, a crocodile, or a combination of a real creature that doubles as a figure for cosmic powers.

Mythological Monsters and Cosmic Creatures

Ironically, many liberals have taken the problematic depictions of 41:18–21 at face value, arguing that a purely mythological creature must be in view.[5] They take the descriptions literally to prove that a nonliteral creature is intended, citing similar descriptions in mythologies of other ancient cultures.[6] Andersen counters that the incontestable mythological use of *leviathan* and *behemoth* in other ancient cultures does not prove a mythological usage in Job. Besides, "Job 40:15 states explicitly that Behemoth and Job are equally God's creatures."[7] The pure mythological view is not an option for anyone who seriously regards the Bible as an authentic, authoritative, and trustworthy revelation from God. In addition to its other problems, a mythological reference would lose all relevance to Job and undermine God's point to Job.

A conservative alternative to the mythological view is the cosmic powers view.[8] Elmer Smick argues extensively that the Old Testament gives no credence to mythological entities.[9] Instead, he sees behemoth and leviathan as "symbolic though their features are drawn from animals like the hippopotamus and crocodile." Ultimately they represent cosmic powers, symbols of Satan presented under the imagery of the beastlike hippopotamus and the dragonlike crocodile. Though distinct from the mythological view, the cosmic view is also driven by a literalistic hermeneutic.

Those who regard these creatures as literal animals must admit that the description given here in Job is an exaggeration of the appearance

> and power of hippopotamuses and crocodiles. Gunkle, Cheyne, and Pope understand them as mythological creatures. The present writer claims only mythological terminology is used to present graphic descriptions of the powers of evil such as Satan in the Prologue.[10]

Why this veiled imagery? Why not provide a more open revelation of the person and presence of Satan? Smick explains that "the Accuser cannot be openly mentioned here without revealing to Job information he must not know if he is to continue as a model to those who also must suffer in ignorance of God's explicit purpose for their suffering."[11] Smick's view is inviting and has been further developed by others.[12]

Less convincing is Henry Morris's dual explanation, combining a dinosaurian interpretation with the cosmic powers view. Morris is confident that "the reason commentators are unable to identify this mighty animal [behemoth] is that it is now extinct," and whatever leviathan may have been, "it was not a crocodile!" Because the descriptions in Job do not match any other creature presently known to man, Morris insists that they must refer to some now-extinct or unknown creature.[13] But Morris's leviathan takes a curious twist when he asserts that behemoth and leviathan symbolize Satan because some of the details "could not literally apply to *any* animal. They could, in fact they *must*, apply ultimately to Satan, *and to him alone*."[14] By interpreting elements of leviathan's description symbolically as references to Satan, Morris dispenses with what he deems problematic details. In the end his view is no closer to a consistently literal interpretation.

These creatures may play some dual, symbolic role; but any such interpretation must exhibit hermeneutical clarity and consistency. Either these passages, in toto, are (1) *literal* descriptions of some unknown and presumably extinct creature or (2) *literal* descriptions of Satan or (3) *primarily poetic* depictions of an extant or extinct creature with *secondary* symbolic application to Satan. To mix (1) and (2), as Morris has done, is to try to have one's hermeneutical pie and eat it too.

Smick's cosmic powers interpretation is more nuanced and lacks the baggage of inconsistency that encumbers Morris's view. Nevertheless, both labor under a common weakness. How is such an abstract description of a cosmic being supposed to impact Job? If he does not and cannot know the *true* identity of this mysterious creature—and Satan is a *creature*, after all—if these two "things" are entirely outside Job's tangible experience, then the divine argument loses all the wind in its sails. The point is to humble Job by showing him how helpless he is even in the face of some of God's creatures. If Job thinks God is talking about a crocodile (or a dinosaur) in 41:1–17 and then, without warning, God throws in details that are bizarre and unearthly (41:18–21)—yet Job does not know, and cannot know (as Smick insists), that this thing is actually a spiritual being—that would only confuse Job and short-circuit the intended effect. For this longest portion of the divine speech to create an impression on Job and make any impact on him at all, Job has to know what on earth God is talking about.

The idea that behemoth and leviathan symbolize the cosmic power of evil, the cosmic personage of Satan, has merit. Some of the parallels are intriguing. However, such an analogous relationship can be only secondary and incidental, not primary and essential. It cannot be essential because it is not adequately required or explained by the handful of difficult details woven into an otherwise highly poetic passage. And it cannot be the primary intent because it does not adequately explain or account for the obvious impact upon Job.

A Dinosaurian Interpretation

The dinosaurian view also arises out of a literalistic hermeneutic, though from the opposite end of the theological spectrum from the mythological view.[15] Some who wish to interpret all the details (particularly 41:18–21) as literally as possible have compared these characteristics to the fire-breathing dragon of ancient legends. Rumors of such a creature must have come from somewhere, they reason. Perhaps some such primeval dinosaurian creature gave rise to long-lived memories even after it became extinct. Or perhaps such a creature managed to survive postdeluvian climate changes up to the time of Job. In any case, the main impetus for the dinosaurian view is a perceived consistently literal approach to a relatively small segment of the description, particularly 41:18–21. I say overly literalistic because the same interpreters recognize the presence of metaphor elsewhere in these chapters, but not here. In that sense, it is also an inconsistently literalistic approach, as I will try to demonstrate.

The dinosaurian option faces several difficulties. First, the assumption that legendary "dragon" descriptions must have come from somewhere, presumably a dinosaur, fails to consider the alternative possibility: perhaps notions of such a creature originated from a literalistic interpretation of this account in Job. Not all mythology arises from a previous reality. Many mythological elements, though perhaps augmented by tales of fearful encounters, are born in the creative human imagination.[16]

Second, the descriptive details that seem to require a dinosaurian interpretation sound surreal even for an extinct creature. "To the possible objection that not even dinosaurs breathed fire," says Henry Morris, "we could answer that no one *knows* what dinosaurs could do."[17] This anything-might-be-true retreat into the misty uncertainty of an extinct species whose characteristics cannot be disproved or proved seems too facile. No reliable evidence of a fire-breathing dinosaur exists, especially one that may have survived as late as the second millennium BC. Moreover, a fire-breathing land-dweller is one thing; but a pyrogenerative creature that lives in *water* is a hopeless anomaly.

Third, whatever the leviathan was, the description repeatedly implies that it was an extant creature known to Job. The divine argument loses all its potency if God is describing a beast Job had never seen. If leviathan was a dinosaur, it had to be "a creature close enough at hand for Job and his compatriots to observe firsthand or even to attack as big game (v. 8). And since he is described right after Behemoth (which is clearly a denizen of the Jordan [see 40:23]), it is most likely a monster that likewise inhabited those waters."[18] Robert Gordis concurs: "We are, therefore, convinced that only a description of actual flesh-and-blood monsters . . . is relevant to the poet's purpose."[19]

Fourth, no one denies that the entire literary atmosphere of Job, including the divine monologue, is highly poetic. If a literal interpretation demands that we take the elements of 41:18–21 at face value, then a consistently literalistic interpretation requires that we also take at face value all such descriptions in the immediate context. I have found no one, however, who insists that a literal interpretation requires the following:

- Lightning bolts speak to God (38:35).
- Baby birds pray for food (38:41).
- Horses talk (39:25) and possess a self-conscious emotional capacity to "rejoice" (39:21).
- Leviathan was capable of actual "laughter" (41:29), along with the wild donkey (39:7), the ostrich (39:18), and the horse (39:22).[20]

Common metaphorical devices are at work here. Indeed, "quite fanciful imagery has already been used in these earlier poems; we are no more required to believe that Behemoth's bones were made of metal (40:18) than that God has water-bottles in the sky (38:37)."[21]

If we are prepared to recognize figures of speech in these cases, what prevents us from doing so in 41:18–21?[22] Those who have no difficulty with other metaphorical features in Job 38–41 must explain why 41:18–21 should be treated differently. Listing various reasons for the poetic use of personification, Ryken notes that "poetry is inherently fictional rather than factual."[23] That is the nature of the poetic genre that God has adopted to communicate some of His revelation to us. We expect divine narrative to function like human narrative—factual with a smattering of the metaphorical. We should expect divine poetry to function like human poetry—metaphorical with a smattering of the factual. Both, of course, are always rooted in a literal reality.

An interpretation of behemoth and leviathan that insists that poetic details be taken literalistically is either hermeneutically inconsistent or else consistently absurd. *Literal* is too easily and often confused with *physical*. Satan, angels, and even God are literal beings but not physical beings. Similarly, a literal interpretation does not demand that we take every detail of this creature in Job physically, any more than it requires us to believe that horses exclaim "Aha!" when they rush into battle (39:25). These are all common figurative patterns that are characteristic of normal literal speech.

A Saurian Interpretation

The arguments above suggest that perhaps something less "spectacular" but just as impressive is in view—not a *dino*saurian identity but a saurian identity nonetheless.[24] The crocodile fits all the other data of the description quite handily. But if it is a crocodile, what *does* one do with the remarkable details in 41:18–21—especially those of us committed to a characteristically literal interpretation of the Bible?[25]

William Bartram was a highly respected eighteenth-century North American naturalist and explorer, who meticulously journaled his discoveries in this strange new world. *The Travels of William Bartram*—a fascinating read in its own right—is the record of a man enthralled by the wild exoticism of plants and animals, topography and even weather, unlike anything any European had ever seen. One creature in particular that earned his fear and respect was the American alligator. His personal experiences furnish a description of alligators in the wilds of Revolutionary-era eastern Florida that is remarkably similar in some details to the portrait of leviathan in Job.

> Behold him rushing forth from the flags and reeds. His enormous body swells. His plaited tail brandished high, floats upon the lake. *The waters like a cataract descend from his opening jaws. Clouds of smoke issue from his dilated nostrils. The earth trembles with his thunder.* When immediately from the opposite coast of the lagoon, emerges from the deep his rival champion. They suddenly dart upon each other. *The boiling surface of the lake marks their rapid course*, and a terrific conflict commences. They now sink to the bottom folded together in horrid wreaths. The water becomes thick and discoloured. Again they rise, their jaws clap together, re-echoing through the deep surrounding forests. . . . The shores and forests resound [the proud victor's] dreadful roar. . . .[26]

Later that evening he witnessed a mass passage of fish across the bay where alligators were assembled in such large numbers that "it would have been easy to walk across [the lake] on their heads, had the animals been harmless."

> How shall I express myself so as to convey an adequate idea of it to the reader, and at the same time avoid raising suspicions of my veracity? . . . What expressions can sufficiently declare the shocking scene that for some minutes continued, whilst this mighty army of fish were forcing the pass? I have seen an alligator take up out of the water several great fish at a time. . . . The horrid noise of their closing jaws . . . *the floods of water and blood rushing out of their mouths*, and *the clouds of vapor issuing from their wide nostrils*, were truly frightful.[27]

The following day, while Bartram was in his boat,

> a huge alligator rushed out of the reeds, and with a tremendous roar came up, and darted as swift as an arrow under my boat, emerging . . . with open jaws, *and belching water and smoke that fell upon me like rain in a hurricane.* I laid soundly about his head with my club, and . . . he went off on a straight line through the water, *seemingly with the rapidity of lightning. . . .*[28]

Crocodilian expert C. A. W. Guggisberg often expresses skepticism toward what he regards as excessive reports of the size or behavior of these creatures. Yet when he cites Bartram's accounts, he never questions the credibility of his descriptions.[29] On the contrary, he defends Bartram's description, which "has sometimes been held up to ridicule, specially the 'clouds of smoke' coming from the saurian's nostrils—but let us remember that it was written in 1791 and about an animal very little known and much feared at the time."

Guggisberg also cites modern herpetologist Raymond Ditmars's similar account: "a 10 to 12 foot specimen lets out *a rattling bellow that shakes the night air* of the lagoon and may be heard for a mile. When so performing, the males *emit vapory jets of musk from the glands on the chin.*" Guggisberg concludes that "what Bartram called 'smoke' in the parlance of his time may have been either watery vapour puffed out into the cooling night air, or the jets of musky secretion mentioned by Ditmars."[30]

These descriptions by Bartram, Ditmars, and others adequately account in realistic terms for the Jobian description of leviathan's smoke-emitting nostrils. Such extrabiblical accounts of crocodiles justify our seeing similar descriptions in Job 41 as consistent with human observation and perception throughout the ages.[31]

The most spectacular feature of the description—the sparks and flames that go out of his mouth (41:19, 21)—can also be accounted for in similar terms, if perhaps less satisfactorily. Bartram above describes blood pouring out of the feeding creatures' mouths. Guggisberg identifies the interior color of the Nile crocodile's mouth as a "deep orange, surprisingly vivid and producing a really beautiful splash of color."[32] And numerous commentators document the spark-like appearance created by a sunning saurian's sneeze.[33]

Nevertheless, the committed literalist may remain unconvinced by such analogies. The explicit terms of the text seem to some to call for actual smoke and fire, not merely the *appearance* of smoke and fire. A literary and experiential observation may provide a more satisfactory explanation for the similarities between the descriptions of Job 41 and those of observers such as Bartram or Ditmars.

Dimensions of a Characteristically Literal Hermeneutic

Much nonsense has been leveled at a literal approach to interpreting the Bible.[34] A literal interpretation, properly and consistently applied, has always acknowledged the presence of figurative devices even in communication that is fundamentally intended to be taken literally. Literal speech, both biblical and modern, employs a variety of figurative devices.[35] A figure of speech is a word or phrase used to communicate a literal meaning in a nonliteral way. Figures of speech are built-in illustrations. Jesus called Herod a "fox" (Luke 13:32), and you may describe a guy on his eighth trip to the food bar as a "pig." Neither remark is intended to be taken "literally"—that is, physically—as though the human referent were, in fact, an animal. Nevertheless, a definite literal meaning and intent underlie both figures.[36]

Metaphor

One of the most common figures of speech is the metaphor, a comparison of two essentially dissimilar things. A pure metaphor is a direct comparison between two nouns joined by a form of the verb *to be*. This is to be distinguished from simile, a more easily identifiable form of metaphor using *like* or *as*. Examples of this species of metaphor surface in the description of leviathan: "his eyes are *like* the eyelids of the morning" (41:18*b*),[37] and smoke ascends from his nostrils "*as* out of a seething pot or cauldron" (41:20). Simile is unambiguous and unarguable; the tip-off term (*like* or *as*) alerts the reader to its presence.

Metaphor is trickier because it "adopts a bolder strategy."[38] Consequently, it is more liable to be missed by the inattentive reader or misunderstood by the literalistic reader. But there is a technical difficulty in describing elements of 41:18–21 as metaphor. Since some form of the verb *to be* is usually the verbal tip-off to metaphor, a strict metaphor would run something like this: "his sneezings are lightning" or "what comes out of his mouth are sparks of fire and smoke." What we have instead is a series of action verbs: "shine . . . go . . . leap out . . . goeth . . . kindleth . . . goeth." Descriptions of clearly figurative language can be identified only as metaphorical, whether their construction includes forms of *to be* or more descriptive action verbs.

Hyperbole

A common feature of literal speech is the use of intentional overstatement.[39] Hyperbole is not deceptive; it is a valid literary device that is commonly understood and widely practiced. Hyperbole is not inaccurate; it is based on an underlying literal intent and reality.

> Is hyperbole error? Is the use of hyperbole consistent with the inerrancy of the Scriptures? If writers using hyperbole were saying more than they intended, is this to be understood as error? No. Error is not reflected by hyperbole because . . . hyperbole is generally readily understood by the reader as an exaggerated statement given for emphasis or impact. Therefore the readers are not misled.[40]

Purposeful overstatement is designed for emphatic intent or dramatic effect. (For example, *everyone* understands that hyperbole is a common feature of characteristically literal language.) "Hyperbole does not pretend to be factual. Indeed, it advertises its lack of literal truth."[41]

Some commentators explain the portrait of leviathan as a hyperbolic description of a crocodile. Generally, however, hyperbole heightens the *dimension* or *proportion* of something that is really true of the object to a lesser degree. For example, Job 40:23 describes behemoth as capable of taking up "Jordan into his mouth."[42] No creature could *literally* (physically) take up a Jordan River into his mouth—not even a dinosaur! And yet the hyperbole does have a basis in reality. Anyone who has seen the gaping maw of a hippopotamus in the water would instantly recognize this as an embellished and graphic way of describing the impressive capacity of this creature's mouth.[43]

In the case of leviathan, then, a technical hyperbole would suggest that a reference to smoke or fire proceeding from the mouth and nostrils of Leviathan is only exaggerating the *dimension* of a phenomenon that is actually there in some smaller proportion. In other words, in a technically hyperbolic portrait of leviathan we would expect a creature that actually does produce sparks from his mouth to be described something like this: "sparks fly out of his mouth in meteoric showers." Therein lies the technical weakness of describing Job 41 as "a hyperbolic portrait of a fearless crocodile."[44]

But hyperbole may also describe a *perceived* phenomenon. In some cases, very little distance may divide the hyperbolic overstatement from the reality as it appears or is perceived—especially by someone who comes face-to-face in a knee-buckling encounter with such a brute. Fear magnifies a terror. Guggisberg mentions the frequency with which the dimensions of live crocodiles are overestimated, until they are actually killed and measured. Consequently, one angle of the hyperbolic dimension could include the *impression* created by such a confrontation.

In a passing reference to the book of Job, Guggisberg admits that our passage "does, in fact, give quite a reasonable description of the crocodile, with which the Hebrews were well acquainted. Not only had they seen it in Egypt, but it also appeared in Palestine itself."[45] Guggisberg describes some saurian species that may well have been known to Job. The Nile crocodile, typically twelve to sixteen feet long, has been documented even in the twentieth century at least up to twenty-five feet.[46] The estuarine, or saltwater, crocodile, typically ranging from eleven to fourteen feet and occasionally up to nineteen feet, has been documented at up to thirty-two feet in Bengal.[47] Who knows the size or range of some of these creatures during the second millennium BC? Guggisberg also includes some hair-raising tales of man-eating estuarine crocodiles in Borneo and New Guinea.[48]

Imagine meeting a creature of that nature and size close up. That is a mammoth saurian monster! What kind of girth must a creature like that possess? What effect would a face-to-face encounter with such a beast create? Archer captures this sense in his description of leviathan: "His frightful appearance as he lunges forward against any would-be attackers throws them all into demoralization and panic."[49] Fabled sailors' tales of sea monsters evidence the impact that a close encounter with even a natural creature of monstrous proportions can have on men's impressions and imaginations. "How should we understand such exaggerations?" asks literary critic Leland Ryken.

"We must avoid foolish attempts to press them into literal statements. Hyperbole does not express literal, factual truth. Instead it expresses emotional truth. . . . It captures the spirit of an event or inner experience."[50]

God describes leviathan as a creature so fearsome that "sparks and flames come out of his mouth, and smoke ascends from his nostrils." To take such language as figurative (metaphorical), or exaggerative (hyperbolic), or some combination of the two, is entirely in keeping with a characteristically literal interpretation and with the figures of speech that pepper the rest of the description—rhetorical questions with a tinge of irony (41:1–7, 13), simile (41:18*b*, 20*b*, 30), and personification (41:29, 34).

God and Leviathan

David's description of God in Psalm 18 contains a stunning parallel to God's description of leviathan in Job 41. This parallel furnishes another argument for a literal-figurative interpretation—as opposed to a literal-physical interpretation—of the description of leviathan.

Psalm 18:8 (NASB)	Job 41:20–21 (NASB)
Smoke went up out of His nostrils, And fire from His mouth devoured; Coals were kindled by it.	Out of his nostrils smoke goes forth . . . his breath kindles coals, And a flame goes forth from his mouth.

The Hebrew wording is not quite as parallel as the English translation might suggest, but some identical terminology links the two passages and the imagery is unquestionably parallel. What, then, do we call David's obviously figurative depiction of God? Anthropomorphism won't work since humans do not spout coal-kindling fire and smoke any more than crocodiles do. Is this a zoomorphism or a leviathamorphism? Since both are poetry, a characteristically literal hermeneutic consistently applied would either require both to be taken literally or allow both to be taken figuratively.[51]

Job 41 is a poetic potpourri of figurative language—rhetorical question, irony, personification, simile, hyperbole, and metaphor—converging to describe the crocodile as one of God's most impressive and intimidating creatures accessible to Job.[52] Beyond merely trying to identity leviathan in Job 41, however, this study has far-reaching ramifications for our whole approach to the figurative dimension of a characteristically literal hermeneutic.

Notes

1—Introducing the Book of Job

[1]The opening scenario is drawn from Job 36:26–38:1.

[2]John Franklin Genung, "Job, Book of," *International Standard Bible Encyclopedia*, vol. 3 (Grand Rapids: Eerdmans, 1956), p. 1685.

[3]H. Wheeler Robinson, *The Cross in the Old Testament* (London: SCM Press Ltd., 1955), p. 19.

[4]Derek Kidner notes the distinctive challenge of Job (along with Proverbs and Ecclesiastes) in this respect: "Where the bulk of the Old Testament calls us simply to obey and to believe, this part of it summons us to think hard as well as humbly; to keep our eyes open, to use our conscience and our common sense, and not to shirk the most disturbing questions" (*The Wisdom of Proverbs, Job & Ecclesiastes* [Downers Grove, Ill.: InterVarsity Press, 1985], p. 11).

[5]Francis I. Andersen, *Job* (Leicester, England: Inter-Varsity Press, n.d.), pp. 15–16.

[6]"Numerous documents, especially from ancient Mesopotamia and Egypt, demonstrate that this genre of wisdom writing was well established in the OT world; but none touch on these matters so eloquently and fully as this OT book" (Elmer Smick, *Expositor's Bible Commentary*, vol. 4 [Grand Rapids: Zondervan, 1988], p. 843). Smick lists several examples, but Kidner does even better by making three of these texts accessible in Appendix A of *The Wisdom of Proverbs, Job & Ecclesiastes*. He notes both comparisons and contrasts between the biblical Job and a Sumerian version of the Job story (ca. 2000 BC) that one scholar has dubbed "The First Job," another Babylonian work (ca. 1500–1200 BC) called "I Will Praise the Lord of Wisdom" (a.k.a. "The Babylonian Job"), and a Babylonian theodicy dating to about 1000 BC. To these examples R. K. Harrison adds others, including

an ancient Indian tale of Harisiandra. But as Harrison observes, "Despite obvious similarities in content, there are equally significant differences" between the Book of Job and these ancient documents (*Introduction to the Old Testament* [Peabody, Mass.: Prince Press, 1969], p. 1026). Indeed, given the defensibly early dating of the historical story (if not the composition) of Job, these ancient international representations of a similar story line may arguably be construed as evidence of national adaptations of the original biblical story of Job.

[7]Harrison, *Introduction to the Old Testament*, p. 1022.

[8]Thomas Carlyle, "The Hero as Prophet," in *Our Heroes, Hero Worship, and the Heroic in History* (Boston: Ginn Press, 1901), p. 56.

[9]Harrison, p. 1022.

[10]John Walvoord, *The Holy Spirit* (Grand Rapids: Zondervan, 1991), p. 45.

[11]"The lecture or the sermon, with its one-way flow, can make its points tidily and at leisure; but a lesson that draws the hearers into answering and asking, into working things out painfully, may well get further into the mind than any discourse, even if at times it deliberately leaves many questions unresolved" (Kidner, *Wisdom*, p. 12).

[12]This produces an A-B-A pattern for the overall literary structure of the book, an essentially poetic work bookended by narrative prose. The fragments of "poetry" that surface in the prose section (e.g., 1:16–19, 21 in the MT) really function as highly structured prose. Similarly, the bits of narrative prose in the poetic section (e.g., 32:1–6) simply provide necessary transitions from speaker to speaker.

[13]See also the diagram "Architectonics of the Book of Job" in Smick, p. 848.

[14]Gleason L. Archer Jr., *Survey of Old Testament Introduction* (Chicago: Moody Press, 1974), p. 464.

[15]Roy Zuck, *Job* (Chicago: Moody Press, 1978), p. 8. Various reasons are attached to most suggestions. Solomon and Hezekiah are often cited as likely candidates because of their close connection to wisdom literature and the book's definite propensities towards that genre. Jeremiah is suspected because of his linguistic similarities to Job and because Job's homeland of Uz (Job 1:1) is mentioned elsewhere only in Jeremiah's writings (Jer. 25:20; Lam. 4:21). Moses is advanced on the basis of a strand of Jewish tradition, as well as the proximity of Uz to Midian, Moses' home for forty years (where, it is suggested, he could have come across this ancient story and eventually translated it into Hebrew). Archer adds that though there is nothing "Mosaic about the style of Job, this theory would at least account for (1) its being possessed by the Hebrews, (2) its attaining canonical status,

(3) its patriarchal flavor and setting, and (4) the Aramaic flavor of some of the terminology and modes of expression exhibited by the text" (ibid.).

[16]Smick, p. 847. To safeguard a theologically accurate view of inspiration, we should note that, technically, the biblical authors were not themselves "inspired." The writers were "moved" (borne along, directed) by the Holy Spirit (2 Pet. 1:21); but only what they wrote, the text itself, is properly designated as "inspired" (lit., breathed out) by God (2 Tim. 3:16).

[17]Archer, *Survey*, p. 466.

[18]"This view was advocated as early as the time of Gregory Nazianzen (fourth century A.D.) and also by Martin Luther, Haevernick, Keil, and Delitzsch." Other conservatives who hold this view include Young and Unger (Archer, *Survey*, p. 467).

[19]Points 2 through 5 are drawn from Archer, ibid.

[20]H. H. Rowley, *Job* (London: Thomas Nelson and Sons, 1970), p. 29.

[21]Besides these 27 appearances of *Yahweh* in the prologue and epilogue, it elsewhere surfaces only once in the dialogue (12:9) and in the narrator's announcement of the divine monologue (38:1; 40:1, 3, 6).

[22]Archer, p. 466.

[23]Ibid., p. 462. "The foreign locale would also account for the comparative rarity of the name *Yahweh* in most chapters of the book. Job shows a distinct preference for the pan-Semitic term *'Eloah* or *'Elohim* for God.... This evidence from the use of the divine names certainly tends to confirm the theory of a non-Israelite background" (Ibid., pp. 464–65). At the same time, as indicated above, the strategic placement of the name *Yahweh* predominantly in the prologue and epilogue suggests a Palestinian composition.

[24]Melchizedek is the most intriguing example since he was a "priest of the most high God" for an entire community of people dwelling in ancient (Jeru)Salem, where he also reigned as king (Gen. 14:18).

[25]The Sabeans were "north Arabian nomads" and the Chaldeans "were roving marauders before they settled down in the south, west of the Tigris, in the ninth century BC" (Smick, p. 883).

[26]E. Dhorme, *A Commentary on the Book of Job*, trans. Harold Knight (London: Thomas Nelson and Sons, 1967), p. 651.

[27]Job lived an additional 140 years *after* his suffering and restoration, probably making his age "around 200" (Zuck, p. 188). "If tradition is correct that he lived to be 210," adds Zuck, "Job's latter years were double his former years (140 as compared to 70). That reckoning is possible though uncertain" (Zuck, ibid.; cf. Andersen, p. 293). Genesis 11 indicates a gradual diminishing of postdiluvian lifespans. Job's age places him chronologically near the end of the genealogy in Genesis 11 (ca. 2200–2000 BC). According to Genesis 11, Noah's son Shem lived to be 600, Arphaxad 438, Salah 433, Eber 464, Peleg 239, Reu 239, Serug 230, Nahor 148, Terah 205.

Cf. Abraham, 175 (Gen. 25:7); Ishmael, 137 (Gen. 25:17); Isaac, 180 (Gen. 36:28); Jacob, 147 (Gen. 47:28); Joseph, 110 (Gen. 50:26).

[28] *Shaddai* appears 30 times in Job, and only 17 times elsewhere—16 of which are traceable to the patriarchal era or back to Job itself: 11 are in the Pentateuch and Ruth, 4 are in the Prophets but are traceable to Job (Isa. 13:6 and Joel 1:15 to Job 31:23; Ezek. 1:24 and 10:5 to Job 37:4–5), and one is in the Mosaic Psalm 91. David's Psalm 68 uses it once.

[29] Archer, p. 465. "This Babylonian account may go back to 1200 BC and may rest upon materials even earlier." See note 6 above.

[30] Harrison, p. 1031.

[31] Andersen, p. 33. He cites, for example, "proverbs, riddles, hymns, laments, curses, [and] lyrical nature poems." He also notes the abundance of the kind of "quasi-juridical rhetoric" common in law courts.

[32] Though "the alternating speeches give the impression of dramatic interchange . . . the form established in the opening and closing sections is that of classical Hebrew narrative," notes Andersen. "There is no evidence that the Israelites had anything in their culture resembling the theatre." Nevertheless, "the idea that Job is some kind of play has often suggested itself. The dramatic quality of Job can be recognized without calling it a drama in the strict sense." Andersen cites Bishop Lowth's conclusion, based on "Aristotelian criteria," that while Job (in terms of drama) was "lacking for want of 'action' . . . it could be called a dramatic poem"—a concession validated "by the fact that the biblical text has actually been staged," in some cases with minimal alteration to the biblical text (Andersen, pp. 33–35).

[33] D. A. Hubbard, "Wisdom Literature," *New Bible Dictionary,* ed. J. D. Douglas (Grand Rapids: Eerdmans, 1962), p. 1334. According to Hubbard, wisdom literature was "a literary genre common in the Ancient Near East in which instructions for successful living are given or the perplexities of human existence are contemplated." Wisdom literature is of two types: (1) proverbial wisdom—short, pithy sayings that state principles for personal happiness and welfare (Proverbs), and (2) speculative wisdom—monologues (Ecclesiastes) or dialogues (Job) that confront the looming philosophical questions of the meaning of life and the relationship between God and man in the context of real-life experiences.

[34] H. Wheeler Robinson, *Inspiration and Revelation in the Old Testament* (London: Oxford University Press, 1946), p. 241.

[35] Our family has enjoyed reading through Job aloud in about 5–7 sittings. In a college course on the Wisdom Books, I had the class take parts and read through Job in one sitting and found it immensely rewarding and enjoyable. The total cast number can be varied somewhat, depending on how many are available for such a reading. Some parts are short and can be overlapped, while some are long and can be shared among more than one person.

The story of Job includes a total of 13 characters. Seven have substantive roles (Narrator, God, Job, Eliphaz, Bildad, Zophar, Elihu) while others disappear after the prologue (Satan, four messengers, Job's wife).

[36]Kidner applies this very method to "The Babylonian Theodicy," an ancient variation on the Job story, in order to "show the progress of the dialogue by summarizing the drift of each 11-line stanza in a sentence or two" (p. 136). See note 6 above.

2—Discovering the Theme of Job

[1]I am excluding what might be called *natural* suffering that is endemic to physical life and human experience—the sting of a cut, the throb of a migraine, the pangs of childbirth—in other words, pain purely conceived as pain. All pain in this sense is an indirect form of judgment as a consequence of the Fall and, as such, forms the platform on which most classes of suffering are played out.

[2]Most Christians are familiar with John Foxe's classic *Book of Martyrs*. Other briefer collections of Christian persecution include J. C. Ryle's superb *Five English Reformers* (Edinburgh: Banner of Truth, rpr. 1994) and Faith Cook's inspiring volume *Singing in the Fire* (Edinburgh: Banner of Truth, 1995).

[3]Peter addressed his first letter to Christians who "were facing suffering and persecution for their faith" and were consequently "disenfranchised, discriminated against, and mistreated" (Thomas Schreiner, *1, 2 Peter, Jude*, The New American Commentary [Nashville: Broadman and Holman, 2003], pp. 38, 41). See, e.g., 1 Pet. 1:6–7; 2:18–23; 3:8–9, 13–17; 4:1–4, 12–19; 5:10.

[4]Schreiner, p. 224.

[5]D. A. Carson, *How Long, O Lord? Reflections on Suffering and Evil* (Grand Rapids: Baker Book House, 1990), p. 154.

[6]The demand that others trust us is adolescent. It is the protest of a teenager to a parent in the face of some imposed restriction. It was *my* protest, as a recently converted teenager, to my mother, who wisely retorted, "It's your flesh I don't trust. And neither should you."

[7]In Acts 15:8, Peter describes the Lord with an intriguing compound participle as "the heart-knowing God" (*ho kardiognōstēs theos*). In Acts 1:24, Peter and the believers pray, "Thou Lord, the heart-knower of all men" (*kardiognōsta pantōn*). The thought is simultaneously terrifying and liberating. We need maintain no pretensions with Him because there can be no pretensions with Him. There is liberty in complete frankness with Someone Who knows us so transparently.

[8]"The Book of Job was revealed for the purpose of answering this tormenting difficulty" (Gleason Archer, *The Book of Job* [Grand Rapids: Baker, 1982], pp. 17–18).

[9]"Every reader . . . realizes that its purpose is to deal . . . with the problem of suffering" (David J. A. Clines, "Job" in *A Bible Commentary for Today,* ed. G. C. D. Howley [London: Pickering and Inglis, 1979], p. 559). The functional word here is *deal* as opposed to *answer*. As simplistic as Clines's assertion initially sounds, he delves satisfactorily deeper by probing into why is there suffering? who suffers? and how are we to respond to suffering?

[10]In *Why Do the Righteous Suffer?* (Findlay, Ohio: Fundamental Truth Publishers, 1942), Henry Thiessen begs to differ with those who argue that the problem of suffering is not solved or that the reasons for Job's sufferings cannot be "safely inferred" (p. 6), but his explanations are less than convincing (pp. 31–40).

[11]R. K. Harrison, p. 1043. Charles Carter concurs: "To solve the problem of suffering is not the purpose of the author of Job. The book does not give us an answer to that problem" (*The Greatest Book Ever Written: The Book of Job* [Grand Rapids: Eerdmans, 1968], p. 21). G. Campbell Morgan backtracked on his original opinion: "In earlier days of dealing with the book, I described [the purpose] as 'the problem of pain.' I think that may abide, but if it presents the problem of pain, it does not afford any solution of the problem" (*The Answers of Jesus to Job* [Grand Rapids: Baker, 1973], pp. 7–8).

[12]Carter (ibid.) argues that "its first and prime purpose is to show that unselfish devotion to God without regard to temporal benefits, and in spite of human calamities and sufferings, is possible for those who know God intimately and have faith in Him for Himself alone."

[13]A supplementary purpose of Job, says Carter (ibid.), is "to demonstrate the falsity of the traditional deterministic religious doctrine that all calamities and human suffering are divine punishments for sin."

[14]Alexander A. DiLella, "An Existential Interpretation of Job," *Biblical Theology Bulletin* 15, no. 2 (April 1985): 54.

[15]Similarly, nineteenth-century liberals who embarked on the quest for the historical Jesus predictably discovered a Jesus Who looked suspiciously like them. George Tyrrell remarked that the Christ they found was "only the reflection of a Liberal Protestant face, seen at the bottom of a deep well" (*Christianity at the Cross-Roads* [London: Longmans, Green, 1910], p. 44).

[16]Carol Newsom concedes the modern temptation to read Job in this way but adds that it is a two-edged sword (*New Interpreter's Bible,* vol. 4 [Nashville: Abingdon Press, 1996], p. 319). She initially describes Job as a "rebel, who debunks the piety of his friends and boldly accuses God of injustice. In contrast to the majority of Jewish and Christian interpreters over the past centuries, who have often seemed somewhat embarrassed by Job's unrestrained blasphemies, many twentieth-century readers, reeling from a century of unparalleled horror, have been drawn to Job's anger as a voice of moral outrage against a God who could permit such atrocities. The attempt to claim Job as the patron saint of religious rebellion, however, also

encounters embarrassment, for at the end of the book . . . Job withdraws his words against God."

[17]Speaking more broadly, Christianity "is not a system into which we have to fit the awkward fact of pain: it is itself one of the awkward facts which have to be fitted into any system we make. In a sense, it creates, rather than solves, the problem of pain." (C. S. Lewis, *The Problem of Pain* in *The Complete C. S. Lewis Signature Classics* [San Francisco: Harper, 2002], p. 377).

[18]Carson, p. 160.

[19]Robert Gordis expresses this view of Job 38–41: "In inviting Job not merely to understand, but rather to revel in the delights of creation, God is not evading, but rather responding to Job's cry of agony. Viewed against the background of the cosmos, man's sufferings do not disappear, but they grow smaller and more bearable as elements within the larger plan of God's world." Job is thus summoned "to steep himself in the beauty of the world and to experience it existentially. By seizing the two staffs of understanding and emotion, man can live wisely, bravely, and joyfully in a world that is miracle as well as mystery" (*The Book of Job* [New York: The Jewish Theological Seminary of America, 1978], p. 560). This seems to be the philosophy that energizes some Jewish approaches to the Holocaust. In Roberto Benigni's film *La Vita e Bella* ("Life Is Beautiful"), the main character, Guido, confronts anti-Semitic persecution and harassment with good humor. When he ends up in a Nazi death camp, he devotes all his wits and energy to helping his 5-year-old son survive by persuading him that the whole thing is a game. The poignant juxtaposition of horror and humor—and even the title (who could guess "Life Is Beautiful" is about the Holocaust?)—exemplifies Gordis's view.

[20]Carson colorfully summarizes Gordis's view as though God were prescribing "the beauty of the world" as "a kind of aesthetic aspirin" to ameliorate the pain of Job's suffering. "When one basks in the world's beauty, one's problems become petty. . . . But to someone suffering intensely, the beauty of the world can just as easily become a brutal contrast that actually intensifies the suffering. . . . This is surely a massive misunderstanding of God's response. Not once does God minimize the reality of Job's suffering" (p. 173).

[21]"Almost every theory that has been adopted has found itself in collision with one or more of the parts of which the book now consists, and has been able to maintain itself only by sacrificing these parts upon the altar" (A. B. Davidson, *The Book of Job* [Cambridge: University Press, 1908], p. xxiii).

[22]*Yahweh* ("LORD") occurs 30 times—all in the mouth of the narrator except four uses by Job (1:20–21; 12:9). It is the only name for God that appears in the epilogue. *'El* ("God") appears 54 times; *'Eloah* ("God") 42 times; *'Elohim* ("God") 17 times (11 times in Job 1–2); *Shaddai* ("Almighty") 30 times; *'Adonai* ("Lord") once (28:28); *Qadosh* ("Holy One") once (6:10); *Go'el* ("Redeemer") once (19:25); *Mishpat* ("Judge") at least twice (9:15;

22:7); "Maker" 4 times (form of *'asah* in 4:17, 32:22, 35:10; form of *pa'al* in 36:3); "Watcher of men" once (7:20).

[23]H. L. Ellison cites W. B. Stevenson's 1947 study (*The Poem of Job*) as demonstrative evidence "that in the poem there is far less allusion to Job's physical sufferings than has often been assumed. . . . Job's problem is not that of pain, nor even suffering in a wider sense, but the theological one, why God had not acted as all theory and his earlier experience demanded He should" ("Job, Book of" in *The New Bible Dictionary,* ed. J. D. Douglas [Grand Rapids: Eerdmans, 1962], p. 637).

[24]Ellison, ibid.

[25]David J. A. Clines (ibid.) dissects the book's focus on suffering into three questions: (1) Why is there suffering? (2) Who suffers (only the deserving, or the innocent as well)? (3) How are we to respond to suffering? The first two questions are the ones we tend to magnify but Job does not. "This third question is the one that it takes the whole book of Job to answer."

[26]"It is this writer's belief that the purpose of the Book of Job is *to show that the proper relationship between God and man is based solely on the sovereign grace of God and man's response of faith and submissive trust*. . . . This statement of purpose involves the assumption that the relationship between God and man is the basic problem of the book. Although there are several subthemes which have been cited by scholars as the main theme, it is the belief of this writer that only *the basis of the proper relationship between God and man* sufficiently encompasses these subthemes and qualifies, therefore, as the central focus of the book. . . . Thus Job's suffering as an innocent party was not the main focus but was introduced only as a means of isolating and intensifying the question of the basis of man's relationship to God. . . . That this is true is demonstrated by the fact that the main problem of the book was posed before suffering entered the scene and was resolved before Job's suffering was removed" (Gregory Parsons, "The Structure and Purpose of the Book of Job," *Bibliotheca Sacra* 138 [April-June 1981]: 139–57).

[27]David Howard, *How Come, God?* (Philadelphia: A. J. Holman, 1972), p. 22. Howard was a close friend and brother-in-law of murdered missionary Jim Elliot; his sister is Elisabeth Elliot.

[28]Philip Yancey, *Disappointment with God: Questions Nobody Asks Aloud* (Grand Rapids: Zondervan, 1988), pp. 162–64, original emphasis. Unfortunately, Yancey proceeds from this valid observation to a dubious application: "Job—and you and I—can join in the struggle to reverse all that is wrong with the universe" by our response of faith.

[29]Rowley, p. 19.

[30]On this point, Rowley is correct: "To Job the supremely important thing is that God has come to him in his suffering, showing him that he

is not isolated from God by his suffering. He has cried for God again and again, and God has come to him . . . to show him that now, when he most needs God, God is with him" (p. 20).

[31]Joni Eareckson Tada, *When God Weeps: Why Our Sufferings Matter to the Almighty* (Grand Rapids: Zondervan, 1997), pp. 124–25. Written with Steve Estes, the book does have some weaknesses; but overall it is one of the most penetrating treatments of suffering in the light of God's providence. For an overview, see my review in *Biblical Viewpoint* 33, no. 1 (April 1999): 97–101.

[32]Tada, p. 128.

3—What Kind of People Suffer

[1]John Piper, *The Misery of Job and the Mercy of God* (Wheaton, Ill.: Crossway, 2002), p. 15. Piper's brief, poignant, and skillful poetic rendering of the heart of Job (both the book and the man) is a fitting way to capsulize the message of a book originally written in poetic form. He does not merely rehash the tale in his own words but reaches for the soul of the story and fleshes it out in original verse that captures the pathos of the account.

[2]The derivation and meaning of Job's name are ambiguous, so suggestions are as useless as they are speculative. The location of Uz is also uncertain, though references elsewhere seem to identify it with either the land of Aram, south of Damascus in what is today southern Syria (Gen. 10:22–23; 22:21; 1 Chron. 1:17), or Edom, due south of the Dead Sea in what is today southwestern Jordan (Gen. 36:28; Jer. 25:19–21; Lam. 4:21). A third option, based on the Arabic name for Esau, may be "what is now North Arabia where the two cultures (Aramean and Edomite) met or divided from a common origin" (Smick, p. 879). G. Frederick Owen spells out a nine-point case for locating Uz along Wadi Sirhan, "a great shallow plain-like depression some 210 miles long and averaging 20 miles wide," which begins about 50 miles east of Amman and runs southeast nearly to Jauf (Al Jawf) in central Saudi Arabia ("The Land of Uz" in *Sitting with Job*, ed. Roy B. Zuck [Grand Rapids: Baker, 1992], pp. 245–47).

[3]Smick, p. 879.

[4]Dhorme, p. 2.

[5]"Unfortunately our culture has trivialized the word by using its derivative 'awesome' to describe everything from the taste of a soft drink to the deafening music of a rock concert—experiences hardly sublime enough to inspire reverence, dread, and wonder in anyone" (Jim Berg, *Created for His Glory* [Greenville, S.C.: BJU Press, 2002], p. 216).

[6]The "fear of God" deserves a fuller treatment than space permits. Whole books have been devoted to the topic. Jerry Bridges's *Joy of Fearing God* (Colorado Springs: Waterbrook Press, 1997) is a helpful study, though his preference for "reverential awe" is disappointing.

[7]E.g., Acts 5:5, 11; Rom. 11:20; 2 Cor. 5:11; Phil. 2:12; Heb. 12:28; 1 Pet. 1:17.

[8]Jim Berg defines the fear of God as "the awe and reverence left over when the frightening vulnerability before the greatness of God is mixed with the joy of security upon experiencing the goodness of God." He qualifies his definition with this caveat: "I use the word 'awe' in its true sense: 'An emotion of mingled reverence, dread, and wonder inspired by something majestic or sublime' (*The American Heritage Dictionary of the English Language,* s.v. awe)" (Berg, ibid.).

[9]James Strahan, *The Book of Job* (Edinburgh: T. and T. Clark, 1914), p. 33.

[10]H. H. Rowley correctly notes that "more important for the understanding of the book than the home or the name of Job is his character. . . . It is essential that the reader should know from the start that Job's misfortunes are not the penalty of his misdeeds, as his friends assume" (p. 29).

[11]The order of the names is not intended to be chronological but climactic since each of these three survived a context of divine destruction. "Noah saved his family along with himself; Daniel was able to save his friends; but Job, [despite] his righteousness, was not even able to save his children" (C. F. Keil, *Commentary on the Old Testament*, vol. 9 [Grand Rapids: Eerdmans, rpr. 1982], pp. 185–86).

[12]"These three men were used as illustrations because of their righteous character" (Ralph H. Alexander, *Expositor's Bible Commentary*, vol. 6 [Grand Rapids: Zondervan, 1986], p. 807). Nevertheless, the repeated reference to their inability to "deliver" anyone emphasizes that the intercessory intervention of even such righteous men as these, who had the ear and attention of God, would not avail to deliver anyone else but themselves.

[13]Zuck, p. 14. Andersen cites Otto Zöckler as favoring this view (p. 80).

[14]"The text, understood simply as it stands, speaks of a weekly round (Oehler and others). The seven sons took it in turn to dine with one another the week round, and did not forget their sisters in the loneliness of the parental home, but added them to their number" (F. Delitzsch on Job in *Commentary on the Old Testament*, vol. 4 [Grand Rapids: Eerdmans, rpr. 1982], p. 50). Cf. also Carter (p. 26), Dhorme (p. 4), Rowley (p. 29), and Strahan (pp. 34–35).

[15]Even though Archer admits that "little is recorded along this line," he proceeds to speculate that the children's spiritual welfare "was more than a little doubtful," that "their relationship with God was rather perfunctory," and that "Job had reason to feel uneasy about their souls" (Archer, p. 29). Rowley, however, stays safely within the bounds of the text: "It is improbable that there is any thought of impropriety, since the whole account is intended to show that the misfortunes that came upon Job had no cause within his family" (p. 29). In fact, any assumption of ungodliness on the part of Job's

children would only support Eliphaz's own probing suggestion (Job 8:4) when the whole thrust of the book is that the three friends had entirely misdiagnosed the cause of Job's circumstances.

[16]Andersen, p. 80.

[17]William Henry Green, *The Argument of the Book of Job Unfolded* (New York: Hurst and Company, 1891), p. 23.

[18]The verb (*qadosh*) may indicate the idea of ceremonial cleansing in order to insure that the burnt offerings would be efficacious for them.

[19]"Job expresses no anxiety" in his actions on behalf of his children (Andersen, p. 80).

[20]Samuel Terrien, "Job" in *The Interpreter's Bible*, p. 877.

[21]Hillel Fine, "The Tradition of a Patient Job," *Journal of Biblical Literature* 74 (March 1955): 28. Job's frank honesty is admirable indeed, but that does not diminish the validity of James's inspired assessment, if one correctly understands the biblical concept of "patience."

[22]The Greek word *hupomonē* derives from the verb *menō* (to abide, remain) and *hupo* (under). Hiebert admits that "'the patience of Job' does not seem to fit the picture of him as he appears in the book bearing his name." His "impassioned outbursts" make it "obvious that Job was not a model of Stoic impassibility. . . . Although he did reveal remarkable patience in his initial acceptance of his calamities, Job's vehement protests against his sufferings can scarcely be described as 'patient.' But the term James uses here is not that found in verse 10 (*makrothumia*), but rather *hupomonē*, that denotes endurance. In the face of all his unexplained sufferings, Job is a memorable model of endurance under tremendous testing, for under it all he remained unswervingly loyal to God" (*The Epistle of James* [Chicago: Moody Press, 1979], p. 304). Hiebert's distinction between these two terms is correct, though he seems to overlook the fact that James is using these words interchangeably and essentially synonymously. In addition, Job's most impassioned outbursts were a long time in coming (which is, after all, the sense of *makrothumia*), largely provoked by (and often aimed at) his friends.

4—What on Earth (and Beyond) Is Going On?

[1]M. H. Abrams, *A Glossary of Literary Terms*, 3rd ed. (New York: Holt, Rinehart and Winston, Inc., 1971), p. 82.

[2]"Many commentators speak of the arrangement as a wager. This goes beyond the text. There were no stakes, such as the soul of Job, as in later trivial imitations" (Andersen, p. 85). D. A. Carson habitually uses wager terminology (pp. 154–55ff.). Although he later acknowledges the dangerous implications of such language ("it may sound as if God is capricious. He plays with the lives of his creatures so that he can win a bet."), he also insists that the "wager" concept is "congruent with other biblical themes," namely,

the "larger, cosmic struggle between God and Satan, in which the outcome is certain while horrible" (p. 177). It is the certainty of outcome that invalidates wager language. Andersen rightly rejects the "wager" terminology since a wager is, by definition, a gamble, a risk ventured on an uncertain outcome. He is also correct to insist that Job's soul was not at stake. But "stakes" do not require an uncertain gamble, only a contest (or, as I have called it, a warfare). There are stakes. But it was not Job's soul that was at stake. The stakes were far higher than that.

[3]The Hebrew word is occasionally used of a human enemy (1 Sam. 29:4; 1 Kings 11:14, 23, 25; Ps. 109:20, 29). The individual in Job is an angelic adversary, translated elsewhere in the OT as a proper name only in Zech. 3:1–2, possibly Ps. 109:6, and 1 Chron. 21:1. In this last reference "Satan has become a proper name, without the article" who "acts as the *agent provocateur*, inciting men to evil" (Rowley, p. 31). "Satan" becomes the standard NT designation for the leader of fallen angels.

[4]Andersen, p. 83.

[5]The frequent OT term "perfect heart" does not denote sinlessness. In Deut. 27:5–6, God commanded the Israelites to build an altar using only "whole" stones that were not cut, fashioned, or shaped with any iron tool. The word *whole* is the word *perfect*—the adjective form of *shalom,* a term that has reference to wholeness, soundness, completeness. First Chronicles describes the men who came "with a perfect heart" to make David king (12:38); they were united in their agreement and loyal in their commitment to David's right to be king. Six kings are described specifically in terms of whether they had a "perfect heart"—David, Solomon, Abijam, Asa, Amaziah, and Hezekiah. Read their biographies carefully and you discover a consistent thread that indicates whether someone had a perfect heart. It was not the presence of mere outward obedience, nor the absence of sin; some of them were guilty of serious moral failure. In every case the possession or absence of a perfect heart involved their rejection or tolerance of *idolatry*—the division of their loyalty to any god other than Yahweh. A perfect heart is undivided, devoted, and loyal only to Yahweh as the one true God.

[6]The New Testament pledges the same perpetual presence of God with His people (Heb. 13:5–6) and in His people (1 John 4:4).

[7]C. S. Lewis, *The Screwtape Letters* (New York: Macmillan Publishing, 1961), p. vii.

[8]Andersen, p. 82.

[9]Walter Kaiser, *More Hard Sayings of the Old Testament* (Downers Grove, Ill.: InterVarsity Press, 1992), p. 186. Walter Kaiser describes this as the "most surprising feature" of this "glimpse [into] a most extraordinary scene in the invisible world."

[10]"Devices" sounds mechanistic, conjuring up images of instruments or weaponry. But this English translation denotes that which is first *devised* by the mind, reflecting the Greek term used in 2 Cor. 2:11 (*noēmata*)—a term that "signifies the function of the intellective faculty (nous)" (Philip E. Hughes, *The Second Epistle to the Corinthians* [Grand Rapids: Eerdmans, 1962], p. 72). The plural form here has a "sinister" (Hughes) or "pejorative sense of 'schemes,' 'designs,' 'plots,' or 'wiles,'" and "one of the Christian's defenses against the devil's stratagems is prior awareness of his purposes and methods, particularly his wish to turn good into evil" (Murray J. Harris, "2 Corinthians" in *The Expositor's Bible Commentary*, vol. 10 [Grand Rapids: Zondervan, 1976], p. 330).

[11]I am indebted for most of these observations to Robert D. Bell in "The Truth About Satan (and God)" in *Biblical Viewpoint* 22, no. 2 (Nov. 1987): 4–8.

[12]Ibid., p. 6.

[13]Robinson, p. 45.

[14]Ibid., p. 46.

[15]For a description and analysis of "prosperity theology" see David Smith, *A Handbook of Contemporary Theology* (Grand Rapids: Baker, 1992), chap. 12.

[16]So speaks Gandalf to the treasonous Saruman when the latter suspects a hook in a genuine and generous offer (J. R. R. Tolkien, *The Two Towers*, Part Two of *The Lord of the Rings* [Boston: Houghton Mifflin, 1965], p. 188). The remark reflects a keen insight into fallen nature. Those who are suspect and untrustworthy are always suspicious and distrustful of others, because they measure all others by their own vices. They assume that everyone else is, deep down, just as self-serving and opportunistic as they are.

[17]Kaiser, p. 187.

[18]The NIV has a more refined ring to it ("that ancient serpent") while the allegedly "wooden" NASB waxes poetic ("the serpent of old"). These renderings are in keeping with Stewart Custer's observation that "the word here is ἀρχαῖος, which means *going back to the beginning* (ἀρχή), the *original* serpent in the Garden of Eden" (*From Patmos to Paradise: A Commentary on Revelation* [Greenville, S.C.: BJU Press, 2004], p. 138). Personally, I like the down-to-earth NCV rendering—"that old snake."

[19]For additional passages and elaboration on this point, see Talbert, *Not by Chance: Learning to Trust a Sovereign God* (Greenville, S.C.: BJU Press, 2001), chap. 9.

[20]I am, of course, borrowing a famous image from C. S. Lewis's *The Lion, the Witch, and the Wardrobe*. In a game of hide-and-seek, Lucy conceals herself in an old wardrobe and "accidentally" discovers at the back of the closet an entrance into the parallel spiritual world of Narnia.

[21]Angels nourish "a strong interest or craving . . . to bend . . . forward to examine more closely" God's redemptive activity for man (Hiebert, p. 71).

Part of Peter's point here is that believers one-up even the angels because of our unparalleled "privilege of enjoying and anticipating salvation. . . . Old Testament prophets saw it from afar, and angels also marvel when gazing upon what God has done in Christ, while the Petrine readers actually experience it" (Schreiner, p. 76).

[22]I. Howard Marshall, *1 Peter* (Downers Grove, Ill.: InterVarsity Press, 1991), p. 47.

[23]Describing the experience of John McAllister, a once-healthy believer suffering from a degenerative disease, Tada vividly applies this truth. "Something dynamic and electrifying is abuzz in John's room, agitating the atmosphere around and above his home. Angels, along with powers and principalities in the heavenly realms, are watching, listening, and *learning.* People may not be noticing John McAllister, but the spiritual world is. Angels—even demons—are intensely interested in the thoughts and affections of every human being." Citing Ephesians 3:10, she continues, "God's purpose is to teach millions of unseen beings about himself; and we are . . . a blackboard upon which God is drawing lessons about himself for the benefit of angels and demons. God gets glory every time the spirit world learns how powerful his everlasting arms are in upholding the weak. . . . My friend's life is not a waste. Although not many people seem to care, someone—a great many someones—care more than John can imagine" (*When God Weeps,* pp. 107–8).

[24]Charles Bridges, *The Christian Ministry,* 1830 (Edinburgh: Banner of Truth Trust, rpr. 1980), p. 1. This classic warrants careful reading from anyone in or entering the ministry.

[25]Anthony C. Thiselton, *The First Epistle to the Corinthians* (Grand Rapids: Eerdmans, 2000), p. 359. "Set forth" is the verb *apodeiknumi*, a different prefix but the same root as *endeiknumi* in Eph. 2:7.

[26]Lit., "'what one sees at a theater,' thus a play or a spectacle" (Gordon Fee, *The First Epistle to the Corinthians* [Grand Rapids: Eerdmans, 1987], p. 174).

[27]"Paul says there is a cosmic dimension to the spectacle: He is on display before the whole universe, as it were—not just human beings, but angels as well" (Fee, p. 175). In the context of 1 Corinthians, Paul is deflating the Corinthians' pride in their wisdom and position in Christ with a splash of the cold water of reality to the face, by reminding them that sometimes God's choicest servants endure brutal suffering. The point for our purpose is the confirmation that angels are in the audience watching, learning as much about God as they are about men.

[28]The LXX renders the phrase "the sons of God" as "the angels of God." The phrase is almost universally understood to be a reference to the angelic hosts. See, e.g., Dhorme, p. 5; Rowley, p. 31; Strahan, p. 37 (though his explanation takes an unusual twist); Keil, pp. 52–53; Smick, p. 880; Kaiser, pp. 186–87. Liberals see in the phraseology of Job 1:6 the use of mythopoeic

language describing a common pagan conception of a "divine council," an assembly of the gods who gather to make cosmic decisions (Bernard F. Batto, *Slaying the Dragon: Mythmaking in the Biblical Tradition* [Louisville: Westminster/John Knox Press, 1992], pp. 93, 214). Gregory Parsons addresses this issue in "Literary Features of the Book of Job" (*Sitting with Job,* ed. Roy B. Zuck, pp. 42–47).

[29]Doesn't the benevolent nature of God *demand* that He rescue the poor, miserable, helpless, drowning sinner? If that were a valid depiction of the case, the point might also be valid. But the analogy is flawed. Humanity is not like an innocent drowning man. Humanity is a boat full of mutineers who have seized the ship, marooned the officers, taken the cargo for themselves, and set sail for a port of their own choosing in order to profit personally from what is not their own. It is a question of rebellion, not morality. So when a storm shipwrecks that vessel and leaves the crew flailing about in the water crying for help, it is a just divine retribution. (I am indebted for this illustration to my pastor, Dr. Mark Minnick, in a sermon titled "Was Atonement Necessary? or Was God Obligated to Provide Salvation?")

[30]The word *freely* in Romans 3:24 is *dōrean*, a form of the word *gift*. A gift compelled or obligated is no longer a gift; it becomes, by definition, a duty. If salvation were God's "duty" compelled by our worth or by His "job description," it would not be the free and undeserved gift it is described to be throughout the NT.

[31]Henry Morris perceives this as half of the purpose of Job. In view of the celestial witnesses to the satanic accusation (1:6ff.), "not only Satan and his demonic hosts but also all the holy angels of God must have been following the developments on earth with intense interest" (*The Remarkable Record of Job* [Grand Rapids: Baker, 1988], p. 92). Citing Eph. 3:9–11, Morris adds, "Job's ordeal and his faithfulness through it was a marvelous testimony—not only to Satan but also to the entire host of heaven" (p. 93). Morris's "second half" of the purpose of Job, though understandable for a creation scientist, is not convincing from either a literary or theological perspective. The importance of the doctrine of creationism in order "to keep the still-believing remnant from drifting into pagan evolution" and "evolutionary humanism" (p. 94) might be better stated as an important byproduct or peripheral truth rather than part of the central purpose of the book of Job.

[32]Kidner, p. 59.

[33]The same word translated "freely" in Rom. 3:24 and "without a cause" in John 15:25 (*dōrean*) also appears in the LXX rendering of Job 1:9 though, unfortunately, it is omitted in 2:3 in favor of a different construction.

[34]The introductory note in the *NIV Study Bible* (Grand Rapids: Zondervan, 1995) is mistaken on this point: "At stake in the suffering of the truly godly is the outcome of the struggle in heaven between the great adversary and God, with the all-encompassing divine purpose in the

balance. Thus the suffering of the righteous has a meaning and value commensurate with the titanic spiritual struggle of the ages" (p. 732).

[35]In the unrelenting vise of suffering, Job will cry out, "Though he slay me, yet will I hope in him" (Job 13:15). "A statement like that speaks highly of Job. But it speaks more highly of God. . . . A sacrifice of praise makes praise more glorious. . . . A sacrifice brightens God's glory" (Tada, pp. 108–10).

[36]Donald S. Whitney, *Simplify Your Spiritual Life* (Colorado Springs: NavPress, 2003), pp. 126–27.

[37]Eric Sigg (*The American T. S. Eliot: A Study of the Early Writings* [Cambridge: Cambridge University Press, 1989], p. 31) documents Eliot's famous remark as occurring in an address to a group of Unitarian ministers in Boston (*Christian Register*, "The Modern Dilemma," October 19, 1933, p. 676).

5—A Model Response to Devastating Loss

[1]Gandalf argues that the plan to destroy a ring of great power would be a strategy beyond Sauron's comprehension, for "the only measure he knows is desire, desire for power; and so he judges all hearts. Into his heart the thought will not enter that any will refuse it, that having the Ring we may seek to destroy it. If we seek this, we shall put him out of reckoning" (J. R. R. Tolkien, *The Fellowship of the Ring* [Boston: Houghton Mifflin, 1965], pp. 282-83).

[2]"Job, while reeling in shock from the news of one loss, was stunned with another" (Zuck, p. 16).

[3]Nearly all commentators agree this is a reference to the lightning of an electrical storm. We need not wonder how lightning could incinerate 7,000 sheep along with the servants. Nothing in the text precludes multiple lightning strikes. Others have suggested that the barn(s) housing the sheep and servants were struck (Zuck, p. 16). I once saw a lightning-struck barn devoured in an almost instantaneous conflagration. Smick argues that the "terminology 'of God' as part of a cliché does not mean God is considered the immediate source in this context. It is simply phenomenological language because it came from heaven" (p. 883). Even insurance companies refer to "acts of God" without any religious intent. However, it is clear from the text that Job and everyone else did see these events as coming from God.

[4]This peculiar language of returning to the womb has elicited considerable comment. Some explain that Job parallels his mother's womb with the womb of the earth from which all men spring: "Man, once dead, enters the matrix of the earth" (Dhorme, p. 13). By "returning thither," Smick agrees, Job had in mind his burial back in the earth from which he was taken (Smick, p. 883). Rowley complains, however, that "commentators bring singularly

prosaic minds to this phrase"; as "this verse is in poetry, and is not addressed to prosaic minds" it means simply, "Naked I came into life and naked I shall die" (Rowley, p. 35). Andersen concurs but adds that "'thither' could be a euphemism for Sheol, 'that place,' as in Job 3:17, 19" (Andersen, p. 88). Cf. Eccles. 5:15; 1 Tim. 6:7.

[5]Andersen, p. 88.

[6]Archer, p. 35.

[7]The phrase, borrowed from John Piper's *Desiring God* (Portland, Ore.: Multnomah, 1986), is drawn from a superb treatment of three stages of worship: (1) the highest stage of worship, "an unencumbered joy" in the presence and "perfections of God"; (2) a transitional stage of yearning for that "unencumbered joy" and fullness of heart; and (3) the lowest form, "the barrenness of soul that scarcely feels any longing, and is still granted the grace of repentant sorrow for having so little love." Even the lowest form glorifies God: "If God were not gloriously desirable, why would we feel sorrowful for not feasting fully on his beauty?" (p. 76).

[8]Andersen, p. 89.

[9]Ibid.

[10]This is the sense of NASB, NCV.

[11]This is the sense of NKJV, NIV, ESV.

[12]"If Job did not charge God with doing anything worthless, he must have believed God had a high purpose" (Smick, 883).

[13]Andersen, p. 89.

[14]Ibid.

[15]The predominant meaning of *barak* is "to bless" (*'arar* is the normal word for "curse"). In fact, Satan himself uses it in this sense in 1:10, when he complains that God has "blessed the work" of Job's hands. *Barak* occurs over 300 times in the OT, and aside from the references cited in Job (1:5, 9, 11; 2:5, 9), it conveys the connotation of "curse" or "blaspheme" in only one other passage (1 Kings 21:10, 13). How the word developed this double use is less certain. Andersen suggests that the word here could have been introduced as a pure euphemism "to avoid even reading such a horrid expression. . . . It could be, however, that out of such a practice the word actually acquires the opposite meaning when the context determines" (p. 81).

[16]I once gave this explanation and illustration to an Ohio congregation, only to be greeted with blank stares. They had no idea what I was talking about. Maybe the South has some long-lost linguistic link to biblical languages. After all, the double negatives of the New Testament are routine in the South, and Paul regularly addressed his readers as "y'all." The formal translations say "you all" (Rom. 1:8; 15:33; 16:24; 1 Cor. 16:24; 2 Cor. 13:14; etc.), but Southerners know what Paul meant.

6—Who Is Responsible for This?

[1]Leland Ryken's concern to highlight the dramatic irony in the story clouds his precision in expressing the theological truth underscored by the text. "As readers," he says, "we know that God is not the cause of Job's suffering (Satan is)" (*How to Read the Bible as Literature* [Grand Rapids: Academie Books, 1984], p. 55). The dramatic irony does not reside in the fact that Job (and the others) think that God was responsible for all this calamity while it was really Satan, but in the reader's awareness of the reason for Job's suffering (a test of the integrity of both man and God) as well as Satan's involvement in his circumstances—while both Job and his friends remain ignorant of both. Their fundamental conviction that God is the One ultimately behind all this is an orthodox echo of God's own affirmation (2:3) and one of the central planks in the sturdy theological platform of the book of Job.

[2]For a discussion of the ramifications of these options, see Talbert, *Not by Chance*, chap. 1, especially pp. 22–24. For a superb apologetical analysis of the age-old "problem of evil" see John Blanchard, *Does God Believe in Atheists* (Auburn, Mass.: Evangelical Press, 2000), chap. 22–23.

[3]This discussion invites an important lesson in our expression of theology. If we are serious about the doctrine of inspiration, we should be equally serious about expressing the Bible's theology in the Bible's terms. Men who believe in election shy away from using the word simply because others might misunderstand it. *Election* is a Bible word. Use it accurately, by all means, but use it. Are we wiser than God in our use of language, or do we suppose that God didn't foresee the theological fallout that would accompany certain terms and concepts? If there is calamity in the city (be it Oklahoma City or New York City, Beijing or Baghdad), then God did it. If He is not afraid to say so (Amos 3:6), should we be? We may need to qualify such biblical terms and phrases with additional biblical explanation (e.g., that God does not originate moral evil or tempt men to commit the sinful acts that contribute to that calamity). That is part of His testimony as well. But in the profoundest providential and biblical sense of the term, He "did" it. He is sovereign and He is in control. He Himself affirms this truth. He is God enough to accept that responsibility.

[4]Few commentators give this verse the theological weight it warrants or its remarkable terminology the attention it deserves. Zuck inexplicably skips 2:3 altogether in his running commentary on the text.

[5]See *tamah* (2:3, 9; 27:5; 31:6); *tam* (1:1, 8; 2:3; 8:20; 9:20, 21, 22); *tōm* (4:6; 21:23); *tamim* (12:4; 36:4; 37:16).

[6]J. Barton Payne in *Theological Wordbook of the Old Testament*, vol. 2, ed. R. Laird Harris, Gleason L. Archer, Jr., and Bruce K. Waltke (Chicago: Moody Press, 1980), p. 974.

[7]The juxtaposition of 2 Sam. 24:1 (which states that God moved David against Israel to number them) and 1 Chron. 21:1 (which states that Satan moved David to number Israel) is not contradictory but theologically complementary. God never prompts anyone to sin (James 1:13). Such an action is contrary to His nature and unnecessary. All God needs to do is withhold His grace and allow human nature to take its natural course (James 1:14–15). Left to himself, anyone is fully capable of initiating all manner of sin on his own. "You and I have enough evil residing in us that if God were to let us have our own way, we would destroy ourselves" (Jim Berg, *Changed into His Image* [Greenville, S.C.: BJU Press, 1999], p. 42). God merely "manages" it for His own ends and glory. In the case of David, God authorized (permitted) Satan to tempt David in keeping with his own voluntary inclination at this time to occasion a divine chastening on the nation. Cf. J. Barton Payne, "1,2 Chronicles" in *Expositor's Bible Commentary,* vol. 4 (Grand Rapids: Zondervan, 1988), pp. 406–7.

[8]This term "needs some clarification. Satan had a cause or reason for doing it—to discredit God, and certainly God was accomplishing his own cause or purpose. In 1:9 Satan used the same word to accuse Job of having an ulterior purpose for serving God. Now God taunts the Accuser with the counteraccusation that Satan himself is the one who wants to see injustice done. The translation of this keyword as 'without any good reason' is good at this point. It means that there was no immediate sinfulness in Job that called for punishment. Another possible translation . . . is 'in vain' (cf. JB). This would suggest that Satan has wasted his energy on Job. But that meaning is rare in the OT" (Smick, p. 884).

[9]Kidner, p. 60.

[10]Henry Morris asserts that Job's troubles, "though allowed by God, did not originate with God" for God "would not deliberately have afflicted such tribulation on one he loved as much as Job," (p. 117). This is theologically tidy but textually (and hence theologically) imprecise. The narrative itself, and particularly God's own statement in 2:3 (which Morris fails to address), insist that Job's experience *did* ultimately "originate" with God. God first brought up Job's name and granted Satan both the permission and the parameters of Job's suffering. God's action here was as "deliberate" as bruising His own Son (Isa. 53:10–11; cf. Acts 4:27–28).

[11]Like other terms and phrases in Job, this proverb has given rise to extended discussion. See Rowley (p. 37) and Andersen (p. 90) for summaries. No one is certain of the origin or precise meaning of this proverb, but the remainder of verse 4 clarifies the intent.

[12]The verb *desired* literally means "to obtain by asking." Christ was not warning the disciples that Satan would like to get his hands on them; He was informing them that Satan had already received God's permission to get

his hands on them. The sifting process had already begun and would continue throughout the next few dark days.

[13]H. H. Rowley, "The Book of Job and Its Meaning," in *From Moses to Qumran* (New York: Association Press, 1963), pp. 176–77.

[14]In His message of comfort and courage to His suffering people in the church at Smyrna, Christ forewarns them of a period of impending persecution. Significantly, the text does *not* read that "the Devil is about to cast some of you into prison in order to test you." The purpose infinitive is cast in the passive tense: "the Devil is about to throw some of you into prison, in order that *you may be tested*" (Rev. 2:10, lit.). Satan does the throwing into prison, but *not* the testing. He doesn't care about "testing"; he seeks only to devour (1 Pet. 5:8). The scene here is Jobian. God gives Satan permission to throw them into prison (whereby he hopes to destroy their faith and devour them), but it is the *Lord's* purpose that they may be tested—proven, strengthened, and graced to endure.

[15]Piper, *The Misery of Job*, p. 39.

[16]Naomi's perception of her sufferings is eventually corrected by the compassion of God's providential provision for both her and Ruth. For more detail see Talbert, *Not by Chance,* pp. 115–17.

[17]Archer, p. 118.

[18]The standard translation that God does not afflict "willingly" (KJV, NKJV, NASB, ESV, NIV) seems almost to infer the theologically and biblically untenable—that He does so against His will. As insipid as it sounds on the surface, the NCV probably comes closest to capturing the sense of the idiom: "He does not like to punish people or make them sad." Emphasis on a sovereign and self-determining God Who always acts according to His good pleasure should not be couched in language that contradicts these kinds of counterpoint expressions of the personality of God. Something as just and right as chastening rebellious Judah may be the pleasure of God, but doing it does not give Him pleasure. If He could, He would rather bless; that is what is in His heart.

[19]Andersen, p. 92.

[20]Green (pp. 93–99) regards the severity with which she is sometimes judged to be "quite undeserved." From all appearances, she has stood with him shoulder to shoulder until now, facing the same losses with the same fortitude and submission. This final stroke simply proved too much for her, as she counsels Job: "Since you must die, die cursing, not blessing, the author of your misery, the source of all our bitter woe." That Job does not call her a foolish woman but says instead that she is speaking *like* one implies, says Green, that this was uncharacteristic of her. "It is unfair to put the worst construction possible upon the language of Job's wife in this case, and then

make her conduct on this occasion the index to her whole life." Strahan concurs (p. 47).

[21]Rowley (p. 39) notes that the early church Fathers "compared the role of Job's wife with that of Eve in tempting Adam." Augustine, he says, dubbed her *diaboli adjutrix* (Devil's helper). Calvin, adds Andersen (p. 92), called her *organum Satani* (an instrument of Satan).

[22]In Piper's poem, Job's wife ("Dinah") is spiritually recovered by Job's pleas (p. 41). In a twist as touching as it is imaginative, Piper has Job explain to her that his disease is actually an answer to prayer. "What prayer?" she asks, "What did you bid him do?" "That I should bear this pain," Job replies, "Not you" (*The Misery of Job*, p. 39).

[23]Delitzsch, pp. 71–72. Long-time missionary in the hills of Kentucky, Mrs. L. C. Easterling, once confided her homespun observation on the preservation of Job's wife. When God finally blessed Job with a new family, she remarked, guess who had to have ten more children all over again?

[24]Green, p. 98.

7—How to Help the Hurting

[1]D. A. Carson's label of choice for the friends is "the miserable comforters," (p. 161ff.).

[2]Morris, p. 75. Morris's cardboard characterizations are disappointing. The three friends are stereotypical, self-righteous finger pointers with no redeeming qualities; Elihu's arrogance is matched only by his ignorance; and Job's response throughout is so flawless that one is almost surprised that God managed to find anything for which to rebuke him (cf. p. 114).

[3]Kidner, pp. 60–61. It is their failure to address Job's situation accurately and convincingly, *despite* their solidarity with the orthodox theology, that highlights a crucial function of the book of Job—to provide a platform on which the *exceptions* to proverbial wisdom and life by law in a moral universe may be addressed.

[4]Tremper Longman III, "Biblical Narrative," *A Complete Literary Guide to the Bible,* ed. Leland Ryken and Tremper Longman III (Grand Rapids: Zondervan, 1993), p. 75. The ellipsis in this quotation deletes Longman's ill-advised expression that "the narrator is *a device used by authors* to shape and guide how the reader responds. . . ." (emphasis added).

[5]Roy Zuck's collection of essays on the book of Job is superbly titled *Sitting with Job.*

[6]Archer (pp. 121-24) concludes his brief commentary on Job with an analysis of the failures of the three friends, from whom "we can learn about what we should *not* do." Some of his points overlap with those I have cited. (1) They "tried to show appropriate sympathy but failed to achieve empathy" in that "they made no effort to see Job's afflictions from his viewpoint."

(2) They "also attempted to argue with Job about theological issues and preach at him in a condemnatory way, rather than encouraging him to pour forth all of his feelings." Both of these failures arise from a third. (3) They "assumed they knew the reason for Job's misfortunes. . . . It was egregiously offensive and insulting for the three critics to conclude without any corroborative evidence that Job was guilty and needed to repent." Archer offers several points to the counselor. (a) "An effective advisor should be very slow to condemn a victim of misfortune for expressing deep grief and bitter complaint." (b) "In general it is best for the comforter to establish an empathetic rapport with his counselee as soon as possible, and to give him full opportunity to unburden his heart and express all of the bitterness pent up inside him before attempting to lead him to theological insights into a possible meaning for his experience." (c) "One should be very cautious about quoting the well-known standard Bible verses that apply to times of misfortune and trial"; the sufferer "may perceive that the counselor has not earned the right, through personal experience, to apply them to the misery of someone else." (d) "If there is an underlying anger toward God in the heart of the sufferer, it is more helpful to wait a while before attempting any kind of full-scale Bible instruction."

[7] John Milton, "Sonnet on His Blindness" in *One Hundred and One Famous Poems* (Chicago: Contemporary Books, 1959), p. 87.

[8] A bit of historical detail does wonders for the twenty-first-century reader trying to imagine this scene. Thanks to a severe drought and a stuck tractor wheel (God's providential tools are amazing), archaeologists in January 1986 discovered along the shore of the Sea of Galilee what turned out to be a fishing vessel dating to the era of Christ (specifically between the first century BC and the late first century AD). It measured 26.5 feet long, 7.5 feet wide, and 4.5 feet high. It had a mast and probably a decked-in bow and stern, like the stern deck under which Jesus slept on "the pillow" (Mark 4:38)—the definite article indicating that "the pillow" was a regular part of the boat's gear, such as a sandbag used for ballast. The discovered ship could have handily accommodated Jesus and His disciples, several of whom were skilled fishermen and sailors. See Shelley Wachsmann, "The Galilee Boat," *Biblical Archaeology Review* 14, no. 5 (September/October 1988): 18–33.

[9] John Bunyan, *The Pilgrim's Progress* (Edinburgh: Banner of Truth, 1977, rpr. 1990), p. 68.

[10] Tada, pp. 131–32.

[11] Alister McGrath, quoted by John Blanchard, *Does God Believe in Atheists?* p. 577.

[12] I have alluded already to Bunyan's account of Christian in the Valley of the Shadow of Death. In the same section, Bunyan shows remarkable insight when he describes Christian as "so confounded that he did not know his own voice." For "one of the Wicked Ones got behind him, and stept up

softly to him, and whisperingly suggested many grievous blasphemies to him, which he verily thought had proceeded from his own mind. This put Christian more to it than anything he met with before, even to think that he should now blaspheme him that loved him so much before; yet, if he could have helped it, he would not have done it: But he had not the discretion either to stop his ears, or to know from whence those Blasphemies came" (ibid.).

8—How to Read the Debate

[1]J. R. R. Tolkien, *The Fellowship of the Ring*, p. 413. Despite the ominous context in which these words were spoken, they do have a ring of good sense.

[2]For a compelling example of the power of intonation of the written word—as well as an enjoyable and edifying experience—see *Behold! The Gospel According to Mark*, a solo reading performance on DVD of the entire Gospel of Mark by Lonnie Polson (Greenville, S.C.: ShowForth Videos, 2003).

[3]David J. A. Clines, "The Arguments of Job's Three Friends," *Sitting with Job*, ed. Roy B. Zuck (Grand Rapids: Baker, 1992), p. 266.

[4]"Perception of tonality depends partly on the subjective impression of the reader," Clines concedes, but "clues to tonality are sometimes given rather unmistakably" in the text (p. 266). Though Clines addresses (in a more sophisticated manner) the role of kernel statements in determining tonality, he does not discuss the "clues" provided by the narrator or by Job's reactions.

[5]D. A. Carson's front-end summary dismissal is disappointing: "Job's friends offer glib answers and a condemning spirit" (p. 161).

[6]H. L. Ellison, *From Tragedy to Triumph* (Grand Rapids: Eerdmans, 1958), p. 87.

[7]Mark Littleton, "Where Job's 'Comforters' Went Wrong," in *Sitting with Job*, ed. Roy B. Zuck (Grand Rapids: Zondervan, 1992), pp. 254–55.

[8]Clines (pp. 266–67) has a more refined treatment of this concept of kernel statements, which he calls "nodal sentences." He cites 4:6 as a good example. On the surface this could be intoned as either "reproachful" or "encouraging," but "the rest of the speech gives us no reason to suppose" that he is saying this "with a sneer" but, rather, affirmingly. Consequently, 4:5 could be intoned aggressively (as Carson suggests below), "but in the shadow of the clear tonality of v. 6, it can only be heard as sympathy." Clines cites 5:8, a second "nodal sentence" in Eliphaz's first speech, as "a crucial sentence for perceiving Eliphaz's mood and message" as sympathetic.

[9]"The Hebrew text of this book is one of the most difficult found in the Hebrew Bible, partly because it contains poetry of high dramatic quality and partly because it may be modeled on [better, reflect] an earlier drama [or

version] that was not Israelite in origin" (James VanderKam and Peter Flint, *The Meaning of the Dead Sea Scrolls* [San Francisco: Harper Collins, 2002], p. 120).

[10]Plainly those translators were struggling as well, despite being natively well versed in Hebrew. The Greek translation of the book of Job is one of the major anomalies of the LXX. It is often one of the loosest translations of the OT. "Dynamic equivalence" would be an understatement. The single statement of Job's wife in the Hebrew text, for example, is a six-verse speech in the LXX. Dhorme catalogues examples in the LXX of paraphrase or explanation, theological speculation, metaphor changes, misunderstanding of the Hebrew text, inversions, redundancies, and lacunae (pp. cxcvi–ccvi). See also Rowley, pp. 25–26; Smick, pp. 855–58. Unfortunately the Dead Sea Scroll discoveries offer minimal help with the book of Job (Martin Abegg Jr., Peter Flint, and Eugene Ulrich, *The Dead Sea Scrolls Bible* [San Francisco: Harper Collins, 1999], p. 590).

[11]Some translations, such as the NASB 1995 update, attempt to mitigate this ambiguity by capitalizing pronominal references to deity. Nevertheless many contexts where the pronoun reference is ambiguous do not involve God at all. A classic example occurs in Luke 22:31–32 (see Talbert, *Not by Chance*, pp. 175–76). Modern translations should devise some unobtrusive way of marking which "you's" are singular and which are plural.

9—Anguish Finds a Voice

[1]Elizabeth Gaskell, *Wives and Daughters* (New York: Penguin Books, 2001), p. 557.

[2]David J. A. Clines, "A Brief Explanation of Job 1–3" in *Sitting with Job*, ed. Roy B. Zuck (Grand Rapids: Baker, 1992), pp. 249–50.

[3]Delitzsch, pp. 84–85. Job "does not despair when he contemplates his affliction, but when he looks at God through it," and all the evidence seems to suggest that God has become his enemy. Job starts out well in "submission to the providence of God." But now that "not only the affliction, but God himself, seems to him to be hostile," despair descends upon Job like a cloudburst.

[4]Delitzsch notes the widely recognized divisions of chapter 3 as 3–10, 11–19, and 20–26, "in the first of which delirious cursing of life is expressed; in the second eager longing for death; in the third, reproachful inquiry after the end of such a life of suffering" (pp. 75–76). Also noteworthy is the two-fold division cited (as the work of Freedman and Habel) by Smick: "A curse (vv. 3–10), followed by a complimentary [sic] lament (vv. 11–26). Each unit has a framing device (inclusio). Each opens by announcing the subject and closes by giving the reason" (p. 890).

[5]Robinson, p. 19.

[6] Thornton Wilder's almost biblical play *Our Town* climaxes with the dead in the cemetery up on the hill, aware of but indifferent to everything going on above them, understanding for the first time the preoccupation of the living with the trivial, and waiting for "something big" to happen. Wittingly or unwittingly, it is woven with much of the same fabric as the OT wisdom books, especially Job and Ecclesiastes.

[7]3:11 (2x), 12 (2x), 16, 20, 23; 7:20, 21; 9:29; 10:2, 18; 13:14, 24; 21:7; 24:1. The question is often implied where it is not stated.

[8]"No one ever told me that grief felt so much like fear." With these words C. S. Lewis opens *A Grief Observed*, his diary of personal pain and loss.

[9]Job's remark in 3:25 "is not a sign that he did not *really* trust God, and therefore got what he deserved: that would subvert the purpose of the entire book—in the third chapter at that!" (Carson, p. 159).

[10]Zuck, p. 27.

[11]Andersen, p. 110.

[12]"Job in his anguish is tortured also by the fear that he has only to think of some new evil and it is sure to come upon him" (Rowley, p. 49).

[13]Carson, p. 159.

[14]Tada provides a number of thoughtful and biblical answers forged in the furnace of her own pursuit of God amid personal suffering (chap. 7–9). Nevertheless, she concludes, even "good answers aren't enough" because "answers are for the head." We need something that penetrates deeper. The best answers are relational, for "reasons reach the head, but relationships reach the soul." In short, suffering is the divinely ordained catalyst to draw, or drive, us to God. That was its net effect on Job.

[15]Pastor Ronald Dunn's son tried to commit suicide and later died in a car accident. As a father and pastor, he has explored on a very personal level why we ask "Why?" (1) Unanswered whys disturb the orderliness of life. The assumption of order gives life predictability, explanations, meaning, and understanding. (2) If we can understand why, we think we can prevent a repetition of the tragedy. "Could it be that our own urgency to know why [calamities befall others] arises from the fear that the same thing could happen to us?" (This appears to be what unnerved Job's friends in the face of his insistent claim to innocence.) (3) We seek absolution from guilt, which often follows grief. (4) We seek moral equalization (when we assume an injustice has been done). But this is a curiously one-way street. We often ask "why me?" but seldom, "why *not* me?" We often ask "why is there evil in the world?" but rarely do we ask "why is there *good* in the world?" (5) We attempt to vindicate God and His actions. (6) We cannot live with mystery. See *When Heaven Is Silent* (Thomas Nelson, 1994).

[16]Tada, p. 22.

[17]Dunn, ibid.

[18]Job's reference to his words as "the speeches of one that is desperate" (6:26) employs the Hebrew word that means (and is elsewhere translated) "to despair" or "to be hopeless" (cf. 1 Sam. 27:1; Eccles. 2:20; Isa. 57:10; Jer. 2:25; 18:12). "Desperate" is simply an adjectival form of the verb "despair."

[19]Archer, p. 123.

[20]Delitzsch insists, "It is inconceivable that a New Testament believer, even under the strongest temptation, should utter such imprecations, or especially such a question of doubt as in ver. 20: Wherefore is light given to the miserable?" Such doubt on the part of an Old Testament believer "may be accounted for by the absence of any express divine revelation to carry his mind beyond the bounds of the present" (pp. 85–86).

[21]The same observation may be made of Joseph, another believer of profound and practical theological depth who antedated written Scripture. For an outline of Joseph's theology, see footnote 7 on pp. 275–76 of my book *Not by Chance.*

[22]Delitzsch feels obliged, in the midst of his discussion of Job, to spend nearly two pages attempting to justify Jeremiah's Job-like language (pp. 86–88). I do not find his explanation convincing.

[23]Smick, pp. 888, 891.

[24]David J. A. Clines dissects the book's focus on suffering into three questions: (1) Why is there suffering? (2) Who suffers (only the deserving, or the innocent as well)? (3) How are we to respond to suffering? "This third question is the one that it takes the whole book of Job to answer." That answer is twofold: (a) With submissive acquiescence. "The sufferer who can identify with Job's [initial] acceptance, neither ignoring the reality of suffering by escaping into the past nor so pre-occupied with the present grief as to forget past blessings, is fortunate indeed. Many sufferers do not come to acceptance so easily," which is why the book provides a second answer to this question of how to respond to suffering, namely (b) with an honest frankness directed toward God. "When acceptance is no longer, or not yet, possible and bitterness and anger and a sense of isolation from God, even persecution by God, are overwhelming, what Job does [in the rest of the book] is what must be done." But Job's reaction "is not some aimless venting of anger and frustration: it is directed towards God. Even though Job speaks rashly and unjustly of God, his protests are in the right direction; he realizes that it is God himself with whom he has to do. It is just because he calls upon God persistently that in the end God reveals himself to him and Job's tensions are resolved by the encounter. And it is just because Job directs himself to God in his suffering, and not toward the secondary causes of his distress (the Sabeans, the natural forces) that God in the end can praise him for speaking of him what is right" ("Job" in *A Bible Commentary for Today,* pp. 559–60).

[25]Carson, p. 160.

[26]"Hypocrisy" comes from a Greek term for playing a part on the stage, thus masquerading as something that one, in reality, is not.

[27]"Tell God all that is in your heart, as one unloads one's heart, its pleasures and its pains, to a dear friend. Tell Him your troubles, that He may comfort you, tell Him your joys, that He may sober them; tell Him your longings, that He may purify them; tell him your dislikes, that He may help you conquer them; talk to Him of your temptations, that He may shield you from them; show Him the wounds of your heart, that He may heal them; lay bare your indifference to good, your depraved tastes for evil, your instability. Tell Him how self-love makes you unjust to others, how vanity tempts you to be insincere, how pride disguises you to yourself and others. If you thus pour out all your weaknesses, needs, troubles, there will be no lack of what to say. You will never exhaust the subject. It is continually being renewed. People who have no secrets from each other never want for subjects of conversation. They do not weigh their words; for there is nothing to be held back; neither do they seek for something to say. They talk out of the abundance of the heart, without consideration they say just what they think. Blessed are they who attain to such familiar, unreserved intercourse with God." Not the kind of approach to prayer you would expect from a seventeenth-century French Catholic archbishop and educator named Francois Fénelon.

[28]"In the last resort it is only when a man experiences a conscious deepening of his relationship with God"—impossible apart from total honesty with Him—"that the therapeutic powers of the divine Being can start to operate effectively within his personality" (R. K. Harrison, pp. 1045–46).

[29]Quoted in Courtney Anderson, *To the Golden Shore* (Valley Forge: Judson Press, 1987), pp. 400–401.

[30]Anderson, p. 413.

[31]Euthanasia is an increasingly hot topic in modern society. The modern term *medicide*, apparently coined by Dr. Jack Kevorkian, is more accurate than he intended. When the suffix *–cide* is appended to a prefix (e.g., sui-, matri-, insecti-, regni-), it invariably denotes the active killing of the object denoted by the prefix (e.g., to kill oneself, to kill one's mother, to kill insects, to murder a king). *Medicide*, therefore, does not mean death *by* medicine (a merciful death with medicinal help), but death *of* medicine (the *killing of medicine*, the *murder of healing*). The pursuit of this form of euthanasia undermines and "kills" everything that the practice of medicine (from the Latin verb meaning "to heal") has historically sought and represented.

[32]Tolkien, *The Fellowship of the Ring*, p. 282. Good fiction is applicably true-to-life.

[33]I have chosen the word *treacherous* purposely. The only clear examples of suicide are two traitors: (1) Ahithophel, David's counselor who betrayed him by joining Absalom's coup (2 Sam. 17:23), and (2) Judas, Jesus' disciple who betrayed him to the elders and chief priests (Matt. 27:3–5). The case of Saul (1 Sam. 31:1–5) seems somewhat debatable, since he appears to have been mortally wounded in battle and feared torture and abuse at the hands of the enemy. Even so, Saul also had shown himself to be a traitor to both God and David.

[34]Bunyan, pp. 129–35. Shortly before dawn on Sunday morning, it was Christian who, "as one half amazed, broke out in a passionate speech: 'What a fool am I thus to lie in a stinking dungeon when I may as well walk at liberty? I have a key in my bosom called PROMISE that will, I am persuaded, open any lock in Doubting Castle.' Then Christian pulled it out of his bosom and began to try at the dungeon door, whose bolt (as he turned the key) gave back, and the door flew open with ease, and Christian and Hopeful both came out."

[35]According to ancient tradition, Peter was not only persecuted numerous times and ways (some of which the book of Acts records) but finally crucified—according to Jerome, upside down at his own request as being unworthy to die in the same manner as his Lord (*Foxe's Book of Martyrs*, ed. William Byron Forbush, [Grand Rapids: Zondervan, 1926], p. 5).

[36]The form of the command in John 21:19 is "Follow me" (*akolouthei moi*). The command is intensified in 21:22 by both word addition and word order: "You me follow" (*su moi akolouthei*).

[37]*World*, May 22, 1999, p. 33.

10—Well-Meaning Friends, Misguided Counselors

[1]Rowley, p. 50.

[2]"In effect, what they planned to do was hear Job's story and agree with him" (Littleton, p. 254).

[3]Andersen describes Eliphaz's initial response to Job's outburst as sympathetic and polite, "tactful in manner and unobjectionable in matter" (p. 110).

[4]According to Henry Morris, Eliphaz pounces on Job's outburst as just "the opening he had wanted. Sadly, instead of trying to comfort and encourage his friend, he spoke sharp words of rebuke and discouragement" (p. 65). Morris's criticism that "there is no indication that they had prayed for Job or about what to say" (ibid.) is as irrelevant as Job's failure to pray about what to say. Carson's analysis is a little more nuanced. Eliphaz, he says, "begins with a sly swipe at Job's distress" by pointing to the inconsistency between Job's counsel to others in affliction and his own response to it now (4:3–5), and progresses in 4:6 to "an ironic suggestion that Job is guilty of rank

hypocrisy" (p. 161). But it is too soon to read Eliphaz this ungenerously. See Andersen's remark in note 5.

[5]Andersen's confirmation of this very point is gratifying: "Since the author has not told us what tone Eliphaz used in making these remarks [4:3–6], commentators [such as Morris and Carson above] have found them smug, sarcastic, hypocritical. I would prefer to give Eliphaz the benefit of the doubt, and find his words, not a taunt, but a kindly reminder that Job's past life of godliness has given him resources for the present crisis" (p. 111).

[6]Robinson, p. 38.

[7]Andersen, p. 110.

[8]Robinson, p. 40.

[9]See J. Barton Payne, *Theology of the Older Testament* (Grand Rapids: Zondervan, 1962), pp. 44–46; Gustav Oehler, *Theology of the Old Testament* (Minneapolis: Klock and Klock, rpr. 1978), pp. 142–44; Gerhardus Vos, *Biblical Theology* (Grand Rapids: Eerdmans, 1948), pp. 70–72; Robert Reymond, *A New Systematic Theology of the Christian Faith* (Nashville; Thomas Nelson, 1998), pp. 4–6.

[10]Henry Morris's arguments that the message of this vision is flawed and doctrinally deficient are specious (pp. 66–68). He misses the fact that Job's words (9:2) repeat nearly verbatim the very message of Eliphaz's dream and that God Himself echoes a corollary sentiment in 40:8.

[11]More than one commentator suggests that Eliphaz is telling this simply to frighten Job into acquiescence or to artificially bolster the authority of his argument. Carter questions whether Eliphaz is even telling the truth or simply fabricating the whole story (pp. 53–54).

[12]The same term is also used of Adam (Gen. 2:21) and Saul (1 Sam. 26:12); in these cases also, the sleep was from God (Andersen, p. 113).

[13]The pronouns in 4:16 are not neuter, but masculine. Andersen explains that *ruach* (4:15), a feminine noun, here takes masculine pronouns and a masculine verb. The use of neuter pronouns in modern translations "has obscured the important fact that the Hebrew '*he* stood' and '*his* appearance' continue the masculine gender. To my mind this proves that it is the Spirit of God" (p. 114). Zuck questions whether the vision was genuinely of divine origin, but his arguments are weak and he nevertheless admits that the content is true (p. 33). Morris is so biased against Eliphaz and the other friends that he is convinced this is a satanic apparition that becomes the basis of their entire argument against Job (pp. 66–68).

[14]So NKJV, NASB, ESV, NIV, NCV.

[15]Other modern versions retaining the traditional translation include the NAV, NIV, NEB. This reading is not only grammatically possible but the normal translation of this grammatical construction.

[16]Dhorme, p. 52. He adds that Job's echo of the same truth in 9:2, where he substitutes for *min* the clearly relational prepositional use of *'im*, removes the ambiguity in 4:17.

[17]The NASB and ESV opt for this rendering. Many commentators (Delitzsch says "all modern expositors") insist that the *min* construction here is not comparative ("more righteous than God") but relational ("righteous before God"). See, e.g., Dhorme, Strahan, Smick, Rowley, Zuck. Other examples of the relational use of *min* as opposed to the comparative can be cited (Smick, p. 897; cf. Ronald J. Williams, *Hebrew Syntax* [Toronto: University of Toronto Press, 1982], p. 56). It is not quite so straightforward a case as some make it.

[18]Strahan, p. 64.

[19]Andersen mistakenly regards the traditional rendering of 4:17 as a "truism . . . so obviously impossible that the banality makes Eliphaz sound pretentious" (p. 114).

[20]5:7 does not imply that such trouble is simply inevitable and inexplicable; that would undermine Eliphaz's whole assumption. Rowley cites Dahood's rendering ("it is man who engenders mischief itself") and concludes that "as surely as sparks fly upward man falls into sin and engenders trouble for himself. He is alone responsible for his misfortunes" (p. 61).

[21]Rowley, p. 62.

[22]Andersen, p. 120. Cf. Smick, p. 896.

[23]Andersen, p. 121.

[24]Rowley provides a literal rendering of 6:7 only to conclude, "This is not very lucid. The ancient versions could only guess at the meaning" (p. 69). Andersen is not convinced that Job's words in 6:6–7 refer to Eliphaz's counsel but acknowledges the difficulty of making contextual sense out of Job's words otherwise (p. 129). "But they seem relevant to the present context if Job is referring to the consolations of Eliphaz, which are tasteless and nauseating to him" (Rowley, p. 69; cf. Smick, p. 901).

[25]The opening word, a *hapax legomenon,* has been translated (or emended) "afflicted," "despairing," "in trouble," "consumed," "ready to faint," "scorned," "he who withholds," etc. Commentators are divided on whether the second stich applies to the hypothetical "friend" or the nonhypothetical Eliphaz (who has forsaken the fear of Shaddai by refusing to show loyalty), or to Job (as being further pushed to forsake the fear of Shaddai through the failure of his friends to show loyalty), or to a hypothetical sinner (even if he has forsaken the fear of Shaddai).

[26]*Loyalty* is the Hebrew word *chesed.* A richly nuanced word, it connotes a loyal love or devotion rooted in a relationship (often officially covenantal) that manifests itself concretely in acts of kindness. Its multifacetedness is evident from the translations it receives even in this single verse: "pity"

(KJV), "kindness" (NKJV), "devotion" (NIV), "gentleness" (Delitzsch), "compassion" (Dhorme). *Chesed* appears only three times in the book of Job. In 6:14 Job's expectation to find it from his friends is disappointed. In 10:12 he testifies to the Lord's loyalty to him all his life long. Finally, in 37:13 Elihu conveys the beautiful idea that the Lord sends storms sometimes for correction, sometimes just to water His land, and sometimes out of loyal kindness to His people. For a profitable and practical discussion of the theological significance of this term, see Randy Jaeggli, *More like the Master* (Greenville, S.C.: Ambassador International, 2004), chap. 9, "More Like His Loyal Love."

[27]One cannot dwell on the imagery of this kind of desertion without thinking of the Lord Jesus, the friend of sinners, Who was willing to risk even the contact of lepers in order to display the healing love and loyalty of God.

[28]"For now you" appears to be a literal translation on the surface. However, the context provides no clear causal connection or relationship. In addition, the combination of *kiy 'attah* carries the idea of "surely now" or "but now" (William L. Holladay, *A Concise Hebrew and Aramaic Lexicon of the Old Testament* [Grand Rapids: Eerdmans, 1971], p. 287), or an asseverative use, reflected in the NASB, "Indeed, you have now become such" (cf. Williams, *Hebrew Syntax,* p. 73).

[29]The word translated *horror* is another *hapax legomenon.* The KJV preserves the sense of the verb root from which this noun comes, "to be shattered, dashed to pieces, struck down" (Holladay, p. 121). Gordis translates 6:21, "Now you have become like that stream; you see my disaster and are seized with fear" (p. 64), and calls attention (p. 76) to the "striking . . . paranomasia in stich b": you see (תִּרְאוּ) . . . and you fear (וַתִּירָאוּ).

[30]Once again, commentators divide over the first stich of 6:25. Some refer it to the words of Eliphaz, while others say Job is drawing a contrast between his words and theirs. The second stich reads literally, "but what (or how) does this reproof from you reprove?" or "what does this demonstration (demonstrative argument) from you demonstrate?" I.e., Job is talking apples and they are arguing oranges.

[31]"The second line is cast in the form of an oath: 'I swear I will not lie.' In the strongest possible way he asseverates his innocence" (Rowley, p. 75).

[32]Lit., "my righteousness is in it" meaning "my righteousness is in this," hence, "my integrity is at stake here."

[33]The last word of v. 30 has been rendered "perverse things" (KJV), "evil things" (Dhorme), "malice" (NIV), "iniquity" (Delitzsch), and "calamity" (Rowley, NASB). The translation "calamity" suggests Job is saying that "he could understand the 'flavor' of his sufferings and know if they were deserved" (Zuck, p. 39). This is, after all, the same word with which Job opens his speech in 6:2, where it is translated "misfortune." That meaning,

however, does not flow very logically with stich a, where he protests that he is not speaking perversity by denying his responsibility for his suffering. Gordis's translation ("Cannot my taste discern falsehood?") makes more sense in this context. Although "the basic meaning of [*hawwoth*] is 'ruin, destruction' (cf. 6:2)," he notes, "here it has the meaning of 'deceit, falsehood'" (p. 78). (For this sense of the word, see Ps. 5:9; 38:12; 52:2; Prov. 17:4; Mic. 7:3.) In other words, Job is continuing the subject (his speech) and protest of stich a: "Don't you think my own palate would discern if I were speaking deceitfully?"

[34]According to Rowley, "the months indicate the duration of his suffering, and the nights the intensity, since they were harder to bear in the night when sleep was denied (cf. 30:17)" (p. 77).

[35]Job's evident passion in this passage, or elsewhere, hardly "disqualifies his claim to godliness. 'A calm and heavenly frame' for 'a closer walk with God' is not the uniform standard for biblical religion. Hannah prayed with the incoherence of a drunken woman (1 Sa. 1:13). 'Jesus offered up prayers and supplications, with loud cries and tears . . . and was heard' (Heb. 5:7). So Job makes his way to God with prayers that are sobs. Narrow and inhuman is the religion that bans weeping from its vocabulary of prayer" (Andersen, p. 136).

[36]Job 7:14 might appear, at first glance, to refer back to the dream-vision dramatically recounted by Eliphaz. He *may* be referring to that vision, but his words are not scolding Eliphaz for trying to terrorize him with such tales. Again, there seems no reason to doubt that the dream-vision came from God. Probably, however, Job is simply referring to the nightmares that plague his troubled sleep (Andersen, p. 137; Zuck, p. 41; Rowley, p. 80). Given his recent life experiences, his mind certainly had plenty of fodder for such dreams. Though God was not the direct source of such nightmares, Job's question implies his conviction that ultimately God is the one behind all his suffering. Whether demonically inspired (Morris, p. 72) or the product of his fevered mind (Delitzsch, p. 124; Strahan, p. 84), they were permitted by God to trouble Job's sleep.

[37]Kidner, p. 64.

[38]Andersen strongly disputes the translation "If I have sinned" (ESV, NIV, NCV). "It gives Job a quite undeserved attitude of self-righteousness to make this hypothetical by adding the word *if,* which is not in the original" (p. 139). *The New Scofield Reference Bible* erroneously includes this translation as the "literal" reading in a marginal note (p. 577).

[39]Andersen, p. 139.

[40]Andersen, p. 139. He adds, "Moffatt's translation—'wild and whirling words'—is very effective."

[41]"It is a pity that the climax of this strophe in verse 19 is clouded by textual obscurities that nobody has been able to penetrate. Nearly every word involved has more than one meaning or connotation. Translations consequently offer the reader a wide range of choice" (Andersen, p. 142).

[42]Carson, p. 163. "The language is forensic. How can a man win a legal dispute with God" (Andersen, p. 144).

[43]The final word of the verse is the verb *shalam,* from which we get the well-known Hebrew term *shalom.* Gordis translates, "Who has ever argued with God and emerged unscathed (or whole)?" (pp. 96, 102).

[44]Smick regards Job's remark in 9:17 (that God multiplies his wounds without cause) as one of the "unfortunate things he had said about God" (p. 922). But Job's perception is exactly right. "Without cause" is the same word God used to describe all He had brought on Job (2:3).

[45]Carson misreads the singular pronoun in 9:30–31 as a plural reference to Job's friends. "No matter how pure he is, his friends would find him impure: their position demands it" (p. 164). But this reading is foreign to the immediate context. Job has been talking *about* God since 9:2; he appears to be speaking *to* God in exactly the same vein beginning at least in 9:27 (note 9:28). In 9:30–31, then, Job refers to God's apparent determination to treat him like one of the guilty wicked. A survey of over a dozen commentators produced none that supported Carson's interpretation. Rowley (p. 99) mentions but rejects the textual emendation of Duhm and Lagarde to produce the meaning "my friends." Job uses the second person plural pronoun whenever he is speaking to the friends but seems to reserve the second person singular pronoun for his frequent and frank interchanges with God.

[46]Andersen, p. 144.

[47]C. S. Lewis, *A Grief Observed* (New York: Seabury Press, 1961), p. 9.

[48]Does Zophar mimic Job's tone of voice here, or mock Job with a faux piousness? See 12:4, comment.

[49]Zophar says literally that "God has forgotten some of your iniquity for you" (11:6); i.e., "God has been gracious enough to ignore some of your sin and not to punish you as fully as He might."

[50]Zophar's assertions are valid up to this point, "but there is no need to . . . call Job a donkey," though "the difficulties in the language make it hard to tell just how insulting Zophar's concluding words are" (Andersen, p. 158). The Hebrew *nabob* means *hollow* and signifies here an empty head. Clearly Job understood the mocking nature of something Zophar said (cf. 12:4).

[51]"Up to this point, we have disagreed with commentators who have found sarcasm in Job's statement. Here, however, it is unmistakable" (Andersen, p. 159).

[52]Robinson, p. 36.

[53]Job 12:9 significantly contains the debate's sole reference to God by His covenant name, Yahweh. Many regard it as a copyist's error or an interpolation from Isa. 41:20 (Dhorme, Strahan, Rowley). Andersen dissents: "The word acquired enormous importance because its rarity makes it so conspicuous. At this key point, Job is still insisting on what he said at first in 1:21, where the sacred name was [also] used" (p. 162).

[54]For a detailed discussion of God's preserving providence of all mankind (viz., holding every person's breath in His hand), see *Not by Chance,* chap. 3. Job 12:10 has become my favorite verse to append to sympathy cards for funerals, for its tasteful and sober reminder of who is in charge of life and death.

[55]In a classic example of acontextual proof-texting, Morris argues that "the creation of animals is the theme of [this] classic passage" (p. 24), where "Job noted that God had created all the animals and that we could learn from them the reality of a Creator" (p. 107).

[56]See Andersen, p. 162.

[57]The KJV "forgers (of lies)" translates the verb *taphal,* "to besmear or plaster over" (Holladay, p. 125). Several translations also assume a personal pronoun ("me"), making Job's accusation more personal: "you besmear me with lies" (NASB, NIV, NCV). But this addition is unnecessary. What they are besmearing is not Job himself; rather, their one-size-fits-all diagnosis besmears the whole situation. They are trying to plaster over Job's unique condition with a standard textbook answer that does not address this situation. ESV translates, "You whitewash with lies."

[58]Kidner, p. 67. "In his bones," Kidner adds, "Job knew what God stood for."

[59]"By presuming to *plead the case for God* (8), *falsely, deceitfully* (7), and with *partiality* (8, 10), they are in grave danger." *Partiality* is literally to "lift up the face"—"That is, show favouritism in judgment, a thing God detests, even if it is showing favouritism to God!" In addition, "the *inclusio* of the same words at the beginning of verse 8 and the end of verse 10 shows structurally that this block is an exposition of verse 7" (Andersen, p. 165).

[60]"Job warned them about lying even while they uttered beautiful words in defense of God. If they were going to plead God's case, they had better do it honestly. God would judge them for their deceit even if they used it in his behalf (vv. 8–9)" (Smick, p. 922).

[61]Cf. Zuck, pp. 60–61.

[62]Referring to 13:15–16, Carson remarks that "in the midst of his confusion and self-justification, Job utters some remarkably assured statements of faith" (p. 166). All is not well with 13:15 in the commentators, however. Andersen notes that "the famous [KJV] translation of verse 15a . . . has been widely abandoned in modern versions" in exchange for the more pessimistic

(but not un-Job-like), "Behold he will slay me; I have no hope"—a rendering with which Zuck agrees (p. 61). After weighing the grammatical arguments thoughtfully, however, Andersen concludes that the KJV rendering "should by all means be retained" (Andersen, pp. 166–67). See also R. Laird Harris, "The Doctrine of God in the Book of Job" in *Sitting with Job,* ed. Roy B. Zuck, p. 175. The traditional rendering is retained in NKJV, NASB, ESV, NCV, and NIV (though this last includes the alternative in a marginal reading).

[63]Andersen, p. 169.

[64]The problem is the vague subject referent in 13:28 (lit., "[And] he decays like a rotten thing"). Job has been talking about himself in the first person to God in the second person but shifts suddenly here to the third person. Some unnecessarily assume the verse to be misplaced and reposition it into the flow of chap. 14 (see Rowley, p. 126, for suggested options). Smick (p. 926) suggests a more satisfying resolution by joining 13:28 with the first line of 14:1 to form the introduction to the poetic musing into which Job's thoughts have flowed. See Smick's balanced structure for the entire poem (13:28–14:4). Here are the first two stanzas:

He wastes away like something rotten,
like a garment eaten by moths—
man born of woman.
Few of days and full of trouble
He springs up like a flower and withers away;
Like a fleeing shadow he does not endure.

[65]Smick makes a point of noting that the word translated "change" or "renewal" in 14:14 is the same root that describes the tree (14:7) *sprouting* or *springing up* to life again. The "basic meaning is 'to have succession'" and here "Job is speaking of succession after death, not the healing of his body in this life"; for again, Job nowhere entertains any expectation of a reversal of fortunes in this life. The connection between 14:7 and 14 is important because it combats a prevailing opinion among many scholars that "any thought of life after death is considered impossible by Job"—an assumption rooted in "their preconceptions about OT theology, which ruled out ideas of resurrection in preexilic and early postexilic Israel" (Smick, pp. 926–27).

[66]The view that the answer to 14:14*a* is "No" need not be considered necessarily wrong; those who take that "No" to mean a denial of resurrection, however, have just seriously misconstrued the import of the question itself. Archer agrees that though the expected answer to Job's question in 14:14 is "No," the point is not to deny resurrection or the intermediate state, "but only to rule out physical resuscitation. . . . Despite much learned discussion encountered in some of the commentaries, no other interpretation of verse 14 does justice to the rights of language" (Archer, pp. 66–67). Zuck's treatment of 14:7–17 is disappointing. After denying the possibility of resurrec-

tion in 14:12, "Job reached out wistfully and longingly for the possibility of life after death" to a "faint prospect of resurrected life" in 14:13–15 (pp. 65–66).

[67]Like Smick (note 65 above), Andersen (pp. 169–70) protests the negative answer to 14:14*a* and the implication it carries for many commentators: "[T]his hope of a personal resurrection is dismissed by many scholars as a fleeting fancy on Job's part, an idea impossible for a person of his time and thought rejected in his concluding words"—leaving one to wonder that if such an idea was patently impossible for a person of his time, how could he have even had such a "fleeting fancy" in the first place? "In arriving at this result, scholars are influenced not only by their *a priori* belief that the idea of resurrection arose quite late in Israel's thought, but also by expecting Job to use western logic in constructing his discourse so that an argument is followed through step by step until the result is reached at the end. By this analysis it is the final word of despair that has the upper hand. We suggest that this approach is wrong." As to the predisposition to reject the early presence of a doctrine of resurrection, Andersen adds: "We believe that this opinion, commonly held by Old Testament scholars, is mistaken. On the contrary, belief in the continuation of personal human life with God after death was, we believe, part of Israel's distinctive faith from its beginnings." The fact that Andersen fails to distinguish adequately between "resurrection" (the raising and reuniting of the body to the spirit) and "the continuation of personal human life with God after death" (the intermediate state of the soul) need not diminish one's appreciation for the sentiment he expresses. For further discussion of resurrection in OT theology, Andersen cites Nicholas J. Tromp's *Primitive Conceptions of Death and the Nether World in the Old Testament*; Smick notes Walter Kaiser's *Toward an Old Testament Theology*, pp. 99, 181, 249.

[68]"Destroy" seems too strong and abrupt a rendering here. Two verses of imagery paint a picture of gradual erosion, slow but steady and sure. In view of the illustration selected, the causative force of the Hiphil should be preserved in translating *abad* here, giving it more the sense of "cause to perish" (cf. Jer. 25:10, "Moreover, *I will take* from them the voice of mirth" = "I will cause to perish"; Ezek. 25:7, where the KJV translates "*I will cause* [them] *to perish* [from] the countries").

11—Waves Crashing Against a Rock

[1]"Proverbs is not afraid to put two clashing counsels side by side." "Naturally they generalize, as a proverb must, and may therefore be charged with making life too tidy to be true. But nobody objects to this in secular sayings, for the very form demands a sweeping statement and looks for a hearer with his wits about him" (Kidner, p. 26).

[2]Even if one wishes to press "the earth" for latent eschatological implications (viz., that the righteous will one day be resurrected and recompensed in the millennial kingdom), the problem of recompensing the wicked and the sinner "in the earth" remains.

[3]"There is no denying that Job's comforters (whose views the book repudiates) rely on the kind of generalizations that abound in Proverbs." But whereas "Proverbs treats them as a spur to faith, the comforters of Job make them a rod for his back" (Kidner, p. 117).

[4]Zuck notes the apparent discrepancies between statements in Proverbs and assertions in Job (and Eccles.): "Are these contradictions? No, because for one thing Proverbs usually looks at the opposites in life without noting exceptions. . . . Job and Ecclesiastes, both wisdom books, demonstrate exceptions to what Proverbs often states in black-and-white fashion. The books, then, are complementary, not contradictory. While the affirmations in Proverbs are normally true, exceptions, as observed in Job and Ecclesiastes, do exist" ("God and Man in Ecclesiastes," *Bibliotheca Sacra* [Jan-Mar 1991], p. 49).

[5]Robinson, p. 35. Strahan absurdly argues that "Job differs from his friends in that he is not the possessor of a formal theological creed, but a seeker after truth" (p. 189). Job clings to his theological creed—what he believes and knows God to be—every bit as tenaciously as his friends cling to theirs.

[6]Robinson, pp. 35–36. Technically, Robinson misstates the main proposition of the syllogism, which should be "All sufferers are evil-doers." One line of argument used by all three friends, however, is that all evil-doers suffer. Thus, the main proposition could be stated, "Only evil-doers are sufferers."

[7]Kidner, pp. 60–61.

[8]Ibid., p. 61.

[9]Some studies on Job organize their whole approach to the dialogue by dividing it up this way. This methodology simplifies handling the heft of material for brief overviews of the story of Job. See, e.g., Leon Wood, *Trusting Through Suffering* (Schaumburg, Ill.: Regular Baptist Press, 1979); Henry Thiessen, *Why Do the Righteous Suffer?* David Howard, *How Come, God?* There are weakness to this approach. Robinson's insightful *The Cross in the Old Testament* (pp. 35–41) illustrates the temptation to oversimplification that is symptomatic of this organization by labeling the friends: Eliphaz the Mystic, Bildad the Traditionalist, and Zophar the Dogmatist (p. 40). Such labels can be misleading. If by "mystic" he means reliant on dreams or visions for disclosure of divine truth at this early stage of prewritten revelation, they are all mystics. They are certainly all traditionalists and dogmatists as well. As helpful as this method can be, it misses the crucial element of interplay and movement that is built into the dialogue format. Overlooking the organic progression of thought and emotion, it mixes and melds the

words of each speaker from different places in the dialogue to form a coherent but often artificial and sometimes inaccurate whole. The dialogue was recorded and preserved in the interactive form in which we find it for good reason.

[10]Andersen, p. 179.

[11]There is no paranomasia here, just a noticeably parallel Hebrew construction:

15:13—you [Job] turn against God (*'el 'ēl)* your spirit
15:25—he [the wicked] stretches out against God (*'el 'ēl)* his hand
See also note 15 below.

[12]John Piper's phrase is memorable: "O spare me now, my friends, your packages of God, your simple adages: 'Be good and strong, but weak when wrong.' They make good rote and clever song, but do not hold the wisdom of our God" (*The Misery of Job and the Mercy of God*, pp. 58–59).

[13]*Consolations* (15:11) and *comforters* (16:2) are forms of the same verb (*nacham*).

[14]Rowley, p. 144.

[15]This is at least the third time the Hebrew word for wind (*ruach*) appears in this sense. Bildad calls Job a "blowhard" in 8:2. Eliphaz calls Job an "airhead" in 15:2 ("vain knowledge" = "knowledge of wind" or "windy knowledge"). Job tosses it back at them in 16:3, calling them "windbags" ("vain words" = "words of wind" or "windy words"). A fourth occasion may be 15:13, where "spirit" (*ruach*) parallels "words" (*milliyn*) so that Eliphaz might be saying, "Will you turn your hot air against God and vent words out of your mouth?"

[16]Andersen (p. 180) notes that "the second phrase in verse 4 is literally, 'Would that your soul was instead of my soul!'"

[17]"Company" refers to all those who previously "companied" with Job ("i.e. those gathered around a prominent person," Holladay, p. 265). It would certainly include his family who is now dead (Archer, p. 69) but also his friends and associates ("the circle of his intimates," Gordis, p. 175) who have deserted him. The piel verb *shammam* means to make desolate or deserted.

[18]Scholars scramble to suggest all kinds of emendations to "fix" the text. Strahan (p. 152) absurdly reasons that "the change from third to second person throws suspicion on the text"—as if the elusive redactor would be so daft as not to notice the discrepancy himself. Dhorme, Rowley, Gordis, et al. change the second person readings to third person to achieve a more satisfactory symmetry. Conversely, the NIV changes the third person in 16:7*a* to second person and inserts "God." A little sympathetic, dramatic imagination goes a long way in appreciating the emotion of the text as it stands in the MT.

[19]Another solution that preserves the MT reading is to translate "He" as "it" referring back to his "pain" or "grief" in 16:6; i.e., "Though I speak my

grief is not assuaged. . . . Instead, it has worn me out. You have desolated all my company" (cf. Zuck, p. 76). This is feasible, though it does not lessen the sudden turn to God in 16:7*b*, and only delays the apparent discrepancy back to the third person reference to God in 16:9ff.

[20]Andersen, p. 180.

[21]Smacking of onomatopoeia, *taraph* depicts wild beasts ripping apart a carcass. Jacob imagines Joseph to have met with such a fate (Gen. 37:33). "Since the word *torn* is commonly used to describe the mutilation of the prey of a rapacious animal . . . the concrete imagery requires that the word *wrath* (lit. 'nose') be taken physically. 'With his snout he ripped me and chased me, He slashed me with his fangs" (Andersen, p. 181). Andersen explains the absence of any preposition with the first word ("snout"): "The preposition that goes with the word *teeth* ["fangs"] does double duty for both nouns. The words for these organs come in chiasmus which confirms the parallelism" (ibid.).

[22]This verb, *satam,* describes Esau's hatred of Jacob (Gen. 27:41), Joseph's brothers' hatred of him (Gen. 49:23, metaphorically described), and the hatred the brothers feared Joseph would harbor against them (Gen. 50:15). All three contexts connote a smoldering hatred fueled by a grudge. Andersen argues instead for the meaning "chase" in keeping with the animalistic imagery (p. 180).

[23]The verb *latash* denotes the whetting of a sword (Ps. 7:12). Here God literally "sharpens his eyes." The NASB renders, "glares at me" while the NEB retains a more literal feel, "looks daggers."

[24]Job 16:10 *may* refer to his three friends as being part of his suffering. The graphic description of their verbal abuse would not be entirely out of place. However, the references to the "ungodly" and the "wicked" in 16:11 are too strong to apply to the three friends. However strongly he feels about them, Job's tenacious commitment to honesty and integrity would not permit him to apply these labels to them. Instead, 16:10–11 seems better understood as his victimization by the wicked men who decimated his flocks and herds (1:15, 17) and "the vilification Job received from the dregs of society (chapter 30)" (Andersen, p. 181).

[25]In Hebrew, the verbs *he broke me* and *he shook me,* "coming in sequence with assonance and rhyme, have terrific poetic force" (Andersen, p. 181): *way*^{e}*pharp*^{e}*rēniy* . . . *way*^{e}*phatsp*^{e}*tsēniy*.

[26]For an extended biblical illustration of misconstruing God's posture towards us based on circumstances, see the discussion of Naomi (Ruth 1) in Talbert, *Not by Chance,* pp. 115–17.

[27]Even Gordis admits that emendations to change the plural to singular here are fraught with difficulty. Feasible explanations of the plural have been suggested. (1) "There are some grounds for assuming that the plural was

used at times in direct address even to one person; cf. Cant. 5:1" (Gordis, p. 190). (2) "Bildad would only treat Job as belonging to the company of the wicked" (Ewald, cited by Rowley, p. 158). (3) "Perhaps Bildad chose to categorize Job as one of the problem people ('you people') who make life difficult by being unreasonable" (Smick, p. 937). Views (2) and (3) correspond to Bildad's exclusive focus on the wicked in a way that implies that Job is obviously among that number.

[28]Andersen, p. 188.

[29]The parallel between 18:4*a* (*tōrēph . . . b^{e}'appō*) and 16:9 (*'appō taraph*) is unmistakable. Whereas Job accused God of tearing him in wrath (or, metaphorically, "with His snout"), Bildad asserts that Job is tearing his own soul in his rage (or, in keeping with Andersen's earlier literalism, with his own "snout" by means of his frenzied words). Likewise, 18:4*c* (*w^{e}ye' ^{e}taq tsur mimqōmō*) ricochets Job's words in 14:18*b* (*w^{e}tsur ye' ^{e}taq mimqōmō*). Does Job suppose that he is so important that heaven and earth—and *truth* long held by the wise—must move for *him*? Bildad "accused Job of being irrationally self-centered. The world was going to remain the same no matter how much Job ranted against the order of things" (Smick, p. 936).

[30]It is frequently pointed out that "while Eliphaz emphasizes the mental worries of the wicked, Bildad focuses on their outward troubles" (Andersen, p. 187; cf. Rowley, pp. 157–58; Zuck, p. 81). This distinction is overplayed. Eliphaz makes only one clear reference to the mental-emotional experience of the wicked (15:24); so does Bildad (18:11).

[31]Smick, p. 937.

[32]Bildad uses the verb in 18:11 as Job did in 7:14 and 9:34. Eliphaz, too, seems to have played off Job's own words (15:24).

[33]"Bildad gives a transparent allegory which is singularly cruel in its obvious reference to Job's bereavement" (Andersen, p. 190).

[34]The "wicked" are a frequent topic of conversation throughout Job. This is not the normal word for the wicked (*rasha'*), which occurs 26 times in Job alone. The word here is *'awwal*, one who deviates from a right standard; it is the exact antonym of *tsadiq*, "righteous" or "just"—precisely what Job has repeatedly claimed to be (6:29; 12:4; 13:18; 17:9), and a claim backed up by God (1:8; 2:3).

[35]Andersen, p. 190. Archer adds: "Bildad has turned a deaf ear to all of Job's protests of innocence, and he has firmly concluded from Job's unwillingness to repent that he must have a lot of repenting to do" (p. 73).

[36]Strahan, p. 171.

[37]"God has overthrown me" (19:6) is possible (cf. the same verb in Ps. 146:9) but seems a bit euphemistic for the context; it fails to convey the element of injustice that surfaces nearly everywhere the word appears (e.g., Job 8:3; 34:12; Ps. 119:78; Amos 8:5). The jurisprudence-saturated context of

Job strongly supports the sense here that God has "wronged me," "*made* me crooked" or "put me in the wrong" (ESV).

[38]The "net" here is not one of Bildad's words but denotes "the hunter's net, into which he drives animals" (Rowley, p. 167).

[39]"It is noteworthy that both he and his colleagues regarded Job's misfortunes as coming from God's hand, but their reasons differed vastly. The three friends looked on the misfortunes as retribution for sin, whereas Job saw them as totally unfair actions" (Zuck, p. 85).

[40]"One can only smile at commentators who are bothered by the picture of *siegeworks* built up around a *tent*" (Andersen, p. 192). Overkill is not the problem with the image; it is the whole point of the image.

[41]The NKJV renders 19:17*b*, "I am repulsive to the children of my own body." How can this be? His children are all dead. The text reads literally, "to the sons of my womb"—i.e., those who emerged from the same womb he did (cf. 3:10). The reference is to his own brothers (Rowley, p. 169; cf. Zuck, p. 87; NASB; ESV; NIV).

[42]It is worth noting, in passing, that Job does not refer to his friends in quotation marks, so to speak. Zuck's tentative suggestion that Job used this term "perhaps in sarcasm, for they had certainly not acted like true friends" (Zuck, p. 88) is a fancy unsupported by the importunate tone of his plea. Nothing here suggests that he is referring to them sarcastically as his so-called friends. They have so disqualified themselves in some people's eyes that they retain no redeeming qualities and are unworthy of being called friends without qualifying quotation marks. Thankfully, God does not see them that way (42:7–9)—or us, when we commit their sins.

[43]The verb *radaph* signifies to pursue, hound, chase down; it often describes a victorious army in hot pursuit of a defeated enemy army on the run. It appears also in 13:25, 19:28, and 30:15.

[44]W. B. MacLeod, cited by Zuck, p. 88.

[45]Andersen, p. 193. Cf. Zuck, p. 89; Strahan, p. 177; Rowley, pp. 172, 174; Carter, p. 106.

[46]Gordis, pp. 206.

[47]Gordis is matter-of-factly confident that 19:26 "cannot refer to Job seeing God after his body decays" (p. 206). The notion of resurrection adduced from this passage is an "older . . . view" that "has been rightly surrendered by modern scholars" (p. 204).

[48]Andersen, p. 193.

[49]Cf. Gordis, p. 204–5; Andersen, p. 193.

[50]Cf. Rowley, p. 174. "To underline his belief that this will happen with full possession of his personal identity, Job uses *I* three times in 27a, once on the verb, once as the emphatic pronoun subject, once as the 'ethic dative':

AV 'Whom I shall see for myself' cannot be improved on" (Andersen, pp. 193–94).

[51]Kidner interjects a uniquely significant datum into the discussion of this phrase: "elsewhere in the OT, *with verbs of seeing, min* always has the sense of 'from,' never of 'without' or 'apart from' (e.g., Gen. 13:14; Job. 36:25; Ps. 14:2; etc.)" (Kidner, p. 69, original emphasis). Smick adds, "The preposition refers to the viewer's vantage point: 'from (within) my flesh I shall see God'" (p. 944).

[52]Smick, p. 943; cf. Andersen, p. 193. The phrase "and not another" is literally "and no[t as a] stranger." This could follow the emphasis that he will see God *for himself* and will not have to rely on a second-hand vision of God through someone else (Dhorme, p. 286; Rowley, pp. 174–75; Smick, p. 944). Or it could reflect the relationship Job anticipates with God at that time (Smick, ibid.)—in the sense that Job will recognize the One he knows so well (Archer, p. 76) or that Job will no longer be a stranger to God as he seems to be now (Zuck, p. 91) or that God will at that point no longer make himself a stranger to Job (Andersen, p. 194; Strahan, p. 178).

[53]Andersen, p. 194. Gordis criticizes "several recent commentators, notably Terrien and Pope, [who] have insisted that Job cannot be referring to God when he speaks of a witness or a redeemer," particularly since "neither Terrien nor Pope has ventured to explicate the identity of the being to whom Job is referring" (Gordis, pp. 526–27). Smick (p. 944) also points to the significance of Job's reference to his Redeemer as "the last" in 19:25, noting that the same Hebrew term is also used as a title for God (e.g., Isa. 48:12).

[54]Smick, pp. 941–42.

[55]Andersen, p. 194.

[56]The very common adverb *'achar*, occurs several hundred times in the OT, almost always in a temporal (i.e., "afterward") or directional (e.g., "after other gods") sense. Gordis chooses a rare locative sense ("behind") to produce the contortionist rendering, "behind my skin, deep in my skin" (p. 206). It should also be observed that the AV reference to "worms" is supplied and is not in the Hebrew text. Smick's literal rendering underscores the difficulty of 19:26*a*: "after my skin they have struck off—this!" (p. 943).

[57]"It begins to appear that, however fitfully and dimly he perceives it, he is speaking here of nothing less than resurrection" (Kidner, p. 69). "And so here we have the doctrine of the bodily resurrection implied even in the first written book of the Old Testament" (Archer, p. 75). Based, among other things, on a faulty view of *min* in 19:26, Zuck disappointingly concludes that Job refers only to seeing God in the afterlife in a nonresurrected state (p. 91). Happily, his later comments are more balanced, if noncommittal ("The Certainty of Seeing God: A Brief Exposition of Job 19:23–29" in *Sitting with Job*, p. 280).

[58]Henry Morris supplies an ample amount of speculation. He concludes from 19:25–27 that Job "believed God's promise to send the Redeemer and believed that through him he would have eternal life" (p. 58). On the other end of the spectrum, Albert Barnes expresses considerable chagrin that, as much as he would like to, he is unable to find in this passage any "distinct prophecy of the Messiah" or even "traces of the early belief of the doctrine of the resurrection of the dead" ("Job 19:25–29" in *Sitting with Job,* p. 295).

[59]See, e.g., Ps. 19:14; 78:35; Isa. 41:14; 43:14; 44:6, 24; 47:4; 48:17; 49:7, 26; 54:5, 8; 59:20; 60:16; 63:16.

[60]See, e.g., Smick, p. 942; Zuck, p. 89.

[61]Michael P. V. Barrett, *Beginning at Moses: A Guide to Finding Christ in the Old Testament* (Greenville, S.C.: Ambassador-Emerald International, 1999), pp. 196–97.

[62]Ibid., p. 197. In view of our quest for precision in the context of our present discussion, the only point at which I would take minor issue with Barrett is his statement that "Job knew this coming Redeemer was Christ" on the basis of Job 16:19. Apart from any other revelation, it would seem that the most we could say on the basis of 16:19 is that Job knew this coming Redeemer was *God.* That in itself is significant, for it shows that Jewish commentator Robert Gordis is, in one sense, righter than he knows when he insists: "In view of the uncompromising monotheism of the Book of Job, there is no basis for postulating a third, intermediate being either as a kinsman in our passage, or as an arbiter (9:33), or as a witness (16:1[9]). It is God to whom Job appeals and whom he sees rising to vindicate him even in the distant future" (Gordis, p. 206). Indeed it is, for Messiah is not merely a "third, intermediate being"; He *is* God.

[63]This scriptural assertion broadsides a common hermeneutical fallacy: the assumption that whatever a given author meant must *necessarily* have been comprehensible and relevant to his immediate audience. That assumption is an outgrowth of a native egocentricity that insists whatever is not immediately relevant to me and my needs is not important.

[64]Morris, p. 127. In calling attention to "the prophets" as "an example of suffering affliction, and of patience," "James cited the specific example of Job and therefore accorded him a place among the prophets and the blessed" (Kurt A. Richardson, *James,* The New American Commentary [Nashville: Broadman and Holman, 1997], p. 225).

[65]Kidner tracks this "ebbing and flowing" in the text (pp. 67–69).

[66]Lions are consummately confident creatures. "A guilty conscience . . . leaves the wicked person perpetually anxious and paranoid" (Duane A. Garrett, *Proverbs, Ecclesiastes, Song of Songs,* The New American Commentary [Nashville: Broadman and Holman, 2003], p. 221). This is precisely what Job does not have. By contrast, the man who has conscien-

tiously fulfilled his obligations (= righteous) can be confident in God's favor. Kidner's comment is vintage: "The straightforward man, like the lion, has no need to look over his shoulder. What is at his heels is not his past (Num. 32:23) but his rearguard: God's goodness and mercy (Ps. 23:6)" (Derek Kidner, *Proverbs* [Downers Grove, Ill.: Inter-Varsity Press, 1964], p. 168).

[67]Smick, p. 946.

[68]Strahan, pp. 181–82. The kind of zealot Strahan describes is perpetuated in an orthodoxy unconformed to the character of Christ.

[69]"Therefore" sounds like a peculiar way to begin a speech. "The ordinary meaning of לָכֵן is 'that is why' (32:10; 34:10; 37:24), referring to what precedes. But at the beginning of a speech, it is an allusion to what follows." Here, therefore, it means "this is why . . ." (Dhorme, p. 289).

[70]A subtle, passing reference to the divine creation of man as an assumed fact. Surprisingly, even Morris misses this one.

[71]Andersen, p. 197. Cf. Smick: "But Zophar . . . had no compassion. He left no room for repentance" (p. 947).

[72]"Despite the error of Zophar's application," Smick says we should "try to appreciate the elements of truth contained herein. As Gordis (*God and Man,* p. 90) notes, Zophar was 'performing a vital task . . . defending man's faith in a moral universe, a world governed by the principle of justice'" (Smick, p. 946).

[73]"There can be no doubt that on the basis of empirical observation the Hebrews were justified in entertaining the operation of cause and effect, since it is a simple fact that the bulk of human suffering, using that term in the widest possible sense, is strictly a product of the relationship between man and his environment" (Harrison, p. 1043).

[74]I do not mean when theology conflicts with mere appearances or interpretations (e.g., alleged evidences for evolution), feelings or impressions of what seems to us is, or ought to be, reality (e.g., the appeals of open theists to what God *must* be like). I mean concrete, incontrovertible, empirical evidence—akin to Job's pointing at wicked people that the others can see who live and die without experiencing the kind of devastating divine decimation that Zophar has described.

[75]Literally, "Listening, listen to my words." This is a standard emphatic construction in Hebrew. The duplication of the main verb by preceding it with the infinitive absolute form intensifies the verbal idea. Gen. 2:17 is a classic example ("dying thou shalt die"). Unfortunately, the literal rendering tempts some to read more theological significance into the construction than is intended. The English translations commonly and correctly express the force of this construction by substituting an adverb for the infinitive absolute, as in "thou shalt *surely* die" (Gen. 2:17), or here, "Hear diligently"

or "Listen carefully." See E. Kautzsch, ed., *Gesenius' Hebrew Grammar,* trans. A. E. Cowley (Oxford: Clarendon Press, 1910), p. 342; Williams, pp. 37–38.

[76]Kidner, p. 64.

[77]Zuck, p. 97.

[78]Commentators are unevenly divided as to Job's intent in 21:4–6. On the surface (depending on the translation), it sounds as if Job is calling them to appalled silence as they look at him and consider the depth of his misery—a contemplation that he himself finds deeply disturbing (cf. Zuck, p. 97). Most, however, interpret this as a kind of caution: "I am not going to complain about man, but God. You do well to clap your hand over your mouth in astonishment! I myself tremble to confront the mystery I am about to describe." See Rowley, pp. 184–85; Strahan, pp. 191–92; Delitzsch, p. 399. Smick (p. 949) explains, "Job was terrified because he knew how awesome a task it is to complain against God (v. 6). Yet in all honesty, he could find no other way out of his predicament." Job is anguished "over not understanding what God was doing"—not only to him, but in the world at large. His friends have shut their eyes to the realities of the world around them while mouthing their theology that God always judges the wicked swiftly. Job will have none of it. He refuses to deny either the reality he sees or the theology he holds. "God would rather have us complain than be indifferent toward him or handle his truths arrogantly" or dishonestly.

[79]Job does not answer in generalities. His repeated quotations and clear allusions to the words of his friends demonstrate that he is addressing and debunking their arguments, one by one, with deadly accuracy. See Smick, p. 949; Andersen, pp. 198–201; Zuck, pp. 97–100 (includes a helpful chart detailing Job's answers to Zophar's charges in particular).

[80]Andersen, p. 197.

[81]Andersen, p. 199.

[82]"The time has come to demolish their position" (Andersen, p. 198).

[83]Gordis, p. 229.

[84]Andersen, p. 200.

[85]Job uses the same words in 21:17 that Bildad did to describe the "putting out" of the light of the wicked in 18:5 and their "destruction" in 18:12.

[86]The AV of Job 21:17–18, expressed not as a question but as an exclamation, initially creates the impression that Job is seriously schizophrenic and self-contradictory. The NKJV, which renders 21:17 as a question but 21:18 as a statement, is almost as confusing. Smick concedes the ambiguity of the Hebrew but insists that "if it is exclamatory, we must assume that Job was being ironic . . . and had already begun to quote his friends" as he does in v. 19 (p. 951). It is preferable to treat both verses as a unit and render them interrogatively (NASB, NIV, NCV). The ASV and the Amplified Bible, along with the NCV, helpfully render the passage as a rapid-fire catena of

abbreviated questions: How often is it that the lamp of the wicked is extinguished? That their calamity comes upon them? That God distributes sorrows to them in His anger? That they are like stubble before a wind and like chaff that a storm carries away?

[87]This is the general sense of 21:19–21 favored by Andersen (p. 200), Zuck (p. 99), Gordis (p. 224), Rowley (pp. 187–88). The idea seems to be that Job is anticipating the standard "explanation" of these "anomalies" in a moral universe. But "this theory . . . that God is saving up *their iniquity for their sons* (verse 19*a*) is a blatant evasion, useless as a demonstration of God's justice (verse 22)" (Andersen, p. 200). Job's whole point is that these cases are not the *exception*; they are the *rule*. The wicked grow up side by side with the righteous, like tares among wheat; rarely are they uprooted prematurely (cf. Matt. 13:24–30, 36–43). What we take for granted as common knowledge was, in that early period prior to written revelation, still being figured out by observation.

[88]The same mystery is expressed more cryptically but explored in more detail in Job's canonical twin, Ecclesiastes (2:14–23; 8:14; 9:1–6, 11–12). Solomon's inspired (12:10–11) resolution is twofold: (1) submissive contentment with one's God-given lot in life (2:24; 3:12–13, 22; 8:15; 9:7–10) coupled with (2) a settled assurance in the ultimate justice of God (2:26; 3:15, 17; 8:12–13). But that is another book.

[89]"Empty" (*hebel*) words are words that promise much but deliver nothing. "Falsehood" (*ma'al*) is faithlessness or treachery, often used of one's betrayal of God or man, but here a "betrayal of the truth" (Gordis, p. 236). "The facts themselves contradict the thesis of his friends. . . . Here the act of infidelity is concerned rather with the way of interpreting reality, their interpretation is disloyal to the facts" (Dhorme, p. 325).

[90]Archer, p. 463.

[91]This is one of God's recurring points all the way through Isaiah. See Isa. 40:18, 25; 43:10–11; 44:6, 8; 45:5–6, 14, 18, 21–22; 46:5, 9.

[92]From "The Royal Crown" by eleventh-century Spanish-Jewish poet Solomon ibn Gabirol, in *Selected Religious Poems of Solomon ibn Gabirol,* ed. Israel Davidson, trans. Israel Zangwill (Philadelphia: Jewish Publication Society, 1944), p. 118. Cited by Gordis, *The Book of Job,* p. 527; see also Gordis, *The Book of God and Man,* pp. 88–89.

12—Looking for God

[1]"On the specific issue of suffering, the basic mistake of these comforters is still with us wherever Christians make projections from their axioms about God, or from their doctrine of redemption, to the effect that the perfect health of the redeemed, here and now, must be what God intends. Like Job's comforters, those who argue in this way are deciding for themselves

what God must surely think and do. . . . This is not to say that Job's case should be seen as the key to all others, or even to any others: simply that it lifts one corner of the curtain beyond which, at any time, there will lie factors of which we have no inkling" (Kidner, p. 62).

[2]Andersen traces the cyclic progression in a little more detail: "In the first cycle the friends are content to talk in generalities, without venturing to apply their doctrine openly to Job. In the second round the main theme is the fate of the wicked and Job's point of view comes into open contradiction with that of his friends. Their relationship noticeably deteriorates and there is a certain amount of vituperation. The inference from Job's resemblance to the state of the wicked, namely that he must be a sinner, has been made, obliquely at first. Now it comes into the open and the breach between them is complete. Once this point has been reached there can be no further dialogue, and the discussion grinds to a halt" (pp. 201–2).

[3]The allusion is to Beatrice in Shakespeare's *Much Ado About Nothing* (Act 2, Scene 1).

[4]"Shocked, instead of shaken, by Job's denials that his suffering is deserved, they pass from gentle probings for some hidden sin, to stern rebuke for his intemperate language (e.g., ch. 15), and finally to inventing a fictitious catalogue of crimes for him (22:5ff.). . . . Small wonder that in the epilogue God charges them with folly and slander (42:8)" (Kidner, p. 61).

[5]Andersen, p. 202.

[6]"Verse 4 is pure irony" (Smick, p. 953).

[7]"None have to do with religion in a formal sense. Job is not charged with any failure in his duty to God" (Andersen, p. 203). Cf. Smick, 953–54. For Eliphaz to link the severity of Job's punishment to these kinds of crimes reveals how seriously such social responsibilities were regarded and how profoundly interconnected man's religion was perceived to be with his treatment of others. This link is a common theme in the Prophets as well. We tend to emphasize spiritual sins such as idolatry, or moral sins such as adultery, and minimize the seriousness of social and humanitarian sins such as oppression and neglect. This fails to give adequate weight to other issues with which God has historically been concerned.

[8]"Brother" (*'ach*) is usually a blood relative or kinsman, who of all people would have "had a claim upon his help" (Gordis, p. 245); but it may also have the wider connotation of fellow countrymen.

[9]"Weary" (*'ayēph*) describes those who are about to faint from dehydration. "Hungry" (*ra'ēb*) is a word for famine and starvation (e.g., Lam. 2:19; 4:9; 5:10). Westerners hardly have the capacity to imagine what it is to be in danger of perishing from dehydration in a hot and arid climate or to linger on the verge of starvation. It is this kind of desperation that Job is accused of callously disregarding when he had abundant means to meet such needs.

[10]22:8 seems out of place to some. Rowley (pp. 194–95) and Andersen (p. 203) see here Eliphaz's implication that Job has come by his wealth and property by cruelly seizing the land of the poor and defenseless (an evil Job denies in 31:38–40). Even that seems a little "between the lines." The comment need signal no more than Eliphaz's pause to underscore the extensive means (prosperity, influence, wealth, property) that Job had at his disposal to meet such needs.

[11]Is 22:15–16 a specific reference to the Flood in Gen. 6–8 (Morris, p. 26)? Quite possibly. That 22:17–18 are a return to Job's words in 21:14, 16 is obvious, but to what intent is not clear.

[12]Andersen, p. 205.

[13]Smick, p. 954.

[14]The precise meaning is not so straightforward. For the KJV, cf. Ps. 139:3. NASB translates, "Yield" or "Know intimately." NIV reads, "Submit." NEB reads, "Come to terms with God." Gordis (p. 240) renders, "Put yourself in harmony with Him." RSV and ESV read, "Agree with God." Delitzsch (p. 440) says, "Make friends with." The element all these options have in common is reconciliation.

[15]The KJV "law" usually gives way to "instruction" (NKJV, NASB, NIV), but the word is *torah.* This is the lone occurrence of this word in Job, and "the terminology of the Mosaic 'law' is surprisingly absent from the book as a whole" (Andersen, p. 205). Given the ubiquity of the Law throughout the rest of the OT, Andersen's observation confirms an early date for the story of Job, if not also the composition.

[16]"Return" (*shub*) is the classic Hebrew term for repentance, signifying not merely a turning to the right or left, but a complete reversal of one's present course.

[17]I will not even attempt to wade through the complexities of 22:29–30. "The Hebrew text is a thicket of thorns, and AV pays the price of honesty by being largely unintelligible. Solutions are almost as numerous as commentators" (Andersen, p. 206).

[18]Gordis, p. 239.

[19]"The irony will be felt at the end when Eliphaz will be the chief beneficiary of Job's power as an intercessor" (Andersen, p. 206).

[20]C. S. Lewis, *A Grief Observed*, pp. 9, 26–27. Lewis's opening words drip with poignancy: "No one ever told me that grief felt so much like fear."

[21]Courtney Anderson, *To the Golden Shore* (Valley Forge: Judson Press, 1987), p. 391, emphasis added. The fuller story is instructive. It took the death of his wife to bring him face-to-face with the pride and ambition that had been his driving motivation to become a pioneer missionary in the first place. He was filled with a sense of guilt and self-loathing that took him years to overcome. For a briefer overview of Judson's life, see Ruth Tucker,

From Jerusalem to Irian Jaya (Grand Rapids: Academie Books, 1983), pp. 121–31.

[22]This suggests not only the contextual significance of 42 for 44 and 46, but a closer link between 44 and 46 than we might otherwise suspect if we assumed that the Psalms are just a random collection arbitrarily arranged.

[23]A number of commentators argue that Psalms 42 and 43 actually form a unit, "two parts of a single, close-knit poem" (Derek Kidner, *Psalms 1–72,* Tyndale Old Testament Commentary, ed. D. J. Wiseman [Downers Grove, Ill.: IVP, 1973], p. 165). Cf. also F. Delitzsch, *Commentary on the Old Testament* and Willem VanGemeren, *Expositor's Bible Commentary.*

[24]The right response to the silence of God when you know He has chastened you for sin is no different. See Lam. 3.

[25]Jesus said, "Ask . . . seek . . . knock" (Matt. 7:7–8). What does this suggest about who *initiates* the dialogue of prayer? *God* does. He speaks first, inviting, encouraging, commanding us to come to Him. "When once we apprehend that the initiative lies with God, we recognize that prayer is not forcing ourselves into the presence of God, but rather accepting His gracious invitation." Prayer is nothing short of obeying the command of a Master or King to report and communicate to Him as His servant and minister. The text reads literally, "*Keep on* asking . . . *keep on* seeking . . . *keep on* knocking." What does this suggest but that we should sometimes *expect delay* when we pray? Finally, Jesus promises, "It *shall* be given . . . ye *shall* find . . . it *shall* be opened." What does this suggest about prayer but that the answer is assured (D. Edmond Hiebert, *Working with God Through Prayer* [Greenville, S.C.: BJU Press, 1991], pp. 4–6)?

[26]Ron Lee Davis, *Gold in the Making: Where Is God When Bad Things Happen to You?* (Nashville: Thomas Nelson, 1983), p. 32.

[27]"Way" (*derek*) can refer to a path or road that one treads; in other passages it connotes *behavior* (Deut. 32:4) or *activity* (Prov. 8:22) (Holladay, p. 74). The construction "way with me" is unusual. No article or suffix is attached to "way" and "although *he knows the way that I take* has gathered a lot of devotional sentiment over the centuries, it has blurred the Hebrew 'with me'" and interpolates too much (Andersen, p. 210).

[28]"Stich b is a hypothetical conditional sentence, with the perfect in the protasis and the imperfect in the apodosis: 'If He tested me, I would emerge pure as gold'" (Gordis, pp. 261–62). Delitzsch describes this construction as the common hypothetical preterite and cites additional examples (Gen. 44:22; Ruth 2:9; Zech. 13:6). Gordis and Delitzsch refer the reader to Gesenius for corroboration.

[29]Others who see 23:10 as an avowal of innocence, rather than an assurance of purification through suffering, include Andersen (p. 210); Smick (p. 959); Zuck (p. 108); Delitzsch (II, pp. 9–10); Gordis (pp. 261–62);

Strahan (pp. 208–9); R. Laird Harris, (p. 178); John E. Hartley ("The Genres and Message of the Book of Job," in *Sitting with Job,* p. 69); Claus Westermann ("Job's Asseveration of Innocence," in *Sitting with Job,* p. 319); Sylvia Huberman Scholnick ("Poetry in the Courtroom: Job 38–41" in *Sitting with Job,* pp. 425–26); A. R. Fausset in Robert Jamieson, A. R. Fausset and David Brown, *A Commentary Critical, Experimental, and Practical on the Old and New Testaments,* vol. 2, part 1 (Grand Rapids: Eerdmans, rpr. 1976), p. 58.

[30]This view is common in devotional hymnody and literature. Cf. Archer, p. 80; Morris, pp. 72, 80; Carter, p. 118; Thiessen, pp. 29–30; and even C. H. Spurgeon, "Believers Tested by Trials" in *The Suffering of Man and the Sovereignty of God* (Oswego, Ill.: Fox River Press, 2001), pp. 195–206.

[31]Taking an unusual tack based on the first word of 23:10 (*kiy,* often "because"), Zuck argues that the meaning is "God is evading me [23:7–9] *because* He knows my ways. He knows I am innocent, and therefore is refusing to appear in court, for once He heard my case He would have to admit to injustice" (p. 108). This is surely reading Job wrongly. *Kiy* also functions as a demonstrative particle used for emphasis ("Indeed" or "Truly"). Apart from this variation, Zuck sees 23:10 as a metaphorical reference to "when God finished with him in court" (*The Bible Knowledge Commentary,* vol. 1 [Victor Books, 1985], p. 747).

[32]"Job's words in vv. 11–12 have to be the words either of a terrible hypocrite or of a deeply committed believer" (Smick, p. 959).

[33]Fausset, p. 58.

[34]Actually, the final phrase in English is the first phrase in the Hebrew of stich b: מֵחֻקִּי צָפַנְתִּי אִמְרֵי־פִיו. Translations vary on the treatment of the last phrase of 23:12—"my necessary *food*" (AV, NKJV); "my daily bread" (NIV); "my prescribed portion" (NASB margin); "my own [words]" (NCV). Gordis, following the LXX and assuming an emendation, renders, "in my bosom I have kept the words of His mouth" (so RSV).

[35]I remember as a teen seeing my mother post this verse on our refrigerator as a spiritual reminder and encouragement to stay on her diet—a commendable goal, but probably not what Job had in mind.

[36]The traditional translation is based on other uses of the term (*chōq*) such as Prov. 30:8 ("feed me with food *convenient* for me," but contextually better "feed me with food *allotted* for me") and Gen. 47:22, taking it in the sense of one's "allowance (of food)," God's provided allotment for one's need (hence, NIV "daily bread"). Others preserve the sense of "statute" or "rule." Delitzsch interprets, "I kept the words of Thy mouth, i.e. esteemed them high and precious, more than my statute, i.e. more than what my own will prescribed for me" (p. 11). Fausset: "'More than my law,' my own will in antithesis to the words of His mouth. How difficult it is for man to prefer God's laws to those of his own will." On balance, however, Fausset

concludes, "Probably, under the general term, 'what is appointed to me' (the same Hebrew is in v. 14), all that ministers to the appetites of the body and carnal will is included" (p. 58).

[37]Centuries later, Jeremiah would affirm the same truth in the midst of horrendous national suffering for sin (Lam. 3:37–38).

[38]For example, see Joseph's remarkable breadth and depth of theology (Talbert, *Not by Chance*, pp. 275–76, note 7).

[39]Smick, pp. 959–60.

[40]"The point would be then that God apparently does nothing to prevent the wrongs that occur every day" (Andersen, p. 211). Zuck confuses Job's frustrated questioning with "lambasting God for being so apathetic toward injustice" (p. 109).

[41]Zuck argues credibly that nothing Job says is directly problematic with his previous assertions (pp. 111–12).

[42]Some, noting the brevity of Bildad's final speech and the absence of Zophar's, suggest that these words have been misplaced and actually belong to one of them. Others offer the possibility that ancient Jewish scribes altered the text to prevent Job from sounding too unorthodox. Smick advises that one consider the possibility that these are Job's unannounced quotations of his friends' views (cf. Gordis, pp. 256, 269). See Smick, pp. 957–58; Andersen, pp. 208, 213. The ESV reflects this: "You say, 'Swift are they on the face of the waters; their portion is cursed in the land."

[43]Andersen believes "that the whole is a string of curses, beginning with verse 18, where an imprecation, not a statement, should be read, as the grammar shows" (p. 214). Another option is that Job may merely be providing a balanced picture of reality. Unlike his friends, who blindly affirm that all the wicked are always cut off on the earth, Job insists that while the wicked sometimes are cut off (24:18–25) this is by no means always the case (21:7–21; 24:2–17). Andersen makes this sound credible (p. 213) but opts for the imprecation interpretation.

[44]The NKJV takes this approach by inserting *should*: "They should be swift on the face of the waters, their portion should be cursed in the earth."

[45]Scholars too clever by half have proposed multiple redivisions of the text to lengthen Bildad's speech and, in some cases, patch together a speech for Zophar out of some of Job's excess words. Rowley notes not less than a dozen reconstructions (pp. 213–14). Andersen remarks, "We shall say nothing further about the dozens of mutually contradictory 'solutions' by which scholars have unscrambled the allegedly disordered speeches at the end of the third round. We do not wish to disdain such efforts. . . . But when there is so little sign of a consensus, it might be better to leave the text as it is, since the onus of proof rests with those who wish to alter it, and so far nothing like proof has been forthcoming" (Andersen, p. 216).

[46]It is interesting to note the overall pattern of the speeches in terms of length. In a number of verses, they run as follows: Eliphaz—48, 35, 30; Bildad—22, 21, 6; Zophar—20, 29, 0. The diminishing pattern, capped by Bildad's briefest and Zophar's no-show, appears to be suggestive that, as Andersen notes, the "point has been reached [where] there can be no further dialogue, and the discussion grinds to a halt" (p. 202).

[47]While some think this doubtful (Rowley, p. 213), others agree it is a logical conclusion (Andersen, p. 214; Zuck, p. 113). Besides being merely logical, it fits the data mentioned. The fact that Elihu noted this problem as the reason for putting in his oar suggests that he, in fact, had something unique to offer to the discussion.

[48]Every reference uses some form of the root *tsadaq*. Even in those few passages where Job complains he would not be found righteous by God, the plain implication is that he believes himself to be righteous but that God has obviously found some occasion against him.

[49]Job's reply to Bildad is described as "biting sarcasm" (Rowley, p. 216; Archer, p. 82) that is "dripping with irony" (L. D. Johnson, cited by Zuck, p. 115).

[50]Andersen, p. 215.

[51]See Archer, p. 83. Morris gives extensive consideration to this aspect of the book of Job. While Smick is correct that "cosmography is not in itself the purpose of this passage" (p. 966), its expressions, though poetic, are consistent with science.

[52]What I am suggesting by the caveat "so far as we know" is not that Job may have lived after the Mosaic era of written revelation but, rather, that there was no written revelation prior to the Mosaic era, *so far as we know*. Pre-Mosaic written revelation is not impossible. Indeed, it is entirely logical that Enoch or Noah or Abraham or even Job may have recorded the words of God to them—it's just not verifiable, since no evidence of such record has been preserved (unless its preservation in the canonical text of Scripture is itself the evidence).

13—The Defense Rests

[1]Andersen, p. 219. The phrase reads literally, "And Job added [continued, or proceeded] to take up his parable and said. . . ." Translations tend to omit either the main verb (NASB, ESV) or the infinitive (AV, NKJV, NIV, NCV).

[2]The word can apply to the pithy proverbs of Solomon (1 Kings 4:32; Prov. 10:1), "an extended didactic discourse" such as Prov. 1:8–19, or a prophetic message of judgment (Isa. 14:4–27). Whatever the length, a *mashal* has "a clearly recognizable purpose: that of quickening an apprehension of the real as distinct from the wished for . . . of compelling the hearer or

reader to form a judgment on himself, his situation, or his conduct" (Victor P. Hamilton in *Theological Wordbook of the Old Testament,* Vol. 1 [Chicago: Moody, 1980], pp. 533–34).

[3]Smick, p. 971; cf. Andersen, p. 220.

[4]Andersen, p. 221.

[5]Ibid. He adds that the penalty in Israel for libel "was the punishment attached to the crime wrongly charged. Hence Job's repudiation of the charges with the oath, 'Let my hater be treated *as the wicked person* he untruthfully says I am.'" Cf. Smick, pp. 971–72.

[6]On this basis many regard 27:13–23 as scribal meddling to reclaim Job's orthodoxy, or as "the lost third speech of Zophar" (a view that "has enjoyed considerable prestige among scholars for two centuries"). But this is unnecessary speculation (Andersen, pp. 219–20; cf. Zuck, p. 121).

[7]"Since Job nowhere denies the justice of God, it is not inconsistent for him to affirm it here. The disagreement between Job and his friends is not whether God is just or not; it is how the justice of God is seen to work out in particular events, and specifically in Job's experiences" (Andersen, p. 220).

[8]Kidner notes Davidson's objection that any distinction between the friends' position and Job's view as he here expresses it "has to be read into his words, for the 'language is as absolute as that of Zophar or any of the three'" (Kidner, pp. 79–80).

[9]"The obstinacy of his friends has gradually driven Job to a position he hates and does not really want to defend. His friends on the other hand can maintain their traditional positions only by shutting their eyes to facts and by repeating platitudes in a loud voice" (Ellison, p. 87).

[10]See, e.g., Job 21:19 in NKJV, NASB, NIV, NCV, Amplified Bible.

[11]Smick argues forcefully elsewhere: "One must not overlook the practice of unannounced quotations. . . . Such an ancient rhetorical device is disturbing to us because we are not used to it, but it may be the correct approach to these verses." Rather than suggesting scribal doctoring or reassigning such passages to a different speaker, "it seems wiser to let the text stand and above all refuse to force modern categories of logic and rhetoric on it" (Smick, p. 958). He is referring to 24:18–24, but I am applying his argument—with even greater merit, I believe—to 27:13–23. In this sense alone, then, the speech really can be "attributed" to Zophar . . . and Bildad and Eliphaz. This is their view as recounted by Job.

[12]Some, of course, go even further than these two options, but given the view here espoused—that the book of Job is a unified and complete entity—there is little value in exploring the theories of men whose imagination is unhampered by any loyalty to the text as it stands.

[13]Cf. Dhorme (p. li), Andersen (p. 224), Smick (p. 974), Kidner (pp. 80–81), Ellison (p. 89).

[14]Andersen, pp. 222–24; Dhorme, p. lii.

[15]Smick, pp. 974–75. For the view that this chapter furnishes the theological as well as symmetrical center of the book, see Michael J. Peterson, "Job 28: The Theological Center of the Book of Job" (unpublished dissertation, Bob Jones University, 1994). The argument is a worthy one but does not seem necessarily dependent on the isolation or narrative authorship of chap. 28.

[16]Andersen, p. 224; the view is that of Junker, cited by both Rowley (p. 226) and Kidner (p. 81).

[17]Personally, I have no difficulty imagining that there was little more than a sigh, a pause, and a conscious shift in Job's spirit between chap. 27 and 28. But this is not necessary even if we accord the words to Job.

[18]Thus Smick's assurance that "the tone is so irenic that one need not assume Job was speaking" (p. 974) may be countered by observing that the tone is so irenic that one need not assume Job was *not* speaking, given the dynamic of narrative selection. It is strange that so few seem to consider narrator discretion as a factor in explaining the shift in the speech's character and content.

[19]Ellison regards 29:1 "as a warning against the supposition" that Job is the speaker in chap. 28 but does not explain why 27:1 is not a warning against the supposition that Job is the speaker in chap. 26 (p. 89).

[20]Those who see chap. 28 as the words of Job include Carter (p. 127), Archer (p. 85), and Zuck (pp. 122–23). For others, see Rowley, p. 226.

[21]"The chapter as the literary apex of the book anticipates the theophany but does so without creating a climax. God alone has the answer or better *is* the answer to the mystery Job and his friends have sought to fathom" (Smick, p. 975).

[22]This name for God, *Adonai* (Master, Lord), appears only here (28:28) in Job. Many commentators have pounced on this peculiarity as proof that this chapter is the work and insertion of some outside source. Andersen notes that "Rowley (p. 234) has trounced the argument that the solitary use of the word 'Lord' here betrays an alien source. Such a sudden twist is often met at the end of a Wisdom poem" (p. 229).

[23]Cf. Prov. 1:7; 9:10; Ps. 111:10. Andersen notes bluntly: "Many commentators do not like this verse. They dismiss it as a platitude that replaces a noble agnosticism with a banal moralism" (p. 229).

[24]In fact, the same contrastive phrase (*w atah*) appears three times (30:1, 9, 16).

[25]Andersen, p. 234.

[26]The word *cruel* in 30:21 (*'akzar*) appears only three other times in the OT in highly charged, emotionally graphic contexts. It depicts the unapproachable *fierceness* of Leviathan (Job 41:10), the *deadly* venom of cobras

(Deut. 32:33), and the *heartlessness* of a mother who refuses to nurse her starving child (Lam. 4:3).

[27]Andersen, p. 234.

[28]Smick, p. 980. Andersen (pp. 238–39) describes this as "an oath of clearance in the form of a negative confession" (a term Smick dislikes). "The form Job uses is, 'If I have done X, then let Y happen to me!' X is the crime; Y is the penalty." But the penalty is not in any human terms of a fitting "fine or reparation. It is some act of God. Its character as punishment for a particular sin takes the form of poetic justice."

[29]Why does this not follow Job's protestation of moral propriety, where it logically belongs? The fact that the sequence of Job's oath of innocence does not follow a neat logical order, Andersen notes wryly, "has annoyed the tidy minds of scholars, some of whom have recomposed the chapter to remove such faults" (p. 239). Andersen provides an ample explanation for this confession's being "neither systematic nor complete. It was not drawn up by an articled clerk" nor is it "a page from a barrister's brief." Rather, "it is a poem, recited by a miserable outcast on the city rubbish dump, not by a prisoner in the dock." Yet even Andersen's observation carries its own irony. He presumes that the author has skillfully woven this quality of "incoherence" into his composition of Job's words for the sake of authenticity. Why not see it as evidence of actual, rather than contrived, authenticity?

[30]"The sin of adultery is here repudiated. **A woman** here means a married woman, as the parallel makes plain" (Rowley, p. 254).

[31]Some have suggested, quite unnecessarily, that the reference to "grinding" may be a euphemism for sexual intercourse, making it more obviously parallel to the obvious reference in v. 10*b* (Gordis, p. 346; Andersen, p. 241). Dhorme identifies this view as a rabbinical interpretation that influenced the Targum and the Latin Vulgate (p. 454). Those who dismiss the euphemistic interpretation of "grinding" seem confident that it is a reference to her becoming another man's slave, since Exod. 11:5 implies that grinding meal is the menial task of the lowest servant (Rowley, p. 254; Zuck, p. 135). But this deduction is not entirely necessary, either. Most households did not have slaves, and in the absence of slaves, the woman of the household did the grinding. It need not imply anything more complicated than the obvious inference that his wife would become another man's wife and the woman of his home rather than Job's.

[32]Strahan complains that Job "imprecated on himself a curse that would fall almost entirely on his innocent and injured wife. When woman has absolutely equal rights with her husband, as she has in Christianity, such a penance becomes preposterous" (p. 259). Ellison dismisses those who are incensed that Job's curse would victimize his wife as "hypercritical," since "there was no greater indignity, no greater confession of impotence, than to be unable to prevent the forcible carrying away of one's wife. Where hon-

our ranked above all else, this dishonour was worse than death" (Ellison, p. 100; see also Gordis, pp. 346–47, who explains the appropriateness of the imprecation "in terms of the ancient doctrine of corporate responsibility and family solidarity"). To suggest that Job viewed this judgment as a form of "penance" is "preposterous."

[33] *Visit* is a common Hebrew term with a potentially misleading English translation. The Hebrew verb (*paqad*) carries two basic connotations: inspection and/or intervention. These concepts may or may not be connected in any given passage. Inspection does not necessarily result in interventional activity but may be merely for the purpose of assessment. On the other hand, intervention presupposes inspection (action based on assessment). When God "visits" iniquity, He is inspecting and assessing human sin and, in some cases, requiting it (i.e., intervening with appropriate judgment). When God "visits" in judgment (e.g., Jer. 5:9; Hos. 2:13; Zeph. 1:8–9), it is not random or capricious; it is God's interventional activity based on God's previous, thorough observation and assessment of human behavior. God may intervene with blessing, also based on His previous observation or "inspection" of human need (Gen. 21:1; Ruth 1:6; Ps. 106:4). Here in Job 31:14, Job expresses his hypothetical speechlessness and his absence of any defense when the time comes for God to inspect his deeds and render a judgment on him, if he were to abuse his fellow man and ignore any just complaint against him of mistreatment.

[34] Zuck, p. 137; Rowley, p. 258; Andersen, p. 243.

[35] Andersen, p. 243.

[36] Those who reject the historicity of Gen. 3 naturally have a vested interest in evicting Adam from Job 31:33. While there is nothing heretical about the NIV (and ESV) translation (cf. also the marginal readings in the NKJV and NASB), the reference to Adam seems at least as natural, if not more so. Meredith Kline argues that an allusion to Adam in 31:33 fits with the imprecation in 31:40, which also carries strong overtones of Gen. 3 (Smick, p. 995). Smick, however, objects that "Job was dealing with hypocrisy here—hiding one's sins. Adam hid himself in shame, but not his sins, as a hypocrite does" (ibid.). But surely this misses the whole point: in hiding *himself* Adam was hiding his sin—pretending it was not there, hoping it might not be noticed, and avoiding God rather than running repentantly in search of Him. Even when God confronted him with a direct question, Adam evaded, prevaricated, and blame-shifted. Even Job's imagery of "covering" or "concealing" his sin is reminiscent of Gen. 3:7.

[37] Smick notes Job's growing confidence from 13:14–16 to the brashness that characterizes his language in this chapter (p. 995). For the essence of Job's challenge in 31:35–37, see also Andersen, p. 244; Ellison, p. 101; Rowley, pp. 260–61; Zuck, pp. 138–39; Howard, pp. 77–78. Archer (p. 90)

seems to think that Job is addressing any potential human accusers in 31:35–37.

[38]"Job would proudly exhibit such a citation of trumped-up charges, because in his innocence he could confidently refute all God's incriminations" and await with certainty "God's verdict of acquittal" (Zuck, pp. 138–39).

[39]Though some regard these verses as out of place (e.g., Rowley, p. 261), Andersen describes them as a recapitulation (p. 244), Zuck (p. 139), and Smick (p. 996) as purposefully anticlimactic in keeping with Job's previous habit (3:23–26; 14:18–22).

[40]Edmund F. Sutcliffe, *Providence and Suffering in the Old and New Testaments* (London: Thomas Nelson and Sons, 1953), pp. 116, 119.

[41]Andersen, p. 240. "Selective," he adds, "it nevertheless highlights matters considered by Job as supremely important as an index of character."

[42]Carson, p. 167.

[43]Cf. Paul in 2 Cor. 11:5–10, 16–18; 12:11 ("I have become a fool in boasting. You have compelled me.").

[44]Smick, p. 990.

14—The Character and Function of Elihu

[1]Disraeli made this remark in a speech at Knightsbridge, London, on July 27, 1878, quoted in the *Times* (July 29, 1878). See Robert Andrews, ed. *Famous Lines: A Columbia Dictionary of Familiar Quotations* (New York: Columbia University Press, 1997), p. 380.

[2]Zuck, p. 142. For some intriguing analysis of the potential significance of the names of Job's counselors, particularly Elihu, see Green (pp. 263–65) and Gordis (*The Book of God and Man* [Chicago: University of Chicago Press, 1965], pp. 115–16).

[3]Cf., e.g., 33:6–7 and 9:34, 34:3, and 12:11. Smick summarizes: "We are not told explicitly why or under what circumstances he was there. The Prologue says nothing of bystanders, though it implies that Job sat in an open public place where the friends could see him at a distance (2:12). These verses (32:1–5) simply imply that Elihu was among the bystanders who listened to Job and his counselors" (p. 999).

[4]From the absence of any divine censure of Elihu, it might be construed "that Elihu's four speeches are intended to be completely normative." Such a conclusion, however, "is an oversimplification of the Elihu speeches" (Robert V. McCabe, "Elihu's Contribution to the Thought of the Book of Job," *Detroit Baptist Seminary Journal* [Fall 1997] p. 64).

[5]Among others (e.g., Zuck, p. 142), McCabe shares this basic view of Elihu as transitional: "the Elihu speeches contribute to the design of Job by

serving primarily as a transition from the dialogue with the three friends to the Yahweh speeches" (p. 49). Although I disagree with McCabe on some key points in our respective interpretations of Elihu, his work in this area is insightful and of the highest scholarly caliber. I owe a great deal to his observations.

[6]David Noel Freedman, "Is It Possible to Understand the Book of Job?" in *Bible Review* (April 1988), p. 29. Freedman proceeds to assert that Elihu—like the other three friends—is not a real person at all but a literary foil fabricated by the writer. But perspective and prejudice are funny things. Keil turns Freedman's argument on its head: "Job is silent because he does not know how to answer Elihu, and therefore feels himself overcome" (p. 241). Job always had an answer to even the most impertinent arguments of the other three, but Elihu leaves him nonplussed.

[7]Green, writing in the 1870s, counters each of these same points (pp. 254–58). Job is silent "because he is convinced of the truth of what [Elihu] says . . . Job yielded to his arguments, and had no reply to make. He tacitly confesses the justice of all Elihu says" (pp. 259, 261). Granted, both Freedman's and Green's explanations argue from silence. That is why we must root our opinions of Elihu in all the textual data we can muster—namely, the narrator's description of Elihu, Elihu's own arguments, and any detectable response or connection to Elihu's words in the following speaker (God).

[8]This liberal argument of the later interpolation of Elihu raises a raft of counterquestions: (1) If Elihu's speeches contribute nothing new, why would anyone bother to interpolate them? (2) What editor could be so inept as to cut and paste a six-chapter section and drop it into an otherwise self-consistent story, yet forget to weave it in convincingly by interpolating some reference to this significant character in the chapters before and after his appearance? (3) How could generations of Jews be so unobservant of this editorial faux pas (so evident to later scholars) as to affirm its canonicity without question? Carson simplifies the problem of these liberal assertions of multiple authorship or editorial patchwork by noting that "such theories solve nothing, for someone put together the speeches with the prologue and epilogue, and if that person did not detect an insuperable difficulty, then why should we think that an original writer would find an insuperable difficulty? Such source theories, even if right, do not solve the theological problem: the book as we have it stands or falls as a literary whole, for that is the only form in which it has come down to us" (Carson, p. 156).

[9]"The Job scrolls also show that the Elihu speeches (chs. 32–37), which many scholars believe were not part of the original composition, were included in this book before the common era" (VanderKam and Flint, p. 120). Portions of the Elihu segment (Job 32–37) comprise over half

of the total text of Job represented in the Dead Sea Scroll fragments (see Abegg, Flint, and Ulrich, *The Dead Sea Scrolls Bible*, pp. 590–93).

[10]Though Job was still trusting God at the end of chap. 31, says Morris, "Satan . . . still had one more trick up his sleeve"—namely, Elihu, who was "impressed with his own spiritual insights and was looking for an opportunity to demonstrate them" (p. 75). According to Morris, both Eliphaz (in his vision in chap. 4) and Elihu (who refers to a constraining "spirit" within him, 32:8–10, 18) were actually influenced by "some alien spirit seeking . . . to destroy Job's faith" (p. 79). For Morris's imaginative suggestion of Elihu as a kind of antichrist, see pp. 79–81.

[11]Rowley refers to "the pompous and irrelevant ideas of Elihu" (p. 20). Norman Habel regards Elihu as the quintessential "fool" ("Literary Features and the Message of the Book of Job" in *Sitting with Job*, ed. Roy B. Zuck, p. 108). Charles Carter can barely contain his disdain for Elihu, who appears "in a spirit of arrogance that sweeps all his peers aside at a single stroke" (p. 140), and includes samples of equally colorful denunciations by other writers. While Kidner's estimation of Elihu is not so searing, it is essentially negative (*Wisdom of Proverbs, Job and Ecclesiastes*, pp. 69–70).

[12]Though he regards the character of Elihu as "written into the book of Job," William P. Brown chides those who have "disparaged" Elihu's character "with almost unmatched vehemence" (*Character in Crisis* [Grand Rapids: Eerdmans, 1996], p. 84). Norman Snaith also disputes the negative impression some have formed of Elihu's speeches (*The Book of Job* [Naperville, Ill.: Alec R. Allenson, 1968], pp. 87ff.). Others who take an essentially positive view of Elihu include Keil, pp. 239ff.; Zuck, *Job*, pp. 140ff.; Dhorme, pp. liv–lvii; Andersen, pp. 245ff.; Smick, pp. 997ff.; Carson, pp. 168ff.; A. R. Faussett, *Commentary*, vol. 2, pp. 77ff.; Thurman Wisdom, "The Message of Elihu" in *Biblical Viewpoint* (November 1987), pp. 27–35; Leon Wood, pp. 103ff.; Archer, *The Book of Job*, (Grand Rapids: Baker, 1982), pp. 90ff.; Green, pp. 245ff.; Howard, pp. 85ff. Andersen and, to a lesser degree, Smick express considerable irritation with Elihu at points as well.

[13]Matthew Henry, *Commentary on the Whole Bible*, vol. 3, (Westwood, N.J.: Revell, n.d.), p. 174. Sadly, many overly sophisticated Bible students harbor as little esteem for Matthew Henry as others do for Elihu. This devaluation springs from a lack of serious interaction with Henry's commentaries and an immaturity that thinks itself capable of producing equally insightful observations on its own. Spurgeon regarded Henry's commentary so highly that he advised young seminarians to read through its entirety at least once within a year of their graduation (*Commenting and Commentaries*, p. 3).

[14]J. Sidlow Baxter, *Explore the Book*, vol. 3 (Grand Rapids: Zondervan, 1960), p. 55.

[15]Smick, pp. 997–98.

[16]A footnote in *The MacArthur Study Bible* ([Nashville: Word, 1997] pp. 728–29) is unhelpfully even-handed. Elihu "had some new thoughts but was very hard on Job." He was "angry, full of self-importance and verbose, but his approach was refreshing . . . though not really helpful to Job." The only reason offered for the inclusion of Elihu's "blustering speeches" is simply "because they happened"! But lots of things happened that the Holy Spirit omitted from the sacred record; surely He had a better reason than that for selecting Elihu's speeches for inclusion. The marginal note in the usually noteworthy *Women's Study Bible* is similarly noncommittal (p. 841).

[17]Green, p. 258: "The difficulties which have been felt with regard to Elihu will, we are persuaded, disappear . . . upon a more careful study of the speech attributed to him, and of the language with which he is introduced."

[18]Longman, p. 75.

[19]McCabe interprets the "strong emphasis on Elihu's anger" as the narrator's way of depicting "Elihu as an impatient individual . . . more emotional than rational." He argues that the juxtaposition of Elihu's "real motives" (angry impatience) with Elihu's self-presentation "as patient" communicates an apparent irony (pp. 66–67). This not only confuses wrath with impatience (surely the narrator's emphasis on God's wrath does not depict Him as impatient and "more emotional than rational") but also artificially psychologizes the narrator's description. It creates a contradiction between the narrator's words and Elihu's where there need not be one. If Elihu is prompted by anger to speak, it is not necessary that he say so; it is usually apparent, as McCabe himself notes.

[20]Andersen admits that "the plain meaning is that Job thought himself to be in the right in his dispute with God, and that God was correspondingly in the wrong" (p. 245). But Andersen undercuts the force of the narrator's observation by assigning it instead to "Elihu's opinion, of course, and an obvious inference." What many miss is that the narrator's report of Elihu's diagnosis agrees with God's diagnosis (40:8). Even if 32:2 is construed not as the narrator's objective analysis but only as Elihu's subjective opinion, 40:8 verifies that Elihu was right.

[21]Rowley acknowledges that "self-righteousness can be found in Job's speeches, indeed" (p. 263).

[22]Henry Morris mistakenly regards this divine question as directed to Job but as referring to Elihu (pp. 85–86). The view that God was talking about Job in 38:2, says Morris, is "impossible" because Elihu, not Job, was the one who had been speaking when God "interrupts." Morris's argument ignores several opposing textual implications: (1) Job had repeatedly asked God to "answer" him (9:16; 13:22; 14:15); so (says the narrator, using the same Hebrew word) God "answered Job." (2) In 38:2 God is actually echoing Elihu's words to Job (34:35; 35:16), just as in 38:3 He quotes Job's own words back to him (13:22; 14:15). (3) The rebuke implied in God's ques-

tion (38:2) is immediately followed by the rebuke to Job implied in God's challenge (38:3). Why would God rail on Elihu then instantly turn on Job Himself? (4) Job's words in 42:3 indicate that he understood that 38:2 was addressed to him and accepts them as applying to him, not to Elihu. This is clear not only from the straightforward sense of Job's words but also from his admitting that he had been guilty of the very kind of speech without knowledge (42:3b) that God had rebuked (42:3*a*). The *Scofield Reference Bible* offers an overall high opinion of Elihu, but sees 38:2 as referring to Elihu—a view the NSRB dropped (p. 592). Other study Bibles correctly refer the words of 38:2 to Job.

[23]Carson, p. 168.

[24]Even Carson, who takes a generally positive view of Elihu's content, concedes: "Perhaps one of the reasons why Elihu does not get a very sympathetic reading in some circles is that he is patently an arrogant and pretentious young man. Probably he is a great wise man in the making, but still far too full of himself and too certain of his opinions" (p. 168). But what makes his alleged arrogance and pretension so "patent"? Do his words actually conflict with the narrator's depiction of Elihu? Or could it be a simpler dynamic at work—intonation based on prejudice or mistaken impression rather than on the textual and contextual markers within the book itself?

[25]Carson notes that "a more sympathetic reading of Elihu teases out his contribution, and shows how this young man avoids the opposing pitfalls into which both Job and his comforters have fallen" (p. 168).

[26]R. J. Williams, "Job, Book of," *Encyclopedia Britannica*, vol. 13 (Chicago: William Benton, 1966), p. 9.

[27]For a six-point contrast between Elihu and the three friends, see Larry J. Waters, "Elihu's Theology and His View of Suffering," *Bibliotheca Sacra* (April-June 1999): 155ff.

[28]Baxter distinguishes Elihu's "new approach . . . from that of Eliphaz, Bildad and Zophar with their hard and fast philosophy and their treatment of Job's problem as detached onlookers. They had wished to be judges; whereas Elihu would be a brother. He would seek to sit with Job in the fellowship of human sympathy, yet at the same time speak the real truth from God's side" (p. 56).

[29]"Elihu's attack on Job was limited to [Job's] statements during the dialogue. He did not accuse Job of a wicked life for which he was being punished" (Smick, p. 998).

[30]"The three counselors had claimed that Job was suffering because he was sinning, but Elihu explained that he was sinning because he was suffering!" (Zuck, p. 141). This does not mean that Satan was right after all. Satan's claim was not that he could get Job to sin (there's little challenge

there), but specifically that Job would curse (i.e., disown and forsake) God for allowing him to suffer undeservedly.

[31]The fact that Rowley admits that Job's speeches betray self-righteousness makes his conclusion baffling: "Whatever may be said of the contribution of the Elihu speeches to the problem of suffering, they are irrelevant to the book of Job" (p. 263).

[32]Gordis (p. 358) also sees this as Elihu's distinctive thrust: "The Friends, as protagonists of the conventional theology, have argued that God is just and that suffering is therefore the consequence and the sign of sin. Job, from his own experience, has denied both propositions, insisting [better, implying] that since he is suffering without being a sinner, God is unjust. Elihu rejects both the Friends' argument that suffering is always the result of sin and Job's contention that God is unjust. He offers a new and significant insight: . . . suffering sometimes comes even to upright men as a discipline, as a warning to prevent them from slipping into sin. For there are some sins to which decent, respectable men are particularly prone, notably the sin of complacency and pride."

[33]Even Andersen, whose criticism of Elihu grows harsh once the monologue begins, admits that Elihu's conclusion (chap. 36–37) reflects this shift: "The full answer to Job's suffering therefore cannot be found in questions about justice. Beyond justice there is a benevolence in God that calls men to trust Him. More simply stated, the issue is whether a person can continue to believe that God is really good" (p. 259). Faith in God's goodness and submission to God's sovereignty are at the heart of the struggle with affliction—a struggle that both Elihu and God address.

[34]"Elihu is as convinced as Job's friends that Job is a great sinner—not, as with them, because of the greatness of his sufferings, but because of the evil of his words" (H. L. Ellison, *From Tragedy to Triumph*, p. 113).

[35]The following chart documenting Elihu's citations of Job is adapted and modified from Roy Zuck in *The Bible Knowledge Commentary* (Wheaton Ill.: Victor Books, 1985), p. 758:

33:9 (cf. 9:20–21; 10:7; 12:4; 16:17; 23:11; 27:6; 31:6)
33:10 (cf. 10:6; 13:24; 16:9; 19:11)
33:11 (cf. 7:17–20; 10:14; 13:27)
34:5 (cf. 9:15, 20; 19:6–7; 27:2, 6)
34:6 (cf. 6:4; 10:7; 16:13; 27:5–6; 31:1ff.)
34:9 (cf. 9:27–31)
35:2–3 (cf. 9:27–31)
[36:23 (cf. 19:6–7)]—But 36:23 is not a citation of Job, per se.

[36]Adapted, modified, and expanded from Roy Zuck in *The Bible Knowledge Commentary*, p. 756.

[37]Elihu's predominant name for God is *'El* (19x in 159 verses); cf. Job (17x in 483 verses), Eliphaz (8x in 113 verses), Bildad (6x in 49 verses), Zophar (2x in 49 verses). He also refers to God as *'Eloah* ("God") 7 times, *Shaddai* ("Almighty") 6 times, and "my Maker" (in different constructions) 3 times.

[38]Rowley, p. 269; Strahan, p. 274.

[39]Eccles. 12:10–11 is one of the most unambiguous claims to inspiration of any book in the Bible. It teaches the genuineness and integrity ("written uprightly"), the reliability and trustworthiness ("words of truth"), the profitability and security ("like goads and fastened nails"), and the divine source and authority ("given by one Shepherd") of the entirety of the book of Ecclesiastes. Perhaps it is precisely because of the difficult nature of this book that God saw fit to inspire so explicit and unmistakable a claim to its divine source, inspiration, authority, and trustworthiness.

[40]McCabe sees this as evidence that "Elihu's presumption seems to have reached a new plateau" (p. 60). Rowley concludes, "Elihu is a stranger to modesty, and frequently finds it necessary to certify his own genius" (p. 291).

[41]Andersen, p. 260. Smick adds that Elihu lays no claim "to superior knowledge but only to eloquence" (p. 997). Smick cites the apparent parallel between the feminine plural "my words" in 36:4*a* and the feminine form of knowledge in 36:4*b* (in the sense of "utterances"). "On this basis Elihu was claiming to be one 'perfect of utterance' because his speech derived from God [v. 3] who is the source of perfect words" (p. 1021). The narrator's depiction of Elihu, along with the features of his speech discussed in this chapter, prevents us from attributing to him an egomaniacal complex of sufficient magnitude as to use language equating himself with God—or rather equating God with himself—in 36:4 and 37:16.

[42]Strahan inadvertently makes this same point: "The poet evidently made a careful study of the great divine speech, and put an imitation of it into the mouth of Elihu; but, fine though his work in some respects is, the general result leaves one in no doubt that there are higher and lower degrees of inspiration" (p. 306). Despite the liberal prejudice that prompts his argument, Strahan's conclusion confirms the internal similarities between the speeches of Elihu and God.

[43]See Larry Waters's eight-point comparison between Elihu's perspective and God's ("Elihu's Theology," pp. 157–58).

[44]Carson, p. 168.

[45]Steven D. Mathewson, *The Art of Preaching Old Testament Narrative* (Grand Rapids: Baker Academic, 2002), p. 58.

[46]Robert McCabe identifies Elihu as a "theological foil" but emphasizes his negative or contrastive function as such: "By emphasizing the tensions between the Joban author's theological emphases and Elihu's deviations

from these, the Joban author's use of Elihu as a rival resolution sets off the true resolution of God." McCabe does, however, see Elihu's shift toward theocentricity near the end of his speech as providing a needed corrective to Job's perspective, "for it restores God to the center of Job's thinking and prepares him to hear from God" (pp. 77, 79).

15—The Argument of Elihu

[1]Robin Richmond, *Michelangelo and the Creation of the Sistine Chapel* (New York: Crescent Books, 1992), p. 20.

[2]Andersen, p. 246.

[3]Showing more sympathetic imagination and attention to biographical detail than most, Green suggests that Elihu's "repetitious and prolix" style "arises from the diffidence of youth and inexperience in the presence of aged and venerable men, which made him feel as though he could not affirm too strongly nor repeat too often his reluctance to obtrude himself or his own views upon them" (pp. 265–66).

[4]McCabe, pp. 50–51. The Hiphil participle of *yakach*, referring to a mediator or negotiator who settles disputes, is translated "convinced" in 32:12. Job uses this participle in 9:33 ("daysman") and the verb in 16:21.

[5]Notwithstanding Andersen, speaking for many, "The irony is that his position is much the same as theirs" (p. 247). McCabe makes the additional argument that the "author's intention by preserving this inconsistency is to suggest that Elihu should not be taken on his own terms" (p. 57). What stands out in Elihu's speech, however, is not the occasional similarity of particular statements, but the wholesale divergence of method and reasoning, emphasis and diagnosis. Even identical truths couched in a different rhetorical method and presuppositional approach can suggest fresh insights, implications, and applications. What underscores the distinctiveness of Elihu's arguments and assessments is God's explicit echo of key statements that only Elihu makes.

[6]"My words are from the uprightness [integrity] of my heart, and my lips speak knowledge sincerely" (NASB). "My words come from an upright heart; my lips sincerely speak what I know" (NIV). "My words declare the uprightness of my heart, and what my lips know they speak sincerely" (ESV).

[7]Smick (p. 1005) notes the flaw in the NIV rendering of 33:8 ("But you have said in my hearing—I heard the very words—"), and clarifies that Elihu quotes Job "with some freedom." Cf. Andersen, pp. 248–49. Since Job never protests the inaccuracy of even the most damaging citations of his words, it seems apparent that Elihu's citations are accurate representations of Job's words and, in some cases, of the logical implications of his words.

[8]Carson, p. 169. "However much Job insists he is innocent, he must therefore put a guard on his tongue and refrain from making God guilty."

[9]The verb in both cases is *riyb*. Every other time the verb (or noun) appears it is in the mouth of Job (9:3; 10:2, 8, 19; 23:6).

[10]It is worth reviewing at this point that there was nothing incorrect or inappropriate in Eliphaz's dream revelation. There is every reason to suppose it was valid divine revelation. The problem with that mode of revelation, however (as Eliphaz demonstrated), is the subjective potential for application. But even more objective modes of revelation are just as susceptible of misapplication.

[11]Abraham (Gen. 15:7–17), Jacob (Gen. 28:12–13; 31:10–13), and Joseph (Gen. 37:5–11) received revelation from God through dreams, as well as other Gentiles outside Israelite ancestry, such as Abimelech (Gen. 20) and Pharaoh (Gen. 41). Even well into the era of written revelation, God continued on occasion to manifest Himself and His will in this way as, for example, to Solomon (I Kings 3:5–15; 9:1–9). Some in the New Testament also received not only directional leading, like Joseph and the magi (Matt. 1:20–25; 2:12), but theological truth, like Peter (Acts 10:9–18).

[12]Carson, p. 169. "This is an advance on the argument between Job and his friends," he adds. "Here is a chastening use of suffering that may be independent of some particular sin." Smick (p. 1006) quotes C. S. Lewis (*The Problem of Pain*): "God whispers to us in our pleasures, speaks in our consciences, but shouts in our pains: it is His megaphone to rouse a deaf world."

[13]The verb *chastened* (*yakach*, here in the hophal) appears in 5:17, leading many to argue that Elihu's suggestion here is nothing but a rehash of Eliphaz. Green considers the parallel "a hasty and superficial view," for Eliphaz regards such suffering "punitive" whereas Elihu sees it as "curative" or preventative. "The two ideas are wide as the poles asunder" (p. 269).

[14]Arthur Bennett, ed., *The Valley of Vision: A Collection of Puritan Prayers and Devotions* (Edinburgh: Banner of Truth, 1975), p. 77. No work on prayer has instructed my spirit, warmed my heart, encouraged my soul, and put words in my empty mouth more than this one.

[15]Andersen (p. 250) disputes whether this section identifies a third mode of revelation, but Smick concedes that it does (p. 1006).

[16]So entrenched is Rowley's prejudice against Elihu that every positive feature is given the worst possible interpretation: "After telling Job to be silent and listen, Elihu tells him to speak if he has anything to say. But," he adds with an eerie psychoanalyticism, "Elihu cannot imagine anyone having any answer to make to him" (p. 276). Elihu is incapable of doing or saying anything to redeem himself in the face of such resolute bias. The result is an unrealistic pseudo-character. Even Smick, generally charitably inclined

toward Elihu, finds him "well-meaning" but "insufferably overbearing" in 33:31–33 (p. 1007).

[17]Green's common-sense explanation best fits the available evidence: Job is silent "because he is convinced of the truth of what he says, and he has therefore nothing to reply" (p. 259). "Job yielded to his arguments, and had no reply to make. He tacitly confesses the justice of all Elihu says" (p. 261).

[18]Smick argues that "Elihu had picked out of Job's speeches those words and ideas that sound particularly damaging" and "only those words that he needed to prove his point" (p. 1010). He is essentially playing the part of God's defense lawyer. There is nothing "unfair" about this.

[19]The only allegations of Elihu that seem to border on either false accusation or misinterpretation of Job's words are 34:7–9, 35:3, and 36:17.

[20]Though 21:15 is sometimes suggested as a cross-reference to 34:9, the connection should be rejected. In the first place, the similarity is purely surface and circumstantial, since the English translation "profit(eth)" in both verses represents entirely different Hebrew words. Secondly, if this is Elihu's "source" for Job's words, it would mean that Elihu has knowingly ripped Job's words out of their context, for Job was expressly describing the attitude of the wicked (21:14–15) and then just as expressly distanced himself from it (21:16).

[21]That this is Elihu's perspective becomes clearer when, in 36:21, he warns Job against responding to his affliction with this kind of iniquitous assessment of God.

[22]The word in both cases is the hiphil form of *rasha'*. It may mean to declare someone guilty, but this is perhaps too strong. The hiphil may also mean to "let someone be condemned" (Holladay, p. 347). I.e., Job's juxtaposition of his own innocence with God's actions could allow God to be condemned in people's minds, by leaving the door open for people to conclude that God was unjust, whether Job drew that conclusion or not.

[23]See the discussion of 31:35–37 in chap. 12. Andersen, Rowley, Smick, et al. are strangely silent on the remarkable correlation between 34:17 and 40:8. Gregory Parsons at least notices the parallel ("The Structure and Purpose in the Book of Job" in *Sitting with Job*, ed. Roy B. Zuck, p. 32). It seems so obvious in the text, especially in combination with the previous and equally unnoticed correlation between 33:13 and 40:2, that the silence of the commentators is inexplicable.

[24]Carson, p. 170.

[25]Though the sense of 34:35 is synonymous, the language of 35:16 (בִּבְלִי־דַעַת מִלִּין) is virtually identical to 38:2 (בְמִלִּין בְּלִי־דָעַת). Once more the silence from the anti-Elihu commentators is deafening. That Andersen makes no comment on the undeniable parallel is astounding.

Rowley skips 34:35 altogether, makes no substantive remark on 35:16, and at 38:2 offers only an unelaborated reference to 35:16.

[26]The word *mishpat* occurs 23 times in Job—once each by Bildad and Eliphaz, 9 times by Job, 11 times by Elihu (of which 2 are in Elihu's citation of Job's words), and once by God. Sylvia Huberman Scholnick argues that, besides the obvious judicial connotation, the word conveys a nonjudicial sense of sovereignty that predominates in the book of Job, and that Job's final response in chap. 42 indicates he finally understands and submits to this aspect of God's *mishpat* ("The Meaning of Mišpat in the Book of Job," *Journal of Biblical Literature* 101, no. 4 [December 1982]: 521–29).

[27]NCV translates, "Do you think this is fair?" NASB provides a sensible translation that preserves the syntax: "Do you think this is according to justice?"

[28]Righteousness is central to the discussion in Job. The Hebrew adjective appears 7 times, the noun 11 times, and the verb 17 times. The essence of righteousness is fulfilling one's obligations, and Job spends chap. 31 arguing that he has. Elihu merely infers what Job leaves unspoken, and probably would never say out loud—that he has fulfilled his obligations to God and man more conscientiously than God has to him.

[29]"Though Job has not explicitly claimed a righteousness greater than God's, Job's consistent claim of innocence and his repeated claim that God has denied him justice may lead to a conclusion that Job was claiming a righteousness that was superior to God's" (McCabe, p. 58). Seeing Elihu's allegations not as quotations, per se, but as inferences drawn from the implications of Job's words prevents us from making the mistake of suggesting that Elihu is falsely accusing Job of things he has not actually said (as, e.g., Carter, p. 147). This is a mistake because Elihu's key inferences are confirmed by God's accusations against Job. If Elihu is misrepresenting Job, then so is God.

[30]Both passages use equivalent terminology, including the same term for righteousness and the comparative min. Some argue that in both passages, the *min* should be translated as "source" or "relationship." Hence Smick (p. 1000) suggests that in 32:2 "Job justified himself in the presence of God"—a reading that Andersen says "softens" the "plain sense" (p. 245). Likewise, Smick reads 35:2, "my vindication (will be) from God" (p. 1017). Besides Smick, those who take *min* as "source" or "relationship" include Rowley (pp. 264, 287) and Dhorme (p. 473), along with the NIV and NCV. Those who read *min* in a comparative sense include Delitzsch (pp. 206, 267), Gordis (pp. 360, 398), Strahan (pp. 269, 292), Andersen (p. 245), Carter (pp. 140, 147), Snaith (p. 86), and McCabe (p. 58), along with (as McCabe notes) the LXX, Syriac, Peshitta, Aramaic Targum, and Vulgate, as well as NKJV and NASB. Most importantly, the latter reading of *min* as comparative is supported by God's inference in 40:8.

[31]First, what link, if any, does the *kiy* suggest at the beginning of 35:3? Does it merely mark another citation (Gordis; RSV)? Or does it signal a contrastive (NCV) or a causal (AV, NKJV, NASB) connection between the inferred quotation in 35:2 and the inferred reasoning in 35:3? Second, who is the "thee" in 35:3*a*? Is it God as the object of a direct quotation? That seems a vague and unnatural way for Elihu to cite Job's words, especially given his penchant for summarizing rather than quoting Job directly. Or is it Job, as an object of indirect discourse?

[32]In 9:27–31, Job vented the frustration of his personal righteousness when, no matter how hard he tried to live righteously, God seemed determined to plunge him into a ditch and treat him as filthy. Elihu probably has that passage in mind here in 35:2–3. But McCabe (p. 58) adds that "Elihu has inferred the question of 35:3 from Job's remarks in . . . 21:7–13" as well, where Job describes the prosperity of many of the wicked and his quandary over the apparent inequities of God's dealings with men (21:22–26).

[33]In view of the storm we know is approaching—the storm that Elihu describes in chap. 36 and 37 and that breaks in 38:1—it is tempting to imagine that even here in 35:5 Elihu actually gestures toward the billowing thunderhead already towering up in the distance.

[34]"The thought here is that the God who is so far above us is beyond the reach of our actions" (Rowley, p. 288).

[35]Andersen, pp. 249, 256; cf. Rowley, p. 289. How is it possible for a theologian to speak of "commonplaces about the greatness of God"? Are even the most basic truths of theology proper irrelevant to any discussion? Such remarks by commentators are *haarsträubend*, "enough to make one's hair stand on end" (Gordis, p. 415); aimed at Elihu, they actually ricochet in God's direction.

[36]Smick, p. 1016.

[37]In the midst of his refined sarcasm aimed at Elihu, Andersen (p. 257) pauses to describe the reference to "God my maker, who giveth songs in the night" (35:10) as "one of the most beautiful tributes to our kindly Father in Scripture"—no thanks, apparently, to Elihu! It would be interesting to know Morris's take on this phrase. The presence of one of Morris's key emphases (God as Creator)—not to mention one of the Bible's warmest depictions of God—in the mouth of one whom Morris describes as the mouthpiece of Satan certainly creates a curious juxtaposition. Unfortunately, Morris neither comments on nor references this verse. Rowley stoops to unforgivable contempt when he comments on 35:11 that "while Elihu is always ready to pick up ideas from the earlier part of the book and put them forward as his own, he is equally able to descend to the commonplace" (p. 289).

[38]"The oppressed who cry out are not moved by the desire to know God" nor "because of a yearning for God's presence" (Gordis, pp. 401, 402), but only with the plea (if not demand) that He act like the omnipotent and

loving God He is supposed to be, by relieving them immediately. For this understanding of 35:9–12 see also Zuck (pp. 154–55), McCabe (p. 59), Delitzsch, (pp. 269–71), et al.

[39]This presumption is symptomatic of contemporary liberation theologies, which canonize the poor and oppressed simply because of their poverty and oppression. The assumption is that God is necessarily and invariably on the side of the oppressed and owes them relief regardless of their personal relationship or attitude towards Him. This perverts the biblical picture of God's posture toward the oppressed. Echoing Deut. 15:9, Jesus said, "The poor always ye have with you" (John 12:8)—the contextual point being that there are higher priorities than the physical needs of the oppressed. Those higher priorities center on people's attitude toward Him (John 12:7–8). Suffering itself is not a virtue that commands the compassion and protection of God, nor does it entitle a person to a claim on God. It is the attitude of the poor that determines God's posture toward them (Ps. 10:14).

[40]The Hebrew *'aph kiy*; appears to be an a fortiori construction "meaning 'how much more/less'" (Williams, *Hebrew Syntax*, p. 64). Cf. McCabe, p. 59; NASB. Gordis, however, rejects the a fortiori sense of 35:14*a* and makes some noteworthy grammatical arguments for an alternative understanding of 35:13–14, as Elihu's refutation of Job's implication of God's inactivity: "But it is not true that God does not hear, and that the Almighty does not see. Although you say that you do not see Him, yield before Him and trust in Him" (pp. 398, 402).

[41]The implication of 35:16*a* seems to be that Job opens his mouth a great deal, yet all that comes out is *hebel*—air, wind, breath.

[42]Andersen sees two major divisions in this final speech (36:1–21; 36:22–27:24) and describes them as "so distinct in tone and content as to give the impression that they are independent compositions and could have been separate speeches" (p. 258).

[43]On the assumption that 36:3 must express synonymous parallelism, Andersen (p. 259) asserts that the traditional interpretation ("ascribe righteousness to my Maker") is erroneous. Rather, "fetch" parallels "give" (*nathan*), "knowledge" parallels "righteousness," and "from afar" parallels "from my Maker" (arguing that the same Hebrew preposition is attached to each object with the same meaning). Hence, Elihu is making a gift to Job of "authentic knowledge" derived from God. But the identical preposition may vary its meaning depending on the sense of the verb used, and there appears to be no precedent for *nathan* with *le* to convey "giving something derived from someone [to someone else]." Few concur with Andersen's analysis of this verse (cf. Mitchell Dahood, cited by Zuck, p. 156).

[44]Andersen, p. 260. Smick suggests instead that Elihu's words represent a claim not "to superior knowledge but only to eloquence" (p. 997). He cites the parallel between the feminine plural "my words" (36:4*a*) and the

feminine form of "knowledge" (36:4*b*) in the sense of "utterances." "On this basis Elihu was claiming to be one 'perfect of utterance' because his speech derived from God [36:3] who is the source of perfect words" (p. 1021).

[45]Mitchell Dahood has suggested that the kinds of titles for deity that surface in the Ebla tablets support reading 36:4 as a reference not to Elihu but to God. One such title, he argues, appears to be employed by Elihu in Job 36:4 as well as 37:16. "Does this phrase refer to God, 'The Perfect in knowledge is with you,' or does it refer to a man [Elihu], 'one perfect in knowledge is with you'? The Ebla material, in which the words are divinities or divine epithets, tends to support those who contend that the Biblical text is using divine appellatives" ("Are the Ebla Tablets Relevant to Biblical Research?" *Biblical Archaeology Review* 6 [September-October 1980]: 58).

[46]If Elihu means to contradict Job's previous argument (21:7–26), then this would be one place where his fallibility shines through. Scripture elsewhere asserts repeatedly that the life of every man, good or evil, is sustained by the breath of God in the providence of God (see Talbert, *Not by Chance*, chap. 3). However, the intent of 36:6*a* seems to be governed by its contrast in 36:6*b*. The opposite of giving justice to the oppressed is not sustaining the life of the wicked but preserving their standing or sustaining them in the context of the judgment implied in 36:6*b*.

[47]That Elihu conceives of the righteous as sustaining a secure relationship to God with eternal ramifications is suggested not only by 36:7 but also by acknowledging that even the righteous may suffer under the chastening hand of God and need to be purged of iniquity (36:8–10).

[48]Though Job does, indeed, "repent in dust and ashes" (42:6), he uses a different term—*nacham* as opposed to *shub*.

[49]Once more, Elihu's conception seems nearly as retributionist as the friends. But even Paul implies a similar disciplinary progression for NT believers (1 Cor. 11:27–34).

[50]Gordis, p. 414.

[51]NCV translates 36:16 as a present appeal: "God is gently calling you from the jaws of trouble to an open place of freedom where he has set your table full of the best food."

[52]Lamentations furnishes a classic and graphic demonstration of this truth. Israel's hope (Lam. 3, 5) lay in her very devastation by God, for it bespoke not hatred but love, not revocation but relationship, not casting off but covenant loyalty.

[53]"In the last two chapters devoted to Elihu, several themes come together, and Elihu begins to appear in more compassionate guise." God is just, "not malicious. He does care for his people. Therefore the proper response to suffering we cannot fathom is faith and perseverance; the response to avoid is bitterness (for it is the godless who harbor resentment, 36:13). Job is in

danger here," for 36:21 suggests that "Job must not turn to evil as a way of alleviating his suffering. Be patient, Elihu is saying" (Carson, pp. 170–71).

[54]Dhorme, p. lvi.

[55]Gordis, p. 405. Andersen adds, "We can almost imagine that Elihu gives his description while a tremendous storm actually breaks over them all" (p. 265).

[56]Andersen, p. 264.

[57]"There is no break between the chapters, except for a sudden ejaculation by Elihu, who is startled into mixed terror and admiration at the awesome spectacle of God's power in the thunderstorm" (Andersen, p. 264).

[58]David Laskin, *The Children's Blizzard* (New York: Harper Collins, 2004), pp. 128–30. Laskin's masterful retelling of this moment in American history is spellbinding, not least because of its intriguing mixture of historical context, journal entries, narrative shifts, and meteorological and physiological explanations.

[59]The assumption of many commentators that between 37:19 and 37:21 the weather shifts almost instantaneously from the darkness of what had been an approaching gale of tornado-like proportions to a sudden and complete clearing of the skies is not realistic, especially since the theophanic whirlwind has yet to strike (38:1). The chapter seems instead to build to the stormy climax of 38:1, with 37:21–22 being an explosion of lightning or a momentary breaking of the sun through the clouds (all the more blinding because of the dilation of their eyes from the surrounding darkness). As the chapter closes, then, "Elihu can speak no further, for the wind and storm have burst upon them all, and only the voice of God can be heard" (Archer, p. 101).

[60]David McKenna, "God's Revelation and Job's Repentance," in *Sitting with Job*, p. 386. McKenna, too, sees the storm break in 37:21–22 and regards the whirlwind as a meteorological interruption (a kind of poststorm spin-off) but a logical progression. But not only does the transitional "then" in 38:1 signal "a natural line of progression from one scene to another" (as McKenna notes), but the reference to "the whirlwind" implies that this phenomenon is not only a logical progression but the meteorological climax spawned by the storm that has been threatening throughout chap. 36–37.

[61]This is the explanation for the Elihu material offered by *The MacArthur Study Bible*, p. 729. The apostle John understates that Jesus did "many other things" that he did not record (John 21:25).

[62]Even though he regards the Elihu material as a later insertion into the book, Roland Murphy particularly notes Elihu's "splendid creation hymn in honor of God's greatness (36:26–37:24), which concludes with questions in the style of the Yahweh speeches in chaps. 38–41. In this respect Elihu can be said to anticipate and provide a transition to the intervention of the

Lord" (*The Tree of Life: An Exploration of Biblical Wisdom Literature* [Grand Rapids: Eerdmans, 1990], p. 42).

[63]Gleason L. Archer, Jr., *The Book of Job*, pp. 90–91.

[64]Cited in Iain Murray, *Jonathan Edwards: A New Biography* (Edinburgh: Banner of Truth, 1987), pp. 36–37.

[65]Ibid.

16—Cleaving the Clamor

[1]Green, pp. 304–5.

[2]For these five men at this relatively early stage of human history, this divine speech represented fresh and direct revelation from God. Here is one sample of how God communicated truth about Himself prior to written revelation—a sample that was itself preserved for subsequent written revelation. It is worth asking, though difficult to dogmatize, whether this theophany is a Christophany. Several factors deserve consideration. (1) The whole divine speech orbits the theme of creation, with frequent assertions that the Speaker is the One Who did the creating (38:4, 9, 10, 11; 39:6); and we know from subsequent revelation that Christ was the special agent of creation (John 1:1ff.; Col. 1:16). (2) Job has bemoaned the lack of a mediator between himself and God (9:32–33); and we know from subsequent revelation that Christ is that Mediator (1 Tim. 2:5). (3) The Speaker in Job 38–41 occasionally refers to God in the third person (38:7, 41; 39:17; 40:2, 9, 19); and we know from subsequent revelation of a distinction of persons within the unity of essence among the members of the Godhead (John 1:1–2). (4) Christ's designation as the "Word of God" supports the idea that God *primarily* reveals Himself *verbally* through the Son. He was not only the final authoritative expression of God (Heb. 1:1–2) but also the characteristic agent of divine revelation; it was "the Spirit of Christ" by Whom the Old Testament prophets spoke (1 Pet. 1:11). (5) Even apart from the arguably Christophanic "angel of the Lord" phenomena, there are other OT passages in which the speaker, Yahweh (cf. Job 38:1; 40:1, 6), is identified in the NT to be none other than Christ Himself (cf. Isa. 6:1ff. and John 12:37–41; Isa. 45:22–23 and Phil. 2:9–11). (6) The most natural contextual implication of James 5:7–11 supports the thought, however subliminally, that the Speaker in Job 38–41 is Christ. James, the half-brother of Jesus, immediately attaches the title "Lord" to Jesus (James 1:1). In chap. 5, he makes a series of references to "the Lord," which we know from a cohesive NT theology denote Christ: (a) The "coming of the Lord" unquestionably denotes the return of Christ (5:7, 8). (b) The "Judge" is none other than Christ (5:9; cf. John 5:22; Acts 10:42; 2 Cor. 5:10). (c) The prophets who spoke "in the name of the Lord" (5:10) were doing so by "the Spirit of Christ, who was in them" (1 Pet. 1:11). (d) So when we arrive at his reference to "the end [outcome]

of the Lord" in connection with Job (5:11), is it too much to suppose—in light of the additional factors listed above—that Christ the Creator, the Mediator, and the Communicator of God is the One addressing Job? My theological instincts suspect that we will one day discover that Christ, in His preincarnate "goings forth" (Mic. 5:2), was far more revelationally interactive throughout human history than we ever dared to imagine.

[3]The Lord's "answer" in 38:1 and 40:6 echoes Job's very word; it is the same verb (*'anah*) that Job uses in requesting an "answer" from God (13:22; 23:5; 30:20; 31:35).

[4]"In answer to Job's plea, God speaks, but in his own time and way" (McKenna, p. 381).

[5]That God is directing the rebuke of 38:2 not at Elihu but at Job is clear from several considerations (see chap. 14 and 15). Job clearly understands and accepts them to have been directed at him (42:3).

[6]Carson, p. 168.

[7]The reference to Job's words is not the more common term, *dabar*, but *milah*. The term is almost exclusively Jobian. Of the total 38 occurrences in the OT, 34 appear in Job.

[8]Carson, ibid.

[9]Terry Rude, "God's Answer to a Complaining Sufferer," *Biblical Viewpoint* 22, no. 2 (November 1987): 38. "The translation 'counsel' in the Authorized and modern versions is too suggestive of 'advice,' whereas God is speaking of His infinitely wise providential workings." Green corroborates this sense of "counsel": "Who and what is he who has been daring to obscure the wise orderings of my gracious and holy providence by the ignorant and empty reflections he has cast upon them. What is his ability, and what his claims to act as censor of the divine proceedings?" (Green, p. 305).

[10]McKenna, p. 386.

[11]The Hebrew phrase is curious. Andersen suggests that *biynah* "is not *understanding* but a noun based on *banah*, 'build'" (p. 274). Dhorme sees *biynah* in this construction as a synonym for *truth*, citing 1 Chron. 12:23 as an example, which he translates "'those who know the truth as to the times' . . . instead of the simple phrase [in Est. 1:13], 'those who know the times'" (p. 576). Perhaps a better solution, however, is to modify the translation (but not the meaning) of *yada'*—"if you are acquainted with understanding," or "if you know [what it is to possess] comprehension." This seems simplest and most consistent with the sense in other passages where the construction appears (e.g., Prov. 4:1; Dan. 2:21).

[12]38:2, 3, 4, 5, 12, 18, 21, 33; 39:1, 2; 40:7; 42:2, 3 (twice), 4

[13]38:4, 18, 20, 36; 39:17, 26; 42:3

[14]God does not despise honest questions nor shy away from hard ones. He is a God of truth with nothing to hide—other than mysteries He has

chosen not yet to reveal. It is encouraging to note the men besides Job who questioned God in Scripture: Asaph (Ps. 73:2–16); Jeremiah (Jer. 12:1–2); Habakkuk (Hab. 1:2–4, 13–17). These men are not defiant or doubtful; still less are they agnostics or unbelievers. They are earnest saints unafraid to pose honest questions. Bound up in each context is a settled affirmation of faith in God's character. It is from within that context that they question some circumstance or experience that seems to contradict what they believe God to be. Only then do they find peace and an answer that satisfies them—even if it doesn't fully resolve the present apparent discrepancy.

[15]Carson, p. 173.

[16]7:11, 13; 9:27; 10:1; 12:8; 21:4; 23:2

[17]God essentially says, "Alright Job, you've wanted to take Me to court; here is your chance" (Rude, pp. 37–38).

[18]The specific juxtaposition of "Who are you?" and "Who am I?" belongs to McKenna, pp. 392–93.

[19]I have purposely reversed the order of the quotation to place the questions in the same order as Job, for the sake of highlighting the similarity. The sense of Paul's argument is the same either way.

[20]"The function of the questions needs to be properly understood. As a rhetorical device, a question can be another way of making a pronouncement" (Andersen, p. 269).

[21]Smick observes that "if the specific and ultimate reason for his suffering had been revealed to Job—even at this point—the value of the account as a value to others who must suffer in ignorance would have been diminished, if not cancelled" (p. 1051).

[22]McKenna, p. 392.

[23]Robinson, p. 43.

[24]Robinson, ibid.

[25]Morris offers an imaginative defense of 38:35 as a reference to "the electrical transmission of communications" (p. 105). Presumably on the basis of what otherwise appears to be a poetic personification of talking lightning, Morris sees an anticipation of the discovery of "principles and devices that can transform electrical energy into sound energy and light energy, transmitting messages and even pictures over vast distances by lightning-fast electronic communications" (p. 47).

[26]Edward Taylor, "The Preface." See Daniel Patterson, ed. *Edward Taylor's God's Determinations and Preparatory Meditations* (Kent, Ohio: Kent State University Press, 2003), p. 49.

[27]M. H. Pope, "Job," *The Interpreter's Dictionary of the Bible,* ed. George Arthur Buttrick (New York: Abingdon Press, 1962), p. 924.

[28]Among others, Henry Rowold notes an overlooked emphasis in God's first speech on His concern for "the joy and well-being of the world"—that

is, His goodness and beneficence (38:7, 13–15, 26–27; 39:3–4), not just His power and majesty ("Yahweh's Challenge to Rival: The Form and Function of the Yahweh Speech in Job 38–39," *The Catholic Biblical Quarterly* [1985], 47: 203).

[29]The pattern immediately raises a question about the exception. What about when animals do die or sparrows fall? Has God failed? Actually, man has. Death is the ultimate consequence of human sin, the result of the Fall. Jesus covers even that eventuality when He assures His disciples that not even one sparrow is forgotten before God (Luke 12:6) or falls to the ground without the Father (Matt. 10:29). The exception underscores the pattern. Even within the context of a sin-cursed world, God faithfully cares for beast and man, believer and unbeliever. For an extended biblical discussion of God's providential preservation of both people and nature, see Talbert, *Not by Chance*, chap. 3 and 4.

[30]"Job's views [of God] were changed. How? By God's natural-science display, which not only deepened Job's impressions of God's wisdom and power, but also dramatically what Job had doubted: God's providential care" (Zuck, p. 184).

[31]It is worth noting the transparently metaphorical nature of some of the descriptions in this passage. Everyone understands that asses, ostriches, and horses do not "laugh" or "mock" or "scorn" (39:7, 18, 22; interestingly the same word used in each case, *sachak,* also appears in 40:20; 41:5, 29); likewise, horses do not say, "Aha!" (39:25). This observation is relevant for the later discussion of behemoth and leviathan.

[32]The independence of seclusion is not all it's cracked up to be. The wild ass may be free from the shouts of a driver and the hubbub of city crowds; but considering its need to "roam far and wide" for anything green to eat, this creature "pays the price of its freedom" (Rowley, p. 319).

[33]The KJV "unicorn" has, of course, given a measure of glee to those devoted to discrediting the Bible. Interestingly, "unicorn" actually reflects a literal rendering of the LXX (*monokeros*), though the precise creature in mind was unclear. Some have suggested the rhinoceros. The context, however, furnishes some clues. "Here there is an implied contrast between the wild ox and the tame ox. This animal (Heb. *rem*; KJV, 'unicorn'; Vul., 'rhinoceros') is believed to be the now extinct aurochs (*Bos primigenius*). Next to the elephant and rhino, it was the largest and most powerful land animal of the Bible world. Most of the nine OT occurrences of the word make reference to it as a symbol of strength (Num. 23:2, 24:8; Deut 33:7; Ps. 29:6, et al.). It was already rare in Palestine in the time of Moses. Thutmose III tells of traveling far to hunt one, and the Assyrians hunted them often in the Lebanon mountains. Once again it is a bit of divine humor even to mention the possibility of this fearsome creature harnessed to Job's plow, or tethered in his barn" (Smick, p. 1038). Andersen (p. 281) concurs: "The beast in ques-

tion is the aurochs, not the fabled "unicorn" of the AV. Extinct since 1627, this enormous animal was the most powerful of all hoofed beasts, exceeded in size only by the hippopotamus and elephant. . . . What is Job to make of such a creature? Is there a hint that its Creator might be more fearsome and unmanageable?" For information on all the animals in the divine speeches, see George Cansdale, *Animals of Bible Lands* (Exeter: Paternoster Press, 1970).

[34]"From the sublime to the ridiculous. It is hard to argue that this hilarious sketch of the ostrich serves any solemn didactic purpose. It is what it is, a silly bird, because God made it so. Why? This comical account suggests that amid the profusion of creatures some were made to be useful to men, but some are there just for God's entertainment and ours. . . . The essential point is made in verse 17. If God is pleased to create a bird deficient in wisdom, so what? Is Job being reminded that some of his behavior [better, words] might be equally lacking in *understanding* (the same word as in 38:4 . . .), unless he receives it as God's gift?" (Andersen, pp. 281–82). But Andersen's own explanation of the significance of this creature's description suggests a "solemn didactic purpose"—namely, God's creative sovereignty and freedom—which, in turn, suggests a didactic application. God's creative gifts vary from person to person. The intellectual equipment that some possess is, it should be remembered, purely the gift of God. Those He "deprives of wisdom" He gifts in other ways instead. Our job as individuals before a Creator Who is both sovereign and all-wise is not to rue what we do not possess but to discover, cultivate, and maximize those gifts He has given us, for His glory.

[35]Though the horse is the only domesticated animal in the passage, this creature "still serves the Lord's purpose, for only one kind of horse is viewed—the charger, the war-horse" (Smick, p. 1039).

[36]I live less than an hour away from Caesar's Head in South Carolina, a natural landmark over which thousands of migrating hawks (about a dozen different species) pass each year. Flight itself is a semimiracle of creation that eluded man for millennia and continues to intrigue him. God asks Job whether he is the one by whose skill design the eagle is able to mount aloft. The unique skeletal construction of birds is brilliant, and even the feather alone "presents a marvel of engineering and design" (Jim Elliott, "Feathers: Form and Function," *South Carolina Wildlife* [March-April 2002], p. 18; ironically, the author juxtaposes references to "engineering" and "design" with references to evolution—a non sequitur). Verse 29 refers to this bird's phenomenal eyesight, which is 4 to 7 times more powerful than human sight, allowing it to hunt from high above and dive on its prey at speeds of 100 miles per hour.

[37]John Piper, *The Pleasures of God* (Portland, Ore.: Multnomah, 1991), pp. 89–95.

[38]The day I inserted the safari motif, I received an e-mail that inspired it. A team from my church's college and career group was in Nairobi on a short-term mission trip. Even though the team's time was relatively short and the ministry needs great, the missionary they went to help insisted on scheduling two days for a safari. He was convinced, said team member Nathan Arnold who sent the e-mail, that "this experience would awe us with an aspect of God's handiwork that would be with us the rest of our lives. I can't tell you how right he was. Truly the wonders of God's creation evidence His mighty power and wondrous works." Describing the incredible abundance and variety of African wildlife they experienced, often just feet away from their vehicle, Nathan noted that "their design and natural beauty surpasses even the most colorful imaginations. . . . Seeing these unusual creatures in their native environment reminds us of our wondrous Creator who is the source of all life." One sight he described was "a mother lion standing over a wildebeest she had just killed to provide food for her cubs, who were playing like kittens in the grass behind her." His conclusion: "Truly we can say with the writer of Job, Hearken unto this . . . stand still and consider the wondrous works of God. Wilt thou hunt the prey for the lion? Or fill the appetite of the young lions, when they couch in their dens, and abide in the covert to lie in wait? . . . Who then is able to stand before me? Whatsoever is under the whole heaven is mine."

17—Behemoth and Leviathan

[1]C. S. Lewis, *The Lion, the Witch, and the Wardrobe* (New York: Scholastic, 1950), pp. 74–76.

[2]"The Lord answered and said" does not imply that Job had said anything between 39:30 and 40:1. It is "formulaic," forming an "*inclusio* that ties together the entire first speech" (Smick, p. 1040).

[3]As already noted, the verb *contend* (*riyb*) and its implied accusation is the same term used by Elihu (33:13). God's use of it here signals that Elihu's evaluation and diagnosis of Job's speech were correct. The term translated "instruct" (KJV) or "correct" (NKJV) is a *hapax legomenon* referring to a critic or fault finder (hence the NASB, "Will the faultfinder contend with the Almighty?"). Cf. Strahan, p. 332.

[4]Sutcliffe, p. 118.

[5]Andersen, p. 285.

[6]It is surely suggestive that even when the Son of God returns in power and glory to destroy His enemies, the sword with which He smites them proceeds "out of His mouth" (Rev. 19:15).

[7]Gordis's translation suggests a valid and helpful tonal interpretation. Instead of the confrontational "Will he . . . ?" (implying "Does he dare . . . ?"), Gordis (p. 440) translates, "Can he who argues with the Almighty

instruct Him? Can he who reproves God answer all this?" Cf. Dhorme, p. 614: "Literally, 'Is a censor (capable of) disputing with the Almighty?'" This dovetails nicely with the interrogation context. Having seen all that God knows and does, can Job possibly offer Him any additional advice on how He ought to run things? Having been bombarded with questions that he did not even know enough to be able to ask, can Job answer these queries? "If Job understands any of these matters better than God, God is willing to learn from him" (Andersen, p. 285).

[8]Smick, p. 1040.

[9]Dismissing Job's reply here as inadequate and evasive, David Howard inaccurately asserts that this term "has no moral overtones" (p. 106). Andersen remarks puzzlingly that Job "rates himself as 'light' but hardly 'contemptible'" (p. 285). Job is on his way to *abhorring himself* and *repenting in dust and ashes* (42:6). "Contemptible" is hardly an overstatement here.

[10]Gordis, I believe, misconstrues Job's words: "Job is not submitting to God or conceding any part of His position" but merely "sets forth his weakness and insignificance and his determination to remain silent" because "he has already spoken more than once and has nothing to add" (p. 466). David Howard even suggests that "Job tried to interrupt hoping that the Lord would stop, because he had had enough" even though "he had not yet come to the point of admitting sin" (p. 106). But Job's response is entirely appropriate to the specific divine challenge in 40:2. Andersen rightly laments the implication of the NEB, which "casts Job in the unpleasant role of 'stubborn' and 'answering back'" since "the verb *answer* does not imply impertinence" (p. 285). Job's demeanor is not that of a resolute, let alone stubborn, witness sticking by his story and pleading the Fifth Amendment. Job is broken, humbled, crushed into contrite silence. Those who have experienced this for themselves should have no difficulty recognizing it in others.

[11]Zuck, p. 175, italics added.

[12]Zuck misconstrues God's continuation: "Because Job did not admit to any sin, God found it necessary to continue with a second speech, to speak not only once, but twice" (p. 176). But Job's response is entirely appropriate to the specific divine challenge. God is not finished, not because of Job but because of God. *He* has more that *He* wants to say, thankfully, or we would be deprived of some stunning revelatory material.

[13]Gordis translates: "Will you deny my justice, put Me in the wrong, so that you may be in the right?" (p. 468).

[14]Zuck, p. 176.

[15]"If you think to contend with Me about the way I deal with men in the light of their innocence or guilt, then you must demonstrate an ability on your own part of unleashing your judicial wrath at all the proud and compelling them to abase themselves before the bar of justice. Then you must

crush them completely and consign them to the grave as retribution for their sin. Only when you have accomplished all of this will I concede your ability to justify your criticism of Me" (Archer, p. 106).

[16]"These verses are presented as an aggressive challenge to Job. . . . But they are lovingly designed . . . to bring him back to reality . . . to shake Job's spirit into realizing God is the only Creator and the only Savior there is" (Smick, p. 1050).

[17]Kidner, p. 84.

[18]Dhorme, p. 619. Cf. Smick , pp. 1050, 1052. Smick, however, proceeds to take a symbolic approach, interpreting behemoth and leviathan as bigger-than-life emblems of evil.

[19]Cf. Zuck, p. 178. Morris is convinced that "the reason commentators are unable to identify this mighty animal is that it is now extinct." "Almost certainly," he concludes, "God was speaking of a mighty dinosaur" that Job and his contemporaries could have seen not long after the Flood before its extinction (hinted at, Morris suggests, in 40:19*b*) due to climatic changes (pp. 115–16). As a confirmed creationist, however, I remain unconvinced. Morris's interpretation is fraught with imaginative speculations on Job's thinking (p. 117).

[20]The hippo is most widely assumed to be the creature in mind. It is a massive beast averaging 5 feet high and ranging in length from 12 to 15 feet. The chief problem with the elephant seems to be the description of the "tail like a cedar" (40:17). However, R. Laird Harris suggests (with some merit it seems to me) that the "tail" could actually be a reference to the elephant's tail like trunk, (p. 167). Cansdale notes, "An interesting case, supported by very early material, can also be made for identifying *behemoth* with the elephant and this is stated well in the Epilogue of *The Natural History of the African Elephant* by Dr. Sylvia Sikes. . . . If this theory is correct it seems likely to refer to the Asiatic rather than the African elephant" (p. 101).

[21]Andersen sees 40:19 as the thematic centerpiece of behemoth's description: "As we have seen so often, a statement of special significance is embedded in the middle of more descriptive material. Verse 19 is different from the rest" (p. 289).

[22]The "first of the ways of God" is not a chronological reference, nor does "chief of the ways of God" imply (as Morris argues, p. 116) that it must be the largest land animal ever created. God is speaking in the context of Job's knowledge and experience, in the same way that Jesus was speaking in the context of His listeners' knowledge and experience when He described the mustard seed as "the smallest of all seeds"—not in a universally absolute sense, but in the context of His audience's experience.

[23]Zuck, p. 180. Assuming leviathan to be a crocodile and behemoth a hippo, Zuck lists a collection of nine "striking parallels" between these creatures.

[24]"The fact that the discussion of Leviathan is longer than any of the other animals and the fact that the crocodile is the most vicious of all the animals recounted by God, sometimes preying even on man, gives chapter 41 a climactic character" (Zuck, p. 180). Cf. Andersen: "The longest poem about the most terrifying animal was deliberately left until last to provide a terrific climax" (p. 291).

[25]The progression is actually a chiasmic structure. Chiasmus is the "sandwich" of literary structures. Picture laying out two pieces of bread. On each slice you lay a piece of ham, then cheese, then one large slice of red-ripe tomato for the center. Now put them together and you have a culinary chiasmus—a progression in which each successive level is mirrored by its structural counterpart. In this case, the chiasmus looks like this:

A1—single-handed capture of leviathan (41:1–2)
B1—cooperative compliance of leviathan (41:3–4)
C—playful harmlessness of leviathan (41:5)
B2—cooperative compliance of leviathan (41:6)
A2—single-handed capture of leviathan (41:7)

[26]It is the details of these four verses that most consternate interpreters. They are thoroughly addressed in the appendix on leviathan.

[27]The appendix cites descriptions of the American alligator by early naturalist and explorer William Bartram that are surprisingly similar to segments of Job 41.

[28]Rowley, p. 341.

[29]The generic verb *to look* (*ra'ah*) in 41:34 is susceptible of different senses, depending on the context. What does it mean that leviathan "*looks at* all the high ones/things"? The implications of 41:33–34 lend weight to the metaphor of "looking down on" (i.e., disdaining), which is conveyed by NIV and NCV (cf. also Zuck, p. 183). The imagery of "staring down," however, is even more evocative of a saurian demeanor and the kind of intimidation that rules in both the human world and the animal kingdom. Dhorme translates, "He gazes at every haughty creature," adding that this creature "is afraid of no one, he lowers his glance before no one whomsoever."

[30]Cf. *ga'ōwn* ("majesty" in 40:10) with *ga'ᵉwah* ("pride" in 41:15; 41:7 Heb); both are from *ga'ah*. Cf. *gōbahh* ("excellency" in 40:10) with *gabōahh* ("high" in 41:34; 41:26 Heb.); both are from *gabahh*.

[31]Kidner, p. 72.

18—Bowing Before God

[1] Elisabeth Elliot, *These Strange Ashes* (Grand Rapids: Fleming H. Revell, 1998), pp. 125–27.

[2]McKenna, p. 382.

[3]"The meaning is that the *realization* of no purpose of God can be withheld from him" (Rowley, p. 341, emphasis added). The rare verb (*batsar*) means to make inaccessible or render impossible. The word *thought* means purpose or plan. An occurrence of the same term in Jer. 23:19–20 is remarkable for its ties to several themes in Job 38–42—"Behold the storm of the Lord has gone forth in wrath, even a whirling tempest; it will swirl down on the head of the wicked. The anger of the Lord will not turn back until He has performed and carried out the purposes of His heart" (NASB).

[4]This understanding does not require a modern version to clarify. It is clear from a full reading of both halves of the verse in the KJV. Still, other versions do elucidate the sense, particularly of 42:2*b*—"no purpose of Yours can be withheld from You" (NKJV); "no purpose of Yours can be thwarted" (NASB, ESV); "no plan of Yours can be thwarted" (NIV).

[5]Zuck, p. 183.

[6]Elisabeth Elliot, *A Chance to Die* (Old Tappan, N.J.: Fleming H. Revell Co., 1987), pp. 219–20, original emphasis.

[7]Sutcliffe, p. 118.

[8]McKenna, p. 409.

[9]A. S. Peake, *The Problem of Suffering in the Old Testament* (London: Kelly, 1904; 1947), p. 88.

[10]Some translations insert these words (or their equivalent) to convey more clearly the sense of Job's echoing them in his mind and with his mouth as he responds to them (e.g., NKJV, NIV, NCV). The ESV accomplishes the same effect by placing the words in single quotation marks, indicating that Job is quoting God. Cf. also Zuck, p. 184; Rowley, p. 342; Andersen, p. 292.

[11]"Indeed" (Gordis, p. 491) or "surely" (NIV, NCV) conveys the sense of admission more clearly than "therefore" (AV, NKJV, NASB, ESV).

[12]Zuck notes this is not physical sight but "spiritual insight" (p. 184).

[13]"Since the root often means 'reject,' the implied object in the light of v. 3 is what he spoke in ignorance" (Smick, p. 1056). Holladay concurs the sense here as "a disavowal (thus rejection) of earlier words" (p. 180). Strahan suggests "I . . . repudiate my words" (p. 348). Cf. also Zuck, pp. 184–85. The term "recantation" (Hassell C. Bullock, *An Introduction to the Old Testament Poetic Books* [Chicago: Moody Press, 1988] p. 109) is an expressive one, but it drops the legal metaphor that has dominated the book of Job and exchanges it for the foreign baggage of ecclesiastical history. See also B. Lynne Newell ("Job: Repentant or Rebellious?" in *Sitting with Job*, ed. Roy

B. Zuck, pp. 453–55), who rebuts J. B. Curtis's outrageous reading of Job's words as a contemptuous rejection of Yahweh Himself.

[14]Rowley, p. 342.

[15]Carson, p. 174.

[16]Ibid.

[17]Modernized excerpt from C. H. Spurgeon's *Morning by Morning* (Grand Rapids: Baker, rpr. 1977) daily devotional (reading for June 6).

[18]Schreiner, p. 285.

[19]Ibid.

[20]Bullock, p. 109 (emphasis added).

[21]"The book of Job, probably the oldest book in the Bible, deals profoundly—and surprisingly—with the world's most pressing and fundamental problems: the place of suffering and man's relationship to God" (Zuck, p. 189).

[22]John Piper, *The Pleasures of God*, p. 94.

[23]It is no accident that Robert Gordis titled his earlier and more conceptual work on Job *The Book of God and Man.*

[24]John Newton, "How Sweet the Name of Jesus Sounds," in *Hymns of Grace and Glory,* ed. Joan J. Pinkston and Sharalynn E. Hicks (Greenville, S.C.: Ambassador Emerald International, 2002), no. 39.

19—The End of Job

[1]See Humphrey Carpenter, *Tolkien: A Biography* (Boston: Houghton Mifflin, 1977), pp. 80–86. Carpenter also discusses how Tolkien's stories rose out of his Christian worldview (pp. 91ff.).

[2]Chris Armstrong, "9/11, History, and the True Story," *Christianity Today* (September 14, 2002), web issue. All "tales of joy snatched from the jaws of tragedy"—whether historical (like Job) or fictional, whether consciously or unconsciously—"point towards the central True Story of Christ's passion and resurrection—the greatest and most complete conceivable eucatastrophe. All stories that hold out hope in the cataclysmic struggle between Good and Evil . . . echo this greatest eucatastrophe."

[3]Robinson acknowledges that the ending may, in fact, reproduce the actual ending of the traditional story. In any case, however, the ending was essential for ancient readers who "had no perspective of life beyond the grave, to which Job might look for the vindication of his faith. The ways of Providence must be justified, here in this world, if they are to be justified at all" (pp. 42–43).

[4]"These gifts at the end are gestures of grace, not rewards for virtue" (Andersen, p. 294). Cf. Zuck, pp. 188–89.

[5]Carson, p. 176.

[6]The context of Ps. 51:4 is particularly striking, since David's confession involves his sins of adultery and murder. It would be difficult to imagine any sins more man-oriented. Cf. Gen. 39:9.

[7]Zuck, p. 186.

[8]Smick, p. 1057.

[9]Archer, p. 113.

[10]Zuck, p. 186. In fairness, this is only a passing observation of Zuck's, not his full position.

[11]"His opinions and feelings were often wrong, but his facts were right. He was not being punished for sins he had committed. But the friends were claiming to know for a certainty things they did not know, and so were falsely accusing Job while mouthing beautiful words about God" (Smick, p. 1057). Similarly, Delitzsch defines "right" rather narrowly as "correct": "The correct in Job's speech consists in his having denied that affliction is always a punishment of sin, and in his holding fast the consciousness of his innocence, without suffering himself to be persuaded of the opposite. That denial was correct, and this truthfulness was more precious to God than the untruthfulness of the friends, who were zealous for the honor of God" (pp. 386–87).

[12]"Job rightly accused them of lying about him and trying to flatter God (13:4, 7–11)" (Smick, p. 1057). The three were willing to "heap accusations on a tormented soul to uphold their theological position" (Pope, quoted by Smick).

[13]"Job has been genuinely groping for the truth, and has not allowed glib answers to deter him" (Carson, p. 177). Kidner (p. 73) agrees that the friends' wayward efforts "to justify God's ways" contrast starkly with "the gritty honesty of Job" so that "we are forcibly reminded that God . . . reads between the lines and listens to the heart." Strahan (p. 351) concurs: "God prefers the honest doubt of the earnest seeker after truth to the zeal of the orthodox believer whose faith has never been tried because he has been afraid to look into the dark mysteries of existence." David Howard takes the application a step further: "God's vindication of Job, who had raised serious doubts about the reality and presence of God in his life, is in striking contrast to the harsh words God reserves for the friends. It indicates that God is more pleased with daring honesty, even when this involves doubt about God and His ways with man, than He is with a superficial attempt to maintain a shallow creed in the face of shattering evidence. It was Job who expressed doubts. The friends never ventured outside the bounds of their creed. They dared not raise the questions that Job raised" (p. 110).

[14]The construction of *dabar* plus the preposition *'el* with the pronominal suffix "me" occurs over one hundred times in the Old Testament. On only *one* occasion is it translated "speak *concerning* me"—Job 42:7, 8. In every

other appearance, this construction means and is translated to "speak to me." The natural question is why must it be translated differently only in Job 42? Matitiahu Tsevet remarks that "to speak of, concerning" is a "rare meaning" for this construction; the standard phrase for this sense would be *dabar 'al* rather than *dabar 'el* ("The Meaning of the Book of Job," in *Sitting with Job*, p. 210). A few cite similar examples such as 1 Sam. 3:12, 2 Sam. 7:19, or Jer. 40:16b. The widespread, unquestioning assumption that "*concerning* me" is the correct sense is curious. I could not locate a commentator who addressed this question of translation, defended the traditional translation, considered the more straightforward translation ("*to* me") or explained why it is unacceptable. Nevertheless, the accuracy of the traditional translation of this phrase in Job 42 deserves more attention than it has received in the literature. It seems that a broadly assumed interpretation has unduly influenced translation, rather than vice versa.

[15]Archer concedes, "we must ask what was so very right about what Job had said of God. After all, Job had been sternly rebuked by the Lord during the four preceding chapters, and had been so overwhelmed by his own guilt in unworthily criticizing and complaining against God that he had completely broken down with confession, repentance, and self-condemnation." In other words, he was censured for, and repented of, *sins* of *speech*. "How could Job then be commended as a true and faithful teacher of the doctrine of God?" Archer asks. How can he be simultaneously *censured* by God for His speech about God and *commended* by God for his speech about God? "Job's repentance was so thoroughgoing and complete that God could cancel out his guilt entirely. Once Job had recognized his folly in judging God's attitude toward him simply on the basis of adverse appearances as altogether wicked and unworthy, it was possible for God to forgive him completely and cleanse him from that sin" (Archer, p. 112).

[16]Zuck, p. 186.

[17]This, too, argues for the interpretation that Job's "right" words "to" God refers to 42:1–6. God does not "accept" Job's priestly intercession on their behalf because he has been sincere but wrong but because he is now back in right relation to Him via repentance and confession.

[18]Kidner, p. 74.

[19]Kidner sees it as "a pregnant statement that the Lord restored Job's fortunes 'when he had prayed for his friends' (who by now had almost the status of enemies)." Even though "nothing is directly made of this" in the text, the fact is that, "had Job's vindication been the only end in view, it could have been achieved" without any mention of Job's intercession for his friends (Kidner, p. 73).

[20]The phrase "turned the captivity" carries its own intrigue. Most interpret it as a restoration of fortunes (NASB), a return to prosperity (NIV). Rowley is certain that "this much discussed phrase, elsewhere used of the

nation cannot well have anything to do with 'captivity' or 'exile' here, and its meaning must be as *RSV* ['restored the fortunes']" (p. 345). The NKJV margin suggests that the phrase refers to the returning of what was captured from Job (e.g., 1:14–15, 17). Gordis argues that it should be "interpreted as using the same root for the verb and the noun; hence 'lit. turn a turning, restore to the previous state'" (p. 495).

[21]Archer, p. 114. The "piece of money" was "a piece of uncoined silver" (Rowley, p. 345), corresponding to the patriarchal setting of the story (e.g., Gen. 33:19; Josh. 24:32). Cf. Zuck, p. 187.

[22]Andersen notes the "wry touch that the Lord, like any thief who has been found out (Exod. 22:4), repays Job double what He took away" (p. 293). This sounds offensive until one remembers the Lord's own admission that He had, in fact, destroyed Job "without cause" (2:3). Cf. Gordis, p. 498.

[23]Job's divinely ordered calamities have resulted in public censure and misunderstanding of Job on a massive scale. It was necessary, therefore, to disabuse the public of their error in unmistakable terms that they will understand. Cf. Ellison, p. 126.

[24]"This is not to suggest that the loss could really be so lightly made good, but the best that could be done in the conditions created by the setting of the trial" (Rowley, p. 343). Archer is unduly cavalier in dismissing Job's first wife as incapable of bearing 10 more children and unwilling to reconcile with Job, so that "we may safely assume that Job obtained a new and younger wife" (p. 116). John Piper's depiction of Job's wife as only momentary in her lapse of faith is nearly as speculative on the other end of the spectrum (*The Misery of Job and the Mercy of God*, pp. 39–41). The biblical record on Job's wife is silent, though in a text that details every other new change one might expect the mention of a new wife as well, if he had received one. There is no textual reason, then, to conjecture a new wife. In that respect, Piper's depiction seems at least closer to the record than Archer's.

[25]Their names underscore their renown: Jemimah ("dove"), Keziah ("cassia, cinnamon"), Keren-happuch ("horn of eye-paint")—an inauspicious-sounding name, but the reference is to "a dark mineral powder" used as eyeliner "to mark them out conspicuously" (Rowley, p. 345), suggesting that she possessed a natural striking beauty of countenance. In Part 4 (pp. 65–78) of *The Misery of Job and the Mercy of God,* John Piper concludes his poetic paraphrase of the story of Job with a hypothetical conversation between Job and little Jemimah. It is one of the touching highlights of his book that crystallizes much of the theology of Job.

[26]Carson, p. 175. The same phrase is used of Abraham (Gen. 25:8), Isaac (Gen. 35:29), David (1 Chron. 29:28), and Jehoiada the priest (2 Chron. 24:15).

[27]Andersen, pp. 72–73.

[28]Derek Kidner, *The Wisdom of Proverbs, Job, and Ecclesiastes*, p. 60.

[29]Carson provides some insightful analysis of the reasons for dissatisfaction with the ending of Job (pp. 175–78).

[30]"In that sense, the epilogue is the Old Testament equivalent to the New Testament anticipation of a new heaven and a new earth" (Carson, pp. 176–77).

[31]Carson, p. 176.

[32]"The restoration of Job's prosperity was not the reward of his piety, but the indication that the trial was over" (Rowley, p. 343).

[33]Zuck offers several suggestions as to the purpose for Job's suffering: (1) to demonstrate the genuineness of human worship; (2) to correct and mature man's perception of God; (3) to teach the necessity of trusting the trustworthy God in the face of inexplicability; (4) to highlight the folly of arguing with God (pp. 189–91).

[34]Armstrong, ibid.

[35]Ibid.

[36]Robert Lewis Dabney, *The Life and Campaigns of Lieutenant General Thomas J. Stonewall Jackson* (Harrisonburg, Pa.: Sprinkle Publications, rpr. 1983), p. 707.

[37]Ibid., p. 708.

[38]Ibid., pp. 722–23.

[39]Ibid., pp. 723–24.

[40]John M. Neale, "Art Thou Weary, Art Thou Languid?" based on an early Greek hymn.

20—The End of the Lord

[1]We explored James's exhortation to patience and the nature of that virtue in chap. 3.

[2]While James 5:11 seems to connect the exhortation to patience with the Lord's compassion and mercy, the context of 5:7–11 clarifies James's larger point. James punctuates his exhortations to patient perseverance with the assurance of the Lord's coming (vv. 7, 8, 9). The "end of the Lord" in v. 11, then, carries a dual implication. It is another reference to His coming (arriving in a whirlwind for Job) but also turns a corner to direct our attention to what we may look forward to when He comes, viz., the same kind of compassion and mercy He showed Job when He arrived to end all his sufferings.

[3]Conclusions may be both logical and erroneous if they are made on the assumption that we have all the data at our disposal. In theological terms, data is revelation; revelation is reliable but limited. In the Bible, and in the Bible alone, we possess absolute truth but not all truth.

[4]Piper, *The Misery of Job and the Mercy of God*, p. 72.

[5]This "is not so much a denial of concern for animals as it is a recognition that even the Law's concern for the oxen was a way of teaching Israel of God's mercy toward all" (Fee, p. 408). Actually, it is not at all a denial of God's concern for animals but a pointer to a deeper concern for man that runs like an undercurrent beneath the surface of such laws.

[6]Kidner, p. 74.

[7]C. S. Lewis, *The Last Battle* (New York: Scholastic, 1956), p. 183.

[8]Robert Fulghum, *It Was on Fire When I Lay Down on It* (New York: Villard Books, 1989), pp. 172–77.

21—Learning Theology with Job

[1]C. S. Lewis, *Mere Christianity* in *The Complete C. S. Lewis Signature Classics* (San Francisco: Harper, 2002), p. 85.

[2]C. C. Ryrie, *Basic Theology* (Colorado Springs: Chariot Victor, n.d.), p. 9.

[3]Lewis *Mere Christianity* in *The Complete C.S. Lewis Signature Classics*, p. 86.

[4]I do not mean to imply that all theological confidence is unwarranted, only that some is when, for example, we speak with certainty on doctrines that have little or ambiguous Scriptural elaboration.

[5]Talbert, *Not by Chance*, Appendix E, "Salvation: Divine Determination or Human Responsibility?"

[6]Robinson, pp. 35–36.

[7]C. S. Lewis, *Mere Christianity* (Nashville: Broadman and Holman, 1980), pp. 47–48.

[8]Ibid., p. 48.

[9]For an excellent argument on the theological responsibility of preachers, see Mark Minnick's two-part series, "Theology Matters," *Frontline* (September-October 2003; November-December 2003), pp. 1–4 of the "Sound Words" insert feature.

[10]Entry for September 5 in Spurgeon's *Evening by Evening* (Grand Rapids: Baker, rpr 1977), p. 251.

[11]Entry for July 20 in Spurgeon's *Morning by Morning*, p. 202.

[12]Edmund F. Sutcliffe, pp. 118–19, emphasis added.

[13]I am well aware that in making such a statement, I am opening myself up to criticism from both sides. Frankly, I am opening myself up to self-criticism, since I am just as prone to this error as anyone else.

[14]This designation will, I am sure, deeply offend those who are committed to the Calvinist label. The fact is, however, that Spurgeon's opponents considered themselves Calvinists not Hyper-Calvinists; and the Hyper-Calvinist position is, after all, the logical extension of Calvinism beyond biblical bounds, just as Hyper-Arminianism (e.g., Open Theism) is the

logical extension of Arminianism beyond biblical bounds. One need only peruse Curt Daniel, *The History and Theology of Calvinism* (Springfield: Good Books, 2003) to see the many versions and varieties of Calvinism historically.

[15]Iain H. Murray, *Spurgeon v. Hyper-Calvinism; The Battle for Gospel Preaching* (Edinburgh: Banner of Truth, 1995), pp. 80–82.

[16]Some protest that this is exactly what we do with other major questions of theology, such as the trinity or the hypostatic union. Historical theology has hammered out extrabiblical formulas for explaining these complex issues. In such cases, however, theology has not sought to reduce or explain the mystery of biblical statements, but to *preserve* it. In the case of the trinity, for instance, *biblical data* (not logic) demands (1) three distinct, coequal, coeval Persons, *and* (2) one God. Similarly with the hypostatic union, *biblical data* (not logic) demands that Christ is (1) fully God, *and* (2) fully man. The historic creeds, therefore, settled on definitions *necessitated* by the biblical data—definitions formulated and designed not to explain or remove mystery (e.g., not to make something "fair" or "sensible") but to preserve the mystery inherent in the biblical data itself and to fence out a heretical overemphasis on either side of that data. (e.g., monotheistic Trinitarianism vs. polytheism or Unitarianism; Theanthropicity vs. docetism or Arianism). To whatever degree that a system's doctrinal formulas are driven by the demands of *logic* (not biblical data), to that degree the result is at best a nonbiblical, unrevealed, and therefore uncertain system. At worst, it risks being an unbiblical system that overexplains or overweights one side of the biblical data to the diminution or distortion of the other side of the biblical data.

[17]Ibid., pp. 150–53, emphasis added.

[18]My five-point friends may want to cover their ears while I wish that Spurgeon was as consistently ruled by this thinking on the extent (intent) of the atonement.

[19]Jon Tal Murphree, *Divine Paradoxes: A Finite View of an Infinite God. A Response to Process and Openness Theologies* (Camp Hill, Pa.: Christian Publications, 1998), p. 131.

[20]Ibid., p. 133.

[21]Andersen, p. 291.

[22]Garrett, p. 205. The observant reader may suspect that I have omitted the remainder of the proverb because it undermines my point. It does not. "The honor of kings is to search out a matter," certainly, but it would be absurd as well as unbiblical to assert that the "matter" they are searching out is the same "matter" that God has determined to conceal (Deut. 29:29). The proverb is constructed as a contrast between the distinctive "glories" of human kings and the King of kings. Cf. Charles Bridges, *Proverbs* (Edinburgh: Banner of Truth, rpr. 1981), p. 463.

[23]Bernard Ramm and Clark Pinnock are two notable examples that come to mind.

[24]Quoted in Murray, p. 154, emphasis added.

[25]Delitzsch, vol. 5, p. 306.

Appendix: Leviathan

[1]Cf. Derek Kidner, *Psalms 73-150* in *Tyndale Old Testament Commentaries,* vol. 14b (Downers Grove: Inter-Varsity, 1975), pp. 268-69; Willem A. VanGemeren, "Psalms" in *The Expositor's Bible Commentary,* vol. 5 (Grand Rapids: Zondervan, 1991), pp. 488-89. Technically, the reference to Egypt as "Leviathan" is an example of hypocatastasis—a comparison of two essentially dissimilar things by direct reference.

[2]Cf. E. J. Young, *The Book of Isaiah,* vol. 2 (Grand Rapids: Eerdmans, 1969), pp. 232-35; Geoffrey W. Grogan, "Isaiah" in *The Expositor's Bible Commentary,* vol. 6 (Grand Rapids: Zondervan, 1986), pp. 169-70. Grogan, however, mistakenly assumes that all the passages that mention leviathan should be combined to form a composite picture of this creature (p. 174).

[3]*The MacArthur Study Bible*, p. 738. This normally helpful study Bible avoids any comment on 41:18-21.

[4]"Crocodile," *World Book Encyclopedia* vol. 4 (Chicago: World Book, 1985), p. 916; "Crocodile," *Compton's Encyclopedia* vol. 5 (Chicago: F. E. Compton, Division of Encyclopedia Britannica, 1969), pp. 610-11.

[5]Smick (1049) cites Gunkle, Cheyne, and Pope as examples of the mythological view.

[6]Cf. Bernard F. Batto, pp. 57-58. The seven-headed monster Lotan in Ugaritic mythology is a favorite parallel (cf. Ps. 74:12-14).

[7]Andersen, p. 289. Andersen regards the inference of Job 40:15 as conclusive.

[8]Carson argues that behemoth and leviathan "may be the hippopotamus and the crocodile, respectively, but they probably also represent primordial cosmic powers that sometimes break out against God" (p. 172).

[9]Smick, "Mythology and the Book of Job" and "Another Look at the Mythological Elements in the Book of Job" in *Sitting with Job,* ed. Roy B. Zuck, pp. 221-44.

[10]Smick in *The Expositor's Bible Commentary,* vol. 4, p. 1049. See Smick's section on "Mythopoeic Language" in the introduction to his commentary on pp. 863-71.

[11]Ibid.

[12]Robert S. Fyall, *Now My Eyes Have Seen You: Images of Creation and Evil in the Book of Job* (Downers Grove: InterVarsity Press, 2002). Fyall sees Behemoth as a symbol of Mot, god of death, and Leviathan as the symbolic

monster of chaos. Both are designed to bring Satan back into the picture in veiled form to underscore his part in Job's suffering as well as God's ultimate control and triumph over him.

[13]Morris, pp. 115-17. Morris speculates, however, that reports "of great sea serpents and plesiosaur-like animals in oceans and deep lakes around the world" suggest that leviathan *may* still exist.

[14]Morris, p. 119, emphasis added. What are these details that can apply only to Satan? Some of them are as mysterious as Morris's interpretation itself. He cites Job 41:3-4 (presumably the power of speech), 9 (?), 25 (?), and 33-34. These descriptions, however, could very easily apply to a creature either directly or via simple personification.

[15]*The MacArthur Study Bible* (p. 738) opts for the dinosaur interpretation. Zuck (p. 180) cites the late George Mulfinger Jr. ("Dinosaurs—The Facts Support Creation," *Faith,* May-June 1976, p. 18), who suggested Plesiosaurus or Mosasauros. Henry Morris's support for this view has already been mentioned.

[16]No one concedes any factual basis for Cyclops or Medusa, unicorns or centaurs, leprechauns or elves, hobbits or orcs.

[17]Morris, p. 118. By way of illustration, Morris mentions "a strange protuberance, with internal cavity, on the top of the head" of some dinosaur fossils, which "could have served as a sort of mixing chamber for combustible gases that would ignite when exhaled into the outside oxygen."

[18]Archer, p. 107.

[19]Gordis, p. 571. "Hence," he concludes, "*Behemoth* is to be identified as the hippopotamus and *Leviathan* as the crocodile."

[20]The same Hebrew verb, *sachaq* (laugh, mock), appears in each of these passages.

[21]Andersen, p. 288.

[22]Part of the problem in 41:18-21, as we will see, is that a more complicated (and hence less immediately recognizable) literary device is employed there.

[23]Leland Ryken, p. 99. He adds: "Poets are always playing the game of make-believe, imagining something that is literally nonexistent or untrue. Poetic license is the liberation of the imagination, for biblical readers as well as biblical poets."

[24]Andersen believes "a naturalistic interpretation is better. And, without trying to count votes, we think that a majority of scholars incline to this view" (p. 288). That majority encompasses, for different reasons, conservatives as well as liberals. In addition to Andersen, others who see leviathan as a crocodile include Archer (pp. 106-7), Bullock (p. 85), Delitzsch (pp. 337ff.), Dhorme (p. 625), Gordis (p. 571), Green (p. 308), McKenna (pp.

400-401), Rowley (p. 332), Strahan (pp. 337ff.), Thiessen (p. 31), Leon Wood (pp. 119-20), Zuck (p. 182), et al.

[25]The phrase "characteristically literal interpretation" is my own and best expresses, in my estimation, the hermeneutic that Bible believers have historically adopted. The reasons for my choice of terminology will become apparent as the discussion progresses.

[26]*The Travels of William Bartram* (New York: Dover, 1955), p. 115, emphasis added. Bartram accents his formal style and penchant for understatement with a wry sense of humor. "My apprehensions were highly alarmed," he writes, after witnessing this spectacle. Later, when an alligator rushed him on the shore, stopped short, and stared at him, Bartram "resolved he should pay for his temerity." Fetching his gun, he reports, "I soon dispatched him by lodging the contents of my gun in his head" (p. 117).

[27]Ibid., pp. 118-19, emphasis added.

[28]Ibid., pp. 120-21, emphasis added.

[29]C.A.W. Guggisberg, *Crocodiles: Their Natural History, Folklore, and Conservation* (Harrisburg, Pa.: Stackpole Books, 1972), pp. 2, 44, 109-10, 180.

[30]Ibid., p. 110, emphasis added.

[31]Thus Rowley (p. 337) speaks matter-of-factly for many commentators (cf. Zuck, p. 182): "When the crocodile issues from the water, it expels its pent-up breath together with water in a hot steam from its mouth, and this looks like a steam of fire in the sunshine."

[32]Ibid., p. 20.

[33]Leviathan "sneezes out spray like sparks of fire in the glint of the sun" (Archer, p. 107). Delitzsch (p. 372) describes the "meteoric appearance" created by the sneeze of a sunning crocodile. "Around the mouth of the crocodile there shoot sprays of water which in the dazzling brilliance of the sunshine seem to be so many flaming torches" (Dhorme, p. 636). Dhorme adds the intriguing suggestion that the term for the creature's "sneezing" (*'atash*) is an onomatopoeia.

[34]Most of the criticism arises from liberals who adopt a simplistic definition of literal interpretation in order more easily to discredit the results of a literal hermeneutic. Some of the criticism, however, comes at times from nonpremillennial believers for the simple reason that a consistently literal hermeneutic inevitably leads to premillennialism. Postmillennialist Greg Bahnsen insists that no one really employs the "literal when possible" principle consistently, since the "beast" in Revelation 13 could possibly be a literal monster but no premillennialist takes it that way ("The Prima Facie Acceptability of Postmillennialism," *Journal of Christian Reconstruction,* 3 [1976-77]: 57). The challenge is absurd, since the monster interpretation

is not "possible" because monsters do not exist. Furthermore, the context (which Bahnsen ignores) attributes activities to the beast (Rev. 13:2, 4-7) that point to a human referent. This is what premillennialists mean when they advocate a *characteristically* literal hermeneutic—an approach that is sensitive to contextual implications and the presence of metaphor in literal language.

[35]For a very helpful overview of some 25 figures of speech, along with biblical examples of each and a discussion of how they affect interpretation, see Roy Zuck, *Basic Bible Interpretation* (Colorado Springs: Chariot Victor Publishing, 1991), chap. 7.

[36]These particular figures of speech are examples of what is known technically as hypocatastasis as opposed to simile or metaphor.

[37]Rowley suggests that "the reference is to the reddish eyes of the crocodile. In Egyptian hieroglyphics the eyes of the crocodile are said to symbolize the dawn" (p. 337). Zuck likens the simile between the eyes and the dawn as a reference to the crocodile's eyes being the first part of the creature to surface in the water.

[38]Ryken, p. 91.

[39]Zuck discusses a number of examples of hyperbole in Scripture, including Deut. 1:28, 1 Sam. 18:7, and Matt. 23:24 (*Basic Bible Interpretation,* pp. 154-56).

[40]Zuck, *Basic Bible Interpretation,* p. 156. "Furthermore," he adds, "the *thought* conveyed by the hyperbole corresponds to fact" and does "in fact accurately portray the truth intended by the statements."

[41]Ryken, p. 99.

[42]There is a reading that sees this verse as a description of the stability of behemoth "though the Jordan should surge against his mouth" (NIV). The preposition is *'el.*

[43]"A hippopotamus has an enormous mouth and can open it to a width of 3 to 4 feet" ("Hippopotamus," *World Book Encyclopedia,* vol. 9, p. 229).

[44]Terry Rude, p. 40. Cf. R. Laird Harris: "The sparks and smoke from his nostrils surely are but hyperbole" (p. 167).

[45]Guggisberg, p. 20.

[46]Ibid., pp. 20-24.

[47]Ibid., pp. 38-39.

[48]Ibid., pp. 148-49. There is a famous World War II incident of Japanese soldiers trapped overnight in a crocodile-infested swamp where they were, to a man, mauled and eaten.

[49]Archer, p. 108.

[50]Ryken, p. 100.

[51]The argument that such descriptions of God must be handled differently because God is spirit and not corporeal is unconvincing and inconsistently applied. The Bible tells us that God is a Spirit (John 4:24). The systematic theologian tells us that that means God cannot have "body parts" such as legs or arms, hands or nose. How do we know that, especially when God keeps saying that He does? Certainly He does not have *corporeal* body parts. But what does a spirit look like, after all? Who says that spirits do not and cannot have "legs" or "arms" or "hands" or "nose" when every description of spirits suggests that they do? Here is another example of confusing "literal" with "physical." The anthropomorphic argument is also inconsistently applied, for those who are careful to qualify that God does not actually have, say, a "back" (Exod. 33:23), never balk at the idea that God has a "face" (Exod. 33:20) or a "mouth" or "eyes"—presumably because these features are most expressive of a communicative personality. But remove all these and you are left with a God Who is what? Pure thought? But "thought" is not "spirit." Moreover, the overlap of anthropomorphism into anthropopathism is just as unconvincing and inconsistent, for if we throw out God's "jealousy" (as proponents of the impassiveness of God are prone to do), we must also throw out His "wrath" and His "love" as anthropopathic expressions of what God would feel if He could but He can't so He doesn't—He just says He does to help us understand and relate to Him better.

[52]The NIVSB uses terminology that mixes hyperbole and metaphor when it describes 41:18-21 as "highly figurative [metaphor], exaggerated [hyperbole] poetic imagery" (p. 779).

Selected Bibliography

(The most helpful works on Job are marked with an asterisk.)

Alden, Robert. *Job.* Vol. 11, The New American Commentary. Nashville: Broadman and Holman, 1993.

*Andersen, Francis I. *Job: An Introduction and Commentary.* Vol. 13, *Tyndale Old Testament Commentaries.* Downers Grove, Ill.: Inter-Varsity Press, 1974.

Archer, Gleason L., Jr. *The Book of Job: God's Answer to the Problem of Undeserved Suffering.* Grand Rapids: Baker Book House, 1982.

Brown, William P. *Character in Crisis: A Fresh Approach to the Wisdom Literature of the Old Testament.* Grand Rapids: Eerdmans, 1996.

Bullock, C. Hassell. *An Introduction to the Old Testament Poetic Books.* Chicago: Moody Press, 1988.

Cansdale, George. *Animals of Bible Lands.* Exeter: Paternoster Press, 1970.

Carson, D. A. *How Long, O Lord? Reflections on Suffering and Evil.* Grand Rapids: Baker Book House, 1990.

Carter, Charles W. *The Greatest Book Ever Written: The Book of Job (A Commentary).* Grand Rapids: Eerdmans, 1968.

Delitzsch, Franz. *Commentary on Job.* Translated by Francis Bolton. Vol. 4, *Commentary on the Old Testament in Ten Volumes* by C. F. Keil and F. Delitzsch. Grand Rapids: Eerdmans, rpr. 1982.

Dhorme, E. *A Commentary on the Book of Job.* Translated by Harold Knight. London: Thomas Nelson and Sons, 1967.

Ellison, H. L. *From Tragedy to Triumph: The Message of the Book of Job.* Grand Rapids: Eerdmans, 1958.

Estes, Daniel. *Handbook on the Wisdom Books and Psalms.* Grand Rapids: Baker Book House, 2005.

Fyall, Robert S. *Now My Eyes Have Seen You: Images of Creation and Evil in the Book of Job.* Downers Grove, Ill.: InterVarsity Press, 2002.

Gordis, Robert. *The Book of God and Man: A Study of Job.* Chicago: University of Chicago Press, 1965.

———. *The Book of Job: Commentary, New Translation and Special Studies.* New York: The Jewish Theological Seminary of America, 1978.

Green, William Henry. *The Argument of the Book of Job Unfolded.* New York: Hurst and Company, 1891.

Habel, Norman C. *The Book of Job.* Cambridge: Cambridge University Press, 1975.

Hartley, John E. *The Book of Job.* The New International Commentary on the Old Testament. Grand Rapids: Eerdmans, 1988.

Howard, David. *How Come, God? Reflections from Job About God and Puzzled Man.* Philadelphia: A. J. Holman, 1972.

*Kidner, Derek. *The Wisdom of Proverbs, Job and Ecclesiastes.* Downers Grove, Ill.: InterVarsity Press, 1985.

Morris, Henry M. *The Remarkable Record of Job.* Grand Rapids: Baker Book House, 1988.

Piper, John. *The Misery of Job and the Mercy of God.* Wheaton, Ill.: Crossway Books, 2002.

Robinson, H. Wheeler. *The Cross in the Old Testament.* London: SCM Press, 1955.

Rowley, H. H. *Job.* London: Thomas Nelson and Sons, 1970.

Ryken, Leland. *How to Read the Bible as Literature.* Grand Rapids: Academie Books, 1984.

*Smick, Elmer B. "Job" in *The Expositor's Bible Commentary*. Vol. 4. Grand Rapids: Zondervan Publishing, 1988.

Snaith, Norman H. *The Book of Job: Its Origin and Purpose*. Naperville, Ill.: Alec R. Allenson, 1968.

Strahan, James. *The Book of Job*. Edinburgh: T. and T. Clark, 1914.

Yancey, Philip. *Disappointment with God*. Grand Rapids: Zondervan, 1988.

Zuck, Roy B. "Job" in *The Bible Knowledge Commentary*. Vol. 1. Colorado Springs: Victor Books, 1985.

*———. *Job*. Everyman's Bible Commentary. Chicago: Moody Press, 1978.

*———, ed. *Sitting with Job: Selected Studies on the Book of Job*. Grand Rapids: Baker Book House, 1992.